A LIFE TORN BY HISTORY

A LIFE TORN BY HISTORY
FRANZ WERFEL 1890-1945

PETER STEPHAN JUNGK

Weidenfeld and Nicolson
London

First published in Great Britain in 1990
by George Weidenfeld and Nicolson Ltd
91 Clapham High St, London sw4 7ta

Copyright © 1987 by S. Fischer Verlag GmbH, Frankfurt am Main
Translation copyright © 1990 by Anselm Hollo

Originally published in German by S. Fischer Verlag

British Library Cataloguing in Publication Data
(applied for)

ISBN 0 297 79551 1

Printed and bound in Great Britain by
Butler & Tanner Ltd, Frome and London

To Anna Mahler

"You know, Felice, Werfel is really miraculous; when I read his book *The Friend of the World* for the first time . . . I thought I was going off my head with enthusiasm."

—Franz Kafka, 1913

"My problem: What business have *I* in a world in which a Werfel finds interpreters?"

—Robert Musil, 1930

Contents

Translator's Note

Throughout the text, titles of Werfel's works are given in English (with the German title in parentheses at first occurrence), whether or not the work in question has been published in English. For editions of Werfel's works in German and English, see the Bibliography. In the Notes, German titles of works cited by the author have been left untranslated; full bibliographic data for these appears at first citation or, in the case of Werfel's works, in the Bibliography.

Acknowledgments

This book would not have been possible without the initiative and active participation of Anna Mahler (1904–1988). I thank her first of all.

Dr. František Kafka deserves much gratitude indeed for his tireless assistance. His assiduous search for documents in Prague archives and his extremely constructive suggestions regarding the description of Franz Werfel's childhood and youth have made an irreplaceable contribution.

My thanks also go to the witnesses of their times who knew Franz Werfel personally and were thus able to give me information and inspiration of a unique kind: Gustave O. Arlt (1895–1986), Los Angeles; Anne Marie Meier-Graefe-Broch, St. Cyr; Anuschka Deutsch (1895–1984), Berlin; Professor Milan Dubrovic, Vienna; Marta Feuchtwanger (1891–1987), Los Angeles; Brigitte Bermann Fischer, Camaiore; Gottfried Bermann Fischer, Camaiore; Adrienne Gessner (1896–1987), Vienna; Alice Herdan-Zuckmayer, Saas-Fee; Albrecht Joseph, Los Angeles; Gina Kaus (1894–1985), Los Angeles; Ernst Křenek, Mödling; Conrad H. Lester, Vienna; Leopold Lindtberg (1902–1984), Zurich; Professor Golo Mann, Kilchberg; Professor Hans Mayer, Tübingen; William W. Melnitz, Los Angeles; Alma Pixner, Vienna; Lady Isolde Radzinowicz, Philadelphia; Gottfried Reinhardt, Salzburg; Dr. Emmy Wellesz (1889–1987), Vienna.

The following libraries have willingly opened their archives to my research: Special Collections, Research Library of the University of California at Los Angeles; Special Collections, Van Pelt Library, University of Pennsylvania, Philadelphia; Beineke Rare Books Library, Yale University, New Haven, Connecticut; Deutsches Literaturarchiv/ Schiller-Nationalmuseum, Marbach am Neckar; Deutsche Bibliothek, Frankfurt am Main, Abteilung IX, Exilliteratur 1933–1945;

Österreichische Nationalbibliothek, Vienna, Handschriften- und Musiksammlung; Wiener Stadtbibliothek, Rathaus, Handschriftensammlung.

Lillian Birnbaum, Marietta Torberg, and Dr. Ulrich Weinzierl were particularly supportive during my years of work on this book—*thank you!*

My thanks to Professor Hilde Spiel, to whom I owe a great deal since my very first literary steps twenty years ago, for reading the completed manuscript.

A LIFE TORN BY HISTORY

City Park

IN THE FIRST week of September 1890, Bohemia and wide tracts of northern Austria were hit by violent rainstorms that caused rivers to rise and afflicted Prague with its most devastating floods in more than four hundred years. There were numerous casualties. Josefstadt, the Jewish ghetto, had already been inundated when in the early hours of September 4 the Karlsbrücke, an ancient stone bridge, was swept away. Not until Wednesday, September 10, did the rain stop and the water begin its slow retreat; it was still cloudy, although by evening the skies had cleared a little.

Shortly before midnight, Franz Viktor Werfel, the first child of Rudolf and Albine Werfel, was born in an apartment at Reitergasse 11, in a pleasant section of Prague's New Town. His paternal ancestors, surnamed either Wörfel or Würfel, had lived in northern Bohemia for more than three centuries. Franz Viktor's great-great-grandfather Gottlieb Würfel, a Jew with "protected" status, had lived in the Bohemian town of Leipa. His son Juda served as a noncommissioned officer in Napoleon's Russian campaign in 1812. Juda Werfel's son Nathan, Franz Viktor's grandfather, was the fifth of seven children. He started out as a weaver in Leipa, then dealt in flour at Jungbunzlau, and finally moved to Prague, where he quickly amassed a considerable fortune with an eiderdown-cleaning business but lost it just as rapidly. His son Rudolf Werfel, born in 1858 in Jungbunzlau, one of nine children, grew up in Prague and was sent to a reputable Bavarian boarding school. Heavily burdened at first by his father's debts, Rudolf still managed to move up in the world in only a few years. In 1882, at the age of twenty-five, he announced the opening of his glove-manufacturing business. Seven years later he married Albine Kussi, nineteen, the daughter of a prosperous mill owner from Pilsen.

The newlyweds' household included their live-in cook, Barbara

Šimůnková, a resolute Czech in her mid-thirties, from Radič near Tábor. Barbara became nursemaid to the newborn Franz, whose earliest impressions were closely linked to her. He spent most of the day in her company. She talked to him in a dialect that was part German babytalk, part kitchen Bohemian; one of his first spoken words was "Bábi." Almost every day Bábi took him in his large white baby carriage to the nearby city park, where a canopy of treetops framed his first view of the sky. As soon as he learned to walk, she took him to the pond to explore its grottoes, inlets, and islands of weeping willows. He played in a sandbox near the monkey cage, gathered Spanish chestnuts, and learned to appreciate the morning dew, the flower beds, the tree shade, the progression of the seasons.

Diagonally across from his parents' apartment was the big Prague Central Railway Station, a building that intrigued Franz Viktor more than any other. From his window he could look down on steam and grime and boxcars, and hear the train whistles and the screeching of brakes. He loved the interior of this fascinating station and always wanted to touch the locomotives. "Maschina! Maschina!" he called the hissing black monsters standing at the ends of the numerous tracks.

On Sundays, very early in the morning, Barbara took the four-year-old to mass at St. Heinrich's Church. Surrounded by cool stone walls and the fragrance of incense, he knelt, stood, and folded his hands in prayer in unison with Bábi. Back in his room, he used whatever came to hand—brooms, hatboxes, newspapers—to construct an altar, and then held something akin to a Roman Catholic service in front of it. A frequent guest at the family dinner table was Father Janko of St. Heinrich's, a good friend of Rudolf Werfel's who gave Barbara special incentive to serve her most imaginative meals. At the same time, Franz Viktor was also exposed to Jewish tradition. Although his parents were far from Orthodox, his ritual circumcision had taken place on the eighth day after his birth, and on the high holy days his father always took him to the Maisel synagogue. The light of a multitude of candles and the shimmering air of the synagogue impressed the boy as evidence of the living presence of God, both exciting and frightening.

In the playgrounds of the city park Franz made his first friend, Willy Haas, who was a year younger. Barbara later told them how they had traveled down the tree-lined gravel paths side by side in their baby carriages. Together they came to know the formidable Kakitz, the stiff-legged park gendarme with his mighty saber, and they liked to tease the "chair lady" who collected a coin from everyone who felt like taking a rest on a park chair. They fed stale bread to the swans, Barbara bought treats from the pretzel man, and once in a while the boys went home with big, colorful balloons. All these joys of early childhood were abruptly terminated when Franz Werfel became a pupil at the private elementary school of the Piarist order.

Jewish families favored this school for their sons. In Franz's first grade, most of the students came from Jewish homes. In the high-vaulted rooms of the monastery's rear wing, black-robed monks taught some sixty boys at a time. Only the periods of religious instruction were held in separate classrooms; for the Jewish boys, Rabbi Salomon Knöpfelmacher came to the Piarist monastery.

Franz sat in a whitewashed classroom, squeezed behind a narrow desk painted a glossy green. Behind the elevated lectern hung a large map of the Austro-Hungarian Empire and a portrait of Emperor Franz Joseph I in a white uniform. Near the door stood a cupboard containing geographical and astronomical globes. Surrounded by dozens of strange, noisy boys, the six-year-old found it hard to endure his first schooldays—he felt abandoned, separated from home by some unfathomable decision. He took refuge in illness: the first months of that school year he spent at home, attended and pampered by Mother, Father, and Barbara. Thus ended the eventful year 1896, marked by the frightening experience of entering school and by two other events in the fall: the death of grandfather Nathan Werfel and the birth of a sister, Hanna.

During his entire time with the Piarists, Franz Werfel remained a sickly child and a poor student. He sat quietly at his desk; in the pockets of his blue-and-white sailor suit he kept some colored marbles and a small notebook listing the names of all his schoolmates and the monks who taught them. Most days, school let out at 4:00 in the afternoon; occasionally Franz and his schoolmates would go to the city park to play cops and robbers or marbles. But other days he hurried home so he would have time for a walk with Barbara. They would go to the Belvedere plateau and look down on the city of a hundred towers with its baroque bridges and large new building sites in the former ghetto, wander through the orchards of Laurenziberg, and rush back to Reitergasse so Barbara could prepare the family's evening meal. They crossed the quiet squares of the Kleinseite, where grass grew between the rough cobblestones, passed by the great palace gardens of the nobility with their guarded gateways, and hurried across the rebuilt Karlsbrücke with its statues of saints and a great crucifix encircled by gilded Hebrew letters. The inscription, Barbara told Franz, had been paid for by a Jew as penance for mocking the cross. On they went, past the smoke-blackened masonry of the Altneu (literally, "Old-new") synagogue, through dark alleys and sinister tenement courtyards redolent of stale beer and salt pork, and on across the Graben, with its horse-drawn tram lines and coachmen who ruthlessly whipped their horses through the dense evening traffic.

Franz absorbed all these colors, sounds, and smells, committing to memory even what seemed mundane: shop signs, streetlights, milk wagons, coal vendors. With equal intensity he engraved on his mind the sights in his own room, where colorful remnants of fabric and yarn, ribbons and ruffles, surrounded his toys as Barbara sat at the whirring sewing machine in the light of an Auer gas lamp. He listened attentively to the conversations of the adults and observed their exaggerated gestures and eccentricities—all the while collecting impressions as other children collect stamps or seashells.

In 1899, when Franz was in fourth grade, his second sister, Marianne Amalia, was born, and the Werfel family moved into a larger and more elegant apartment on Hybernergasse, near the Gunpowder Tower. This new abode was also close to the main railway station, from which Rudolf Werfel started out on his frequent trips to Tuschkau, near Pilsen, the site of one of his factories and his most important branch office.

With his round face, bushy moustache, and gold-rimmed pince-nez, this distinguished businessman with a fondness for cards was a familiar figure in Prague. His passion for music was well known, and he was often seen at the Neue Deutsche Theater, accompanied by his attractive young wife. Albine Werfel was a head taller than her stocky husband, and her features had character and animation.

Rudolf Werfel had taken his brother-in-law Benedikt Böhm as a partner, and Werfel & Böhm, manufacturers of leather gloves, had gained a reputation far beyond the boundaries of the Austrian Empire. The business, which was expanding steadily and had branches in London, Paris, Brussels, and Berlin, was mainly based on exports to Switzerland and the United States.

During these years, Franz knew his father as an extremely nervous and quick-tempered man. Even if he could guess at one reason for the tension at home, he was not yet able to understand it. Excesses against Germans as well as Jews had become increasingly frequent in Prague. At the end of the nineteenth century, the city had roughly 400,000 inhabitants, with a German-speaking population of about 35,000. Within this minority, there was a further minority of 12,000 German-speaking Jews. Yet even the Jewish citizens of Prague who spoke only Czech at home were not immune from the crass anti-Semitism of some Czech nationalists: Jews and Germans were loathed equally as exploiters of the Czech people, and it was commonly believed that in collusion with the hated aristocracy, they had simply divided up the best positions in the state among themselves. The great majority of the population of Prague felt like strangers in their own land, and mistrust, hatred, and lust for revenge were rampant.

In the spring of 1897, hundreds of Czech workers staged anti-Semitic demonstrations. The core of their movement consisted of members of the glovemakers' union, and thus, to a great extent, employees of the Werfel factories in Prague and Tuschkau. At the end of the year, the "December Storm" swept through the city; some German-owned property was destroyed, but it was Jewish shops and dwellings in particular that were looted and set on fire. The government in Vienna took days to impose martial law on the city. Two years later, a trial concerning a ritual murder allegedly committed by Jews plunged all Bohemia into renewed anti-Semitic hysteria and markedly poisoned relations between Jews and Germans. Rudolf Werfel was deeply distressed by these developments. On the eve of the twentieth century, Prague was permeated by an atmosphere of terror reminiscent of the days of Rabbi Bezalel Löw, the great Kabbalist and scholar who had taken mud from the Vltava River and fashioned the Golem to protect the ghetto Jews.

In the fall of 1900 Franz Werfel entered the Royal and Imperial German Gymnasium on the Graben, practically next door to the Piarist school at the corner of Herrengasse. He was a weak, listless, and far from clever student. Here, too, more than half the boys came from Jewish homes; here, too, Salomon Knöpfelmacher came to give them religious instruction; and here, too, ten-year-old Franz was one of his worst students. The rabbi did manage to teach him to read and write Hebrew, and also instructed him in the biblical history of Israel from Genesis to the Prophets. One day Knöpfelmacher remarked that he considered King David's musicality far superior to that of, say, Wolfgang Amadeus Mozart—and from then on Franz regarded religious instruction as a sham.

His entire interest was focused on Karl May's series of adventure novels, with their Wild West and oriental settings, and on the weekly illustrated boys' magazine *Der Gute Kamerad*, in which he read serialized stories about trappers and Indians, fascinating facts about China and Siam, India and Afghanistan, and instructions for building a camera. The tale of Erich the plucky cabin boy was a particular favorite. That deeply tanned North German lad, the hero of a story in the *Der Gute Kamerad*, became his friend and role model. Erich taught him sea chanteys, mariners' yarns, and all about rigging a mast. A Sunday steamboat excursion on the river with his mother became a fantastic ocean voyage for Franz: islanders surrounded the ship, their arrowheads dipped in poison; typhoons threatened Erich and his friend with shipwreck; and on the horizon was a majestic procession of smoking volcanoes.

While reading, Franz indulged in frequent snacks; he had become a plump child. When Barbara banned eating between meals, he just looked at her with guilty little-boy eyes and kept right on eating.

His parents had already taken him to plays and operas at the Neue Deutsche Theater near the city park. The high point of each season was the May Festival, created by Angelo Neumann, one of Europe's most renowned opera impresarios and theater managers. Every year Neumann engaged the best singers and most famous actors from the great cities of neighboring countries for a five-week season at his theater in Prague. In May 1900, Josef Kainz came and performed his Hamlet; the following year, the year of Giuseppe Verdi's death, the theater had a Verdi festival, followed by a great Wagner festival in 1902. These five spring weeks, when one could become totally immersed in drama and grand opera, were the absolute high point of the year for cultured German-speaking citizens of Prague. On the other hand, Czechs never participated in the May Festival, nor would any German-speaking inhabitant of the city ever stray into the Czech national theater, not even when Diaghilev or Nijinsky made guest appearances.

Time and again Franz begged to be taken along to the festival events. But every time, a great sadness would overwhelm him during the very first act, because he knew that there was no stopping the progression of the plays and operas, and that in just a little while the performance would have to come to an end. He was happiest in the joy of expectation before one of these evenings at the theater, and he always yearned for that feeling of excited anticipation.

He built a puppet theater and began to give performances of plays from the repertory of world drama. Georg Weber, Werfel's closest friend at the gymnasium, shared his enthusiasm for the theater. They spent hours in the kitchen making cardboard figures, spears, shields, armor, and creating the special effects for their performances—colophony lightning, vapors of foul-smelling cooking fat—all according to the instructions given in *Der Gute Kamerad*. They invited schoolmates and relatives to performances of entire dramatic works and operas—*Faust* and *Der Freischütz*, *The Magic Flute* and *William Tell*—but what mattered most to the boys was the success or failure of their stage effects.

Another schoolmate, Franz Jarosy, also played an important part in Franz's first years at the gymnasium. He was the very opposite of

Franz's Christian friend Georg Weber and impressed Franz with his air of superiority, his joie de vivre, and his cynicism. Though Jarosy was a Jew, most of his classmates thought of him as nondenominational or converted—he certainly succeeded in shirking religious instruction. Son of an insurance company director in Trieste, the twelve-year-old was already an accomplished actor who treated his contemporaries with pronounced arrogance; for example, he sold Franz an ordinary trouser button, claiming it had been Napoleon's.

Jarosy was willing to participate in his friends' theatrical performances, but only on condition that the boys themselves take the place of the puppets; Jarosy would specialize exclusively in princes and men of noble birth. Franz agreed readily: he himself wanted to play only villains, schemers, and demons.

A very different theatrical event took place in Prague in the middle of 1901. Children were given the day off from school, and the populace packed the sidewalks of all major streets: for the first time in a decade, His Apostolic Majesty, Emperor Franz Joseph I of Austria, King of Hungary, King of Bohemia and Moravia, was paying a visit to Prague. Thus, Werfel, Jarosy, Weber, and Haas were among those who glimpsed him for seconds as his carriage rumbled across the Wenzelsplatz. The city's public buildings and many private ones had been decorated festively; the decorations on the main office of Werfel & Böhm on Mariengasse were especially outstanding.

The gymnasium, with its strict bureaucratic disciplinary principles, depressed and frightened Franz more and more. He experienced the school's coerciveness as a torture that threatened to suffocate him, and the weeks of summer vacation provided intense relief. The Werfel family usually spent those weeks in the Salzkammergut, in Austria. Franz loved swimming in the lake, hiking in the mountains, and taking afternoon naps in high meadows or shady forests. But vacation was always overshadowed by the Damocles' sword of the return to school, and its end broke over him like a natural catastrophe. As in the early days at the Piarist school, illness seemed the best way to escape occasionally from gymnasium life; he managed to contract almost every existing childhood disease.

During the second semester of his third year of secondary schooling, having missed a great many classes, the debilitated Franz found himself engaged in a hopeless battle against his adversaries: Royal and Imperial Professors Konthe, Krespin, Löffler, and Rotter. His mother paid frequent visits to these gentlemen during their office hours and did her best to save what might still be saved. Nevertheless, Franz failed

Latin and mathematics, and had to repeat his third year of gymnasium.

In mid-September 1903, after his thirteenth birthday, Franz was bar mitzvahed. This confirmation—as the assimilated Jews of Prague called the event—consoled him a little for his defeat at school. Alexander Kisch, the Maisel synagogue's rabbi, had been preparing the boy for months, and now he elevated Franz to the status of son of the Jewish commandments and prohibitions, enjoying equal rights and duties with adults.

Franz had always found the teeming crowds in the synagogue and the constant murmuring of the congregation unpleasant. When he encountered Polish or Russian Hasidim on the streets of Prague, refugees from the pogroms, with their long sidelocks, black caftans, and the fringes of their prayer shawls dangling from their waistbands, he had to admit to himself that he did not feel any kinship with these people. But to touch the velvet-wrapped scrolls of the Torah with his fingertips; to listen to the cantor singing, or to the blowing of the shofar during Rosh Hashanah; to watch his mother descend the synagogue steps on Yom Kippur, weak from fasting—these moments of Jewish life he loved, and he certainly wanted to be part of that tradition.

Now he stood on the *bimah*, the wide, raised platform facing the congregation, the books of Moses open before him. In a voice both excited and plaintive, he sang out the Hebrew words, a prayer shawl wrapped around his shoulders. Then he loudly recited the blessing that precedes the weekly reading from the Prophets: "Praised be Thou, O Lord, our God, King of the Universe, who hath chosen the prophets, the richly gifted, and taketh pleasure in their words which they have spoken in truthfulness." And finally he said the Shema, the prayer at the heart of Israel since the ancestral days of Moses.

The Werfel family moved again, this time from Hybernergasse to Mariengasse, into a building in the immediate vicinity of the main offices of Werfel & Böhm. They now lived in the most exclusive part of town, on the edge of the city park, with a view of the tall Spanish chestnut trees and the Neue Deutsche Theater on the far side of the park. The large rooms of the apartment were fragrant with cleanliness, and everything had been painted a dazzling white, including the corridor walls and doors; even the moldings had a glossy coat of white enamel. The floors were covered with costly carpets, and valuable paintings adorned the walls. However, Franz's own room, located between the kitchen and Barbara's room, was very small.

To ease Bábi's burden, the Werfels hired governesses to attend to the two girls, Hanna and Marianne, and to make sure that the son of the family, that disappointing scholar, did his homework and turned his light out at the proper time. Anna Wrtal was one of these women, but Erna Tschepper was Franz's favorite. Around thirty when she began working for the Werfels, she wore her beautiful blond hair in a demure chignon. Almost every day Fräulein Erna accompanied Franz to the park, and often a young admirer joined them on their walks along the gravel paths; Fräulein Erna also spent the night with this admirer quite frequently, a secret that she and Franz kept well.

Franz enjoyed being bathed and dried by Erna, and he was happy as long as he was allowed to read. While ill with the various childhood diseases, often for weeks at a time, he had become addicted to reading. Now, every night and often long into the night, he studied Gustav Schwab's massive work on the legends of classical antiquity, immersed himself in Bulwer-Lytton's *Last Days of Pompeii* and Gustav Freytag's *Debit and Credit*. But, this happy state of affairs did not last long: Erna became pregnant, and Albine Werfel dismissed her without notice. Franz cried for two nights after Fräulein Erna told him that she would have to leave.

It was in Los Angeles, California, where Franz Werfel died at the age of fifty-five, that I began my search for the story of his life. My intention was to end the quest in the city of his birth and childhood, but I was not permitted to enter the Socialist Republic of Czechoslovakia, despite multiple applications. The shared culture that once joined Trieste and Prague, Trent and Lemberg, Vienna and Czernowitz, into one coherent space no longer exists. Before World War I it was possible to travel the continent without identification papers and even to visit India and the United States without ever owning a passport.

I wanted to set foot in Werfel's houses, see his school, walk through his streets, parks, and theaters, but each new attempt to gain access to Prague failed. Finally, I contacted an acquaintance from that city whom I had met many years before and asked him for advice.

This gruffly amiable old gentleman replied by return mail, under the letterhead "Dr. František Kafka, Author, Prague" (no relation to Franz Kafka), that he was indeed familiar with the archives of the Golden City, but that he had to warn me: "Documentary research takes a very long time because one is not permitted to enter the archives oneself but can only apply for copies that have to be notarized and duly paid for." From then on, I received one letter after another from Dr. Kafka, who calls himself the last survivor of the Prague circle.

According to Dr. Kafka, Franz Werfel's birthplace near the Prague Central Railway Station, on what was formerly called Reitergasse and is now Havlíčkova, has been used as an office building for many years. The site is currently being prepared for a new underground station of the B line, Revolution Square. In the lobby of Havlíčkova 11, Dr. Kafka noted some oriental landscape paintings, and "at the foot of the stairs, in a niche, the black figure of a knight in armor, made of plaster of Paris." After some initial difficulties in gaining the doorman's confidence, he managed to penetrate the upper regions of the building: "The present-day floor plan is far removed from that of 1889, as the original rooms have been divided up into smaller office spaces."

Franz Werfel's first school, the monastery of the Piarist order at the corner of the Graben and Herrengasse, now contains about thirty rental apartments, a "well-established industrial enterprise for machine manufacture," and the wine bar U Piaristů. The former German gymnasium now accommodates an electrical engineering school, whose courtyard is still connected to that of the Piarist building by means of a passageway.

Alas, the city park opposite the gates of the modern main railway station has been reduced to a narrow strip of lawn leading up to the magnificently restored Smetana Theater, the former Neue Deutsche Theater. The construction of metro line A has claimed what used to be the largest green area in the inner city, with its pond, grottoes, waterfalls, and playgrounds.

On my desk is a pile of single-spaced typed letters Dr. Kafka has sent me over the years. Looking through them, I find his reply to my inquiry whether there is any information in Prague about Barbara Šimůnková, of whom I know only that she died in 1935 in the hospital of the Sisters of St. Elizabeth. "She died at the age of eighty years, six months, and three days," Dr. Kafka wrote, "and was buried on March 26, 1935, in Olschan Cemetery. There, I noted that she still lies in cemetery 3, burial plot 2, grave 782. In the register, her profession is listed as 'cook.' The fees have not been paid for twenty years, and the grave has become state property, including headstone and accessories."

Caruso

IN MAY 1904, Verdi's *Rigoletto* was on the festival program at Angelo Neumann's Neue Deutsche Theater. This first visit to Prague by the world-famous tenor Enrico Caruso had been advertised for weeks. Franz Werfel accompanied his parents that evening and witnessed a unique performance that far surpassed the Italian highlights of past years. The elegance of Caruso's timbre, his effortless legato, his powerful crescendos drove the audience wild. The tenor had to repeat the Duke's aria three times, stressing new nuances every time. For hours after the performance, groups of Caruso-intoxicated people strode through the night and "La Donna è mobile" resounded in the city's streets and courtyards.

No theatrical experience had ever moved Franz as much. The arts, above all his passion for the theater, now began to absorb him completely, even—at least temporarily—making his scholastic worries recede. At Rosenthal's, the court optician on the Graben, he spent his allowance on Caruso's phonograph records on the Schreibender Engel label: Verdi's *Rigoletto, Il Trovatore, La Traviata*, Bellini's *Norma*, Donizetti's *Lucia di Lammermoor*. By listening to them over and over again, he slowly memorized the melodies and librettos. Before long, the fourteen-year-old knew entire arias by heart.

He stuffed his coat pockets with Reclam pocket editions of Goethe's *Faust* and Byron's *Manfred*. Portraits of Verdi and Dante adorned the walls of his room. He read poetry, especially Novalis, Hölderlin, Lenau, Rilke, and Walt Whitman and Jules Laforgue in translation. He loved to listen to his mother read to him at bedtime, always the same odes, sonnets, and ballads, and he had soon memorized every word of them. With Georg Weber he continued to improvise puppet performances on his now quite elaborate Punch and Judy stage. Hanna, the older of his sisters, also participated.

13

Werfel's talent for imitating adults was astonishing; he reproduced their gestures, inflections, and vocabulary to near perfection. His greatest hit was the impersonation of the cantor at the Maisel synagogue. With a bath towel wrapped around his shoulders, he reproduced the worthy cantor's unwittingly comic lamentations. Hanna pretended to be a devout girl in the congregation, and even Marianne, the youngest, was allowed a part in the game.

In September 1904, after repeating his third year at the German gymnasium, Franz changed schools. He now went to the Royal and Imperial Stefansgymnasium on Stefansgasse, where Willy Haas, his gentle, dark-eyed friend from city park days was his classmate. The two often read secretly during class, hiding books borrowed from their parents' libraries under their desks; thus, a dog-eared copy of Arthur Schnitzler's *La Ronde* soon circulated in class, as did the latest works of Stefan George, Hofmannsthal, Strindberg, and Hauptmann.

Their teacher, Karl Kyovsky, soon developed a certain fondness for the new student Werfel. One afternoon, when an organ-grinder was playing in the schoolyard, disrupting Latin class, Kyovsky wanted to know if anyone recognized the melody. Franz immediately popped up and declared, "That's the sextet, Herr Professor, from *Lucia di Lammermoor,* by Gaetano Donizetti." The schoolmaster smiled, and from that day on, Franz was assured of at least a "satisfactory" grade, even when his academic accomplishments were poor.

The theater performances and evenings at the opera of the past years, especially the works of Verdi; the practically constant reading of poetry, prose, and plays; the first, only semiconscious excitement caused by Woman, that alien being—all these fused into one element in Franz's consciousness, and he reached out for it, trying to give it words, a language. Formulating sentences, he was writing poetry before he knew it—spontaneously, without premeditation. It happened, and the creator was taken by surprise. He channeled the power that flowed into him from the arias, duets, quartets of Italian opera—not least in the form of Caruso's bel canto—into language. He invented the world anew, recreated the cosmos line by line, adorning the lines with exclamation points—he wrote an entire poem! He versified his anxieties, joys, memories; he sang words. Soon he was writing a new poem every day.

Willy Haas was a daily visitor. His first duty was to greet Barbara and exchange a few words with her—Franz insisted on that—before entering his friend's room, a scene of great disarray, with bits of paper and sketches for poems scattered everywhere—in the wardrobe, on the washstand and the bedside table, stuck between pages of books, or crumpled in jacket and trouser pockets. Franz recited his poems to

Willy from memory. His friend was enchanted by Franz's first lines of verse and encouraged him to keep writing, to keep writing without fail.

Suspecting that Willy Haas was the instigator of her son's sudden and unceasing production of poems, Frau Werfel banned him from the house. Franz kept on writing. During this initial exploratory period he received encouragement from the renowned Prague poet and physician Hugo Salus, a family friend. Once, when they took a train ride together, Salus sat staring out the compartment window for a long while, then suddenly turned to the schoolboy and suggested that he write a poem titled "Graveyard in a Field."

During vacations in the Salzkammergut, Franz wrote dramatic dialogues and staged them in a garden pavilion with Hanna and other children, reserving the starring roles for himself. *Aphrodite* was one of these mini-dramas, *Barseba* another; *Classical Philistines* (*Klassische Philister*) mocked the professors at the Stefansgymnasium. Poems, too, kept coming in profusion.

In the garden of the rented summer villa was a fountain with a basin eminently suitable for sailing toy boats. Franz also liked to play cowboys and Indians, and particularly enjoyed being tied to the stake, mocked, and humiliated. One evening, with a thunderstorm in the air, he and Hanna took refuge in a small log cabin where their pet kitten had also found shelter. While bolts of lightning lit up the dusk, Franz tortured the softly meowing cat until it became a lifeless ball of fur in his hands—a cruel and disgusting primal event with which the fifteen-year-old Franz tried to come to terms soon afterward in his first literary prose piece. "The Cat" ("Die Katze") transforms this revolting act into one of mythical dimensions: "My muscles went into spasms in the voluptuous experience of digging into soft life, and my ears yearned for the sharp outcry of a victim. . . . With treacherous tenderness I finally picked up the kitten's almost weightless body and obscured its eyes with my thumbs. . . . And I pushed ever deeper until I felt warm liquid run down my fingers and, with unprecedented pleasure, uttered small cries through my clenched teeth. . . . Then I heard myself, whipped into rage by thunder and lightning, cry out fearfully, 'Dear God, protect me from the Devil, God help us.' "

During the winter, upper-middle-class German-speaking families in Prague held regular soirees. Franz Werfel and Willy Haas were old enough now to be invited to these gatherings, which were governed by rigid protocol: first came the written reply to the invitation, then a formal visit to the host family's house, and finally, a week after the party, yet another of these ritual calls. Cutaway and top hat were required dress. Franz took it all in his stride: he was hoping to meet a certain girl again, his first passionate love of some years before, whom he had seen every day in the dining room of a large hotel in the Alps as they both sat at the same table next to their parents. Maria Glaser, daughter of an assimilated Jewish chocolate manufacturer, Adolf Glaser, was an exceptionally pretty black-haired girl with dark blue eyes. Wearing a rumpled dress shirt and equally rumpled dinner jacket, Franz now encountered her again at these dances; he felt awkward and hardly said a word. He believed himself to be insincere and unclean, and considered his plumpness repulsive. On the other hand, Maria, who was his own age, seemed to him noble, honest, and kind. The boy who joyfully sang Verdi arias to his friends, sometimes even whole scenes from operas, who had memorized entire acts of plays, was speechless in Fräulein Mitzi's presence.

On fine spring days, the Glaser family arranged so-called aesthetic Sunday afternoons in the garden of their villa. All guests were asked to recite either a poem or something else they had written. This was Franz's first opportunity to present his verses to a wider public, and to impress Maria in particular. But when he met her again alone, he simply could not utter one sensible word. The same thing happened at the tennis court, where he sat watching her graceful and energetic play. He listened to her voice as she spoke to her numerous admirers, hardly deigning to glance at him. He grew more attached to her with every wound she inflicted on him.

Back home in his room he wrote: "You gave me a wicked, wicked word. / Not out of a wicked heart, but I was struck by that wicked word. / I was quite embarrassed, red and mute, / And the others nudged each other and laughed all around us . . ." And he complained: "You play with many / But do not notice me. / I stand in the background / Close to you every moment / With a mouth frozen shut / And a face of iron."

Franz's performance at school remained disturbingly poor, especially in Latin and mathematics. His parents hired a tutor, but instead of letting this Dr. Holzner prepare him for his math tests, Franz engaged him in philosophical debates.

His mother kept trying to intervene with the professors on his behalf. His choleric father, on the other hand, told his son to desist from writing those silly verses. He would sometimes present Franz with mathematical test questions, and if the boy did not know the answers, Rudolf Werfel glared at him disdainfully and sent him back to his room. More and more often, he asked his son to accompany him to the factory, to watch the tanners, cutters, seamstresses, and packers working on the skins of doe, kid, pig, and calf. Dozens of sewing machines whirred away, thousands of strips of leather were joined and finally stretched, smoothed, and pressed into their definitive shape before being packed in large crates for export. Franz liked the pleasant smell of the piles of men's and women's gloves in different colors, and there were moments when he even enjoyed the heartbeat of the big enterprise, the radical opposite of his own word-music. Nevertheless, he found it hard to imagine his future as heir to and director of Werfel & Böhm, a role he was naturally expected to assume.

In addition to Willy Haas, Werfel's close circle of friends included Paul Kornfeld, Ernst Deutsch, Franz Janowitz, Fritz Pollak, and Ernst Popper. Like Franz, Kornfeld, Janowitz, and Popper wrote poetry, prose, and plays, read their works to each other, and criticized each other ruthlessly. Ernst Deutsch was a highly talented actor; for four years, he had been Werfel's schoolmate at the Piarist monastery, and the two would always try to outdo each other in their impersonations of Rabbi Knöpfelmacher. In addition, the sixteen-year-old Deutsch, an ace tennis player known all over town, was able to boast of great success with the girls.

Werfel's classmate Paul Kornfeld seemed somber and introverted. Like Franz, he suffered in school, particularly under the narrow-mindedness of their German teacher, who refused even to look at papers if the writing ran over the red line in the margin and never discussed works that the class found really interesting. Thus, Goethe's *Götz von Berlichingen* was read instead of *Faust*, Hoffmann von Fallersleben instead of Heine, Klopstock instead of Hebbel.

In his seventh year of gymnasium, Werfel started playing hooky with his friends. They boldly spent mornings in the parks, sat in pastry shops and coffeehouses, visited dimly lit beer halls in the suburbs, or flirted with waitresses in garden restaurants under old chestnut trees. Later they presented forged parental excuses to their teachers.

Evenings were spent in frequent visits to the Neue Deutsche Theater to enjoy performances by Irene Triesch, Alexander Moissi, Rudolph Schildkraut, Adolf Sonnenthal; they saw guest performances by the Deutsche Theater of Berlin, directed by Max Reinhardt, such as *A Midsummer Night's Dream* or *The Merchant of Venice*. Maria Immisch was the star of a Schiller festival that ran for several weeks, and in her Franz believed he had found the incarnation of the ideal woman. One evening he wanted to surprise her at the stage door with a huge bouquet of flowers. The plan misfired; overjoyed—because the unattainable had remained unattained—he flung the bouquet into the city park pond.

Willy Haas continued to be regaled with his friend's new poems: love songs and complaints dedicated to Maria Glaser, memories of playing in the park, of feeling safe near Barbara, nursery moments, relived riverboat trips, images of sailor suits, shop signs, soccer games, Kakitz the park guard. Haas urged Franz to revise and collect these poems, which were still quite disorganized, in many cases just sketchy fragments. Perhaps, he said, it would even be possible to submit one or two to the editors of some journal.

Franz agreed, but on one condition: he would have to use Haas's address, to avoid his father's renewed ire if a returned manuscript should appear in the Werfel mailbox. Each and every one of the journals did indeed reject the beautifully handwritten poems by return mail. To Willy Haas's address. Franz kept on writing, his friend kept on sending out manuscripts.

One sunny winter afternoon in late February 1908, the two friends were sitting in their new favorite café, the Arco, across the street from Willy's house on Hybernergasse. They were planning a ride out to the Baumgarten, a park in Bubeneč, but Haas wanted to get a clean handkerchief from his room, and Werfel waited for him in the lobby. Moments later, his breathless and suddenly speechless friend handed him the Sunday edition of the Vienna daily *Die Zeit:* there, on the first pink page of the literary supplement, was the poem "The Gardens of the City" ("Die Gärten der Stadt"), by Franz Werfel—who promptly had an attack of nausea and palpitations when he saw his name in print for the first time, and not just in print but in a respected newspaper with wide European distribution. The published poem was not, in fact, one of his own favorites; it was a rather ponderous piece of work that began with the lines "Wilted ivy twines around fountains / Which long ago renounced the play of water. / Only the tears of a shower still roll / Down marble hermae in hidden gardens."

In the Baumgarten, Werfel walked as if in a trance. He kept staring at the newspaper, proud as never before. He imagined that this was fame, this was what had attracted him so strongly ever since he heard Caruso's voice for the first time and witnessed the tumultuous applause on that evening of *Rigoletto.* The hopeful vision of his schooldays had been the dream of one day achieving even a little bit of that fame. From now on, he would have to be counted among those born to be poets. . . .

Sporadically at first, then with increasing courage, Werfel, Haas, Deutsch, and the rest caroused their way through the city's nightclubs— the Hamlet, the Montmartre, the Napoleon, the Eldorado. The Gogo, on Gemsengasse by the city market, was Prague's oldest and most expensive brothel. Well-to-do businessmen, high-ranking civil servants, artists, academics, and military men could be seen in its parlor with the red wallpaper, velvet curtains, and mirrors in gilded frames. For the gymnasium students, the brothel was first and foremost an inspiring venue for discussion, and the exciting atmosphere of the Gogo's parlor heightened their sense of joining the adult world—with wine, liqueurs, and cigarettes providing an additional boost.

Musical entertainment was provided by an aged piano player who used to mark the entrance of young Werfel with the first bars of some Italian opera; Franz was known at the nightspots for his ad hoc performances, in a pleasant tenor voice, of practically every vocal piece in the vast opera repertoire. "Caruso" was his nickname, and the better-educated ladies of the night were given to enthusiastic shouts of "Carousseau!"—they believed their idol's name sounded more correct in this French pronunciation.

The girls liked their youngest visitors and bantered with them, sometimes allowing them to share their communal early-morning breakfasts and possibly even granting further intimacies free of charge. Then the friends staggered home and to bed, where they remained until late morning, hours after their classmates arrived at school. Incredibly enough, both Franz's teachers and his parents let him get away with this behavior.

More excitement was provided by spiritualist séances in which the boys huddled around a small table calling up the souls of the dead. Paul Kornfeld was regarded as a talented medium, and the sessions were frequently held in his apartment. Often they waited for hours before the table leapt into the air and started dancing jerkily across the floor. The spirits communicated by knocking on or tilting the table; they described life in the beyond and made predictions about the future. Once, a woman who said she was freezing to death called for help: she was about to give birth, would someone please save her, she was in Semlin, on a bank of the Danube! In a panic, the friends rushed to the main post office through empty streets at 3:00 A.M. and sent a telegram to the police station in Semlin, demanding that the unfortunate woman be rescued.

By 1908 twenty-four-year-old Max Brod had laid his first claim to literary fame, and the young writers of Prague regarded him as their leader. After Werfel's poem appeared in *Die Zeit*, Willy Haas contacted Brod and gave him a manuscript collection of his friend's verses. Brod, himself an alumnus of the Piarist school and the Stefansgymnasium, had also taken his first literary steps as an adolescent; he found Franz's work exceptional and immediately asked to be introduced to the eighteen-year-old, defying the common belief that an age difference of six years was too great a gap to bridge.

Franz was very anxious when he met Brod for the first time, but when he started reciting his favorite poems by heart—tentatively at first, then with increasing bravura and assurance—he quickly won over the influential writer. Brod was enthusiastic and promised that he would do his best to ensure further publication of Werfel's work. Only once before had he given anyone such an accolade: Franz Kafka, the twenty-five-year-old insurance company employee whose eight prose pieces—his first publication—had appeared not long before in the Munich journal *Hyperion.*

Brod began to participate in the séances and sometimes brought his friends Franz Kafka and Felix Weltsch along. "I have been in such a state of confusion the last three days," Werfel told Brod in one of his letters of invitation, "that I'm surprised to find myself able to write." He went on to say that the new series of experiments had yielded "such striking phenomena" that he was now expecting, particularly because of Brod's presence, "some very special things." Sometimes these séances took place in Werfel's favorite café on Hybernergasse: "For tonight [we have] reserved the cellar in the Café Arko [*sic*] and would be most grateful to you if you could come and notify the other gentlemen as well."

The triumvirate Brod-Kafka-Weltsch was unanimous in its approval of Werfel, the chubby student. They liked his poems, they particularly appreciated his musical accomplishments, and they invited him to join them in their weekly excursions to the outskirts of Prague. Usually on Sundays, they hiked through the Bohemian forests and went skinny-dipping in the rivers. Tall, thin, and olive-skinned, Franz Kafka was the strongest and bravest swimmer among them. Werfel, however, was not up to strenuous hikes and hours of swimming; after one such weekend in early summer 1909, he returned home exhausted and severely sunburned, and took to his bed for several days with a high fever. His mother was furious and took Brod to task; it had been irresponsible of him, she scolded, not to have taken better care of his younger friend, especially at this critical juncture when Werfel, a weak scholar at best, was just about to take his graduation exams.

West Berlin, seventy-five years later: Knesebeckstrasse, at the corner of Kurfür-
stendamm. Anuschka Deutsch from Prague lives here, on the second floor of a
town house. Very slowly, the delicate, fragile lady moves through the light of the
drawing room. "You know, in my normal state I probably could have told you
some things of importance to your project," says the eighty-seven-year-old
woman in a deep, very hoarse voice, "but at the moment, I'm afraid, I'm just too
weak."

In 1922 Fräulein Fuchs married Ernst Deutsch, by then a very famous actor.
"I'm afraid you've come just a little too late," she says, "because I am not well

now." She sinks into an easy chair. Her eyes are alert. "Well, this photograph here, I can show you this: it's my husband and Werfel on their trip after passing their exams. My husband passed his at the German gymnasium on the Graben at the same time that Werfel sat for his on Stefansgasse. They used to argue about who had gone to the better school, and of course they did have the same religious instructor, and both of them were good at imitating him. Each one would claim some story as his, and they would get into huge arguments about it, many, many years later. Since both of them were such good children, their families paid the way of an indigent classmate to go with them on that trip as a chaperone. They had all sorts of adventures. For instance, they wanted to get into the Tivoli in Copenhagen, even though their money had run out—they just tried to sneak in for free! If you ask me, both of them look really dissipated in that picture.

"I knew Werfel's sisters well," Frau Deutsch continues after shaking her head one more time over the photograph. "Both of them were pretty girls, really, Marianne and Hanna. But their mother, Werfel's mother, I'm sorry to say, didn't have much character. The younger sister, Marianne—she was four years younger than I—we went to the same school, but she was a modern girl, one who ran around with men. We didn't do that. Not that we wouldn't have liked to; it just didn't happen. I think it was a musician Marianne was going with, but I have no idea what his name was. If I'm not mistaken, she left gymnasium after her fourth year. The other one, Hanna, was a schoolmate of my older sister's. She looked a lot like Werfel. Later she married a cousin of mine, Fuchs-Robetin, but my family wanted nothing to do with him. I mostly knew the Werfel sisters from parties; I went to a lot of dances and garden parties from the time I was ten years old. And I knew one of Werfel's great loves really well—she was pretty as a picture, Mitzi Glaser. She always looked down her nose at me. I knew her family, too—her sister Freda and their four brothers. You know, my husband had a big crush on Freda, he confessed to me much later. But we all knew that Werfel was very much in love with Mitzi. Of course it was all platonic! What else? You have to realize, this was before World War I; no one paid any attention to provocative girls, although there were some of those too. To make a date with a girl to go to some coffeehouse—that was as impossible as . . . as crawling up these walls would be. In our circles all encounters took place in people's homes, at parties. Werfel grew up in this bourgeois society, and that's why he started going to the Arco and so on, as a sort of protest. And started writing poems. Everybody thought that was very amusing. The very idea of writing poetry was totally alien to anyone from that part of society. I remember, when his first volume of poems came out, our family physician, who was also the Werfels' doctor—a real scandalmonger he was—came to see my mother and said, 'Can you imagine the nerve of that Franz, he has gone and published a book, The Friend of the World [Der Weltfreund]!*' He then went on to read it to us, to demonstrate how terrible it was. A little later I got a copy of the book and liked it a great deal. I was still so incredibly young. But to my mind Franzl was one of the sweetest*

people I've ever known—except for his looks, which really weren't too great. So they all sat in the coffeehouses then, my husband and Werfel and Kafka, Brod, Kisch. I knew Kisch really well. Mitzi Glaser became Mitzi Bondy, poor thing. Her husband, of the Bohemian copper dynasty, only shaved every other day, and on the unshaven days Herbert refused to go out, so Mitzi, too, could only go out every other day. She died fairly young, I think. Breast cancer, was it? I'm not sure. . . . Just ten minutes of talking makes me tired, it's ridiculous. I have to go lie down again. You should have come sooner, when my husband was still alive. The things he could have told you about Werfel and everything! . . ."

Café Arco

As soon as Franz Werfel gained his freedom from school, his father insisted that he attend university or enter a business apprenticeship. Although Franz did not register, he occasionally audited philosophy and law lectures at Karlsuniversität in Prague. He also took a course at the business college but continued spending his nights on the town, sleeping late, and writing poems, short stories, and theatrical dialogues.

He visited the coffeehouses daily—the Corso, the Edison, the Continental—but spent most of his time in the Café Arco, where he read dozens of literary journals, secretly paying for the subscriptions for some of them when he settled his monthly accounts with Herr Pošta, the headwaiter.

New faces appeared around Werfel's special table, where he sat with his friends, most of them young poets: Otto Pick and Rudolf Fuchs, Johannes Urzidil, Oskar Baum and Ernst Polak, the bank employee bitten by the literary bug. Like Kafka, Brod, Kornfeld, and Haas, all of them belonged to the small German-speaking Jewish minority of Prague.

As often as not, Werfel's works were created in the Arco's smoke-filled hubbub; as soon as a poem was completed, he would read it to his admirers. Traveling businessmen or brokers from the nearby Corn Exchange became an involuntary audience and had to interrupt their conversation as soon as Werfel started declaiming his verses.

Since his graduation, the number of poems he considered good had grown appreciably. Once again Willy Haas was his adviser and encouraged him to put together a first volume of poetry. Early in 1910 they sent the manuscript—which contained "5 Songs to Fräulein Mitzi" ("5 Lieder an Fräulein Mitzi")—to Ernst Rowohlt Verlag, a publishing house that had been founded in Leipzig two years earlier. Its initial lists, with their surprising number of avant-garde titles, had caught the attention of the Arco group. The Rowohlt editors soon returned Werfel's poems without comment. Brod then advised his friend to send the book to Brod's publisher in Berlin, Danish-born Axel Juncker, a wealthy older gentleman who was regarded as the leading publisher of modern poetry. "At the urging of Dr. Max Brod," Werfel wrote to Juncker in the summer of 1910, he was submitting a book of poems to which he "would like to give the title *The Good Comrade* [*Der gute Kamerad*]." Werfel went on to lie that another publisher was interested in the volume and had even begun "negotiations." Nevertheless, he was asking Juncker to consider the book, as he greatly valued his opinion and "the possibility of becoming part of your highly esteemed publishing program."

The atmosphere was far from pleasant around the family table at Mariengasse. A year had passed since Franz finished school, yet he had not started university studies or begun any commercial training. Recently, he had even failed in his father's place of business; he had been told to make a glove, but even with help from one of the workers, the journeyman piece had been a dismal failure. Rudolf Werfel was convinced that only a separation from the circle of friends in Prague and from the Arco and the Gogo would put Franz on the straight and narrow. He therefore got in touch with an import-export firm in Hamburg with which he was on friendly terms, the house of Brasch & Rothenstein, and arranged for Franz to start with them in the fall of 1910 as an intern. A minor until age twenty-three under Austrian law, the twenty-year-old Franz had no choice but to bow to his father's decision, in sadness and anger.

The summer vacation preceding his projected move was spent with his parents and sisters in Marienbad at the Grand Etablissement Egerländer, where he waited impatiently for a reply from Axel Juncker. Worried that the publisher might not see the "nature" of his poems clearly, Werfel wrote again to Berlin, saying that in the event of a favorable decision he would like to add "newer and more mature" poems and "replace and complete many things." The publisher, however, did not react to either letter.

Early in September, Franz and his family went to Munich and attended numerous theatrical performances and concerts. The world premiere of the *Symphony of a Thousand*, Gustav Mahler's Eighth, conducted by the composer, impressed Werfel most.

Alone, he then traveled north to Hamburg and took lodgings in the Pension Schröder on Hansastrasse, on his own for the first time in his life. The vitality of the Hanseatic city—the proximity of the North Sea, the great seaport, the markets, hotels, and theaters—was much to his liking, but his daily duties at Brasch & Rothenstein soon threatened to cast a shadow on these pleasures. Werfel responded to the demands of his job with passive resistance. During working hours in the firm's office he drafted poems, prose texts, and dialogues, pretended to be stupid, and deliberately bungled many of his assignments. One day he tossed an entire bundle of bills of lading into the toilet and flushed them out to sea, fantasizing that without the documents, the freighters would get lost on the high seas.

After only a few weeks, the manager asked the new intern to leave his post voluntarily and as soon as possible, to avoid the embarrassment of being summarily fired. Franz was delighted to agree to this proposal, jotting the equation "job = vice" into his notebook.

In the meantime, Axel Juncker had rejected Werfel's unconventional hymns. Max Brod then wrote Juncker a letter informing him that he no longer wanted to be published by a house that was unwilling to take a chance on a talent such as Franz Werfel's, and Juncker changed his mind. Although Juncker still wanted some changes, Werfel ignored the demand and wrote to the publisher in late October 1910 that he had chosen a new title for his book: "I would like to call it *The Friend of the World*. A good title, don't you think?" Impatiently hoping to placate his father at least a little with the publication of his first book of poems, Werfel urged Axel Juncker to get the volume out before the end of the year, but the publisher was not able to comply.

After his departure from the import-export firm, Franz stayed in Hamburg for several months, partly to avoid a confrontation with his parents, partly out of curiosity about bachelor life in the big North German city. He was attracted to St. Pauli and its cabarets. He went to seamen's bars, stood on swaying landing stages, gazed at the great steamships as they left harbor. Aimlessly he wandered through town, watched the feeding of the sharks in the zoo, sat in seedy smoke-filled cafés, jotted down conversational fragments and observations. He wrote poems and short stories and reflections on his work so far: "Too great a reliance on effects, I know that well." He planned a "Praise of Idleness" ("Lob der Faulenzer") and a "Hymn to Kitsch" ("Loblied auf den Kitsch").

Unexpectedly, he also found himself quite homesick. He sketched the heads of his parents on the back pages of his small notebook and often talked to them and his sisters and Barbara on the telephone. After these long-distance calls, he usually felt even worse.

One evening he ran into Mitzi Glaser in the lobby of the Lübeck Stadttheater and was appalled by the changes in his recently married heartthrob's appearance; now she seemed quite common to him. Each pretended not to recognize the other. Under the influence of this meeting Werfel wrote a one-act play, *The Visit from Elysium* (*Der Besuch aus dem Elysium*), set against a background of tennis, dancing school, and "the cosmos." Lukas, formerly Hedwig's platonic lover, has died and now appears as a ghost to thank his erstwhile tormentor for having been so lacking in empathy: "Had you loved me in return and granted me your greatest favor, my love could never have achieved the fulfillment it found when you did not invite it; thus you unleashed the most powerful force in my nature—*longing!*"

In early April 1911, on a Sunday walk through a cemetery, Werfel saw the dedication on the headstone of Annie Kalmar, a well-known actress: "In eternal memory—Karl Kraus." He stopped at the grave and read the chiseled words over and over, unable to explain what kept him there. He hardly knew the voluminous works of the poet, satirist, and pamphleteer Kraus; at this point he had only seen a few issues of *Die Fackel*, the journal Kraus was publishing in Vienna.

Werfel went back to his pension and to bed. He dreamed of the funeral of a young man: the coffin lid was open, he was able to memorize the features of the corpse. He saw wire-rimmed glasses, close-cropped hair, a curiously twisted mouth. He loved this stranger so much that he jumped into the grave, shouting ecstatically, "Who is this whose pain resounds here with such emphasis?"

The next morning, his mail at the pension contained a letter from Karl Kraus informing him that *Die Fackel* was going to print five poems from his as yet unpublished collection. Werfel considered the acceptance a great honor: the criteria of this polemical Viennese journal were regarded as particularly stringent. Only six weeks later, Kraus, until then known only by hearsay, had become an important person in Werfel's life. "All I need to be happy," he wrote to Kraus, enclosing some new poems, "is to know that you whom I revere and love (perhaps this declaration sounds a little bold) are reading my stuff." Kraus responded kindly, giving the young poet more encouragement. "The praise you bestow on that one stanza of my poems," Werfel replied, "has made me giddy with joy tonight."

At the end of May 1911 he returned to Prague. His father's position was unchanged: Franz would have to complete a course of academic study and enter a solid profession. Rudolf Werfel considered the publishing contract with Axel Juncker an irrelevant frill and even expressed doubts as to whether the announced book would actually appear. He now insisted that Franz do his military service.

In the fall, the twenty-one-year-old Werfel began his year of voluntary service in a barracks in Prague's Hradčany Castle, as an artilleryman in the Eighth Heavy Howitzer Division. In the course of his military training, he often spent time in detention. Harmless pranks and small derelictions were enough to earn hours of solitary. Werfel suffered from the stupidity and crudity of his superiors, and loathed the strenuous battle exercises and the daily preoccupation with rifles, artillery, ammunition. He hated the all-pervasive spirit of servility and its manifestations, such as having to beg for a pass to leave the barracks area.

During his months of military service, Franz Werfel became sympathetic to Czech irredentism, which was close to Bakunin's anarchism and strove for the secession of Bohemia and Moravia from the Austro-Hungarian Empire. The longer he served, the more resolute became his rejection of established power structures, whether familial or political. The very city of Prague became more and more alien to him, and he found its provincial restrictiveness, particularly for a non-Czech, increasingly insufferable. Angelo Neumann had died at the end of the previous year, and with his passing even the glamour and magic of the annual opera festivals were gradually fading. Werfel began to think seriously about leaving his native city on completion of his military service.

But there were good moments too. At the end of a reading from his own work in Berlin, in mid-December 1911, Max Brod read a few poems from Werfel's *Friend of the World* and told the audience that the book would be available in just a few days. The audience responded well to these samples, and the *Berliner Tageblatt* reviewer, Albert Ehrenstein, reported that the most enjoyable part of a reading given by the author Max Brod had been his recitation of poems by someone far more significant: the unknown young poet from Prague, Franz Werfel. In the December issue of *Die Fackel*, Karl Kraus printed five more poems by Werfel and made a point of calling his readers' attention to the long-awaited publication of the book.

The Friend of the World came out in a first edition of four thousand copies that sold out immediately. During the following three weeks it had to be reprinted several times, and the name Franz Werfel became instantly known and admired in the German-speaking world. A new sound, said the laudatory reviews, was heard in Werfel's hymnodic verses; the apparently simplest, most soulless things were elevated into living poetic images in these songs of feeling. Fame, once the schoolboy's wildest dream, had now come to him: overnight the young son of a Prague glove manufacturer had become one of the most widely discussed poets of the German language.

Franz Kafka envied his friend the ease of his success, his abundance of talent, and the wealthy background that had permitted Werfel, so Kafka believed, the freedom from care that he himself longed for yet saw himself utterly incapable of achieving. For his part, Werfel was not very excited by Kafka's prose. When Brod read him some of Kafka's texts, Werfel expressed disappointment: "That will never play outside Tetschen-Bodenbach!" (a small border crossing between Bohemia and the German Empire).

It was not simply this judgment that caused a temporary estrangement between Werfel and Brod; more divisive was an argument about Richard Wagner. On one of their frequent walks in the city park, Brod called the German composer the greatest in the history of opera—an opinion that Werfel, the Verdi enthusiast, could not leave unchallenged. When he dared to say something derogatory about Wagner and poked fun at the Wagnerian style of composition, Brod lost his temper and withdrew his patronage.

Some diversion from the detestable routine of military training, which was to continue until the end of September 1912, was provided by the occasional maneuvers in which the Eighth Heavy Howitzer Division engaged. Werfel enjoyed sleeping out in the fields and forests of the Bohemian countryside, and he loved marching through the villages in the morning light, talking to the farmers. Undetected by his superiors, he was sometimes even able to write. One of these exercises saw the creation of a one-act play, *The Temptation* (*Die Versuchung*), a bombastic three-way conversation between a poet alter ego, an archangel, and Lucifer, dedicated "to the memory of Giuseppe Verdi."

"And why is it mine, this terrible gift of poetry?" That is the poet's rhetorical question, to which Lucifer replies: "Triumphs will be yours before which those of kings and tenors pale.... Pindar's Olympic laurel [is] of a lesser mythic power than your tenfold Nobel Prizes." When the archangel describes the impetuous poet as "one of ours, one of the infinite spirits," the poet's enthusiasm for himself knows no bounds: "I admire myself. I am great. . . . For look, I am the Annunciation!"

In the uniform of a one-year volunteer, wearing a wide cavalry saber, Werfel would hurry down from the Hradčany into town, back to the Café Arco, during his few hours of leave. His friends and admirers esteemed him more than ever; they were proud of him, the famous writer they had known when hardly anyone outside the café walls had heard of him. As before, they immersed themselves in discussions of Dostoyevsky and Tolstoy, Nietzsche and Kierkegaard. Werfel recited his new drama, *The Temptation*, to the assembled friends from memory.

Today, the erstwhile cradle of literary expressionism and main gathering place of the Prague avant-garde is a petit-bourgeois restaurant with adjoining spaces for variety shows and a student cafeteria. "Today's Café Arco is much smaller than the original," Dr. František Kafka says in one of his letters. "Being a corner building, it was damaged by the construction of the new pedestrian walkway on Hybernergasse and Dlážděná." He also tells me that the old leaseholder of the establishment kept the Arco going until his death in the mid-1930s—and that this same Suchanek is one of the main characters in Johannes Urzidil's well-known story "A Night of Terror" ("Eine Schreckensnacht").

Not only young German-speaking authors frequented the Arco. Situated across from the Central Railway Station, and not far from the newly constructed main station, it was often used by business people and salesmen as "an ideal place to meet and relax." Young women from Czech Bohemia also frequented the café, such as the beautiful Milena Jesenská, who later married Ernst Polak and corresponded with Franz Kafka. Willy Haas, too, first met his wife, Jarmila Ambrožová, in the Café Arco. The "Arconauts"—as Karl Kraus called the circle around Werfel—chose the café as their headquarters for yet another reason: unlike the well-established cafés on the Graben, says Dr. Kafka, the Arco "was not burdened by old enmities between the Czech and German nations. This generation was looking for something new, and thus the café became a bridge builder between the young Germans (= Jews!) and the young Czechs of Prague." A lively exchange of ideas took place between these two groups in the Arco, where authors, painters, and musicians of both nationalities gathered, providing Werfel and his friends with a special escape route from the linguistic and cultural ghetto in which they would have existed otherwise.

The famous saying "Es brodelt und werfelt und kafkat und kischt," a description of the Arco circle, was not coined by Karl Kraus or Anton Kuh, as is commonly supposed. Dr. Kafka writes: "Max Brod, with whom I had an interview in 1967 in Flims, attributed it to Egon Erwin Kisch, who was thus trying to attract more attention to himself than he really deserved."

The building in which Franz Werfel lived until he left Prague in the fall of 1912 is still standing. The former Mariengasse on the edge of the city park is now named Opletalova Ulice, after a Czech student who was shot and killed by the Nazis in 1939. Dr. Kafka visited the former Werfel family apartment at Opletalova 41: "The doors and interior surfaces of this apartment, painted a high-gloss white, are still preserved in what are now the offices of the Průmstav construction company, and it is even possible to guess where Barbara's little room was. It is a large luxury apartment with many rooms, in what was then the most elegant street of the haute bourgeoisie." Rudolf Werfel always lived in modern Prague's New Town, with its wide streets and sanitary new buildings, whereas Hermann Kafka, Franz Kafka's father, was reduced to renting small, dark apartments in the former ghetto, on the narrow streets of the Old Town. "The Werfel family," Dr. Kafka informs me, "was not only a notch above the Kafka family in its material living conditions, it was also more open in its thinking: liberal, tolerant—and as un-Jewish in life's outward forms as possible."

The Day of Judgment

Max Brod had left his publisher, Axel Juncker, and joined Ernst Rowohlt Verlag in the summer of 1912. Rowohlt was the house that two years earlier had rejected the first version of Werfel's *Friend of the World* without comment. Now Brod praised his friend Werfel to both Rowohlt and his financial backer, Kurt Wolff, describing him as one of the most talented of the younger generation and, what was more, a poet who could be very profitable to a newly emerging publishing house. Wolff himself had rejected the manuscript back then but now regretted the decision and wanted to patch things up by inviting Werfel on a no-strings-attached visit to Leipzig. The latter knew how to turn that meeting to his advantage, impressing Wolff, a slender, elegant young man, with his tales of childhood and youth, of the strict father who expected his son to take over the family glove business one day; he even told Wolff an amusing version of the Hamburg interlude at Brasch & Rothenstein. He also spoke of his passion for the theater, Italian opera, and literature. He told Wolff that if it was possible for him to land a job that had the appearance of regular employment, his father's resistance and fears could be allayed at least for a while.

Instantly charmed by his visitor, Kurt Wolff acted on the spot. He offered Werfel a contract to work for the publishing house as an author and editor, with an annual starting salary of eighteen hundred marks. The contract pointedly did not mention that the publisher was giving his new employee a great deal of freedom and wouldn't even insist on regular office hours.

Very soon after this discussion, Wolff and Rowohlt had a falling-out. Business relations between the two had been extremely tense for some time, and this one incident was enough to bring about a final separation. Rowohlt, the founder, felt that his partner had gone over his head; he could not tolerate Wolff's meeting with Werfel behind his back, so to speak, as if he were the sole proprietor and decision maker. At the beginning of November 1912, Wolff and Rowohlt formalized the break, and Wolff became the sole owner of Ernst Rowohlt Verlag, whose name he changed to Kurt Wolff Verlag in 1913.

A few weeks after completing his military training, in October 1912, Franz Werfel left his native city and moved to Leipzig. In two large cupboards in his parents' apartment he left what he now called his literary estate—everything he had produced since he began writing at the age of fourteen.

Rudolf Werfel had been informed of his son's new employment and gradually relented. Thus, Franz's plan had worked perfectly. His father wrote to Wolff, saying that he had resigned himself, after a long struggle, to the fact that his heir would pursue a profession so very far removed from his own. However, he urged the publisher (the twenty-five-year-old Wolff must have impressed him as a very responsible person) to make absolutely sure that Franz did indeed work regularly for several hours a day. In addition, Rudolf Werfel had begun to act in his son's business interests; for example, he threatened Axel Juncker that he would withdraw the rights to a third edition of *The Friend of the World* if the Berlin publisher did not agree to certain conditions.

The young editor Franz Werfel, wearing his long hair combed straight back and otherwise looking remarkably disheveled at all times, rented accommodations from Frau Seyfert on Haydnstrasse. He became known as an extremely unreliable and forgetful person who often misplaced important things and was apt to burst into Verdi arias or recitations of his own poems, a dreamy visionary who adored beautiful women, a coffeehouse addict who slept through the mornings and occasionally put in an appearance at the publisher's office in the afternoon. He dined at Wilhelms Weinstuben, the wine cellar that had become the meeting place of Leipzig's poets and thinkers. There he encountered, enthroned at their regular table, Carl Sternheim and Frank Wedekind, Martin Buber and Kurt Hiller, and also made the acquaintance of Else Lasker-Schüler, who called herself Prince Yousuf of Thebes and wrote him love letters in which she, fourteen years his senior, addressed him as "schoolboy" and "Franzlaff" (Franzl-ape).

He was preparing a new collection of poems that he wanted to call *We Are* (*Wir sind*); in this first Leipzig period he also wrote several prose pieces, among them "The Season" ("Die Stagione"), in which he drew on his memories of the May Festival in Prague and the military year in the Hradčany. Occasionally he attended lectures at the famous University of Leipzig, particularly those of the old psychologist Wilhelm Wundt and the historian Karl Lamprecht. Now that he no longer felt coerced by his father, he enjoyed the academic world, seeing himself in the tradition of Goethe and Lessing, both of whom had studied in Leipzig.

He usually went to the Café Felsche or the theater in the evenings, then spent the night making the rounds of bars, cabarets, and brothels. His new friends were other editors at Kurt Wolff's: there was his contemporary Walter Hasenclever, a poet from Aachen, high-strung and very talented, whose conflicts with his father had been similar to Franz's; and Kurt Pinthus, a little older than his colleagues, a heavy-set, ponderous, rather more settled young man, also a writer, as well as a reviewer and correspondent for the *Berliner Tageblatt*.

Early in 1913, as the three of them sat with Kurt Wolff in the wee hours in the so-called Intimate Bar, a decision was made for which Werfel had been pushing from the moment he joined the publishing house: to give unknown writers their first chance at publication by means of a new series of avant-garde literature in slim paperbound volumes. It would be a series, Werfel proposed, that could be published inexpensively at irregular intervals, and that would stand out from the literary production of other publishing companies. On that February night in 1913 Kurt Wolff for the first time seemed willing to agree to the proposals of his three editors: the new series would be presented to the public that spring. The galleys of Werfel's collection *We Are* happened to be lying on the marble-topped bar table; Pinthus stabbed at them with a pencil, hitting a line from the dramatic sketch "The Sacrifice" ("Das Opfer"): "O Day of Judgment! O reunion!" That night the series was titled Day of Judgment.

Its first volume was Werfel's own one-act play *The Temptation*, written one day on maneuvers in 1912; the second was Hasenclever's *Endless Conversation (Das unendliche Gespräch)*. The new series, the public was told in an advertisement written by Werfel for the German book trade journal, had been created "by the collective experience of our time." In another slightly confused ad, also written by Werfel and distributed as a leaflet, we read: "In these little books we welcome the true, true poet . . . who every moment bleeds with the knowledge that . . . the act of realization itself obscures and blinds. . . . The world begins anew every second—let us forget literature!!"

Around this time, Franz Werfel gave his first public reading, in the Mirror Room of the Deutsches Haus in Prague. He read from *The Friend of the World* and *We Are*, and the audience was receptive to his natural pathos. The daily papers reviewed the event most favorably. During his visit to Prague, Werfel met frequently with his friends from the Café Arco and renewed his friendship with Franz Kafka, in whose work he was far more interested now, since he was able to see it more clearly than he had a few years before. At this time, Kafka wrote to his fiancée, Felice Bauer, in Berlin and told her that he was growing ever fonder of Werfel, also rhapsodizing about his friend's practically paradisiacal new existence as an editor in Leipzig. Together Kafka and Werfel attended a guest performance by the Ballets Russes and saw Nijinsky and Lydia Kyasht, an event that made a lasting impression on Werfel. He was impressed by the wonderful non-nationalness and the mad *being-beside-oneself* (freedom from preconceived form) of the Russian ballet. "I did not experience these as aesthetic stimulation but as the symbol of [a] new humanity. All emotions swell up to a rage 'to be in the world,' to celebrate."

Werfel and Kafka read their latest works to each other. Over and over again, Kafka told the younger man how impressed he was by his poetry. In November 1912 Kafka's first volume of prose, *Meditation*, had been published by Ernst Rowohlt Verlag in an edition of eight hundred copies. After his return from Prague, Werfel told Wolff about Kafka's new stories, praising them highly. Wolff then wrote to Kafka, asking to see these works. When Kafka visited Leipzig not long after and met with Wolff at Werfel's urging, he told the publisher about a novel-length work in progress. The first chapter of that novel (*Amerika*) appeared under the title *The Stoker* in May 1913 as volume 3 of the Day of Judgment series. *The Metamorphosis* and *The Judgment* followed in 1915 and 1916, as volumes 22–23 and 34 of the series.

It was Werfel who first brought Karl Kraus to Kurt Wolff's attention. As the audience for Kraus's journal *Die Fackel* consisted almost exclusively of readers in the states of the Danube monarchy, Wolff had never heard of him. Werfel insisted that he try all means at his disposal to make Kraus one of his authors. He spoke obsessively about his idol and kept at it until Wolff actually went to Vienna in Werfel's company and persuaded Kraus to publish his future writings exclusively with Kurt Wolff Verlag in Leipzig.

While Wolff was away on vacation in April 1913, Werfel ran the house practically single-handed. He now received manuscripts by unknown authors daily and saw how popular the new series was becoming. A voluminous bundle of poems by a young writer from Salzburg, Georg Trakl, pleased him particularly. He wrote the unknown poet to tell him that he had read the poems "with great admiration" and that "I have—the publisher tells me that he is already negotiating with you—selected a number of poems. I hope you will find the selection agreeable."

Werfel's second volume, *We Are*, came out that spring and was favorably received by the critics, although they did not find the work as startling and fresh as *The Friend of the World*. The book, Werfel stated in an afterword, was "the first in a succession of volumes that will eventually, as *one* work, bear the title *Paradise* [*Das Paradies*]." Domestics and prostitutes, dogs and telephone conversations, ladies' orchestras and theater scandals—all enlivened its pages as subject matter wholly novel to German-language lyric poetry. The Dionysiac-expressionist style, breathless and hyperbolic, was clearly reminiscent of Werfel's idol Walt Whitman, whose *Leaves of Grass* he had adored since his schooldays, and whose influence had been unmistakable even in Werfel's first book. A saying of the revered poet's, uttered on his deathbed, provided the epigraph for *We Are:* "Well then, now I'll go sit on the porch and enjoy life!"

Werfel spent May 1913 with his friends Hasenclever and Pinthus in Malcesine, on Lake Garda. At the publisher's expense, they stayed at a pension by the lakeshore and lived the life of Riley, ingesting huge bowls of asparagus at fifty centesimi a bowl, savoring wonderful meals in the osterias, enjoying excursions to the beautiful countryside, to Riva del Garda, Sirmione, Verona.

During these weeks in Italy, Werfel was already preparing a third volume of poems, writing numerous odes and hymns. For the first time his poems included subject matter to which he had been curiously attracted from his earliest childhood; now his writing began to draw closer to that strange yet familiar religion of Catholicism, with which Barbara Šimůnková had once acquainted him when she took the little boy to morning mass. One of these new poems was "Jesus and the Carrion Road" ("Jesus und der Äser-Weg"), another "The Procession" ("Die Prozession"), whose third stanza read: "Up the stairs into the church they dive / A thousand, praying and kneeling wildly. / Chaotic candlelight bursts out of blue smoke, / Under a picture, a bell is rung. / There—and horns and organs roar under the vaults."

In the summer of 1913 Werfel received a letter from Rainer Maria Rilke. The verses in *The Friend of the World* and *We Are* had moved him to an extraordinary degree, Rilke wrote; moreover he believed that he had found a kindred spirit in the young poet, whose senior he was by fifteen years. Werfel considered this praise the highest honor yet bestowed on him in his life. As a schoolboy, he had regarded Rilke as the very embodiment of the Poet and looked up to him as if to a saint. Rilke's poetry had fired his will and compulsion to write. "How can I tell you how many tears I have to thank you for since the days of my awakening?" he replied to Rilke's first letter. "How, years ago, when you gave a reading in Prague, I was unable to breathe and almost swooned in your presence. Those long, pure-as-rain consolations I received from you in my schooldays! And now, this man is writing to me!!"

The two agreed on a first meeting in October, at the festival in

Hellerau near Dresden. Both looked forward to it: the quiet older man with the peaceful smile, blue eyes, drooping moustache, and delicate features, so careful in every gesture, so exquisitely attired, an aesthete through and through; and the loud, chubby younger man, always sweaty, always shabby, always full to bursting with the joy of reciting and telling stories. Rilke had decided, so he told his friend Hugo von Hofmannsthal, to embrace Werfel on their first encounter, but when they actually met, he just shook hands quickly and then, embarrassed, put his arms behind his back. They took a walk, and Werfel sensed a remoteness on Rilke's part; only later, after lunch at a vegetarian restaurant, did the older man yield to Werfel's urging and start telling him, tentatively at first, about his own childhood in Prague and his time at the Piarist school. He talked about his sense of being condemned to spiritual homelessness by the fact of being a German from Prague, and about the indignities to which he had been subjected during his time in the military. He never looked directly at his companion but sat there with downcast eyes.

After the festival performance of Paul Claudel's play *The Annunciation,* a large group of people proceeded to Dresden's noble Palast Hotel, among them Werfel, Rilke, Lou Andreas-Salomé, and Baroness Sidonie Nádherný of Castle Janowitz in Bohemia, an admirer and close acquaintance of Rilke's. Baroness Nádherný knew about Rilke's enthusiasm for Werfel; he had told her in a recent letter that he was reading and rereading Werfel's poems. Now, however, as Werfel was introduced to her, she immediately pulled Rilke aside and let him know how much she disliked this "Jewboy." All evening long, she treated Werfel with marked condescension, making her contempt quite clear. Anti-Semitism alone cannot have been the reason for such behavior. Only a few weeks earlier, Sidonie Nádherný had met a man who, according to her diary, "understood" her like no one ever before—a simply unforgettable man: Karl Kraus.

The deeply offended Werfel, aware of that liaison, took care to let Kraus know as soon as possible that Rilke seemed to be very close to the baroness, going in and out of Castle Janowitz at all hours. He also spread some other rumors, partly invented, partly assumed, such as the piquant morsel that Baroness Nádherný had to be a fascinating lady, since at one point in her life she had spent months traveling with a rather derelict circus troupe. . . .

During his visit to Hellerau, Werfel met several times with Jakob Hegner, the initiator and organizer of the festival. Although Hegner was a Jew and entertained no thought of conversion, he was particularly interested in Christian subjects. In conversation with Werfel he mentioned that he regarded Euripides as an early forerunner of Christianity. He urged Werfel to do a new adaptation of *The Trojan Women*, saying that there had been no truly stageworthy German version of the tragedy since Schiller's antiquated translation. Hegner told Werfel that such work would give him a chance to deal intensely with questions of dramatic structures, and also to introduce his own ecstatic and hymnodic language to the German stage.

Hegner's suggestion resulted in Werfel's translation of *The Trojan Women* (*Die Troerinnen*), on which he worked from the fall of 1913 until the beginning of the following year. It marked a great leap in Werfel's development. Since his departure from Prague, this childlike dreamer, the sheltered, dependent son of the haute bourgeoisie, had become a writer with an analytical bent, well read in philosophy, and an editor who bore the great responsibility of participating in decisions on the fate of other writers. His blunder in regard to Baroness Nádherný and Karl Kraus, however, was indicative of a regression to late adolescence.

In his introductory note to *The Trojan Women*, Werfel pointed out that the fall of Troy could be seen as a metaphor for the present. Then as now, the world was suffering a period of upheaval and the dissolution of value and meaning: "In its cyclical course, human history once again passes through the conditions out of which this work may well have been created"—thus he justified his decision to retranslate Euripides' tragedy. He said that he had seen in the figure of Hecuba, tried by suffering, an anticipation of the passion of Jesus Christ; by carefully altering the original, probably with Hegner's encouragement, he had the Queen of Troy act and argue like an early Christian. Thanks not least to this delicate manipulation, he came to the conclusion: "And thus we see the notorious atheist Euripides as a harbinger, a prophet, an early dove of Christianity."

For years, Werfel had felt alienated from his Jewishness but unable to express the reasons for that alienation. His relationship to Judaism was characterized not so much by self-loathing or conscious rejection as by an indifference that he himself did not see as a problem. He had hardly set foot in a synagogue since his schooldays. His world consisted of the writers and composers of Europe, most of whom had strong ties to Christianity. Yet he did not really belong to this world: like Rilke, Werfel saw himself as a man without roots who had to find his home in his work.

At the beginning of 1914, Willy Haas dropped his law studies in Prague and followed his friend to Leipzig, where Werfel found him a position as an editor with Kurt Wolff. Haas had had some publishing experience as the editor of the *Herder-Blätter*, a literary journal with a very small circulation; it had published works by Werfel, Brod, Kafka, Janowitz, Pick, and others, but had ceased publication at the time of Werfel's departure from Prague.

Haas shared a large Haydnstrasse apartment with Werfel, Hasenclever, and Pinthus. After a night of partying they were usually roused by their secretary, Karl Weissenstein, a colorful character who had been a habitué of the Café Arco and had found Prague unbearable without his friends. He slyly coaxed the young gentlemen out of bed by telling each that the others had risen long ago and had been hard at work for hours.

On the same spring day in 1914 that Franz Werfel was giving a reading in his hometown, his father addressed a dramatic appeal to Kurt Wolff, urging the publisher to make sure that Franz began working toward a doctorate, and saying that it was high time he understood the necessity of a secure profession. It was inconceivable, Rudolf Werfel wrote, that Franz would ever be able to start a family of his own if he went on living at night and sleeping away his days. His parents were deeply concerned about their son. However, it was imperative not to let Franz know that his father was the initiator of this idea: Wolff was to act as "go-between." Two months earlier, the publisher had made yet another attempt to pacify Rudolf Werfel, telling him that his son was about to receive a raise, and that he, Wolff, was particularly proud to count Franz Werfel among his authors and was more than satisfied with his work as an editor. Evidently, none of this had been enough to allay the father's fundamental misgivings.

Soon after Werfel's reading, Karl Kraus came to Prague to give a lecture. In delighted anticipation of a reunion, Werfel left a note of welcome at his hotel. But when he rushed to greet Kraus at the end of the lecture, he encountered conspicuous reserve. "From the coolness of your handshake . . . I surmise what has come between us," the unhappy Werfel wrote to Kraus, asking to see him as soon as possible. While admitting that he had been "imprudent" in spreading gossip about Baroness Nádherný, he nevertheless claimed "the purest of intentions."

"I am Franz Werfel," he says in the letter, which Kraus immediately sent on to Sidonie, after underlining Werfel's stylistic blunders with obvious relish, "and . . . if you can believe even for a moment that I would have been capable of an indecency, of intentional malice, you also declare my work . . . to be a lie and a fraud." Kraus asked his lady friend to advise him how to reply to this "disgusting" letter. By agreement with Sidonie, he had given Herr Werfel "the cold shoulder" when he saw him in Prague. But how to react now, after receiving the enclosed?

In the next issue of *Die Fackel,* which contained Kraus's report on his lecture in Prague, readers were informed that in the capital of Bohemia the German-language poets were now multiplying like "muskrats," "pollinated" by that "child virtuoso" Werfel. This slur on the poet once praised so highly by Kraus must have been quite incomprehensible to the journal's subscribers.

On June 28, 1914, the Serbian nationalists Princip and Čabrinović succeeded in assassinating Franz Ferdinand, heir to the Austrian throne, and Werfel's quarrel with Kraus faded in importance. Now political events struck Werfel as the fulfillment of his own prophecy: "Even in our souls, faith has lost its form," he had written three months earlier in his introduction to *The Trojan Women,* "and we have to regard that as a portent of the upheaval that is in the making . . . Tragedy and hapless Hecuba may now return; their time has come."

Werfel's gradual attempts to free himself from obligations to family and state had been in vain. On the last day of July, in the wake of general mobilization, the one-year volunteer reservist had to report to his regiment in Prague and return to the hated barracks of the Hradčany, transferred from Leipzig's atmosphere of freedom to Battery 2, demoted from poet and editor to lowly gunner.

One week later, the Austro-Hungarian Empire declared war on Russia.

The greater part of Franz Werfel's literary estate is in the custody of the University of California at Los Angeles, located in Westwood Village. On a hot, cloudless day I cross the parklike campus to the Research Library and descend, now chilled by air-conditioning, to the basement, where large, windowless rooms lit by fluorescent light house the Special Collections.

An extremely shy, fragile-looking young librarian introduces herself as the cataloguer of Franz Werfel's unpublished works. Of Japanese descent, she was born in the United States, she tells me in a quiet voice, blushing a little when she admits her ignorance of German—this explains the numerous spelling errors that occurred when she was typing the catalogue lists, she says. She also admits that she is totally unfamiliar with Werfel's oeuvre. As silently and imperceptibly as she appeared, Mrs. Hatayama retires again.

I sit at a work table in the Special Collections room, dozens of shoebox-sized containers of letters, diaries, notebooks, sketches, and original manuscripts by Franz Werfel stacked before me. His life's work of fantasizing and philosophizing is preserved in these shabby cardboard boxes—cardboard tombs in which I look for signs of life, feeling like a grave robber, digging through papers that were never intended for the eyes of strangers.

A supervisor watches me from some distance, while I leaf through hundreds of unknown letters from Werfel to his beloved—and later, wife—Alma Maria Mahler. I keep on opening boxes, feeling rather greedy. I discover some of the earliest poems, written in almost illegible pencil in thin exercise books that are now falling apart. I find dried flowers between manuscript pages, dramatic sketches, bits of prose, thought fragments . . .

The notebook "Leipzig 1913" comes to hand. It contains, among other things, a list of long-lost Werfel texts: "The Town by the Sea" ("Seestadt"), "A Soldier's Letter" ("Ein Soldaten-Brief"), "Jesus and Hatred" ("Jesus und der Hass"). During his Leipzig days, Werfel was planning a dramatic work titled Theresa; *there is an outline for thirteen scenes. His serious involvement with Christianity first becomes apparent in this notebook: "Redemption! The world can only be redeemed from the world," reads one entry. "Christianity gets by with an illusionary pessimism. The church performs the magic of a retrospective utopia that has taken place in the past." Elsewhere, Werfel quotes—probably at the time he was translating* The Trojan Women—*a verse from the Second Epistle of Peter: "For the prophecy came not in old time by the will of man: but holy men of God spake as they were moved by the Holy Ghost."*

Before the beginning of the war he wrote, "Logic of the state. Because blood has been shed, more blood has to flow, so that the blood already shed won't have been shed in vain." And when the Great War broke out, he noted laconically, "The modern state, well designed for war, really presupposes war as the true challenge of its organism. . . . created for war, as a cholera hospital was built for cholera—this state denies, one grows pale at the thought, any responsibility for the creation of the war." During his renewed service in the barracks, where he saw countless casualties "suppurating, feverish, delirious, dying," he wrote, "The war an experience? It is the opposite of all experience. A destruction of all differentiation, all harmonies and discords, a department store, a going-out-of-business sale of all experiences—it devalues them by cheapness, mass, and inevitability."

The Good Soldier

Franz Werfel had never cherished the ideals of fidelity to the fatherland and bravery under fire. He did not hesitate to feign physical illness and mental instability to his military superiors. To him, it was a matter of indifference whether officers and comrades regarded him as a weakling or a coward. He was excused from active military duty as early as the end of November 1914, initially for three months, until the "handing down" of a "superarbitration finding," as noted in the official memorandum of the Royal and Imperial Army.

More than happy to have escaped from the military machine at least temporarily, Werfel moved in with his parents on Mariengasse. Here he wrote the first act of a play, *Esther, Empress of Persia* (*Esther, Kaiserin von Persien*), in which he used the biblical subject to refine his sense of the dramatic and to practice writing consistent dialogue. Using methods similar to those he had applied to *The Trojan Women,* his apprentice piece, he now assimilated the rules of classical theater and attempted to emulate Shakespeare, Lessing, and Grillparzer.

He worked on the dialogue *Euripides, or On the War* (*Euripides oder über den Krieg*), in which he blamed "the fathers," the old men, for the outbreak of martial conflict. The old men, argues Euripides in Werfel's text, sent "the young men to war in order to redeem their own vices. . . . All states are the symbol of the old men."

Before the end of the year he had completed the collection of poems *Each Other* (*Einander*), which he had begun a year earlier in Malcesine on Lake Garda. The confusions and anxieties he observed in himself during the first months of the war were reflected in his latest poems, which now stood contrasted with earlier expressions of religious exuberance: "But God's music is mercy / . . . O mankind, highest curved wave, / Soprano in God's entirely endless orchestra!"

Werfel worried that this new volume would not succeed without the personal involvement of Kurt Wolff, who was now serving as an aide-de-camp in an artillery regiment on the French front. Wolff had left all business matters to Georg Heinrich Meyer, an experienced publisher, whom he considered entirely trustworthy. In January 1915 Werfel met Meyer in Leipzig and felt some liking for the new director of his publishing house, even though the latter let him know that Werfel's kind of poetry was not his cup of tea.

In February 1915 the Prague military command found Werfel still unfit for service and deferred him another two months. He traveled to Berlin to visit Martin Buber, whom he had revered for years. Buber had presented his "Three Lectures on Jewry" ("Drei Reden über das Judentum") in Prague, and Werfel had met him on that occasion. They exchanged some letters, met several times in Leipzig, and had last seen each other in the spring of 1914, after a reading Werfel gave in Berlin.

Immediately after the outbreak of the war, Buber, Gustav Landauer, and Max Scheler had formed a secret antimilitarist group. Werfel was invited to their meetings; at twenty-four, he was extremely proud to be accepted as an equal in this circle of far older men and truly felt like a conspirator as he listened to the talks and animated discussions in Landauer's home. They confirmed him in his own anitmilitarist views.

The deferment Werfel had been granted was to end on April 1. Afraid that he would wind up in the trenches after all, he put in a personal appearance at the offices of the Supreme Command in Vienna. He pointed out that his nerves would be unable to stand the stress of frontline service, enumerated his literary successes, and explained the precariousness of his health. He claimed that he wanted to serve but asked to be assigned duties commensurate with his exceptional status. Surprisingly enough, the Supreme Command actually agreed to these special requests by the well-known antiwar poet and assigned Private Werfel to office duty in Bozen (Bolzano). At that time, the capital of the province of South Tyrol was still far removed from the battle lines.

Shortly before his transfer to Bozen, Werfel saw Karl Kraus sitting in a restaurant in Vienna and went to greet him. When the gaunt man with the small round spectacles saw Werfel, he jumped to his feet and launched into a long tirade, accusing his former protégé of fabricating all the scandalous stories about Rilke and Sidonie, slanderous lies based only on Werfel's injured vanity. Werfel replied haltingly that he really couldn't remember those events in Dresden all that well, then shame-facedly admitted that he was now unable to comprehend "what he had been thinking of at the time." As a poet, Kraus countered, he should take care to think of better things in the future—whereupon Werfel apologized once again, begging Kraus not to treat him with such

biblical severity and to give him credit for his contrition. But the furious
Kraus was implacable and turned away in disgust.

In mid-April 1915, Private Werfel moved into the Erbacher Hof, an inn
in Bozen—at his own expense, as was duly noted in his record. He
considered his posting an undeserved stroke of luck; he had a lot of
free time and was able to read, write, and make excursions into the
Dolomites. One day, he was walking through a gorge not far from town,
carrying a Reclam edition of Dante's *Divine Comedy*, which had become
a kind of second Bible to him. He was suddenly overwhelmed by the
certainty that past and future, birth and death, this world and the next
were simultaneous, and that distinctions between them were purely
conventional, designed to keep people from losing their sanity. He
thought that heaven and hell—as Dante, too, described them—were
not to be located exclusively in life after death, but that they were
already unfolding in this life. Enchanted by this idea, he returned to
his room at the inn and immediately began to write "Dream of a New
Hell" ("Traum von einer neuen Hölle") in terza rima, following Dante's
example.

He spent the following days in a trance. Each moment gave him new
proof of the existence of hell in this world, even a ride in the funicular
from Bozen to Kohlern. "He feels condemned to such a hell," he wrote
a little later in his somewhat overwrought "Bozen Journal" ("Das
Bozener Buch") "as he steps into the small carriage of the funicular
railway. He is surrounded by hostile petits bourgeois. To get away from
them, he steps out onto the platform . . ." And before the funicular
reached its terminal on the mountaintop, he jumped off, was dragged
along for some distance, and suffered severe injuries to both legs,
especially his right foot. He was rushed from Kohlern to the hospital in
Bozen.

Although he was suffering intense pain, he felt curiously happy in
the bright hospital room: "He is filled by a wonderful feeling of having
done penance. . . . With this event (whether it was a punishment or not,
I did not ponder the mysterious chain of events), with this event, my
soul had rid itself of all guilt, all sense of sin. . . . Now I belonged to the
suffering, to the poor, to the not-so-fortunate of this earth—I thought,
with joyful satisfaction." Subconsciously, he may well have inflicted this
damage on himself in hopes of being excused from frontline duty for
the duration—surely the war would be over by the fall or winter at the
latest. He spent several weeks in the Bozen hospital before he was
allowed to return to Prague. As late as mid-June 1915 he still had to use
crutches and put up with the inevitable questions of Prague acquaintances as to what battle he had been wounded in.

In the meantime *Each Other* and the translation of *The Trojan Women* had appeared. Neither book sold at all well, although G. H. Meyer mounted the most intensive publicity campaign the German publishing world had ever seen: big red posters advertising Kurt Wolff Verlag were plastered on kiosks and columns everywhere.

Werfel consoled Meyer, saying that many of his readers were in the trenches and that the "spontaneity" of sales was not as important as their "continuity"; furthermore, he was working on a book that was "sure to put the house back on its feet"—so convinced was he of the potential of the project begun in Bozen, "Dream of a New Hell." However, the work proceeded only by fits and starts. Convalescence made Werfel tired, apathetic; a novella about Montezuma, the Aztec ruler, did not get past its initial pages either.

Most of Werfel's friends from the Café Arco—except Kafka, Brod, Urzidil, and the blind poet Oskar Baum—were now in military service. During the summer of 1915, Werfel and Max Brod engaged in vehement disputes about Judaism and Zionism. Brod had become an enthusiastic supporter of Theodor Herzl's ideas and dreamed of the founding of a Jewish state in Palestine. Werfel, on the other hand, felt increasingly drawn to Catholicism; he loved the wealth of imagery, the opulence of the Church, in which he thought he discerned a kinship to the intoxicating sumptuousness of Italian opera. Judaism—Torah and Talmud—appeared too abstract, so much arid theory. He was intensely preoccupied with Christian theology, studying the Church Fathers and Scholastics, reading Thomas Aquinas and Augustine, the *Confessions of St. Francis,* the writings of Albertus Magnus.

Werfel advocated a once-and-for-all dispersion of the Jews among all other nations, hoping that everyone of Jewish descent would sooner or later convert to Christianity. Brod was outraged by his friend's opinions and passionately urged him to give up this aberration and return to Judaism. Werfel's mind remained unchanged even after discussions that lasted for days—they only tended to reinforce his convictions. Deeply disappointed, Brod finally gave up. He incorporated the conflict with Werfel into his novel *Tycho Brahe's Road to God (Tycho Brahes Weg zu Gott),* on which he was working at the time, giving his Johannes Kepler character traits that were clearly those of the apostate Werfel and identifying himself with Tycho Brahe, Kepler's mentor and one-time idol.

In the spring, Werfel had been granted another four months of leave because of his leg wound. There was, however, the threat of a court-martial on charges of self-mutilation. It never came to that, but in early September 1915 the final call-up loomed large: Werfel had run out of excuses.

He spent the last week before that dreaded date in Marienbad with his family; then, a few days before his twenty-fifth birthday, he proceeded to Trebnitz, near Lobovič in Bohemia, where his regiment, the Eighth Heavy Howitzer Division, was stationed. Just as in Bozen, he did not live with the other soldiers in the barracks but took lodgings at an inn at his own expense. And once again he succeeded in achieving what he himself had hardly thought possible: by complaining ceaselessly about severe pain in his right foot and imploring his superiors to release him from combat exercises, he managed to get discharged in a mere six weeks—only days before his unit was sent to the front.

In November 1915 the leg injury obliged him to undergo an examination in the Prague garrison hospital. During his stay there he saw, if only for a few moments, one of the two assassins of Sarajevo, Čabrinović, who was being held in an observation cell at the hospital before being transported back to Theresienstadt to serve his life sentence. Werfel wrote a prose piece about the Serbian anarchist that read like a diary entry but was nevertheless mature and accomplished. Rather than depicting Čabrinović as a fiendish murderer, he made him a reticent and dignified hero, an instrument of God, a plaything of God's great game plan: "The guilt had been laid on a lamb."

One of the surgical nurses who took care of Werfel while he was in the orthopedic ward caught his eye. The two had met briefly, years ago, and she recognized him and reminded him of their first meeting, which he no longer remembered. Her name was Gertrud Spirk. She was thirty years old, unmarried, a Prague German from an Evangelical Lutheran family. Franz was delighted when she appeared in his room at all hours of the day and night, sat down on the edge of his bed and talked to him, or sometimes just took a break from her work, in silence. There was a peculiarity to Gertrud's appearance that Franz found most attractive: as a result of a mishap at the hairdresser's, her hair had turned entirely white at an early age. He was charmed by her happy, unspoiled nature and the slightly chaotic life-style she told him about. Her Christian background was not the least of her attractions for Werfel. After his discharge from the hospital, he spent as much time as possible with his new friend. They took long walks together, visited the Café Arco, went to the theater, the opera, the movies. Nevertheless, they tried to keep their relationship as secret as possible. Gertrud's mother did not tolerate illicit affairs, and it was important not to let other members of the Spirk family know about their liaison either. Franz and Gertrud toyed with the idea of moving to Vienna as soon as the war was over; they began to discuss a shared future.

Werfel did not write much during these months. He felt suddenly estranged from everything he had done so far; it seemed immature and flawed. "Dream of a New Hell," for which he had held such high hopes only six months before, never got beyond its fifth canto. He wrote occasional poems, and their titles reflected his current mood: "Weariness" ("Müdigkeit"), "Ballad of a Guilt" ("Ballade von einer Schuld"), "Ballad of Madness and Death" ("Ballade von Wahn und Tod").

At the beginning of March 1916 he wrote G. H. Meyer to tell him that he was working on a new book of odes and ballads—the first of his works to hold its own "not by chance but by necessity." Otherwise, he told Meyer, he was "not exactly in wonderful shape," being once again condemned to lie about in a hospital that was "dirty as well as boring." At the end of February, all those who had been declared unfit for military service had been ordered to report for another examination. Franz lived in fear of it for weeks, drinking endless cups of black coffee and chain-smoking strong cigars, hoping to present the examining physicians with evidence of a weak heart and poor circulation. As a schoolboy he had often suffered from fainting spells that were heralded by an acute fear of death; half-jokingly, Willy Haas had referred to these as his heart attacks. He had no such luck when he stood in front of the detested draft board: he was found to be somewhat weak but quite capable of light duties as a soldier.

The weeks before his transfer to Elbe-Kostelec, not far from Prague, passed in a state of deep melancholic anxiety. His parents, sisters, and Barbara worried about him. The impending separation from Gertrud Spirk certainly depressed Werfel at least as much as the prospect of parting from his family.

Even the news of the wonderfully successful first night of his adaptation of *The Trojan Women* at the Lessing Theater in Berlin did not console him. A congratulatory letter from Kurt Wolff reached him at the beginning of May, during the first days of his new tour of duty. The publisher, on a short furlough to Leipzig after nearly two years of uninterrupted combat duty, informed Werfel that he regarded both him and his work as the central and most important factors in the existence of his publishing house. Despite his "extremely low spirits," Werfel responded with gratitude: "Your loyalty to my work is one of those immensely valued reassurances I need in my present state of uncertainty."

Serving in the Nineteenth Heavy Field Artillery Regiment in Elbe-Kostelec, Werfel lost the privilege of private accommodations and had to live in the barracks. Even though his duties included the training of recruits, sentry duty, and office chores, he managed to find time to write, among other things the poem "The Blessed Elizabeth" ("Die heilige Elisabeth"), inspired by Gertrud and dedicated to her: "She floats there still, the tall German / . . . O twilight of her hair, / O step, O gaze, / How she walks, the sister of the fifth hour!" In a letter he tells his beloved that he composed these verses for her: "For me, you are a *great measure of abundance* and *melody,* ever growing and sounding."

He outlined a dramatic legend told in twelve dreams, "Man's Life" ("Das Leben des Menschen"). The fragment, inspired by auto-biographical elements, tells of a young man who is far wiser and more famous than his father. Nevertheless, the father constantly demon-strates to him how stupid and inferior he really is. Finally the confused son decides to leave his fatherland and emigrates overseas.

After about a month in Elbe-Kostelec, Werfel received word that he was considered fit not only for light military duty but for combat as well. He was told to be ready for a transfer to one of the fronts. "It really isn't clear to me how this has come about," the desperate Franz wrote to Gertrud, apostrophizing her as his "eternal, most beloved." "Truly, I had not expected this. I had made plans for work, for Vienna." Then he consoled her: "I will and must be grateful even for suffering, for it, too, is a rain that spawns fertility."

Days of worry and waiting followed. Parents and sisters came to Elbe-Kostelec to say goodbye. Gertrud too came to visit him one more time. His pain at parting and fear of death grew immense.

Early one morning Werfel's company received its marching orders. Packed into boxcars like cattle, the men were shipped to Galicia, on the Russian front. Franz's head was shaved; he wore a scratchy uniform and dog tags around his neck with the address of next of kin to be notified in case of his death. His heavy rucksack contained ammunition, canned goods, a spare pair of boots—and books, many books. After a strenuous journey of several days, interrupted by stops at numerous stations, the company arrived in the ugly, war-damaged township of Hodóv, near Jezierna, a forbidding, flat landscape in the easternmost province of the Austro-Hungarian Empire.

Many of his superior officers treated Werfel with surprising courtesy, and he did his best to establish good relations with them, hoping that this would make life easier for him even at the front. Only a few days after his arrival in Hodóv he was assigned a duty much envied by his comrades: he was to be the telephone operator and dispatch rider at regimental headquarters. "In spite of it all, things are still extraordi-narily favorable," he wrote to Gertrud. "I've been incredibly lucky."

Although this assignment kept him out of the trenches, a few hun-dred yards behind the lines, the spoiled young man suffered from the dirt in the hut where he slept with seven other men; suffered because he never had a moment to himself even in the daytime; suffered because of the miserable food and the constant fear of battle.

It did not take him long, however, to rent a fairly decent private room in a peasant family's house in Hodóv. His parents and Gertrud regularly sent packages containing food and smoking materials. All things considered, Werfel was not doing too badly during the advance of the Russian general Brusilov. He was even getting used to the incessant thunder of heavy artillery. In the middle of August, he told his beloved in a letter that he was doing better than ever—an attempt to reassure Gertrud, who was losing sleep over him. But he may have been sincere when he stressed that the "Gypsy" in him was content to experience the primitive nature of life in eastern Galicia. He really did enjoy his nocturnal duties, laying miles of telephone line all by himself under a starry sky: "My rudimentary Red Indian strain was well satisfied, and the long-forgotten Old Shatterhand in me said something in typical Karl May English!"

Here, of all places, at the front in a world war, he was writing more, and more regularly, than ever before. "But I am working! Every day," he informed Gertrud. "By the phone, with ten thousand barbarians dancing all around me. God knows it doesn't turn out to be much, as rage tends to interrupt the flow of logic only too often! But sometimes I do believe that a guardian spirit is guiding me, that some of my words are being given to me." His tour of duty usually lasted from 4:00 A.M. until 10:00 P.M., and he often used the first hours of the morning for his own work: polemical essays, narrative prose, poems, and daily letters to Gertrud came into being while he was transmitting information about ammunition dumps, targets, and burning cities over the field telephone.

In the midst of this inferno of national hatred, he also wrote an introduction to the German-language edition of the *Silesian Songs* (*Schlesische Lieder*) of the famous Czech poet Petr Bezruč. He knew the work from his Café Arco days. "Petr Bezruč is the . . . last outcry of a destroyed tribe," Werfel wrote in his declaration of solidarity with the Czech people and their language. "Our heart feels that it belongs to the same people as the oppressed of all nations. Our spirit hates the might and arrogance of all nations."

In the fall of 1916 Werfel sent the Berlin journal *Die Neue Rundschau* a full-page open letter to Kurt Hiller, a cultural critic and pamphleteer. Titled "The Mission of Christianity" ("Die christliche Sendung"), the letter attacked the "activism" advocated by Hiller and the doctrine of the saving grace of *the deed*. Werfel defended the idea of Christianity, claiming that it was "entirely accepting" of the "I." According to Werfel, Christianity was the most sensible of all philosophies, and he opposed what he took to be Hiller's hostility to individualism: "The mission of Christianity completes its work in the I, in the consciousness of man, because it recognizes in its wisdom that one cannot bring about transformation, 'change,' from outside."

It seemed important to Werfel not just to confess his adherence to Christianity to Max Brod in private, but to present himself to the public as a Christian writer. This was the true motive for his open letter. His letters to Gertrud Spirk bear further evidence of how deeply committed he had become to his newfound faith: "My love, there is only one way in which we will be able to endure life," he wrote at about the same time he was writing "The Mission of Christianity." "*Indestructible greatness, imitation of Christ, the greatest degree of incorruptibility*. I shall bind you to me more deeply than any worldly bond."

Werfel was assailed by severe self-doubt about his work so far; true, many were hailing him as the spokesman of his generation, a pioneer of literary expressionism—and yet, he wrote plaintively to Gertrud, he himself saw his work as only a weak reflection of what other young poets were creating. He asked himself why he was regarded as a representative of his generation when he had really written "so little" and such "minor, ephemeral" things.

Werfel's evaluation of his work seemed to find confirmation in a satirical poem Karl Kraus published in *Die Fackel* in November 1916. Titled "Elysian Matters, Melancholia: To Kurt Wolff" ("Elysisches, Melancholie an Kurt Wolff"), it imitated Werfel's bathetic style, deriding all the authors whose work had appeared in the Day of Judgment series. Kraus called them copyists and plagiarists, a gang whose headquarters was the Café Arco, their leader "the other Schiller."

Kraus's verses served to "humiliate the man and declare the artist bankrupt," Werfel wrote to Gertrud; nevertheless, he found time to sit down in his telephone hut and compose a personal letter to his new enemy. As if unaware that Kraus had quite deliberately used some remarkably clumsy turns of phrase and Prague-German allusions in his poem, Werfel proceeded to point out grave violations of style and grammar: "Is this truly the language of someone who wants to avenge language on all who speak it?" In addition, he severely chastised Kraus for denigrating Wolff, "our common host," and finally reminded him that it had been he, Werfel, who had urged Wolff to publish Kraus.

At the end of the year, Werfel had been promised a short leave for a lecture he was to give in Berlin. Overjoyed, he had told his parents and Gertrud that he would also visit them in Prague. But only a few days before his departure, his leave was canceled. The telephone operator had forgotten to salute a colonel on horseback; this omission was reported to his regimental commander, who instantly revoked his leave.

Winter was coming on; the freezing cold became a problem. The small stove in Werfel's hut did not provide enough heat, though it belched smoke "like the stage in *Götterdämmerung*. But General Brusilov had halted his offensive, and it was a little quieter on the front. Werfel was able to spend almost the entire day reading books his father, Kurt Wolff, and others had sent him. He read the memoirs of the Russian revolutionary Alexander Herzen; he devoured Strindberg and Tolstoy, Swedenborg and Kierkegaard, Flaubert, Zola, and Balzac. Max Brod sent him works on Judaism, such as Martin Buber's latest book and a Talmud anthology published by the Universal Jewish Library.

Werfel worked in a room nine feet wide, its space almost completely taken up by the stove, a table, and a cot. The telephone, liable to ring at any moment of the day or night, seemed to him a sinister, hateful creature, a large insect that kept buzzing aggressively. The view from his window was a clump of dying trees, piles of garbage, latrines. "When I have to work," he wrote to Gertrud, "I am in such a foul mood that I have become the holy *telephone terror* of this entire sector. I don't believe the most hysterical lady operator in Prague is my match in delivering threats, insults, and libelous remarks."

After six months at the front, Werfel was close to despair, only somewhat relieved by the photographs of herself that Gertrud occasionally enclosed in her daily letters. He wrote back by return mail, adopting a tone both boyish and magisterial. His days and nights seemed to him like a "long prison sentence with few privileges," he felt "half crazed," his apathy was increasing: "This is an existence of slow atrophy." Yet he tried to convince himself that the years this war was stealing from him were a kind of "surrogate time" that did not really age him: they would be returned to him, miraculously, at a later date.

Shortly before Christmas, his longed-for leave was reinstated, and he spent deliriously happy days on Mariengasse and with Gertrud before traveling to Berlin with his sister Hanna in early January to give a reading. They spent a week in the capital of the Reich. Werfel again saw Martin Buber, who tried in the course of long conversations to lead the renegade back to the path of Jewish ethics and philosophy. Werfel's "Mission of Christianity" had just been published, and its message had shocked Buber just as Max Brod had once been shocked in Prague when the two young men debated Werfel's fundamentally Christian view of life. Buber, however, treated Werfel far more gently, and when the apostate returned to Hodóv, he in turn tried to reassure Buber by mail that his feelings as a Jew were "completely nationalistic," even if he was vehemently opposed to certain "Zionists of Prague." Two months earlier, he had expressed similar views to Max Brod, with whom he kept up a friendly correspondence in spite of their occasional disagreements. He told Brod that he had reconsidered his theory of assimilation and now agreed with the idea of Zionism. Indeed, it now struck him as "the only Jewish form" in which he found himself able to believe.

In a later letter to Brod he justified his dislike of Theodor Herzl by saying that the latter was Viennese, and worse, a journalist in the pay of *Die Neue Freie Presse.* Werfel concluded: "Our Ahasuerian fate really only began with emancipation: it forced us to become two-faced until Weininger's death finally happened almost as a symbol."

Brod, in turn, published a response to "The Mission of Christianity" in Buber's monthly *Der Jude* at the beginning of 1917. In it he tried to demonstrate that his friend's theories were really marked by an un-Christian attitude, and sounded the warning that Werfel's ideology was harmful to the already endangered Jewish community. Werfel wrote to Gertrud that Brod's essay was written "from an entirely partisan Zionist viewpoint" and said that he did not feel like replying to it, even though Buber had invited him to do so: "I really have no desire to discuss these things when there is no inner need to do so." At the same time, however, he reassured Buber that he would try his very best to get his position on Judaism down in writing. "What I call Christianity consists of conducting one's life according to Christ's example, as an imitatio Christi," he stated in a letter promising Buber an essay on the subject. "It would seem to be historically accurate that Christianity is an ancient and vital form of Judaism, perhaps even more, its own polarization, the eternal protest, the revolution against the *Law.*"

At the beginning of 1917, Werfel found his monotonous and, to him, entirely absurd existence at the front even harder to endure than it had been before his short leave. He had made a large calendar, out of which he snipped every day he had survived. On the brief visit to Prague, his relationship with Gertrud had become closer, and the tone of his letters was much warmer than before. They contained increasingly frequent hints that he wanted to marry Gertrud as soon as the war was over. However, he told her that the most important thing was to achieve financial security before the wedding: he wanted to complete several books in order to get as much money as possible in advances from Kurt Wolff, and he was also contemplating a return to his job as an editor with the publishing house. The next step—Werfel referred to this as a "step-by-step policy"—would be to present his parents and Gertrud's family with a *fait accompli,* in which case, or so he hoped, his father would not entirely abandon him financially. He was determined to leave Prague and move to Munich, Leipzig, or Berlin after their marriage and then he fantasized about the appearance of their future living room, the select books that would adorn their library shelves, the exact spot for the large peasant chest Gertrud had acquired: "We'll be together for a lifetime. Do you feel that?"

At the beginning of 1917 Karl Kraus printed Werfel's personal letter from the front, dated November 1916, in *Die Fackel,* under the title "Over There" ("Dorten"), adding a full page of satirical commentary. It was another demonstration of Kraus's cutting wit in matters of linguistic purity, and it heaped relentless mockery on his favorite adversary.

"I really feel sorry for the man," Werfel wrote to Gertrud. "He is not evil, he has just built himself up so boundlessly on false foundations. In the final analysis, he is like a criminal on the run who uses all his criminal wits to build ever new structures around a deed that remains in the dark. His entire work consists of the uninterrupted recitation of an alibi by someone who was never asked for an alibi in the first place."

This time he responded with an open letter titled "The Metaphysics of the Twist" ("Die Metaphysik des Drehs"). He sent it to *Die Aktion*, a Berlin literary journal that had dedicated a special issue to Werfel the previous fall. "If you were an I-am," the offended author writes in his somewhat confused and not very convincing response, "you could go on conjugating and say: You are. But you resist the We-are, because it is painful to see others be without being yourself." He admitted to Gertrud that his text was not really successful but added that he simply did not believe in "false refinement" and that it would be "quite misplaced in regard to this man" to remain silent, as practically everybody targeted by Kraus had done. Moreover, he felt that his response would act as a protective spell "against an evil eye (mal occhio)."

At the end of February 1917 Werfel was promoted to the rank of corporal "with two stars" and moved, with some other men of his company, to a building on the outskirts of the village, hidden behind some trees next to a military cemetery. The move meant the loss of the little hut in which he had been working and spending most of his nights; true, he now had a much larger and more comfortable room, but he had to share it with an artillery engineer and suffered from the lack of solitude. As the telephone had also been installed in this room, there were no more quiet moments, and he felt that he was living in a train station. He was mostly on night duty and did not have much to do in the daytime, but he still found it impossible to concentrate on creative work as he had been able to the year before.

A ray of hope came with the news that the German diplomat and patron of the arts Count Harry Kessler had set wheels in motion to have Werfel recalled from the front. Count Kessler tried to have the young poet invited to lecture and give readings in Switzerland, a country completely untouched by the war, and he had the support of numerous other cultural figures, such as Kurt Wolff and the writers Annette Kolb and René Schickele.

The decision of his sister Hanna to announce her engagement to Herbert von Fuchs-Robetin, a paper manufacturer from Prague, took Franz by surprise. Hanna was only twenty, and he regretted that she had not had a chance to learn much about life. He wished that she could spend some time in a great city like Berlin, where she would meet people with a sense of freedom, far away from Prague and its German-Jewish milieu. He tried to dissuade her from the marriage, asking her to think things over, but the wedding took place only a few weeks later, in the middle of March 1917.

Werfel managed to get leave at short notice, and on the wedding day he arrived in Prague at five in the morning, surprising the family. Hanna helped him dress; his father lent him a tailcoat and a top hat. During the days he spent in Prague he was haunted by the feeling that Hanna's marriage marked the irrevocable loss of his own childhood.

"It's hard to believe that I went to Prague," he wrote to Gertrud the day he returned to the front, "and that we were able to experience so much during these long days. . . . My love, I know, it is the most certain thing in my life, that we are meant for each other."

Spring weather transformed the countryside around Hodóv, first into a sea of mud, then into a flowering landscape, and Werfel's frame of mind underwent a similar slow change for the better. As his roommate had been transferred away from the front, he had the room to himself at night, and even though the "telephone vultures" were still "picking away" at his nerves, he tried to write again after a break of several months. Without asking his superiors for permission, he went for two-hour walks in the afternoon, rested in the shade of a tall tree, read Montaigne's travel journal, and wrote first drafts of many new poems.

At the end of May he spent whole afternoons outdoors and resumed work on a large new book of poems that he had originally conceived in the spring of 1916, before he was called up. The book was to be called *The Last Judgment* (*Der Gerichtstag*) and to consist of five sections, after Baudelaire's *Fleurs du mal*.

He told Gertrud that he felt a "great urge" to write, to let his "discontent coalesce into verses." "This Last Judgment will be a monument of interior devastations, truly a book of the war!" He would find it hard to publish the work, but "*beauty*" was not to be expected from a "galley slave."

Every day in early June 1917 brought new indications of an imminent Russian offensive. After the czar's abdication and the transfer of power to a provisional government, Alexander Kerensky, the Russian minister of war, laid plans for a decisive battle on the eastern border of Austria-Hungary. Werfel feared that the summer leave he had already been granted—in practically every one of his letters, he spoke to Gertrud about these coming holiday weeks—might be canceled. At the same time, he received news from his father that was both confusing and heartening. The propaganda section of the Military Press Bureau in Vienna had asked Rudolf Werfel for his son's field address, indicating that they were considering Franz as a propaganda lecturer in Switzerland. "I still can't believe it'll work out just like that," he wrote to his beloved. Days passed without further news, and Werfel's hopes, never high to begin with, began to fade.

"With a thousand interruptions, little by little every day," Werfel was now working on a theatrical piece called *Stockleinen*. In this futuristic vision of Europe after the war, a tumultuous celebration of peace suddenly turns into the moment of birth of a new totalitarianism. A civil servant dressed in brown steps into a circle of friends and insists on dancing with Fräulein Gertrud. And suddenly, while Stockleinen circles the dance floor with the girl, "something evil" happens, "an injustice. . . . People are no longer enjoying themselves. . . . It is all the fault of the man in brown." The second act takes place shortly after Stockleinen's rise to power. The populace is divided into work crews doomed to spend the rest of their existence at forced labor operating huge banks of machines. Thousands try to escape from the dictator's reign of terror, but the country's borders are sealed. Wearing his brown uniform, Stockleinen personally supervises the monotonously rhythmic assembly lines. "Man will become perfect!" he proclaims, and to that end he forces the closure of all opera houses and bans all musical performances.

At the end of June the feared Russian offensive began, with considerable ferocity. Werfel had to interrupt his work on the play. As fate would have it, Hodóv was in the midst of the first great artillery battle when an inquiry came from Corps Command: Was Private Werfel available? Vienna wanted to send him to lecture in Switzerland. "Once again, my incredibly bad luck in the military," he wrote to Gertrud. Because the telegram had arrived in the midst of battle, "everybody was up in arms against me, thinking that I had . . . made a trip to Corps Command and 'fixed' things in my favor." On the previous day, he had visited his friend Otto Pick, who was stationed nearby, but that visit had nothing to do with the inquiry. His superiors and comrades remained suspicious, however, and his regular furlough as well as his transfer to Switzerland became doubtful. Werfel feared that the whole matter would end up with the higher authorities in an inactive file, never to arise again: "They'll consider the telegram tomorrow and decide."

The following day he was told—to his great relief—that he was now under the jurisdiction of the Royal and Imperial Military Press Bureau in Vienna, authorized to leave the front without delay. Back in Prague, he was to await orders for his journey to Switzerland.

He had hardly left Hodóv, traveling west, when the building in which he had lived and worked as a telephone operator for months suffered a direct hit from Russian artillery and was completely destroyed.

In the research room of the military archive in Vienna, I sit turning the pages of a bundle of official documents labeled "Werfel, Franz." Through the open window I see a massive air-raid bunker in the courtyard of the Stiftskaserne; it was built shortly before the end of World War II by the forced labor of prisoners of war. "I doubt that we'll have a whole lot here," says Herr Lipič, a jovial elderly gentleman wearing the gray dustcoat still favored by many Austrian civil servants. He speaks a broad Carinthian dialect; the words are spaced out slowly, and so are his physical motions. "I'm sure those brownshirts destroyed most of it," he says as he ascends once more to the attic. Thousands of bundles of papers, documents, and war reports reaching back at least to the fifteenth century are stored in this administrative building. In the midst of tremendous clutter and mounds of dust, Herr Lipič continues his search for papers documenting Franz Werfel's employment with the Military Press Bureau.

"Here—took a while to dig that up!" Herr Lipič hands me a Werfel manuscript titled "Report on my LECTURE TOUR IN SWITZERLAND*" and a document signed by Major Baron Schramm-Schiessl in which the Ministry of War is petitioned to grant Private Werfel a permanent assignment with the Military Press Bureau. Schramm-Schiessl points out that since the outbreak of the war it has repeatedly been necessary to release the poet from his duties for reasons of health, and that his only active duty has been as a telephone operator in the office of the Regimental Command. Thus it would be most inadvisable to send Werfel to reserve officer's school: he would be able to serve the fatherland far better as a propagandist than he could in the field. On September 27, 1917, Schramm-Schiessl's urgent petition was approved by the Supreme Command.*

"Now you should go down to the basement," Herr Lipič advises me. "Go see Herr Tepperberg, he should be able to give you a little more help."

Dr. Tepperberg, a young, very cooperative military historian, receives me in his dark cubbyhole of an office. The odors and dust clouds of centuries have settled on the furnishings. Dr. Tepperberg searches in wide Biedermeier cupboards for a copy of Franz Werfel's "Hauptgrundbuchblatt," his "main registration record."

Once he has found it, we peruse this document of the Royal and Imperial Military Administration for Bohemia. With a fine nib, in Gothic script, Private Werfel's height has been recorded as 166 centimeters. His "size of footwear," hair color (brown), and eye color (gray) are also recorded; the shape of his face, we learn, was "round," his nose "proportional." A "moderate deficiency of vision" is mentioned as a "possible defect."

"It appears he was inducted in the usual way in the general mobilization of

July 31, 1914," Dr. Tepperberg *notes, and then proceeds to help me with the registration record's section of "Changes." The Austro-Hungarian monarchy's bureaucratese is well-nigh incomprehensible. "But then, right after that, he's 'superarbitrated'? That means declared unfit for service. . . . So, released, until September 1915? And then, on October 18, he's released again?* Incredible! *So he didn't have to go to the front until May 1916! Telephone operator—not one day in the trenches! But see here: promoted twice. But that didn't necessarily mean a reward. He didn't make it very far: first to corporal, and then, in the beginning of June 1917, to platoon leader. Three stars. But platoon leader isn't a very high rank for someone with a gymnasium education and, well, his level of culture. But wait a minute. After eleven months in the field, he receives the Iron Cross of Merit with the ribbon of the Medal for Bravery? I don't believe it. How did he manage that? What did he get that for?"*

Alma Maria Mahler-Gropius

THE MILITARY PRESS Bureau in Vienna was a safe haven for renowned Austrian writers—Rainer Maria Rilke, Stefan Zweig, and Robert Musil worked there as propagandists, along with Peter Altenberg, Roda Roda, Franz Blei, Leo Perutz, and Hugo von Hofmannsthal. In early August 1917 Franz Werfel joined it as well, after his lecture tour of Switzerland had been postponed until late fall.

He arrived in the war-scarred capital of the monarchy in the high heat of summer. He rented a little room in the Graben Hotel, in the heart of town, close to St. Stephen's Cathedral. Gertrud Spirk accompanied him to Vienna but then traveled on to the Tyrol. The hardships of the last months had taken their toll on her: she had lost so much weight that Werfel insisted she take leave from her hospital duties and go to a health resort.

In the press office Werfel wrote his first texts for the war machine he detested, mostly long newspaper articles, obediently sentimental fairy tales of the front that nauseated him. However, he was willing to produce them as the price of his release from that front. Among other things, he described newly opened retirement homes for soldiers and discussed the journals of deserters. "I have been given an incredible number of assignments by the office," he wrote to Gertrud, "and I sit up late writing introductions for war exhibitions and similar delightful matters." One of these introductions was for a children's book, a collection of illustrations and marching songs intended to demonstrate to the youngest of the nation how "the man of their fatherland" defended his home at the front in an "indestructible and joyful" manner, being able to "do a great deal and endure a great deal."

He had to stay in the office until 6:00 P.M. Then it was time to seek better surroundings than his tiny den in the hotel; it was always easy to let his friend from Prague, Egon Erwin Kisch, take him to his favorite

56

haunt, the Café Central on Herrengasse. (The "Raging Reporter" was also working for the Military Press Bureau, despite his well-known antigovernment views.) Werfel liked Kisch's enthusiasm and extreme temperament, and spent almost every free evening in his company.

Kisch introduced the newcomer to his circle of friends at the Central: the cocaine-addicted anarchist psychoanalyst Otto Gross; the *littérateur* and magazine publisher Franz Blei and his friend Gina, the adopted daughter and lover of Josef Kranz, president of the Depositenbank; Otfried Krzyzanowski, the impoverished poet and expert in the art of getting by; and many other characters of the Viennese *vie de Bohème*. Like its predecessor the Arco, the Central now became Werfel's surrogate home. It was a large room with high ceilings and gray stone walls, full of cigarette smoke and dimly lit, a meeting place for artists and intellectuals, chess and card players. Robert Musil, Peter Altenberg, Alfred Polgar, and Egon Friedell came every day, as did the painter Paris Gütersloh, the actor Max Pallenberg, the composer Leo Fall, and many others for whom this café was home and office, gambling casino and restaurant all in one.

Werfel often spent the whole night with this new circle. After the late closing of the Café Central, they kept on going—arguing, telling stories, pursuing amorous escapades. Werfel entertained the group by reciting his own poems or singing arias from Italian operas. After those months in the field, he had an insatiable "hunger for people." But he also had a bad conscience: in his letters to Gertrud, which he wrote surreptitiously during office hours, he proclaimed over and over again his longing for purity, rigor, and discipline. He beseeched his beloved to save him from the "atmosphere of corruption" into which he said he had fallen after his move to Vienna. "Is it base of me," he asked, "to rely on you to such a degree in matters of morality?" And he kept going to the café every day.

At the end of August 1917 Gertrud came to Vienna for a couple of weeks. The vacation in the Tyrol did not seem to have improved her health much, and she came down with a case of food poisoning. The lovers felt ill at ease, devoid of passion, almost like strangers. Franz made an effort to reconcile his ideal of the bride-to-be with the reality of the emaciated, sickly nurse. At first he took the responsibility for the tension between them: "I must live through this period of moral crisis in which a new man beats against my old grimaces, struggling to be born," he wrote to Gertrud at the end of September, after her return to Prague. "You mustn't think that I am changing in regard to you. It is just that the entire content of my heart has to go through this hell with me."

A further postponement of his Swiss lecture tour worried him: once again the Austrian military attaché in Bern had canceled his dates. Intrigues between Major Schramm-Schiessl, Werfel's patron, and some officers in the Supreme Command were endangering his position in the propaganda office: the Military Press Bureau had suddenly arranged a trip for him to the Italian war zone, during which he was to write reports from the front and also present himself to an inspection commission that would decide whether he was still unfit for active service.

He had hardly gotten over the news of this assignment when he was informed that his childhood friend Franz Janowitz had fallen on the Italian front. "Only we, the more brutal ones, remain. . . . The truly noble will be exterminated in this war," Werfel wrote to Gertrud. Karl Kraus, a particular champion of Janowitz's writing, had built him up as the antidote to the hated sentimentalist Werfel. Only a few hours before Janowitz died of his wounds in a small field hospital, he had converted to Catholicism. The conversion of his Jewish friend, with whom he had once played hooky and shared adventures at nightclubs and séances, preoccupied Werfel for weeks; he kept pondering the twin facts of his friend's death and his decision to embrace Christianity.

Werfel's friend from the Central, Franz Blei, had an exceptionally large circle of friends and acquaintances that included Gustav Mahler's widow, a well-known figure in Viennese society. When Blei asked Alma Mahler whether he could introduce her to his friend from the press office, the music fanatic and poet Franz Werfel, she responded favorably: in view of her deep appreciation of Werfel's work, which had inspired her to set his poem "The Seer" ("Der Erkennende") to music two years earlier, she would be delighted to make the poet's personal acquaintance.

In 1915, after her notoriously stormy affair with the painter Oskar Kokoschka, Alma Mahler had married the German architect Walter Gropius. With her daughters Anna and Manon, she divided her time between a handsome villa in Breitenstein am Semmering and a large apartment in the Inner City of Vienna, not far from the Ringstrasse. While Gropius was at the front, his wife continued her distinguished salon; everyone of rank and name in Central Europe was invited to Frau Alma's apartment and its red music room. She competed for guests with her friend Berta Zuckerkandl, who also held a salon in Vienna.

In mid-November, a few days before Werfel's propaganda journey to Italy, Blei took him along to an afternoon reception at Alma Mahler's. Franz immediately felt very much at ease in his hostess's presence.

During this first meeting he spoke to her nonstop, told her about his passion for Italian opera and the Russian Revolution, for Christianity and socialism, and stayed well into the night.

The "fat, bow-legged Jew" with his "thick lips," "liquid slit-eyes," and nicotine-yellow fingers had not displeased Alma at all, as she confided to her diary; his socialist "affectation" and his "babble" about love for humanity and willingness to sacrifice, however, had irritated her a great deal—she noted that she had never quite been able to believe similar talk from the late Gustav Mahler.

"Imagine, yesterday Blei took me to see Frau Mahler in the afternoon," Werfel immediately reported to Gertrud. "It was really wonderful. . . . I learned much about Gustav Mahler—and sensed that he had all my conflicts. They were interesting hours; she is tremendously warm and alive, a woman of quality."

On his return from Italy, he soon went back to Frau Mahler's salon, making the acquaintance of Walter Gropius, who was on a short furlough in Vienna. In the presence of her husband and Franz Blei, Werfel flirted uninhibitedly with his hostess, recited his poems, sang arias in his pleasant tenor voice; on an impulse, Alma sat down at the piano and accompanied the troubadour, immersing herself in music, the basic force in her life.

In early December 1917 Werfel went on another official trip at the invitation of the governor of Trieste, the main port of the Royal and Imperial Navy. He visited the destroyed war zone of Friuli, saw demolished outposts and towns that had been burned to their foundations; "on the hills," he told Gertrud in a letter, "there are still many unburied corpses; there are graveyards that are completely torn up, a sight that like some frightful scar will never disappear from the face of the earth." In Görz, not a single building had been left standing along the Corso Verdi, the main thoroughfare, and rats the size of cats were scurrying about. "It was the spitting image of a medieval plague site."

Back in Vienna, Werfel's visits to Frau Mahler-Gropius grew ever more frequent. He began to share his ideas, wishes, and dreams with her. They often made music together, and hardly a day went by without at least some kind of message from her admirer—her junior by eleven years. True, she did not refrain from making anti-Semitic remarks and others specifically directed at Werfel's obesity; nonetheless, Werfel had never felt as comfortable, as well understood, as happy in a woman's presence as he now did with Alma Mahler. She felt the same way; Werfel stimulated her greatly. He was a *miraculous miracle*, she noted in her diary.

After each reunion Werfel felt more strongly that their meeting had been fated. He loved Alma's extremely powerful personality and was overjoyed that she told him what to do and what not to do; he believed that in her he had found everything Gertrud Spirk was not able to give him. She would succeed where Gertrud, because of her weakness, had failed. She would save Franz from that "atmosphere of corruption." In the Café Central he boasted about his conquest like any playboy, and his friends smiled half mockingly, half in admiration. In reality, however, he saw Alma as his savior, an earth mother, *magna mater*—indeed, a goddess whom he could worship.

His relationship with his beloved in Prague grew ever more burdensome. In her letters, to which Werfel replied less and less frequently, Gertrud for the first time voiced suspicions, frightening dreams, and premonitions that had reinforced her worst fears. "There is so much pain and anxiety in all those dream images you tell me about," Werfel wrote to her at the end of 1917. "You see, this melancholy of yours frightens me. . . . Your disposition for pain, which is really so much in your nature, . . . always makes me fear that I'm mistreating you." In the future, he continued, Gertrud would have to find a way to tolerate the character of her friend "without immediately becoming unhappy." To attach herself to him meant "stepping onto the ice; like being a rider on Lake Constance."

At the turn of 1917–18, Walter Gropius spent another short leave in Vienna and found his wife rather frosty. A projected cycle of Mahler's works, which Willem Mengelberg was rehearsing in the concert hall of the Vienna Music Society, and her interest in Werfel and his work seemed to take up Alma's entire strength and powers of concentration. A few hours after his departure, Gropius sent his wife a telegram from a border station: "Break the ice in our faces!" This was a quotation from a poem in Werfel's *Each Other* collection, "Veni Creator Spiritus."

While Mengelberg conducted Mahler's Fourth Symphony, Alma and Franz exchanged passionate glances from their respective boxes. After the concert, Alma took her young admirer home to her apartment on Elisabethstrasse. Had she been twenty years younger, Alma admitted to herself the following morning, she would immediately have disregarded everything else and followed Franz Werfel, her "*beloved of the gods,*" to the ends of the earth.

"I feel that I want to kill all that is evil in me, and want nothing but to have you be happy, rid of all difficult things," he now wrote to Gertrud in a letter that contained a coded confession: he said that "many signs of change" had occurred in the last few days. The ambiguous phrase referred primarily to a sudden order from his superiors to leave for Switzerland in January on a tour of Zurich and six other cities. Shortly before that tour, he visited Prague for a few days and saw Gertrud and his family. In mid-January 1918 he traveled to Zurich, via Vienna and Feldkirch.

He wrote to Alma from Feldkirch: "Homesickness, homesickness all the way on this trip, you my giver of life, keeper of the flame!!!" He told her he was constantly humming the theme of a trio of Pfitzner's, the one she played so beautifully by heart. "If you don't see me for a long time," he asked anxiously, "will you forget me?"

Gertrud, too, received a letter from Feldkirch: "I am with you very, very much," he reassured her. That night on the train she had appeared in the strangest dreams, the likes of which he hadn't experienced since his time at the front. "I believe my heart gives only what it has and cannot lie. . . . You are with me and walk hand in hand with me."

In Zurich the poet, no doubt inspired by his amorous Viennese adventures, experienced the greatest public success of his life to that date. In the Tonhallesaal, an auditorium with a thousand seats, he read to a full house from his own works. Two days later, the Zurich Stadt theater presented the Swiss premiere of his translation of *The Trojan Women*. Both events were highly praised in the daily press, and every Zurich newspaper carried long articles and reports about him. Most of his free time was spent in the Café Odéon, the meeting place of the dadaists and numerous other colleagues. He met Else Lasker-Schüler, whom he had known well in Leipzig, again, and saw Annette Kolb and Frank Wedekind, Leonhard Frank and Albert Ehrenstein, and, above all, his friend Stefan Zweig. Zweig, too, had been sent to Zurich by the Military Press Bureau and was impatiently awaiting the premiere of his play *Jeremiah*.

Werfel gave a total of twelve lectures in Switzerland. Their subjects included Ferdinand Raimund's drama *King of the Alps and Misanthrope* (*Alpenkönig und Menschenfeind*) and the history of psychology in Austria. In Davos, at an adult-education institute, he read poems that he introduced to his audience of mostly workers with a short speech. "Comrades!" he cried. "That which today calls itself art is just an iridescent blob of fat floating on top of the capitalist broth." Time and again, only those in bourgeois circles heard the artists' "outcry," not the working classes who had sunk to being "slaves of militarism," numbed by phrasemongering and obedience to the state. Werfel, who had obviously graduated to socialism under the tutelage of Egon Erwin Kisch and was impressed by the success of the Russian Revolution, contrasted this state of affairs with the model of the Soviet Union, where great authors like Tolstoy and Dostoyevsky had been able to reach the people to make them "move forward." "Spirituality and socialism," he said, had happily "merged into one" in the new Russia, and he hoped that his own verses, which he was about to read, would also contribute "to the dissolution of the bourgeois world . . . to the renewal of socialism."

It took a good deal of courage in early 1918 to give a public lecture portraying the archenemy of the Austrian Empire, Bolshevik Russia, as a paragon—the more so if you had been sent abroad to propagandize for the Austrian cause. The Austrian military attaché in Bern received immediate word of Werfel's allegedly treasonous words. It was also becoming public knowledge that the press office emissary had frequently made unequivocally pacifist remarks before, during, and after his lectures, thus quite consciously undermining his propaganda mission.

In mid-March Werfel wrote to Alma from Davos that as soon as his final lectures were over he would immediately return to her—that he was, in fact, cutting his tour short. *"Only because of you!* Do you hear?" He feared that Alma would treat him unkindly on his return, would be unable to understand how he had been able to endure life without her for so long. Why else had she hardly written him during the past two months? "You hate me and will no longer be glad to suddenly hear my voice on the telephone."

As soon as Werfel arrived back in Zurich, the Austrian military attaché presented him with an order from the Military Press Bureau to break off his Swiss tour immediately. Well-publicized readings in Zurich, Winterthur, and Chur had to be canceled. Three days later Werfel arrived in Vienna and reported to the press office. He was immediately told of a rumor according to which his Swiss lectures had roused the ire of certain gentlemen in the Foreign Office and that he could expect severe punishment.

Alma Mahler-Gropius was in her third month of pregnancy when Franz Werfel returned to Vienna in the second half of March. She wasn't sure whether her lover was the child's father but assumed that it had been conceived in January, before Werfel's departure, not in December, when Walter Gropius had spent a few days in Vienna. In any case, she left Werfel in a state of doubt but insisted on spending as much time as possible with him. She visited him at the Hotel Bristol, his new domicile across from the opera house, where he had moved from the Graben Hotel, and also invited him quite openly to her apartment, introducing him to her friends and acquaintances in the red music room. He regaled the members of her salon with entertainingly hyperbolic reports of his Swiss adventures.

As the anticipated reprisals for his antimilitarist behavior were not forthcoming, at least for the time being, he could devote himself to his own work for the first time in a long while. At the end of his working day, rather than visit the Café Central, he went home to his hotel room on the Kärntnerring to work on *The Last Judgment,* a book of poems he had begun years ago, added to at the front, and wanted to finish at last. He told Kurt Wolff in late April 1918 that he regarded this book as his most important to date. He compared it to Nietzsche's *Thus Spake Zarathustra* and expected it to find a large readership.

Gertrud Spirk, still in the dark about the changed circumstances of her lover's life but amazed at his long absence from Prague, told Werfel that she wanted to visit him in Vienna. Franz assured her that he longed greatly for her company: "All the things we'll have to tell each other when we meet again!" He continued, "I have to learn how to muster my interior powers. And you'll help me with that!"

When Gertrud arrived in Vienna, Alma Mahler was at a health spa. Alma had invited her lover to accompany her, but, as he was expecting Gertrud's arrival, he declined. "I did not want to go to Göding," he explained later, because it took him "a long time to get used to strange surroundings."

The reunion with Gertrud, who stayed with her sister and brother-in-law, was totally overshadowed by Werfel's doubly bad conscience. He was impatient in the company of his former lover and tortured her with his irritability during her entire visit. Only when he was certain of her imminent departure did he write to her, at her sister's address. "Do not curse these days too much. I am such a nervous wreck myself that I can no longer be used as *medicine.*"

Nevertheless, when she returned to Prague, she sent him new photographs of herself, and he replied, "Don't believe that I'll vanish from your life—that is impossible." On the contrary, he would visit her soon in Prague, he dreamed of her so often. . . . Such language at a time when he was also having "*hot, sweet, and painful*" dreams of Alma Mahler. In one of these, he saw himself as a child, dressed up in a stage costume and playing with other children while Alma, an adult, was sitting in an adjoining room with the other adults. "You are to me what I felt as *home* when I was a boy," he wrote her. "*I adore you*—you are the greatest rapture I have ever experienced—I am yours in wonderful *humility.*"

At the beginning of July 1918, Gina Kranz, a friend from the Café Central, found him an apartment on Boltzmanngasse, in the ninth district of Vienna. It had housed the editorial offices of a short-lived journal, *Summa,* financed by Gina's adoptive father. A large, light studio space with a view of Boltzmann Park and Maria de Mercedes Church, it became Werfel's home—the first apartment he had had to himself in his life. Gina even provided a cleaning woman, and Franz immediately sent his mother a telegram asking for bed linen. However, he claimed he would stay in the mansard apartment only if Alma agreed to it. To live there without her permission pained him, and he asked her to let him know as soon as possible what he should do. To his delight, Alma agreed to the move.

When his sister Hanna gave birth to a son at the end of June, the family insisted that Franz try to get a few days' leave to come to Prague. At a time when Alma Mahler-Gropius was in her sixth month of pregnancy, Werfel wrote Gertrud Spirk that he wanted to make plans for their future while he was in Prague. He suggested that they try to figure out a way to live together in his new and really lovely apartment on Boltz-manngasse. This letter was written in a particularly messy scrawl and splattered with ink. *"Beloved, come to me soon!"* he exhorted. *"We won't ever have to leave the house.* We'll talk about it all in Prague."

But during his short stay in the city of his birth, at the height of summer 1918, he confessed that he had given his heart to another woman some eight months before. He admitted that he had been lying to and cheating Gertrud all that time. He denounced himself, described himself as a good-for-nothing, a monster, yet begged for her forgiveness like a repentant schoolboy. After this meeting, their correspondence came to an abrupt end.

Two hours from Vienna by train, Alma Mahler had a second home, acquired in 1914. The villa, Haus Mahler, stood on a plot that Gustav Mahler himself had chosen for it, in a magnificent mountain landscape about a thousand meters above sea level. Franz visited Alma there at the end of July. Freed from his oppressive relationship with Gertrud, he was able to treat Alma with newly won confidence. She was very pleased to see him, and even her fourteen-year-old daughter Anna Mahler liked her mother's new friend. In the company of a lady of Viennese society who was visiting Breitenstein, the three had to engage in a bit of play-acting in order to conceal Alma's adultery. First of all, they took Emmy Redlich on a strenuous walk up the Kreuzberg, and in the evening Alma fulfilled Frau Redlich's dearest wish by playing the entire second movement of Mahler's Eighth Symphony on the harmonium. "When bedtime came," Werfel wrote a few days later in his "Secret Diary" ("Geheimes Tagebuch"), "Frau R. didn't budge from Alma's room for almost two hours." Only then was Werfel able to appear in Alma's bedroom: "We made love! I did not go easy on her. In the small hours, I returned to my room."

He had hardly fallen asleep, at dawn, when Alma's English maid, Maude, woke him to say that her mistress was suddenly feeling very ill.

Would Herr Werfel please get a doctor; Madame Mahler had just had a severe hemorrhage. Panic-stricken, he ran across meadows and fields still damp from the rain on that Sunday morning, fearing the worst for his beloved, blaming himself as the cause of the hemorrhage. He lost his way in the fields and woods, ran on, shouting, praying—"Let Alma live!"—fell down a hill, made a vow on his mad run never again to desire any other woman but Alma. At last he reached a road leading to a nearby sanatorium, where he roused the physician on duty. As this man was a tuberculosis patient himself, he took his time climbing the steep path to Haus Mahler.

Werfel left Breitenstein that afternoon. A longer stay might have aroused Frau Redlich's suspicions. When he parted from his lover, she was in considerable pain and afraid she might lose the baby she had been carrying for seven months. She would hear nothing of Franz's guilt and tried to reassure him, saying that she was equally responsible for anything that had happened.

While Werfel waited for his train at Breitenstein station, Lieutenant Walter Gropius stepped off a military train. Early that morning Anna had called her stepfather, who had brought a gynecologist from the city. The two men passed close by Werfel without noticing him.

In the days that followed, Werfel wrote conscientiously in his diary, recording practically every moment of his existence and repeating the vow he had made that morning when he feared for his loved one's life: "To remain always true to Alma. . . . Not to let my eyes dwell on sexually exciting things in the street."

A telegram notified him that Alma had to be taken to a hospital in Vienna and that her condition remained serious. Werfel decided to fast, hoping to help his beloved by doing penance. He despaired over his own shortcomings: "I'm still not mature, I slide back only too easily into the world of sleaze." On August 1, four days after the hemorrhage began, he was able to speak to Alma on the telephone. She had been taken to the Löw Sanatorium, the hospital in which Gustav Mahler had died in May 1911. Werfel was told that she was still in serious danger, and the physicians did not hold out much hope for the survival of the unborn child.

When he returned home that evening, he fell asleep for hours, an "undoubtedly hypnotic" and "paralyzed sleep" filled with mortal anxiety. As soon as he woke up, he called the Löw Sanatorium and was told that Alma had been taken to the delivery room at the very same time he had been in that trancelike sleep.

The next morning, he called the hospital again. This time he talked to Walter Gropius, who told him that Alma had had a very difficult night but had given birth to a boy. All things considered, she was doing quite well. "O Lord of Life, never again shall I lose you," he wrote in a letter addressed to Alma, "and all my doing and not doing shall not cease to praise Thee and sanctify Thee." And he informed his beloved, "Through you alone I am reborn, sweet holy mother!"

Werfel was still not certain whether the newborn was his or not. As soon as Alma had revived a little, she wrote Werfel and confirmed that he was undoubtedly the child's father. But in his diary Werfel goes on questioning: "Is it my child? . . . That it is a boy, makes me feel . . . Yes! I haven't been able to imagine that a girl would come from my seed."

Eight days after his departure from Breitenstein he was able to see Alma again. He visited her in the sanatorium, pretending to be just a friend while the nurses were present. Only when they had a moment alone did he dare to look at the rapidly breathing baby that lay sleeping in a small basket. He noted that the diminutive creature not only resembled him but resembled even more—and this really moved him—his father, Rudolf Werfel, "to a frightening degree."

Alma, too, had noticed the likeness between the baby and her lover, and every time she had visitors she was afraid that someone would mention it. One day Walter Gropius and his rival stood side by side in the hospital room, admiring the baby. "The *deep poignancy* of the situation made me tremble," Werfel confessed in one of his daily letters. He regretted that Alma's architect-husband, whom he regarded as one of "the most distinguished, most noble of men," was living "in a state of ignorance," and he felt guilty about it. True, it had been Alma's right to choose the father of her child, he wrote to her, "but it wasn't my right to become the father." Alma had told Werfel that Gropius was delighted with the boy and anxious that he should survive; she admitted that this caused her heartache. In her letter she asked her lover whether he thought that her husband would ever find out the truth; at the same time, she did not hesitate to sign the letters she wrote from the hospital "Alma Maria Werfel."

Werfel had permission to visit her room, number 190, at any time, but he always felt embarrassed when he could not be alone with Alma. Thus, when her mother and stepfather, the painter Carl Moll, were present, his gestures became awkward and he hardly dared utter a word or even cast a glance at his own child. As soon as he returned home he would write Alma to lament this almost insupportable situation. The lovers corresponded about a name for their son, vacillating between Martin and Daniel, Lukas and Benvenuto. Werfel declared that the boy would "not be a weakling" and "not a hysteric," and claimed to perceive traits of maturity, courage, and sensitivity in him at this early stage. "These days," he wrote to Alma, "I often feel that—even if I am a disaster—he'll be the perfection of what is only hinted at in me."

At the end of August, while Alma Mahler was still in the sanatorium, Walter Gropius overheard his wife in a very intimate telephone conversation. When he asked her who had been at the other end of this ardent discourse, Alma remained silent ". . . and he knew everything," Werfel noted in his diary. That same afternoon the betrayed husband made his way to his rival's apartment, but Werfel did not answer the door. Their confrontation took place the next day, in a calm and reasonable atmosphere; Gropius even felt sympathy for his rival. However, the architect could not imagine giving up the woman he adored as a goddess; his plan was to take her and the children to Germany after the war, to begin a new life. Nevertheless, he also discussed matters with Alma's mother and consulted lawyers. Then he received sudden marching orders: he had to get back to his unit. During the past few weeks, the Allies had forced the Germans to retreat from all their defensive positions on the Western front. The last great decisive battles of World War I had begun.

Gropius wrote to Werfel from the front and said that now they both had a duty to support the "divine woman" who had come so close to dying. He mentioned that he had started reading Werfel's works and was extraordinarily moved by them. "I love him and feel friendship for him," Franz told Alma, and asked her if she thought it possible "that we do not have to be jealous!? That there can be a brotherhood of love for the divine being Alma?"

In his next letter, Gropius went one step further: after reading everything Werfel had published so far, he recognized in his rival a "*genius of fate*," sent to scourge him so that he, Gropius, could become better. He paid tribute to Werfel and hoped that Alma's wisdom would now find the right word and the right road for both men.

In the meantime, Alma had returned to the city apartment on Elisabethstrasse, together with the baby, which was still extremely sickly. Werfel was working on a fairy-tale drama in which he tried to incorporate the events in Breitenstein and their prehistory in allegorical form. So that he could write without distraction, he prevailed on the Military Press Bureau's doctor now and then to put him on the sick list for several days, and in a short time he finished the first act of the play *The Midday Goddess* (*Die Mittagsgöttin*). Werfel had to rush because he absolutely wanted to include the play in his book *The Last Judgment*, which had already been set in proof and about which he felt very differently now than he had in the spring. The volume now seemed to him, he wrote in his diary, "sterile down to the bones, barren, even deficient in music. . . . Coquettish fluff. But I have to let them do it. For Kurt Wolff's sake." He felt too weak to "suppress . . . this evidence of my existence after two or three years of silence."

The Midday Goddess had as its main character Mara, the earth goddess, the primary pagan principle, who manages to attract to herself
the aimless, decadent vagabond Laurentin. Mara shows him the way
out of the "chaos of the I," making a new man of him. She bears a child,
Laurentin's son, whose birth causes the vagabond to feel reborn, this
time with the strength and maturity to choose his own path in life, in
sincerity and purity.

The three-act play was completed by the end of September 1918.
Werfel sent it to his publisher with a note stating that *The Last Judgment*
had been lacking this particular element of male-female relationship:
thus the play would truly complete the large volume. Now, he wrote to
Georg Heinrich Meyer, he was praying "to the gods that a few insight-
ful people will understand what I have concealed within this book."
(Financial and contractual matters were still in the hands of Rudolf
Werfel, who acted as his son's agent in all negotiations with Kurt Wolff
Verlag.)

In October 1918, Walter Gropius received a medical release from
frontline duty and traveled to Berlin to prepare for the reopening of
his architectural office. At the very beginning of November—the German Reich was in the initial throes of revolution—he came to Vienna.
He had decided to ask Alma for custody of Manon, their two-year-old
daughter, and to suggest that Alma start a family of her own with
Anna, the new baby, and Franz Werfel.

The three protagonists of this real-life drama talked things over.
Alma announced her decision to bid farewell to both men: she said that
this was irrevocable and that she wanted to raise her three children by
herself. On bended knee Gropius begged his wife to forgive him for his
threat to deprive her of Manon. Werfel managed to calm the other two
down with a few carefully chosen words. However, they did not make
any progress toward a resolution of their triangular problem that day
in November 1918.

*"If you were thinking of using my mother's memoirs as a basis for your research,
you'd better forget it," says Anna Mahler. I am visiting the sculptor in her home
in the medieval town of Spoleto, near Rome. "There was an original manuscript
of the autobiography," she continues. "It was nine hundred pages long, but out
of consideration for certain people—and for Mammi herself—most of it was
toned down a lot and even drastically changed before the book was published.
For instance, practically all of her horrendous anti-Semitism was edited out.
And also what she really thought of Mahler, Gropius, Kokoschka, and Werfel."*

Alma Mahler's daughter spends six months of the year in Los Angeles, the other six in Italy. Her two-story house on the narrow Via degli Eremiti is sparsely furnished. The rooms have stone floors. In the front yard, surrounded by dry clumps of grass, lies the white sculpture of a nude male under large, semi-opaque sheets of plastic. The atmosphere of the high-ceilinged rooms is cool and spare, but the kitchen and study are a little warmer.

There is a long wooden table covered with piles of books, newspapers, correspondence. "Alma kept calling Kokoschka a coward until he finally 'volunteered' for military service in the war," Anna relates in her deep, slightly hoarse voice. "Well, she couldn't tell the world that, could she? Kokoschka really did not want to go to war, but she was already fed up with him by then. He was too demanding for her. Then, when he was hospitalized in Vienna with a severe head wound, she refused to go and see him. But she really did fall in love with Werfel, even physically, absolutely. *He did have a beautiful head. . . . I made a bust of him, in the thirties in Vienna. And he had a wonderful forehead, light blue eyes. . . . But he was very stout and muscle-bound. A large mouth, muscular, typical for a man who likes to talk a lot. But* terrible *teeth! And his chin looked very weak when he was talking."*

There is an album of photographs, inherited from Alma Mahler. The book looks full to bursting—it contains hundreds of images of long-gone life stories. They parade before my eyes like fragments of dreams. Alma's father, the famous landscape painter Emil Schindler; her mother; her stepfather Carl Moll; her siblings and her daughters; her husbands, lovers, and friends. "See here, that's the Haus Mahler in Breitenstein," says Anna, pointing at a slightly yellowed photograph. "Not really a very handsome building, is it? But it was lovely inside. Paneling everywhere—and, at first, no electric light at all. It was so lovely at night in the room with the fireplace: only the flickering fire and many, many candles. Above the fireplace there was a fresco by Kokoschka that continued the flames upward, with Kokoschka himself sitting in their midst. To the right, some monsters, very dark. To the left, a figure of light, pointing—as it were—to the way out. And that figure, of course, was Alma."

"I always liked Werfel, from the very beginning. Of course I remember that terrible episode with the hemorrhage. I'm sure that much of that was due to poor nutrition—we had hardly anything to eat during the war. Our cook—her name was Agnes—used to prepare a kind of ersatz meat for us, a concoction of mushrooms and tree bark, with polenta and potatoes on the side. That was more or less it—surely not enough nutrition for the fetus. And after the hemorrhage, until the birth, there were three days during which the baby hardly got any oxygen. No wonder it became so ill later. Those weeks of anxiety about Alma and the child preoccupied Werfel to the end of his life. He hardly ever spoke of them, but that period keeps cropping up in his work. I don't know, maybe it wasn't all that good for him to fall under Mammi's influence. She made him into a novelist, that's for sure. Without her—I'm pretty sure of this—he would have

remained a poet and a bohemian to the end of his life. I don't think he would have been too concerned about making money."

Anna's husband, Albrecht Joseph, a writer, theater director, and film editor in his time, has joined us at the big table. After listening to his wife for a while, he comments, "Werfel told a friend in later years: 'If I hadn't met Alma, I would have written a few more good poems and gone to the dogs, happily.' "

"But you mustn't imagine that Alma was some kind of monster—that wouldn't be right at all," Anna says. "If you don't know both sides of her, you can't understand her; she was an incredibly passionate woman who was able to give an incredible amount. When she entered a room, or just stopped in the doorway, you could immediately feel an electric charge. There was a glow when she came into a room."

"Yes, she had this amazing magnetic energy, and it served her hunger for power," Albrecht agrees. "At first sight, she looked like a successful opera singer, a Wagnerian. She always wore these gowns shaped like potato sacks so that you couldn't see her figure at all, only her imposing head."

"Still, she had magic," Anna Mahler insists. "You can't deny that! And her enthusiasm for everything in the arts—she was like a volcano! And she really paid attention to everyone she spoke to. And encouraged them. Gave people courage to be themselves and to pursue their art. You experienced it yourself: she really had a great personality, she was able to enchant people in a matter of seconds."

"Your father, Gustav Mahler, was a remarkable man even before he met Alma," Albrecht says. "Kokoschka would have become Kokoschka, Alma or no Alma. And Gropius would have founded the Bauhaus even without Alma. Speaking of Gropius—when reminiscing, she used to say, 'Oh, but he was so boring!' "

Breitenstein am Semmering

Today, against the superior force of these mounted police, we are still too weak!" Franz Werfel shouted to the crowd surrounding him. But soon, the twenty-eight-year-old assured his audience, waving his hat in operatic fashion, soon, like an avalanche, the proletariat would crush the rulers who were still exploiting it: "Then *we'll* own these palaces of money!" he shouted, and pointed at the massive Bankverein building behind him. It was the beginning of November 1918, near the Schottentor in the Inner City of Vienna. Werfel sympathized with the Red Guard, called into life a short while before by Egon Erwin Kisch and modeled on the Bolshevik example. With his friend, its leader, he roamed the streets in great excitement, staying away from his post in the Military Press Bureau more and more. In military barracks, exercise yards, newspaper offices, he participated in heated discussions, attended gatherings of soldiers and workers, and went to illegal meetings to plan the overthrow of the monarchy by the dispossessed classes. At the same time, the Austro-Hungarian Empire was collapsing on all fronts, and the greatest slaughter humanity had yet seen was drawing to a close.

Some of the agitators in the Red Guard had participated in the Russian Revolution. They pushed through a resolution proclaiming that blood would have to flow in future clashes with the state. When Werfel voiced his strong opposition to the resolution, he was threatened with expulsion from the military committee. The threat did not seem to faze him—he had other worries. His call to storm the banks had quickly reached the ears of the authorities, and he was summoned to a hearing. Werfel said that he was a supporter of Tolstoy and of primitive Christianity, and was therefore strictly opposed to any use of violence; his brief speech, he claimed, had simply served to calm the excited mob—and in particular to stop it from marching on the Rossauer

Barracks. Police Commissioner Johann Presser countered that the accused was hardly in a position to gauge the dangerous effect of his incendiary words and pointed out that Werfel had lost his right to reside in Austria: his permanent domicile was in Prague, the city that a fortnight ago had become the capital of a new and independent Czech state. Werfel replied that he was a well-known poet and that any restrictions on his freedom would lead to a furor in the press all over Austria and Germany—surely Commissioner Presser did not want to risk such a scandal?

On November 12, 1918, one day after the abdication of Emperor Karl I, the Austrian Republic was proclaimed on the Ringstrasse in Vienna, in front of Parliament. Hundreds of thousands streamed in from all districts of the city and gathered between City Hall and the opera house. Only the members of the Red Guard, whom the crowd took to be security forces, were still wearing their field gray uniforms. During a speech by the president of Parliament, the Guard unfurled red flags: they had simply torn the white strips of fabric off their newly manufactured red-and-white Republican flags. A sudden commotion broke out when it was rumored that a machine-gun post had been set up on the roof of Parliament to open fire on the Red Guard. A few Guard members tried to enter the building, firing their weapons at random. In the ensuing panic, two people were killed and several demonstrators seriously wounded by small-arms fire.

The Austrian press accused the Red Guard of having instigated the bloodshed and condemned its leader, Egon Erwin Kisch, as an irresponsible adventurer. Franz Werfel, too, was linked to the events and painted as an active member of a gang of criminals, a sympathizer of looters and arsonists.

On the morning of that historic day, Franz Werfel had visited Alma Mahler in her apartment to ask for her blessing, refusing to leave until she gave him a kiss. When he returned late at night, exhausted and disheveled, his beloved—who was a monarchist—showed him the door, turning her back on him in a gesture of revulsion. Walter Gropius, however, took care to see that the police did not get their hands on his rival. He intervened on his behalf in high places and even went to Werfel's apartment on Boltzmanngasse several times to warn him of possible raids.

After the waves of public outrage had died down a little, Werfel retired to the "netherworld" of coffeehouses and—now that his duties at the Military Press Bureau had ended and he no longer had regular working hours—fell once again under the influence of his friends.

He paid daily visits to the Café Central and to the year-old Café Herrenhof, only a few steps away on the same street, the dark and narrow Herrengasse. In the Herrenhof, dim light filtered through a yellow glass ceiling; the café had numerous spacious booths, arranged in a star pattern, each with its own presiding spirit. One of them was a friend from Prague, Ernst Polak, Werfel's intellectual mentor in the happy Café Arco days, who had moved to Vienna a short while before. Polak had married a Czech woman, Milena Jesenská, thus freeing her from the mental institution to which her father had committed her. A foreign-currency clerk at the Austrian National Bank in the mornings, Polak spent the rest of his days in the Herrenhof. Milena, who had had a large circle of admirers in Prague, did not find it easy to adjust to the postwar austerity of Vienna; she felt lonely, insecure, unloved. She gave private Czech lessons, worked as a maid, and was even a porter at the Western Railway Station, while her husband sat and philosophized in the Café Herrenhof, always gathering new disciples of both sexes.

Alma Mahler's premature child survived the aftereffects of its difficult birth surprisingly well, but at the end of November 1918, when the baby was four months old, its condition took a drastic turn for the worse. It suddenly developed water on the brain, and its head swelled alarmingly. Deeply anxious about the survival of her child, Alma now permitted Werfel to visit her occasionally.

He told her about the large-scale play he had been planning in recent days. Its title was *Mirror Man: A Magical Trilogy* (*Spiegelmensch: Magische Trilogie*), and Alma took an instant liking to the idea. She suggested that Werfel move to her house in Breitenstein for the winter to complete the play there, in peaceful and undisturbed surroundings—a prospect that closely matched his own longing to get away from the chaos of the city. Even before meeting Alma, he had told Gertrud Spirk that he hoped to be able to leave Vienna one day when the war was over, for a place where he could do nothing but write, in peace and without distractions.

Shortly after Christmas 1918 he arrived in Prague and spent two weeks with his parents. More than ever he realized, there in the city of his birth, that Alma had become the absolute center of his life—and he told her this in ever new variations in each of his daily letters. For instance: "Back here, I realize that I have become a man without a fatherland. It is a deeply alien city!" In conversations with his family he now echoed Alma's opinions and enthusiasms. Thus he, once a Verdi fanatic, suddenly considered Richard Wagner the greatest dramatist of all time. His mother shook her head sadly and summed it all up by saying, "He has become a total stranger."

During his visit, some Czech nationalists heard him speaking German in the street and beat him up. After the dissolution of the empire, Jews and Germans had become even less popular than before; from now on, fear was Werfel's constant companion in Prague. He met Gertrud Spirk again. She treated him with great reserve but showed surprising empathy when Werfel told her about his ailing son. "My feelings for G.S. are those for a remote acquaintance," he claimed in a letter to Alma. "I feel incredibly alienated." His former love was becoming "an ever more ghostly apparition . . . like all of Prague." At the same time he expressed anxiety that Alma might distance herself from him now that he was gone; indeed, he had not received a single letter from her during his time in Prague. "Why," he asked, "are you so mean, so cold, and do not give me any news of my son?" And he exhorted her, "Woe unto you if you do not, while I am away, declare every day that Jesus of Nazareth is the one you love most!"

In the meantime the child's condition had grown worse. When Werfel returned to Vienna in January and saw the baby again, he was horrified: the boy's hydrocephalic head had assumed nightmarish dimensions. Cerebral and spinal taps were performed several times, but the condition persisted.

Once again Alma withdrew from Werfel. Now she promised Walter Gropius that she would soon stop seeing Werfel and wrote in her diary that she had never really loved anyone except Gustav Mahler; compared to *him,* men like Kokoschka, Gropius, or Werfel seemed insignificant, negligible, "mites." She picked fights with her lover, made mountains out of molehills. Once she forced him to justify his decision to ask some café friends to his apartment on Boltzmanngasse, a group that included two women whom he had certainly not invited. In despair he defended himself, saying that he had already "given up so much" since he had known Alma and that he no longer had a *serious relationship with anyone,"* not even his own family.

In spite of all this ill feeling, Werfel was allowed to retire to Breitenstein, to Haus Mahler. Vienna was still suffering the miseries and grave shortages of a lost war. Basic foods could only be purchased at exorbitant prices on the black market, and there was hardly any coal. A great many Viennese starved or froze to death that winter, while others perished in an insidious Spanish flu epidemic.

In the Semmering hills, Werfel led the life of a hermit. The caretaker couple next door attended to his needs sporadically. When the weather warmed up, he went on long walks, up the Kreuzberg, the Rax, and Schneeberg, down to the Adlitz valleys or through imposing forests to Payerbach-Reichenau. In a few weeks he completed the first act of his fantasy play *Mirror Man,* a "magical trilogy" whose protagonist, Thamal, retires into a monastic cell in some legendary highlands, isolated from the world, determined to find his way back to himself. In a fit of self-loathing, he fires a shot at his own reflection, but from the splinters of the mirror is born a Mephistophelian alter ego, the Mirror Man. At first Thamal totally succumbs to this creature's seductive wiles. As he had done in his one-act *The Midday Goddess,* Werfel wove autobiographical elements into the plot: Thamal declines to accept his father's heritage and seduces the wife of a friend; she, Ampheh, gives birth to a boy, but the child "is ill, lame, broken in the bud."

"I am leading the life of the monks in *Mirror Man.* Insane loneliness!" Werfel wrote to Alma, complaining of his incessant, almost unbearable longing for her. He claimed to be working on the play for eight to ten hours every day, often feeling so "like a medium, so electrified" in the evenings that he almost frightened himself. He was also following a milk diet for weight loss that Alma had prescribed; on some days, he assured her, he even fasted. However, even these desperate measures did not in the long run change his characteristic corpulence.

Meanwhile, Alma noted in her diary that her resolve to love Werfel had blinded her for months. In actuality he was the cause of all her misfortunes; the child's malformation in particular had alienated her from him. She did not wish to see Werfel again.

The boy had been christened Martin Carl Johannes. His condition was deteriorating so rapidly that he had to be kept under constant observation in a hospital. Surgery was performed on his head, without result. "Twice, Alma spent a week on the verge of suicide," Werfel wrote in his diary. "Even though she has been vehemently claiming otherwise in recent times, we are tied to one another by an incomparable physical enchantment. . . . What will become of us? . . . In one year, we have shared an entire lifetime."

In March 1919 Werfel visited Vienna briefly. Alma told him on that occasion that she intended to join Walter Gropius in Germany. She had also decided to suppress radically any passion that she still felt for Werfel. Sad and completely at a loss, the rejected lover returned to Breitenstein. Slowly he recovered and then took up his work again in Alma's house, which he now called his "true home." First he wrote two fairy tales, "The Djinn" ("Der Dschin") and "Play Yard" ("Spielhof"), the latter clearly inspired by his relationship with Alma. "I had to put *Mirror Man* aside because it doesn't concern the two of us," he told Alma. Instead, he had written a fairy tale "in which our entire story is told in dreams. Does that make you angry? Is it indelicate of me to have written down words that were spoken by us?"

In late April, Walter Gropius founded the Bauhaus in Weimar, a state institution that combined the Weimar School of Crafts with the Academy for the Visual Arts. Alma and Manon traveled to Weimar for the occasion. They were staying with Gropius, and Werfel wrote daily letters. "*Do not do anything against me and against yourself,*" he pleaded. "Please, Alma, make sure to come back at the beginning of June. *I can't stand it much longer!*"

In mid-May he received a letter from Alma's friend Berta Zucker-kandl informing him of the death of his ten-month-old son. The child's mother received the news in Berlin but did not interrupt her stay in Germany. She returned to Vienna a month later. Alma had not made a final break with her husband, but they were both considering a divorce. With increasing urgency Werfel asserted his desire to forge a perma-nent bond. "It would be ridiculous," he wrote to her in Germany, "not to get *married* as soon as possible."

Mirror Man was once again on the back burner. Werfel applied all his energies to his longest and stylistically most brilliant prose piece yet, a fantasy inspired by Gustav Meyrink, Edgar Allan Poe, and E. T. A. Hoffmann. Titled *The Black Mass* (*Die Schwarze Messe*), it in-corporated elements from *Mirror Man* as well as Werfel's passion for Italian opera, intermingled with dream images from Babylonian my-thology and biblical history. But as soon as he returned to the play, he abandoned the "magic novella" and never completed it.

After Alma's return from Germany, she surprised Werfel by not keeping her distance but, on the contrary, joining him in Breitenstein and thus granting her "man-child" his heart's desire. Overjoyed, Werfel kept working through the summer with great vigor. He had hardly felt so happy and sure of himself in his life. In a few weeks, they would celebrate Alma's fortieth birthday. She admitted that she was longing to have another child with Werfel—a son, if possible. It seemed as if they had finally surmounted all the dark and threatening events of the year.

During a brief stay in Vienna, the lovers spent an evening in the Prater amusement park. Alma wanted to revisit one of the stalls where, years before in the company of Oskar Kokoschka, she had observed a boy handing the patrons of his father's concession the wooden balls to be thrown at the bizarre faces of life-size character puppets. Kokoschka had remarked that it would be almost a miracle if the boy did not grow up to be a murderer. When Alma and Franz entered the amusement park that summer's evening, they found a crowd gathered around this particular stall: the night before, its operator had been killed with a pickax—by his son. Werfel instantly saw the literary potential of this well-nigh unbelievable story, and on their return to Breitenstein he wrote, in record time, his first complete novella, *Not the Murderer* (*Nicht der Mörder, der Ermordete ist schuldig*). The title for this father-and-son tragedy was provided by Alma; "Not the murderer, the victim is guilty" was a proverb she had heard from an Albanian diplomat.

"All these fathers aren't . . . givers and bearers of love and wisdom," read a key sentence of the tale, "but [they are] weak and addicted . . . poisoned monsters of authority." Werfel had presented similar views back in 1914 in his dialogue *Euripides, or On the War,* but they only became effective in this new text, the tale of Lieutenant Karl Duschek and his unbridled hatred for his father. The book's philosophical underpinnings were derived from the anarchist credo of Otto Gross, psychoanalyst and bohemian, Werfel's friend from the Café Central. Gross's attack on a patriarchal world order that he found guilty of war, hatred, and malice was combined in *Murderer* with aspects of Franz's own often unharmonious relationship with Rudolf Werfel (although the actual relationship between the Werfels was by no means as grim as the novella would seem to indicate). There were also traces of Martin Buber's and his friends' cabal against militarism, whose meetings Werfel had been allowed to attend several times; even his former sympathy for the Czech irredentist movement was reflected here. A certain atmospheric similarity to Dostoyevsky's *Brothers Karamazov* and Turgenev's *Fathers and Sons* was clear indication that Werfel was still very insecure as a stylist, greatly dependent on the giants that had gone before him.

"For God's sake, please, I do not intend to have a 'tendentious success' à la *Son* by friend Hasenclever," Werfel wrote to Kurt Wolff after receiving galley proofs of the novella in the fall of 1919. Walter Hasenclever's play *The Son (Der Sohn)* premiered in 1916 and was staged at every important German-language theater. It was impossible to overlook the influence of this play about a father-son conflict on Werfel's own text. "The *Last Judgment* phase is all over now," he informed Georg Heinrich Meyer, the publisher's managing director. "I am taking pains to become more accessible." But he confessed to himself in his diary, "I still don't have, or will never acquire, the *cunning* of the true novelist." As in everything he had written so far, "the mathematics of the story" were "problematical."

Alma had ordered the conversion of Haus Mahler's attic into a spacious studio, an ideal workplace for her lover. In the fall of 1919 Werfel resumed his work on *Mirror Man.* Chain-smoking, he sat under the shingled roof, looking down at flowering meadows and distant larch forests, but often he worked at night, to the point of exhaustion, which gave him a feeling he knew from his schooldays—one of frightening powerlessness accompanied by panic. Sometimes it could even give rise to thoughts of suicide. "Feeling of impotence," he noted in his diary, "of not being able to write a serious book. Then shortness of breath, queasiness, inability to think, and the sudden sense that I can't take it anymore."

Alma Mahler thought she knew one of the reasons for these debilitating attacks. She claimed that her lover had destroyed himself by indulging in "insane masturbation" from the time he was ten years old until he met her. No wonder, she thought, that he often felt so exhausted, having weakened his heart and body cells; she even worried about a "softening of the brain." She decided to take good care to see that her "Franzl" led an ascetic life from now on and decided to put fewer demands on his vitality.

After months of living together in Breitenstein in great harmony, Werfel and Alma returned to Vienna in mid-November 1919. Gina Kranz had evicted her tenant from the Boltzmanngasse apartment after numerous arguments, but Werfel no longer needed a pied-à-terre in the city. When he came to town, he either stayed in Alma's apartment or took a room at the Hotel Bristol. Alma suffered greatly from the cold that winter; even she was hardly able to obtain fuel during the worst of the coal shortage. Austria, now a small country, seemed to be paralyzed; train service was curtailed, and industry had ground to a halt.

Werfel went to Prague to apply for a Czech passport. In a Europe of sudden new national boundaries, such a document had become a necessity of life; after the end of World War I, Werfel could no longer claim Austrian citizenship. He spent four weeks in the city of his birth, and they were once again painful. He counted the days as he had done at the front, slept most of the time, and was unable to work. His fear that Alma would slip away from him as soon as he left her seemed to be confirmed.

He wrote her that he was suffering because she could not give up meeting people who were "antithetical" to him and his work. She had given breakfast parties for people who were not, in his opinion, "worthy of the woman in whose domain *Mirror Man* is being created." He himself—he added reproachfully—was leading "an *orthodox* life in the Almasium." He had refused all invitations up to now because he did not want to sit around with "women" and generally found all "females" disgusting. Otherwise, he had paid only two visits to a "neutral" coffeehouse—which was meant to indicate that he had avoided the Arco—and was seeing, apart from his own family, only his old friends Oskar Baum, Max Brod, Willy Haas, and Franz Kafka. "Max Brod shyly asked me about you," he wrote to Alma. "Then he started singing your praises! He can't wait to meet you. For him, Mahler is the greatest art experience in this life."

In recent months Gertrud Spirk had begun a relationship with another man, to Werfel's tremendous relief. Now he was free of all obligations; he did not even need to write her the formal letter that Alma had recommended. But he was less than delighted to find out that his sister Mizzi had become best friends with Gertrud. Twenty-year-old Mizzi was the cause of great displeasure in the Werfel family: although her engagement to a non-Jewish Czech had broken off, she was still passionately in love with the man. Unresponsive, ill, and gaunt, she moped around her parents' apartment. Franz urgently asked for Alma's advice: she had met his sister briefly in Vienna—perhaps she would be able to help the girl. Somewhat surprisingly, Alma did write to Marianne Werfel and even relieved her depression a little. Without any correspondence addressed to himself, her brother read this letter "over and over" just so he could see the handwriting of his beloved.

"To win you forever and tie you to myself, that is now my only goal in life," he told Alma; and if only she got her divorce, he would no longer be plagued by the constant fear of losing the love of his life. "Alma, I implore you," he insisted, "help me during these coming years! Do not leave me for a minute!" He promised her he would work hard and earn so much money that she would never lack for anything. After finishing *Mirror Man,* he would write "one book after another" in order to be more useful to Alma. He did not think that his father would have too many objections to their marriage. While the two never talked "about anything personal," he nevertheless felt that Rudolf Werfel was "well content with my love for you."

At the end of January 1920 Werfel returned to snow-covered Breitenstein, alone. "In the city I'm no longer able to pick up a pen," he wrote in his diary, "not even for a letter." He pushed the first draft of *Mirror Man* to a conclusion. It was a piece, he wrote to Alma, who had stayed behind in Vienna, in which he felt he had combined "straight" theater with elements of farce, opera, and ballet. It was also his most vicious attack on Karl Kraus to date: he let his Mephistophelian Mirror Man slip into the role of the publisher of *Die Fackel* and wrote lines for him that were those of a self-important, fraudulent "East European backwoods lawyer" who inflated "any local gossip into a cosmic occurrence"—all this in a provocatively offensive musical number with a strong tinge of Jewish self-loathing. It ended with the words: "In short, because I . . . can't . . . look people in the eye, I'll look up their asses to see how good their ethics are."

After completing the first draft of the play, Werfel wrote to Kurt Wolff that the *Magical Trilogy* confirmed him in his conviction that none of his contemporaries had as much "theater blood" in their veins as he. He would soon travel to Munich (the new location of the publishing house) and read the "monster" to Wolff in several sessions. His friend Ernst Polak, to whom Werfel read isolated scenes from the play during a brief visit to Vienna, in his room in the Hotel Bristol, told Werfel that the work was superior even to Ibsen's *Peer Gynt*. Fired by such encouragement, Werfel finished the second draft in the spring of 1920, in Breitenstein, paying particular attention to Alma's suggestions for changes and improvements. She had, in fact, made deletions in her own hand in the original manuscript: at first, Werfel thought this an incomprehensible act of "irreverence," but now he cut and revised as much as possible while adding a few newly invented scenes. He told Alma that rewriting only produced "lame things." "I am someone who gets it right the first time or not at all. Unfortunately!"

At this time Alma Mahler was back in Germany, visiting Walter Gropius. Once again she received daily letters from Werfel, documenting his longing, which seemed almost unbearable to him, and his panic that his beloved would withdraw from him or perhaps even leave him altogether. These visions were not entirely unfounded: in her latest letters to her husband, Alma had emphasized that she no longer wanted a divorce but, on the contrary, was definitely planning to return to him. Werfel's nerves were so frazzled that he developed insomnia and often woke up in the middle of the night, picked up a pistol, and searched the house from top to bottom for burglars.

In mid-March 1920 right-wing radicals attempted a coup d'état in Berlin. The uprising, led by Wolfgang Kapp (whose men wore the Indian swastika symbol on their steel helmets), was put down by the Socialist government in only a few days, but during this time a general strike paralyzed the whole country. As postal and telephone communications were severed, Werfel trembled for Alma's and Manon's safety, and a week passed after the Kapp Putsch before he heard anything from Weimar.

In the meantime Alma and her daughter had moved into Walter Gropius's new apartment in Weimar. "You belong to me," Werfel cried out to her in a letter. "Even spiritually! Don't let them belittle the Jewish spirit! . . . My *life!* I am in such pain, to know you *there!*"

A few days before he had finished the second draft of *Mirror Man*, he received a telegram from the director of the Deutsche Theater in Berlin: Max Reinhardt invited him to read from his new play in a series of events titled "Young Germany." This invitation was the crowning glory of Werfel's most productive year so far: he would be able to read from the *Magical Trilogy* on one of the most prestigious stages in the German-speaking world.

In the thirteen-month period since Werfel's move to Breitenstein, he had produced—in addition to *Mirror Man*—the *Murderer* novella that was now doing well in the bookstores, *The Black Mass,* and numerous short stories, fairy tales, and essays. The love of his life had indeed liberated him from the Viennese "atmosphere of corruption" and transplanted him into monkish isolation: she had also succeeded in encouraging him to work on a daily and regular basis.

In the middle of April he recited long passages from his play at the Deutsche Theater. Max Reinhardt liked the *Magical Trilogy* and offered to produce it the following fall—on condition that Werfel cut the play considerably and revise it once more, as its present long chain of dreams and fairy-tale episodes was far too long for an evening at the theater.

After those painful weeks of separation, Werfel met Alma again in Berlin. To Walter Gropius's dismay, his wife now appeared in public with her lover in Germany—in *his* country, his own backyard.... Unabashed, she visited the cafés and theaters of the Reich's capital in Werfel's company and also came along to his conferences and private discussions with Max Reinhardt. They then traveled to Munich together, where Werfel delivered his play to Kurt Wolff in person. He had not, however, paid any attention to Reinhardt's suggestions for changes in the text.

At the beginning of May 1920, Alma Mahler left her lover once again; she had been invited to a Gustav Mahler festival in Amsterdam. She sent Franz back to Breitenstein, back to his desk in the large wood-paneled studio of her country house.

By way of Gloggnitz and Schottwien and through the Adlitz valleys, I drive in the direction of Kreuzberg, following the signs to Speckbacherhütte. Behind the small railway station in Breitenstein, a steep road winds uphill; after a kilometer or so I reach the turnoff, a narrow road lined with flowering fruit trees. The three-story Haus Mahler has been visibly altered by renovations and additions made in the course of past decades; from the outside, one can only guess at its original form. At the end of World War II, Red Army soldiers were stationed in the building. After the Allied forces withdrew from Austria, the house was acquired by a shipyard in Korneuburg and has since been used as a vacation home for employees of that company.

The first guests of the year will be arriving the coming week, during the Easter holidays. The K.'s, the caretaker family, are busy sprucing the place up for them. Herr K. shows me the large, white-tiled kitchen: it does not seem to have changed much at all, this former domain of Agnes Hvizd, the cook. Her pleasant little room was right above the kitchen, and a wrought-iron spiral staircase still leads to the upper floor. I make my way through a dark corridor to a roofed veranda: in Alma Mahler's day, this was a large wooden deck lined

*with tall pillars where she received her guests, who could relax in deck chairs
and rattan seats around a cozy coffee table. Now it is the dining room of the
shipyard workers' recreation home—an addition of glass and concrete furnished with Formica tables and plastic chairs on a linoleum floor.*

"And this used to be the fireplace room," says the caretaker. We are standing in
a bare room. The paneled walls have been covered over with yellow-gray
wallpaper, even where the open fireplace used to be. "Yes, the fireplace," Herr K.
says, "it was bricked up." He tells me that a shipyard executive found Oskar
Kokoschka's fire fresco above the mantel morally offensive and had it destroyed.
As soon as that had been done, the fireplace was bricked up. Now that space is
taken up by a color photograph of Kurt Waldheim, president of Austria, and
next to it stands a plastic sign showing the varieties of ice-cream bars available
here. Fairly drastic changes, in a spot where, among many others, Hugo von
Hofmannsthal and Arthur Schnitzler, Gerhart Hauptmann and Carl Zuckmayer, Alban Berg, Arnold Schoenberg, Hans Pfitzner, and Ernst Křenek came
to visit Alma, to talk to her and to trade jokes and arguments with Werfel—or
simply came to Breitenstein for rest and inspiration at Haus Mahler.

Pumuckl's Journey to Master Eder *is the title of a fairy-tale record that
Barbara, the caretakers' nine-year-old daughter, has put on a portable record
player, the volume turned up as far as it will go, here in the fireplace room.
Barbara sings along, takes a few tentative dance steps, and then bites into a
chunk of bacon and a stale, dry roll.*

On my way upstairs I scan the shelves of the home's library: Julia, Sylvia, and
doctor novels, Westerns and "Jerry Cotton" books. "This is room number five,"
says Frau K., opening the door to a room filled with bunk beds. Here, too, the
handsome paneled walls have been papered over, as they have been in rooms
three and seven. Bunk beds and faded wallpaper everywhere. In Alma Mahler
and Franz Werfel's former bathroom, three long-necked shower heads hover
above a bare stone floor: it looks like the washroom of a jail or a mental
institution.

The third floor—the attic that Alma Mahler-Gropius had redesigned as a
spacious studio, where Werfel had his desk and high desk, where the rough board
walls were covered with large posters for his plays—has been divided up into
four little mansard rooms for the use of shipyard employees. "In that room with
its board walls," Werfel noted in his diary in 1922, "I sense, time and again, my
spirits welcoming me." Many of his works were created here, in addition to
Mirror Man: Goat Song (Bocksgesang), Paul Among the Jews (Paulus
unter den Juden), Juarez and Maximilian (Juarez und Maximilian),
The Pascarella Family (Die Geschwister von Neapel), and The Forty
Days of Musa Dagh (Die vierzig Tage des Musa Dagh). Chain-smoking,
he wrote and wrote here, for twenty years, until the Anschluss—the annexation
of Austria by the German Reich—deprived him of his workplace. Not a speck of
dust, not a single vibration in the air is left to remind anyone of what took place

here, who lived, suffered, and rejoiced here, only fifty or sixty years ago. There are NO SMOKING *signs in big black letters above each of the doors to the mansard rooms.*

A subdued babble of high-pitched voices rises from the ground floor: Barbara's fairy-tale record. "Some days, all she does is read, that Barbara," her mother tells me. "Last Christmas, she read the whole newspaper, even the stuff in parentheses." I find myself staring at a notice that is posted in every room of the house, even here, in the former attic:

Austrian Shipyards AG
Linz-Korneuburg, Korneuburg Yard
Shipyard Home—Breitenstein No. 102

Dear Vacation Guests!

A most cordial welcome to our vacation home. We wish you a wonderful stay.

Every year, funds permitting, we make improvements to render our guests' stay more pleasant.

To guarantee order in the home, we have to ask that you obey the following house rules.

HOUSE RULES

Please observe the following mealtimes:
    0800 breakfast and pickup of picnic lunches
    1200 lunch
    1830 dinner
Drinks served only during meals and in the evenings until 2130.
If you plan an extended excursion and hence a later return, please
    notify management in advance.
Afternoon rest period: 1330–1530.
During this time, please refrain from playing the radio, walk quietly
    on the stairs, and close doors quietly. In the immediate vicinity of
    the house, children are also required to play quietly.
The night rest period begins at 2200.
After this time, television sets must be turned down to a volume
    audible only within your room, so as not to disturb other guests.
Please wear slippers when in the house.
Use the electric-shaver outlets only for electric shavers.
Standing and sitting on the radiators is not permitted.
If your room is not fully occupied, please use only 1 bed.
Lying on the beds in day clothes is not permitted.
Furniture, bed linen, etc., have been newly acquired and should be
    treated with care.

*As the walls in the mansard rooms are wood, smoking is not
permitted in these rooms. There is no smoking in the dining
room.*

*Trash must not be deposited on the surrounding paths or on the
lawn or in the toilet bowl. It should be deposited in the containers
provided.*

*Books and games should be treated with care and returned.
Newspapers and journals are for common use. They must not be
taken to rooms before the evening and should be returned to the
rack in the morning.*

Lawn chairs and outdoor games are to be returned after use.

*The house manager is responsible for the enforcement of these house
rules.*

Requests and complaints should be addressed to the house manager.

*Austrian Shipyards AG
Linz-Korneuburg, Korneuburg Yard*

"I Am Goat Song"

LATE FALL 1919 saw the publication of *The Last Judgment*. Franz Werfel had not felt close to this work for quite some time—it seemed to confirm him as a literary expressionist, and since he had been following his Catholic and conservative leanings more and more in the past months, he wanted to dissociate himself from that radical artistic stance. In the spring of 1920 he used a newspaper interview, on the occasion of the successful premiere of *The Trojan Women* at the Vienna Burgtheater, to declare himself "quite consciously opposed to dramatic expressionism." He attacked the movement as a North European fad that he, a man of the South, intended to combat from then on. "Our heart," he went on to say, "more than ever belongs to the music of the vaulting arches, the *stretti,* the *finali,* the splendid breathtaking absurdities of the theater—in short, our heart belongs to the divine Verdi!"

Now that *Mirror Man* was finished, he was casting around for new material. *Not the Murderer* was selling steadily and had received some enthusiastic reviews. It also provided Werfel with the first substantial income of his life. *The Trojan Women* ran for many months in Vienna, yet Werfel felt depressed and impotent without an idea for a new work. He made an outline for a novel directed against Karl Kraus: the latter's desperate attempts to become assimilated are put in jeopardy by the unexpected appearance of an Orthodox Jewish relative; appalled, "Karl Kalans," man of letters, decides to resolve the problem by simply poisoning his unwanted cousin.

Werfel spent most of the summer of 1920 in Vienna, until Alma sent him back to Breitenstein. She believed that he was capable of concentrated creative work only in the solitude of her house when she was not staying there. A few days after his thirtieth birthday he did indeed start working on an idea for a play with literary symbolism that had preoccupied him for a while: what if his hydrocephalic son Martin Carl

85

Johannes had survived and reached maturity? He wrapped the idea into a plot about Slovenian landowners at the beginning of the nineteenth century, a time when popular uprisings had been bloodily suppressed by the Turkish military. The protagonist of the play, half man, half Pan-like creature, would never appear onstage but would simply be reflected in the reactions of the other characters. This Werfelian Golem became a personification of revolution, a symbolic idol of the dispossessed, disenfranchised, and weak, spreading panic among the high and mighty.

Werfel called the project *Goat Song*, a direct translation of the Greek term *tragoidia*. In an arresting sequence of short scenes, far more accomplished in terms of both language and content than the *Mirror Man* experiment, he joined the private tragedy of his own son's deformity to his former vehement political engagement in the cause of the proletariat. The character Juvan, for instance, the self-appointed leader of the disenfranchised, was a composite of anarchist Red Guards and Russian propagandists Werfel had met during those weeks of revolt in Vienna.

Werfel may have wanted to please Alma by deprecating his own enthusiasm on the barricades as an aberration of youth. While working on *Goat Song*, however, he realized that he still felt responsive to the demands of the dispossessed and oppressed of all nations. The socialist revolution was both glorified and damned in Werfel's fascinating new play as it began to take shape. As Werfel himself put it later, the play symbolized "the theme of *our* time, the *sense of destruction*."

In October 1920 Alma Mahler and Walter Gropius were divorced in Weimar. "There is one human being in this world," Werfel thereupon wrote to his beloved from Prague, "to whom I say Yes more than I say it to God." Every day, he said, he gave thanks on his knees for her being in the world: "I could just weep incessantly." He wanted to take her to Venice to celebrate her divorce, and he even studied a little Italian during his stay in Prague.

At that time he was working on a "Dramaturgy and Explication for the Magical Play *Mirror Man*" ("Dramaturgie und Deutung des Zauberspiels *Spiegelmensch*"), creating a kind of guide for his future audience through the turmoil of the *Magical Trilogy* and its characters. In the meantime, galley proofs of the play had been mailed to the most important German-language theaters in Europe. Kurt Wolff regarded the sarcastic song about Karl Kraus as a total failure and had tried to persuade his favorite author to delete it, but Werfel insisted on leaving the embarrassing monologue in the text. *Mirror Man* was bound to be a success, he wrote to the disgruntled publisher at the end of October, "simply because there is no drama in a polyphonic style these days, just a lot of barren verbiage!"

Alma, now a divorcée, visited her lover's parents for the first time, something she had managed to avoid until then. She was a house guest on Mariengasse, staying with Franz, his father and mother, Mizzi, and Barbara. That year Albine Werfel turned fifty; thus, she was only nine years older than her son's mistress. The relationship between Franz and Alma probably became clear to all concerned during those days, but Alma was treated with the utmost respect and great sympathy. She was now regarded as a member of the family.

Werfel and Alma traveled to Venice at the end of 1920, taking lodgings at the Grand Hotel Luna and spending wonderful weeks in the city they both loved more than any other. Finances permitting, they decided to visit Italy and the city on the lagoon much more frequently in coming years.

Werfel began the new year with an extended reading tour of Germany. He wrote Kurt Wolff that the country had become "unspeakably terrifying! . . . Do you sense this too? Never before have I felt so keenly the question: 'For whom?' " His many readings were well attended and successful, but he was angered by the lukewarm and to some extent even hostile reactions of German critics to *Mirror Man,* which had now appeared in book form. In a letter to Alma, he claimed to be "pursued by hatred from all sides" in Germany. "Terrible country, terrible people!" He even feared that his lover might be adversely influenced by the Reich's prevalent opinion of him.

He did not return to the Semmering until May 1921, to continue work on *Goat Song.* He had had news from Leipzig that *Mirror Man* would have its world premiere there in the fall. In an "Autobiographical Note" ("Autobiographische Skizze"), probably intended for a press release by Kurt Wolff Verlag, Werfel confessed, "The consuming art sensation of my youth was the theater," and said that the most important experience in that context had been "the presentation of Verdi's operas by visiting Italian companies." It had been a key experience whose "aesthetic perspectives are still far from exhausted or intellectually charted." In the note he moved the year of his graduation from the gymnasium back to 1908, thus trying to conceal the embarrassing fact that he had repeated grades. Similarly, the fact that he had served only as a telephone operator on the East Galician front—without a day in the trenches—was buried in the sentence "The war years 1915–17 I spent serving in an artillery regiment." The note ended with the words: "Since the fall of 1917 I have lived in Vienna. I have found the great happiness for which, unknowingly, I had always been looking."

After *Mirror Man* premiered in Leipzig and Stuttgart, not very successfully, there was hardly a cultural page in any German-language paper that did not report on the poet, playwright, and prose writer Franz Werfel. Among these, not a few attacked him as an intellectual con artist, facile and money hungry. Even Karl Kraus succumbed to the temptation of revenge. In his playful operetta *Literature, or Let's See Now* (*Literatur oder Man wird doch da sehn*), the "Werfel family" engaged in stereotypically Jewish literary machinations in a coffeehouse reminiscent of the Café Herrenhof. Kraus accused young "Johann Wolfgang Werfel" of plagiarizing *Faust, Peer Gynt,* and *To Damascus,* describing his adversary as a sophisticated businessman who simply served literary fashion. The operetta matched Werfel's tasteless attacks on Kraus in every way.

When Werfel returned to Prague at the end of October to visit his parents, the city seemed more than ever a "phantom." Even the apartment of his childhood was more alien than ever. His mother was pained to see her son was turning away from her world and even had a crying fit over it. "I had to remain quite cold," Franz reported to his "only queen." He was constantly comparing his mother and father to Alma Mahler and deploring the almost insufferable discrepancy between these two worlds. "I don't belong anywhere, anywhere at all, to no city, no country, no time—I belong only to you," he wrote her. "I want to live with my back turned to the world!" This decision was not so easy to realize: about five hundred reviews of *Mirror Man* were forwarded to him in Prague. He didn't hear from his beloved for days: "I am quite at a loss. Good God! Why aren't you writing to me! . . . My mother keeps asking me why you aren't writing to me. . . . I swear to you, if you don't write to me this instant, you'll get a taste of what it feels like to be disappointed by the mailman."

Goat Song premiered at the Raimund Theater in Vienna on March 10, 1922. The daily newspapers reacted to the bizarre and unconventional piece approvingly but with confusion. Thus Robert Musil, who knew Werfel well from the Herrenhof, remarked in the *Prager Presse* that the play reminded him of a successful opera libretto, but as it did not go beyond allegory, it was not a work of great symbolic power. He went on to say that the poet Werfel, as was well known, had been struggling for years to achieve depth and significance without being able to convince his theatrical audience. "My line of credit has been exhausted. How come? I have become too familiar to those snobs and journalists," Werfel wrote in his diary after the premiere of *Goat Song*. As he was apparently no longer capable of surprises, he complained, those people were now debunking him. The press needed to discover a new talent every other year, and his "moment" had simply passed. But, he wrote, there was a consolation: "It comes again," that moment.

*   *   *

In order to spend time with her daughter Manon, Alma Mahler visited Walter Gropius in Weimar for a fortnight at the end of March. "I can't live *alone!*" Werfel pleaded, imploring her, as he had the previous year, not to allow the general German antipathy against him and his work to influence her. The Germans, he insisted, had not understood his passion and longing in the least. There was nothing "more mendacious and hypocritical . . . than this 'spiritual' Germany: Goethe or Bauhaus." His letter culminated with the statement: "*I* am (thank God) *Goat Song.* The primal chaos of insatiable *desire.*"

"All loneliness is illness" was one of the first notes for a play he was outlining during Alma's absence. No doubt it arose from the feeling of total lack of meaning and direction that overwhelmed him as soon as his beloved left him to himself. The main character of *Mass Murderer (Der Massenmörder)*, later retitled *Schweiger,* was a well-respected master watchmaker who had once, in a fit of insanity, opened fire on a crowd, undergone psychiatric treatment, and then been released as completely cured. Now, Franz Schweiger was not even able to remember the darkest moment of his life.

Distracted by rehearsals at the Burgtheater for the Austrian premiere of *Mirror Man,* Werfel interrupted work on the new play. Although the passage against Karl Kraus had been deleted by the play's director, the theater administration, headed by Anton Wildgans, still feared violent protests by fanatical Kraus supporters. On the first night, police security was provided in the auditorium, but the anticipated scandal did not occur. Apart from a few hisses, the audience reacted with great applause and demanded repeated curtain calls for the author with its shouts of "Bravo!"

In early May Werfel followed Alma to Venice, where she had already stayed several weeks in a small hotel on the Grand Canal. On their first visit to Venice, Alma had decided to purchase a small palazzo, and she was now actively looking for one even though her U.S. investments had been sequestered. To actually buy such a house, she would have to rely on the financial assistance of her stepfather, Carl Moll. True, Werfel wanted to contribute—his book and theater royalties were increasing steadily—but the disastrous effect of inflation in both Germany and Austria was rapidly devaluing his income.

After about a month of intense effort, Alma managed the almost impossible: she found the palazzo she coveted, in its own little garden. The three-story building was not far from the Grand Canal on one of the prettiest squares of the city, right next to the Basilica dei Frari in the Campo San Polo district. Repairs were needed, the previous owners were troublesome, but the dream of a house in Venice—Alma immediately called it Casa Mahler—was about to come true.

Franz Werfel spent peaceful and happy days in the city on the lagoon. On walks, on *vaporetto* trips, and in hotel lounges he made notes for a projected large-scale novel, based on a notion harking back to his schooldays and visits to the opera: to write, one day, about his idol Giuseppe Verdi. Until now, a vague fear of not being able to do justice to the venerated figure of "the Maestro" had held him back.

With Alma's help, he even began to compose music himself. For instance, he set Friedrich Nietzsche's poem "Venice" to a tune in six-eight time, the rhythm of the barcarole. His mentor admittedly regarded the result as "utterly devoid of inspiration and talent," as he noted in his diary—"but I often have such a great yearning for notes written by myself."

On her return to Vienna, Alma Mahler wrote a letter to Kurt Wolff, whom she had not yet met. She told him that Werfel was in dire straits: for the 3,500 German marks he received every month (the equivalent of 105,000 Austrian crowns), he was barely able to buy cigarettes and certainly not in a position to defray living expenses, for which he was entirely dependent on her. She asked Wolff to permit her to pay off any debts Werfel had incurred through various advances, saying that her friend felt uneasiness toward his publisher because of these unresolved financial matters. Was not Werfel head and shoulders above most of his colleagues, she asked, and should he not be remunerated accordingly?

Wolff defended himself vehemently, declaring that Werfel was his favorite author and that he was more than willing to discuss modifications of their contracts. On the other hand, he pointed out, Werfel had received three times as much money in the past year as Frau Mahler quoted in her letter. Besides—and here the publisher attempted to justify himself in a somewhat curious manner—Werfel had repeatedly assured him that his father was making considerable contributions to his finances on a regular basis.

Werfel spent the summer of 1922 in Breitenstein, working on the first draft of *Schweiger*. Franz Schweiger, a mass murderer, has been released from an insane asylum, as completely cured. Professor Viereck, director of the asylum, suddenly appears in Schweiger's workshop, after learning that his former model patient is going to become active as a speaker and candidate for the Socialist Party. The psychiatrist, a German nationalist, reminds the murderer of his deed, destroys his marriage to Anna (who is pregnant), and generally transforms the good watchmaker's newly idyllic life into a living hell. But then Dr. Ottokar Grund, a university instructor, somnambulist medium, and slave of the evil professor, shoots and kills his master. "We shall never,

never stop hating!" he shouts at Schweiger. "Down with the human race! We, you and I, shall organize the boundless hatred of the diseased millions!" The character was modeled on Otto Gross, Werfel's friend from Café Central days, and drawn as a "singularly unpleasant person," a dangerous psychopath and anarchist.

Dr. Grund is Schweiger's alter ego, just as the Mirror Man personified Thamal's split personality. Looking back, Werfel probably saw Otto Gross as his own antiego: if Alma had not saved him from the coffeehouse milieu, his life might have followed the pattern set by the passionate father-hater and brilliant disciple of Freud, who had died a painful death at the beginning of 1920 in the wake of withdrawal from his drug addiction.

The first draft of the play was finished in two months. In October, when the second draft had been completed, Werfel wrote in his diary, which he kept sporadically: "Generally speaking less confident than last year, after *Goat Song*." He seemed more content with a number of new poems written in 1922 and due to be published under the title *Incantations (Beschwörungen)*. "And yet writing poems often makes me unhappy, *fills me with suspicion*," he wrote to his friend in Prague, the poet and translator Rudolf Fuchs. "If one used this kind of careless intensity and vague suppression of inner voices in the construction of a physical apparatus, one would really be in trouble."

"It's just not possible anymore for you to go to Weimar," he clamored in a letter from Prague when Alma and Manon once again visited Walter Gropius. After—once again—hearing nothing from her for days on end, he wrote, "I am Schweiger [the Silent One]. A paralyzing indifference crawls through my entire being. I don't care for anybody. . . . *And I love you*." He pleaded with Alma to come to Prague, even tried a little blackmail, saying that he had been asked to give a reading for 2,000 crowns but would refuse to give it unless his beloved came to attend. "I can't read without you. (And it would be a shame to lose the money.)" His father, by the way, had guaranteed him a private monthly income of 1,500 Czech crowns—a lifesaver at a time when inflation in Germany was assuming ever more frightening proportions.

Arthur Schnitzler came to give a lecture in Prague at the end of October and met Werfel several times. They saw each other quite often in Vienna and Breitenstein; on these occasions, Schnitzler discussed his own work with the much younger man, whom he regarded as a friend. In Prague he was the guest of Werfel's parents and spent a particularly pleasant evening on Mariengasse. Franz Werfel, however, felt a need to apologize to Alma for having invited Schnitzler. "I just couldn't help it," he wrote, "because I felt that he expected it. Don't be angry with me." Alma had become estranged from Schnitzler after he divorced his wife

Olga in 1921. In the Schnitzlers' continuous marital battles, Alma had taken Olga's side.

Surprisingly enough, Alma did come to Prague to attend Werfel's reading, but she did not stay long. Soon after the reading, she returned to Weimar. She had become the main subject of conversation in the Werfel home. "*You've made an incredible impression,*" Franz informed her. Mizzi was constantly bothering her brother to tell her more about Alma. His mother was happy to have become much closer to her son's friend. According to Werfel, his mother had said that she now understood Frau Mahler and recognized her "nature" as it had been depicted in *The Midday Goddess.* And he thanked Alma for her efforts: "You made a great sacrifice for me."

He stayed in Prague for two more weeks, spending time with Max Brod, Otto Pick, and, first and foremost, Franz Kafka. Kafka's tuberculosis was now in an advanced stage. Werfel invited Kafka to visit him, either in the bracing mountain air of Breitenstein or in Alma's house in Venice, if he was well enough to come. Werfel had long since revised his initial mistaken view that Kafka's work would never get beyond Teschen-Bodenbach: after the publication of "A Report to the Academy" in 1917, he even wrote to Max Brod that he considered Franz Kafka "the greatest German author." Kafka had not changed his estimation of Werfel and defended him against anyone who dared question his significance. He praised *Mirror Man,* and *Goat Song,* and later recalled one of his dreams in which he gave Werfel a kiss.

But when the two met again at the end of 1922, Kafka's disapproval of *Schweiger* cast a pall over the reunion. The play had just appeared in book form and was to have its world premiere in a few weeks at the Neue Deutsche Theater in Prague. Kafka told Werfel that he found the main characters entirely inhuman and the invented story of Schweiger's psychosis utterly unbelievable. He was particularly offended by Werfel's characterization of a man he had once revered and befriended—who had, after all, had some influence on his own work: Otto Gross. Kafka identified with Gross's desperate battle against his father, the professor of criminology Hans Gross of Graz; he identified with Gross's vehement rejection of the patriarchal world order and agreed in some respects with his anarchic desire for political and private license. All the more reason for him to be outraged by Werfel's decision to make the revolting Dr. Ottokar Grund the spokesman of these ideas in his play.

Werfel tried to defend himself, arguing as well as he could, without being able to change Kafka's mind. On the verge of tears, Werfel ran out of the house. Kafka spent a bad evening and a sleepless night, and then wrote a long explanatory letter—which he never mailed. In it he said that he had always seen his younger friend as the leader of his generation but was now compelled to realize that Werfel had betrayed this calling; what was more, the tragedy of Franz Schweiger had offended him, and he considered the play an outright "cheapening" of a whole generation's suffering. Kafka added that he would not have expressed his anger so clearly if he hadn't regarded Werfel as a close friend. On a conciliatory note, he finished by saying that he was grateful for the invitation to Italy but doubtful that his condition would allow him to accept.

Schweiger also met with rejection from Arthur Schnitzler. He called it "a tortured, confused play—socialistic, occultist, religious, psychiatric," and told Werfel how little he liked it when he saw him again in Vienna that December. He noted that Alma Mahler had been glad to hear someone speak honestly to Werfel about the play, which she, too, regarded as a failure.

The play premiered in Prague on January 6, 1923, in a well-staged production at the Neue Deutsche Theater, and opened a few nights later in Stuttgart. Although the critics generally dismissed *Schweiger* as a slick fantasy with sensationalistic overtones, the tragedy was a big hit with the public.

"I met Ernst Polak in the Café Herrenhof when I was about eighteen," says Milan Dubrovic, a retired journalist and embassy counselor, once a habitué of the cafés Central and Herrenhof. "Polak probably was the very best friend of my whole life, and he was Franz Werfel's best friend. Incredibly smart and well read, Polak had a lot of charisma, and that made me venerate him. In the Herrenhof, I even became a member of 'his' booth, with—among others—Anton Kuh and Gustl Grüner. Alfred Polgar visited occasionally, and Robert Musil quite often. And Werfel, not every day but quite frequently. As soon as Alma took off, he really relished it; he became an instant recidivist."

I am visiting Milan Dubrovic in his large apartment on Minoritenplatz in Vienna, only a minute away from Herrengasse, only a minute away from Dubrovic's memories. The Café Central is still there today, but Dubrovic takes pains to avoid it. The notorious smoke-filled netherworld of yesteryear has been transformed into a tourist trap: brightly lit and squeaky clean, it now sports a life-size papier-mâché figure of Peter Altenberg reading the newspaper at his table. The only remaining fragment of the once spacious Herrenhof is a small espresso bar with plastic and Plexiglas decor.

"Back then, we lived in the café," the eighty-three-year-old gentleman reminisces. "You have to imagine it a bit like the academies of ancient Greece, where they tried to solve all the problems of philosophy. That was the kind of thing we did in the cafés. We discussed everything—religion, sexuality, politics, the gossip

*of the city. There were times when we really thrashed things out in a very brutal
psychoanalytical manner, for instance after the first night of Werfel's* Goat
Song—*which I attended, at the Raimund Theater. Of course, everybody tried to
figure out what Werfel was really talking about in that play. His coffeehouse
friends said to themselves and each other, There just has to be some reason why
he chose this fascinating but really quite horrendous subject. And Ernst Polak
told us that Alma had yelled at Werfel more than once that the deformity of her
son was his fault. 'It's all because of your degenerate seed!' She really treated him
abominably. And in* Goat Song *he was able to rid himself of all that in writing.*

"*I was totally enthralled by Werfel. He was a truly fascinating man. He had
exceptionally large eyes and a strong erotic aura. Sometimes, when he was in
form, he could go on for hours telling stories, impersonating people, reconstruct-
ing situations. One never knew about those stories—how much had his imagination embellished them? We didn't really care, they were always good stories!
When Werfel began to tell them, everybody fell silent. Kuh once said, 'When
Franz is talking, it's not like hearing a solo instrument but a whole orchestra!'
He would think of five subjects at once—it was tremendous. A splendid person,
obsessed by ideas and ways to present them. He was like a fireworks display. One
night we were leaving the Herrenhof after all the other places had closed, and
Werfel said, 'Let's get a hotel room, I'll pay for it.' The hotel clerk was quite
puzzled: 'What can I do for you gentlemen?' Werfel gave him an enormous tip
and said, 'All we need is a bottle of red wine and a lot of coffee.' And then we sat
listening to him in that little room until dawn. But those weren't just stories,
those monologues of his: they were often well-founded explanations of the world.
He was phenomenal. Sometimes we visited Werfel in the apartment on Elisabethstrasse, only if Alma wasn't there. Or we went to Gina's, to the grandiose
mansion of Kranz, her adoptive father. Or to Polak's apartment on Lerchenfelderstrasse. And Werfel would start playing the piano and singing Verdi arias.
He knew them all by heart. But even when we had stayed up all night, at nine
o'clock in the morning at the latest he would be at his desk—he was incredibly
industrious; you know the saying 'Genius is industry.' In Breitenstein, where he
worked often and in total isolation, he had a huge collection of phonograph
records. He had practically everything by Verdi. Even though, if I'm not
mistaken, his favorite opera wasn't one of Verdi's at all, but Bellini's* Norma.

"*He was a cantor at heart, a singer of praises, of God and the world. Religion
was very important to him—for instance, he was deeply involved with the
thoughts of Thomas Aquinas, pondering the compartmentalized world view of
Thomism. He knew many priests and was always analyzing Catholic philosophy.
That was one of his obsessions. A very different one was his interest in girls who
did not appear erotic at all. 'Strange,' we used to say, 'the kind of woman Werfel
falls for!' It was a rather common type, really, apart from Alma. He was capable
of starting a conversation with one of these young ladies right there in the street,
and then they would vanish into a hotel. Well, in those days between the wars it*

really wasn't difficult to have these erotic adventures—and that was due not least to the influence of Otto Gross. His theories were very much alive in the Herrenhof, and he was a propagandist of free love. Gross thought that one shouldn't even have a conversation with a woman before getting to know her sexually.

"We coffeehouse people strongly condemned the influence Alma Mahler had on Werfel. We used to say, *That's a different Werfel, he's become a 'success boy' [in English in the original]!* But he seemed happy. One evening we were sitting there discussing what those present would term the highest happiness on earth. And Werfel said, quite openly, 'Success! To me, success is practically identical with happiness.' He had to admit that. 'What wouldn't I give,' he once said, 'to have been Puccini! To have written Tosca and to live to experience its world-wide success, to conduct it in person at La Scala in Milan, and here comes the thunderous *applause from the audience! Well, if not Puccini,'* he added a little wistfully, *'then I'd be content to have been Caruso.'* "

A Novel of the Opera

AFTER THE PREMIERES of *Schweiger* in Prague and Stuttgart, Franz Werfel returned once more to Breitenstein, his voluntary exile, at the end of January 1923. Surrounded by snowdrifts many feet high, the house was almost impossible to heat. "Let's move to Venice, *at long last*," he wrote to Alma, who had stayed in Vienna, "to America, even farther away." But he soon got company on the Semmering: Frau Mahler offered her hospitality to Richard Specht, a journalist and music critic, whom she had asked to make a preliminary selection for a projected edition of Gustav Mahler's letters.

Werfel complained about the houseguest, finding him a constant irritation. He claimed he could hardly concentrate on his work and that Specht was in fact a "terrible old maid," a cautionary example of "yesterday's impotent generation." Werfel soon abandoned a play he had begun, *The Rebellion of the Dead (Der Aufruhr der Toten)*, in which he combined memories of World War I with mythical images of a mysterious mining town. He found himself unable to start anything else and traveled restlessly back and forth between Breitenstein and Vienna.

Only months later, staying in Alma's Venetian palazzo, was he able to calm down and concentrate. His plan of the previous year—to dedicate a large prose work to his idol Verdi—assumed more definite outlines, although Werfel still feared the problems he would encounter in combining historical facts with a fictional plot.

"I have converted A. to Verdi," Werfel had written in his diary at the end of 1922. "Of Verdi's lesser-known works, we played *Don Carlos, Macbeth, Aroldo, Simon Boccanegra*. The others, only cursorily. But the great works, forever. . . . I would like to collaborate with Alma on a new version of *Macbeth*. Edit, delete, compress." Alma Mahler's evident conversion to Giuseppe Verdi's world—she was an ardent Wagnerian—must have encouraged Werfel to get on with the task of the novel, an adventure upon which he would hardly have embarked without her approval.

In the spring of 1923 Werfel wrote in the preface to his novel in progress that Verdi "would not have suffered the smallest infringement of the truth concerning himself. But the truth of a life is not to be found in the strictest analysis of its biographical material, nor in the sum of all its doings and sayings." Hence his book would result in "the purer, essential, mystical truth" of "the Maestro" and thus "the *legend* of a man."

For his leitmotiv he chose a personal conflict between Giuseppe Verdi and Richard Wagner, which might theoretically have taken place but for which there is no historical evidence. It is not even known whether the two ever met. Werfel devised a scenario set in Venice only a few weeks before Wagner's death. Verdi has arranged a secret stay in the city on the lagoon in order finally to meet his adversary, whom he blames for his creative crisis of many years. Time and again Verdi finds himself in Wagner's immediate vicinity but never musters the courage to speak to him. On the very day when he decides at last to visit the revered and detested rival in his home, the Palazzo Vendramin, he receives the news that Wagner has died that morning. Only after Wagner's death, in February 1883, does the Maestro in Werfel's story overcome his creative impasse, find the way back to his true self, and complete masterpieces like *Falstaff* and *Othello*.

Werfel had become acquainted with the music of Richard Wagner as a gymnasium student, during the May Festivals. Wagner was considered the declared enemy of Italian opera, and Werfel had had to defend his own passion for Verdi against the Wagner cult prevalent among Prague Germans of Jewish extraction, often suffering ridicule in the process. He had first considered writing a biography of Verdi when he was twenty-one, during his year of military training. In subsequent years, Werfel experienced at first hand the contrast between the German North and the Italian South, and it became a theme of his writing. His disdain for cool stoicism and abstraction, his passion for emotion and ecstasy—these found their ideal reflections in this contradictory pair, Verdi and Wagner. Moreover, it was an ideological conflict of great personal relevance when he compared his own work with the ideas of Walter Gropius and the Bauhaus group.

Drafting the Verdi novel, Werfel now took daily walks through the streets and alleys of Venice, looking, as he had the year before, for sights, colors, smells, and, not least, original "types" to use as models for the characters in the book. He visited the beautiful gardens on the Giudecca, went to the Lido, visited the Palazzo Vendramin where Wagner had died. Studying the history of Italy in the nineteenth century, he read the works of the poets Manzoni and Carducci, as well as the writings of Garibaldi and Mazzini, the leaders of the Italian unification movement who had chosen the Freedom Chorus from Verdi's *Nabucco* as their anthem. For additional inspiration, he read Thomas Mann's *Death in Venice*.

"Returned mid-June 1923. Cold here, windy, flowering meadows," Werfel noted in his "Occasional Diary" in Breitenstein as he began his first draft of the novel. In five weeks, six chapters, more than four hundred pages, piled up on his desk. At first, there were diary entries such as "A propos the V. book, doubts, doubts, doubts. I feel strong inhibitions, even a kind of shame, toward this work!" But he kept on writing, day and night, often for twelve hours without interruption, much like Giuseppe Verdi, of whom it was said that he composed like a man pursued by furies, using a metronome to pace himself. Convinced he had failed, Werfel once handed the nearly completed manuscript to Alma and asked her to burn it immediately.

At the height of summer in 1923, while Werfel was still working on the first draft, Alma's nineteen-year-old daughter Anna Mahler came to Breitenstein for a visit and brought her friend, the composer Ernst Křenek—an admirer of Karl Kraus. In letters to Vienna, Werfel complained about the houseguest: "K. is an idolater of Nothing!" he wrote, claiming that if the twenty-three-year-old Křenek represented "the youth of our time—then heaven help us!" In any case, this fellow was "one of the most horrible types" imaginable, "conceited as a Ludendorff, presumptuous as an officer." "Only the devil could see the world" the way the young composer did.

However, after Anna and her friend had left, Werfel gave one of the characters in the novel, the ultramodern composer Mathias Fischböck (diametrically opposed to both Verdi and Wagner) certain traits of Ernst Křenek's. "Yesterday, I started writing about K.," he wrote to Alma. "I judged him harshly. But my nerves had been ... *outraged* ... by his mechanistic Satanism!"

Fischböck owed his character to yet another Austrian composer, Josef Matthias Hauer, the man who had invented a twelve-tone system years before (and independently of) Arnold Schoenberg. As he told Alma, Werfel used Hauer's book on musical theory, *Interpretation of the Melos* (*Deutung des Melos*), to "rewrite the Fischböck scenes."

"The end. Thank God! Praised be! On September 25, 1923, at 4 in the morning," he noted below the final line of the first draft of *Verdi*. The week before, he had informed Max Brod that the book had become far longer than originally planned and that it had caused him "more anxiety, doubt, and trouble than all my previous ones put together." While writing, he had often thought of Brod's *Tycho Brahe*—he even believed that a sentence from that novel had "snuck" into his book.

Werfel began to rewrite without a break, and the second draft was finished in six weeks. "The book is suspenseful, moving, and important," he wrote to Kurt Wolff, but to Alma he admitted that there were flaws, "partly because of the genre, partly because of the subject, and partly because of me." After five months in Breitenstein, he was "starved for the city," as he confessed to his diary. "I've been so faithful to this novel, yet it's not enough, still not enough!!!!" In addition, "this business" had "cost him [his] eyes." From now on, he claimed, he would never again be able to read or write without glasses.

Jakob Wassermann, whose work Werfel admired and whom he valued as a friend, read the second draft of the novel. He liked it but made numerous suggestions for changes, and Werfel accepted his advice with gratitude. He revised the whole book one more time, making particularly radical changes in the ending.

Verdi was a turning point in Werfel's literary development. It was the first clear demonstration of his abilities as a novelist. He seemed to find this form of fiction as easy to write as he had found poetry or drama. But his prose was still too purple, the "hymnodic" quality of his style unmistakable. A typical sentence from the novel reads: "Then, lest their [the violins'] fragile forms should crumble in his mortal grasp, Claudio Monteverdi laid the lovely sisters reverently by and tore himself away, whimpering and weeping in an unbearable ecstasy of pain and pleasure."

Side by side with arresting and effective scenes were glaring disasters, deeply embarrassing passages next to writing that could sweep readers off their feet. Venice, the fascinating stage on which the characters act out their joys and sorrows, was captured very convincingly in all its dreamlike uniqueness. And yet, this "novel of the opera" (that was now its subtitle) was its author's first move into, or close to, the realm of light popular literature—precisely the sphere to which Karl Kraus had contemptuously consigned him years before.

"I know for certain," Werfel declared triumphantly in a letter to Kurt Wolff, on completion of the book, "that I, for one, have surmounted the crisis that has destroyed the entire production of so-called expressionism (all the Unruhs, Bechers, etc., e tutti quanti) so far."

Paul von Zsolnay, the scion of a well-to-do Jewish family in the tobacco import business, had almost finished his university studies when he decided to start an Austrian publishing house specializing in belles lettres. Zsolnay knew Alma Mahler's stepfather, Carl Moll, and asked him to act as mediator with Werfel, to whom he wanted to make a serious offer. He also contacted many other authors, including Arthur Schnitzler, Felix Salten, and Richard Coudenhove-Kalergi.

At their first meeting Werfel and Zsolnay discussed a subject that had made the headlines practically every day for many months— inflation, which had assumed almost unbelievable dimensions in both Germany and Austria. One American dollar was now worth 4 trillion marks. A one-pound loaf of bread cost 260 billion marks. Postage stamps no longer carried a denomination, since the rate changed daily. During this time of hourly devaluation, Werfel's book and theater royalties hardly paid for the bare necessities: even the sensational success of *Schweiger* did not change that, although the play was being performed on twenty-odd German provincial stages and was in the repertory of one of the largest theaters in Berlin. In the autumn of 1923 Werfel wrote to Max Brod that his treatment at the hands of Kurt Wolff had been "disgraceful." "This year, I have been cheated out of three-quarters of my income." For the new editions of his works, Werfel claimed, Wolff had "fraudulently paid me a ridiculously low advance."

Zsolnay, on the other hand, offered an advance of 5,000 Swiss francs for the Verdi novel, provided that Werfel left Kurt Wolff Verlag and took the risk of entrusting his work to an entirely unknown and inexperienced publisher. At the end of 1923, that sum represented a small fortune, as the Swiss franc—like the U.S. dollar—was a stable currency. With regrets about Kurt Wolff but strongly encouraged by Alma Mahler, Werfel accepted Zsolnay's offer. The young publisher, for his part, decided to make *Verdi: A Novel of the Opera* (*Verdi: Roman der Oper*) the cornerstone of his enterprise. He still hadn't come up with a name for his publishing house; he was vacillating between Verlag der Autoren (House of the Authors) and Hohe Warte (Lofty Point).

In a letter full of excuses and explanations, Werfel asked Wolff, his friend and publisher for eleven years, for advice regarding this delicate situation, and he also tried to clarify his own motives. Wolff reacted with great understanding: right then, he said, he would have been unable to come up with 1,000 francs, let alone 5,000, and he could understand why Werfel wanted to accept Zsolnay's proposal. Wolff must have been expecting news of this sort for some time, ever since Alma Mahler's letter the previous year in which she demanded money and paid off Werfel's debts. In August 1923 another author had announced his separation from Kurt Wolff: Karl Kraus, whose main complaint against Wolff was that he had published Werfel's *Mirror Man* without insisting that Werfel delete the satirical passage against Kraus.

Only a few days after its publication in early April 1924, *Verdi* became a best-seller: its first printing of twenty thousand copies sold out in no time, and a second edition followed immediately. This audience reaction by far exceeded Werfel's expectations. His work had not been received with comparable enthusiasm since his success with *The Friend of the World* twelve years earlier. Now he could sense it again—that whiff of fame and power that had attracted him so strongly since the fourteenth year of his life.

In April 1924 Franz Kafka was admitted to the ward for diseases of the throat and larynx at the University Clinic in Vienna. Dr. Markus Hajek, the director of the clinic, Arthur Schnitzler's brother-in-law, diagnosed tuberculosis of the larynx. For the first time in his life, Kafka slept in a room with several others, and when one of his fellow patients died, he found life in the ward almost unbearable. Max Brod asked Werfel to use his and Alma's influence to secure a private room for Kafka. Werfel wrote to Dr. Hajek and also pleaded with Vienna's city councillor in charge of public health, his friend Dr. Julius Tandler, and Tandler's lover, Frau Dr. Bien, to use their influence in the matter. The director of the clinic, however, was not impressed by any of these interventions, and Kafka remained in the open ward. Mortally ill, he left the hospital and moved to a recommended private sanatorium in the country, at Kierling, near Klosterneuburg, where he was able to get a private room. Only six months earlier, Werfel had written to Max Brod, "Can't anything be done to save this rare human being? He will write the most wonderful things, but they'll become ever further removed from life, and thus perishable. The *dream* alone can't sustain a man past forty. No hunger artist can go hungry for that long."

Werfel sent the "novel of the opera" to Kafka in Kierling, with a big bouquet of red roses. Kafka, hungry for acceptable reading matter, now read nothing but that book, very slowly but regularly. "To *Franz Kafka*, deeply revered author and friend, with a thousand wishes for a quick recovery" was Werfel's dedication. Only a few weeks later, on June 3, 1924, Kafka died, in the presence of his beloved Dora Diamant and his friend Robert Klopstock. *Verdi* was the last book he read.

"I'm sure I don't have anything to do with that Fischböck," says Ernst Křenek. Our meeting takes place in Vienna, in the sunny conference room of Universal Edition, the music publishers. The composer, whose works now number more than 230, divides his time between Palm Springs and Mödling, near Vienna, in a house that Arnold Schoenberg inhabited in the early twenties. "At the time I visited Breitenstein, Werfel couldn't have used me as a model for Fischböck," Křenek continues. The eighty-five-year-old composer speaks slowly and quietly. "You see, he didn't really know anything of mine then. In her fairy tale Poetry and Truth *(that's what I call Alma Mahler's autobiography), she describes how I appeared there on the Semmering as Anna's, her daughter's, new lover and*

proceeded to spread out these enormous sheets of music paper, covering the whole house with them, so that she and poor Werfel had to seek refuge in the attic. All I brought was quite ordinary paper—there wasn't any other kind to be had—and I don't think I composed very much that summer."

Křenek is a curmudgeon with an ironic twinkle. I watch his eyes; they are in constant motion. The features of his face are immobile, determined not to reveal any emotion. In his quiet monotone, he continues, "Those Fischböck descriptions in the Verdi novel—they could fit Webern maybe, or maybe Josef Matthias Hauer. I hadn't done anything with twelve-tone series at that time. For me, that came much later. I didn't know anything then about twelve-tone music, that's simply nonsense—even Schoenberg had hardly published anything yet. He only revealed his invention of the twelve-tone series to his students in 1922. And his own serenade composed in that twelve-tone form came out a year later. I didn't know that music then, didn't even know the word for it. And the music that Werfel describes as Fischböck's—those supposedly horrible chords that bump into one another like drunks—that's a description of music à la Schoenberg.

"Of course, my feelings about Werfel are colored by the fact that I was a great supporter and admirer of Karl Kraus, and so there was enmity, even though I was politically more of Werfel's persuasion. Earlier on, he had been much further to the left. He'd been at the barricades, everyone knew that. At the Bankverein building he made speeches and urged people to take it by storm! We all heard those stories. But Alma tried to tame him, little by little. At the time of our meeting, his leftward leanings had already been modified. In any case, I can't remember any arguments with Werfel. Why would he have worked on the libretto of my opera The Fortress (Die Zwingburg) if everything I did was so repulsive to him? He worked on it in 1922. It certainly was modern music, The Fortress was; in any case it doesn't sound like Verdi. And it certainly was atonal—that seems to have been enough to arouse his antipathy. But he did work on it, nevertheless—I really can't understand why.

"Alma and I never really got along. And that terrible book of hers! What a disaster. All those affairs she had—I really don't think they had anything to do with love. She just wanted to rule. A terrible person! In the thirties, there was a coup attempt by right-wingers, led by a certain Rintelen, with whom Alma was on friendly terms. Werfel accused her of flirting with this Rintelen, but Alma just said, 'Oh, Franzl, you know a woman can pray in many churches!' But she did have a certain presence. She was the Brünnhilde type, and I never liked those particularly. Nor did I like her daughter Manon; she had such a sneaky air, as if she were always spying on people. I couldn't stand it.

"But wait, I just remembered—it must have been the fall of 1923: I visited Breitenstein a second time and started working on my Fourth String Quartet. For Christmas that year, Anna and I went and stayed in Switzerland, in Zurich. And I remember that the Verdi novel must have been finished that fall, because Werfel read to us from the manuscript, a chapter or two. I must say, there was *something very warm and lovable about the man. But you have to know one thing: I'm not very good at describing people. That is why I've never written anything in the epic mode. No talent for it. It bores me. What else should I tell you about Werfel? He so loved to sing! Alma would sit down at the piano, and he'd perform entire operas from memory. That was really pleasant. And I can't remember his ever being surly around me."*

Success and Crisis

VENICE—IN ALMA'S house! Wonderful," Franz Werfel noted in his "Occasional Diary" in the spring of 1924, although he was bothered by the noise around Casa Mahler, even late at night. Carl Moll had added two rooms at the top of the building so he could visit at any time without feeling like a guest in his stepdaughter's house. "*Will I be able to work?*" Werfel wondered. "*Here? A vital question.*"

Inspired by the great success of *Verdi*, he drafted outlines for two major works of fiction. One was to be a "novel of theosophy," a fictional biography of Helena P. Blavatsky, the Russian-born founder of the Theosophical Society, whose goal was the brotherhood of man without distinctions of class, race, or religion; the other, the history of a Jewish family "from the Toleration Edict up to the present, the so-called world domination by the Jews," from the ghetto in a small Bohemian town to the Jewish politicians and capitalists of the present, scapegoats of the anti-Semitic hatred that had grown ever more vociferous since the early twenties.

Werfel never embarked on either of these projects: he was not one of those writers who map out their oeuvre in their youth and then feel compelled to realize it, piece by piece, driven by the fear of not having reached the self-imposed goal. Moreover, Alma probably did not approve of either one of the projects, and that was reason enough for Werfel to abandon them.

He was now in his mid-thirties and better known than ever. "How short, the moment given to a man. But there is one consolation—it comes again," he had noted in his diary two years earlier, after the premiere of *Goat Song*. Now that this prediction had come true, Werfel wanted to prove both to himself and to Alma, who kept pushing him, that he was capable of holding on to his success—as long as he was able to find subjects the public would like. Financial security was not the least consideration in these plans. Alma expected her lover to take care of her material needs and to become independent at last of his family. At the end of June 1924 she sent him away from Venice to Breitenstein, where he was to begin a new work.

"No plan this time! What now?" was the first entry on his return to the Semmering, but it took only twenty-four hours for an idea to come to the rescue: "As I was reading books I had brought with me, the idea came to me like a flash of lightning: the historical tragedy *Juarez and Maximilian of Mexico*." The subject seemed without visible connection to anything Werfel had written so far; but hope that it might be best-seller material must have played a decisive role. It was also a factual and realistic subject, and by dealing with it he hoped to put an even greater distance between himself and literary expressionism, a movement he now detested. The final break with the avant-garde was to be sealed with a story about the tragic fate of the Austrian archduke Maximilian.

It did not take Werfel long to finish the first, technically very conventional draft of the play that told of that Hapsburg scion's adventure and downfall: Napoleon III cajoled Maximilian into going to Mexico, but the French troops soon abandoned him, and he was executed by firing squad on the orders of the Mexican revolutionary and President of the People Benito Juarez.

As in *Verdi*, Werfel again combined historical fact with intuitive insight, and the method is noticeable in the way he treats the main characters and key events. In his very first notes, Werfel still considered Maximilian's adversary the main character of the play, but later he remarked, "He is too colossal a figure and would lose his effect by becoming visible." As with the Pan-like monster in *Goat Song*, the President of the People, also the incarnation of a revolution, never appears on stage in person. Juarez remains the powerful commander of fate, untouchable, godlike.

Werfel described Maximilian's downfall with great sympathy for the politically naive Austrian, characterizing him not as a man with a desire to rule but as a good-natured idealist. The play does not criticize the gullibility that led him to become an accomplice in the murder of thousands of Mexicans, nor does it consider his blindness toward the power politics of Napoleon III and Mexico's reactionary princes of church and finance. This is surprising—the more so considering Werfel's own attacks on the house of Hapsburg and his infatuation with the ideas of the Red Guard only six years earlier. In his notebook we read that he did not doubt that it had indeed been Maximilian's noble intention to improve the lot of the Indian proletariat. Inspired by "mystical love of the enemy," he had vied for Juarez's favor: "I bowed down to him," Werfel has Maximilian cry out. "For what am I, by myself? But he is as great as this country."

Werfel told Alma that a woman would have the last word in this "play about men." Princess Salm, who played a part in Maximilian's passion reminiscent of the biblical Mary Magdalene, was to speak the final sentence. "But no," he then corrected himself—the end would be marked by a rousing revolutionary marching tune: "Boom, Boom, Boom! Vulgar but nice! I hope you'll agree."

One day before his thirty-fourth birthday, in early September 1924, Werfel completed the second draft of the historical drama. "An aloof play," he noted in his diary, adding that he felt it "wasn't bad, generally speaking," although he was aware of "many flaws, mistakes, dilettantisms. The drama is well constructed. Its scenes are intense and pointed." When he read *Juarez and Maximilian* to his friend Julius Tandler, who came to visit him in Breitenstein, the latter called the play Shakespearean, and Dr. Bien, Tandler's mistress, burst into tears.

Rehearsals for the world premiere of the play were to begin at the Volkstheater in Vienna in mid-September, and thus Werfel did not have time to revise it again. To have his "wonderful manuscript" typed, he traveled to Vienna, where "these stinky female typist animals" of Paul Zsolnay Verlag did their work "in a bestially cretinous fashion," as Werfel wrote to Alma, who was residing in Venice. The typescript was then rushed to the printer, as the publication of the book was scheduled for the beginning of October. As soon as the galleys were ready, Werfel had to read them in a great hurry. "I'm afraid, so afraid," he whined to Alma. "I'll never write another play."

When he heard that Max Reinhardt was interested in producing the play in Vienna the following spring, he quickly withdrew it from the Volkstheater, only a few days before rehearsals were to start.

In mid-January 1925, after months in Venice, Werfel and Alma embarked on their first long trip outside Germany and Italy. The initiative for this trip had been entirely Alma's, as Werfel was loath to leave familiar surroundings: he had to be presented with a *fait accompli.* But as soon as preparations had been made, tickets and reservations acquired, he enjoyed the project immensely and became the enthusiastic world traveler. They embarked on the steamship *Vienna* in Trieste, and the first leg of their journey took them via Brindisi to the Egyptian port of Alexandria.

On board the *Vienna* were also a great many Jewish emigrants en route to Palestine to settle their old—and new—homeland. True, that homeland was under a British mandate, as was Egypt, but the Balfour Declaration of 1917 allowed Jews to start their own settlements in Palestine and thus move considerably closer to Theodor Herzl's dream of the return to Israel. Still aboard the *Vienna,* Werfel noted in his "Egyptian Diary" ("Ägyptisches Tagebuch") that the Zionists were regrettably repeating the anachronistic mistake of nationalism: the Jews believed, Werfel wrote, that they were compelled to prove that they, too, could "do the same thing they have so despised and mocked in other nations."

Werfel and Alma spent three weeks in Upper and Lower Egypt. They visited the royal tombs at Thebes, went to Heliopolis, Memphis, Karnak, and Luxor, on to Cairo and the pyramids at Giza. They saw a performance of Verdi's *Aida* on the stage of its world premiere, the Italian Opera House in Cairo. The palm trees, orange groves, and fellahin villages along the Nile enchanted Werfel, and he found the quality of the light and the exotic landscape inspiring. An idea for a play that had preoccupied him years before resurfaced in Egypt: a play with Akhenaton, the pharaoh who embraced the Sun God, as its central character. Werfel also pondered the Islamic religion, about which he did not know much: "What is the nature of the Muslim's fanaticism?" he wrote in the diary. The Muslim "has to observe more prayers, rules, laws, and formulas than the devout person of any other religion!!" He became preoccupied with the figure of the *mahdi,* the Muslims' messianic renewer of the world, thinking that it might provide material for a novel. In a small suburban mosque in Cairo he witnessed the ancient, ecstatic dance of the dervishes and was fascinated: "The noble form of the sheik of the dervishes in his blue cape shakes with a sudden convulsion. . . . And suddenly the sheik glides away from his spot with an unspeakably holy grace. . . . Effortlessly the blue one has gained the center. And now he bobs up and down, as if he were not supported by the floorboards but by the waves of a magical sea."

After a few days, Werfel found the contrast between the upper-class hotel in Luxor, mostly inhabited by British and German tourists, and the alien and mysterious land surrounding it, with its "pitch-black people" and horrifying poverty, hard to endure. Furthermore, he found "this rushing through temples and landscapes boorish and soul-killing." More and more he disliked being a tourist among other tourists.

After he and Alma had returned once more to Cairo, they took the train to Palestine. For Werfel, the two weeks that followed were characterized by extreme anxiety and a tumult of emotions, a seesaw of feelings the likes of which he had hardly ever experienced. "From the very first moment, I felt torn," he noted. "My hand is no longer free. My mind is no longer at peace." While he had not sympathized much with Zionism in his youth, he now found himself, due to Alma's anti-Semitism—which she made particularly plain on this trip—as well as her virulent hatred of communism, defending a cause that really was not his. "Those were days of deep anxiety," he later wrote.

Apart from side trips to the northern part of the country and to the Dead Sea, Werfel spent most of the time in Jerusalem. He visited the church of Christ's grave and the Wailing Wall, as well as the Islamic Temple Mount, Mount Moriah of the Old Testament, where Abraham went to sacrifice Isaac, the site of Solomon's Temple and the Second Temple. He took daily walks through the narrow streets of the Old City, returning over and over again to the places of worship of the world's three monotheistic religions. He met the Kabbalah scholar Gershom Scholem; talked to physicians, architects, and philosophers, arguing with them about the pros and cons of Zionism; and visited numerous agricultural schools and cooperatives in the countryside surrounding Jerusalem.

"Today I lost my interest in the Jews," Werfel had noted on board the *Vienna*, with its passengers bound for Palestine. In reality his alienation from his own Jewishness had begun years ago, long before he met Alma Mahler—who indeed approved of it wholeheartedly. Bar mitzvah not-withstanding, Werfel had long seen himself as a believer in Christ to whom Judaism had become an alien world, one that even embarrassed him. "What did I have to do with these people," he argued in an unpublished essay written in 1920, "with this *alien world*? My world was the great European artists with all their contradictions, from Dostoyevsky to Verdi."

In Jerusalem, at the source of all theology, Werfel searched his memory for the point at which he had become conscious of turning away from the religion of his forefathers. He saw himself at four or five years old, walking to Sunday morning mass with Barbara Šimůnková; he heard again the solo soprano voice in the choir of the Maisel synagogue in Prague—which had struck him as "mortally indecent" when he was ten, so that the entire Jewish service suddenly made him "uncomfortable" and would henceforth seem an embarrassment. He remembered his religious instructors, his later arguments with Max Brod, his meetings with Martin Buber.

The journey through Old Testament lands shocked Werfel into an intense preoccupation with his Jewish origins that went far beyond his admitted interest in Israel's religion and history. In the months following his return from the Near East, he spent time almost every day reading about Jewish history, customs, and rituals; he relearned Hebrew, written and spoken, and studied German translations of the books of the Old Testament and the Talmud.

At the beginning of April 1925 Werfel returned to Breitenstein, once again separated from his beloved after a long time in her company. He wrote a new scene for Max Reinhardt's production of *Juarez and Maximilian,* but as soon as that was done, he was overwhelmed by a serious artistic crisis. After surveying all his creative work to date, he arrived at the conclusion that he had to "make an *entirely new* start." He felt that he had never succeeded in *"pure creation"*—every page he had written now seemed to him, as he wrote to Alma, "crowded with the abominable accidents" of his own ego. He felt paralyzed, perhaps "incapable of working for years!" And he implored Alma to help him—only she would be able to save him from this abyss of depression and anxieties.

Some temporary relief was provided by the first nights of *Juarez and Maximilian* in Düsseldorf and Dresden. After a rather unsuccessful world premiere in Magdeburg, the Dresden performance, at which Werfel was present, was a triumph for the author. Reinhardt's Vienna production was also very well received: on the first night, there were over sixty curtain calls for the popular company. Only rarely before (and never for a play) had Werfel received more enthusiastic reviews in Germany and Austria; the tragedy of Maximilian of Hapsburg was his first genuine theatrical hit. His plan to achieve, by means of subject matter pleasing to an audience, not only artistic but material success (inflation was now receding) seemed to have worked out perfectly.

Nevertheless, the creative crisis had not been overcome. His extensive readings in the Talmud and Torah had made him an expert in biblical matters, but his creative powers seemed to be in abeyance. His engagement with the doctrine of Israel and the Bible commentaries of Rashi, Maimonides, and Nachmanides had not brought him closer to Judaism, as he had perhaps hoped, but had rather reinforced his rejection of Orthodox Judaism and his sympathy for a Christian world view.

Only at the height of the summer of 1925, four months after his return from Palestine, did he slowly work his way toward the concept of a new play which had surely germinated during his stay in Jerusalem. He wanted to describe the historical moment of the separation of primitive Christianity from the Jewish religion by telling the story of Rabbi Saul, a former student of the high priest Gamaliel, who became transformed into Paul, the first missionary of Jesus, in the Jerusalem of the first century A.D. In the character of this Paul of Tarsus, without whose life's work Christianity would probably never have become a world religion, Werfel saw a crystallization of the same conflict he had been experiencing ever since he was a child. When he created his dramatic legend *Paul Among the Jews,* it was chiefly to explore his predilection for Catholicism, which had been the source of so much private confusion.

"No one is Israel's friend, not even Israel" was one of Werfel's first notes for the play. He decorated the title page of his *Paul* notebook with a drawing of Mount Sinai, with the two stone tablets of the Law that Moses had received from God enthroned upon it—yet crowned by a mighty crucifix. Christ's Cross and the Ten Commandments, synagogue and church—these were contrasts that to Franz Werfel had seemed to form a coherent whole ever since he was a child.

"Before embarking on a new work, I always go through a period of terrible despondency," he wrote to Hugo von Hofmannsthal only a few days before he began the first draft of *Paul*. Less than a month later, in early September 1925, he had already completed two drafts of the play but was still so dissatisfied with the result that he decided to put it aside for a while, hoping that he would find a new approach to the subject later on. For the first time in his life, he did not pass a completed work on to his publisher the very moment it was finished. Alma Mahler considered this a clear indication that he had matured a great deal during the last few years.

Alma was planning a journey to India with Werfel that fall; it was something she had wanted to do for a long time. Ullstein Verlag in Berlin was willing to pay for everything if Werfel would write travel impressions from India for the newspapers and journals of the large publishing house. But the confusion triggered by his experiences in Egypt and Palestine was still too fresh in Werfel's memory; he needed time to absorb it. Resisting the idea of having to deal with yet another utterly alien world, he canceled the trip at short notice. Instead, he took the disappointed Alma to Venice and worked on a new treatment and translation of Verdi's opera *La Forza del Destino*. The Maestro's oeuvre was still relatively unknown in the German-speaking world, and it was Werfel's declared goal to bring about a breakthrough and introduce his idol's works in German-language opera houses. In his adaptation of *La Forza del Destino,* he clarified motivations, tightened up the action, but also deleted all songs in praise of war.

During the summer and fall of 1925, Franz Werfel was interviewed extensively by Richard Specht. Paul Zsolnay Verlag had commissioned Specht—the biographer of Gustav Mahler, Arthur Schnitzler, and Richard Strauss—to write the first biography of the thirty-five-year-old Werfel. Worshipful in tone and devoid of any criticism of its subject, Specht's panegyric *Franz Werfel: An Attempt at Mirroring Time* (*Franz Werfel: Versuch einer Zeitspiegelung*) was remarkable mainly for its stylistic excess and bitter invective against Werfel's contemporaries. When the book came out in 1926, Werfel found himself compelled to apologize to all concerned, among them Fritz von Unruh, Kurt Hiller, and

Paul Kornfeld, in each case swearing that he had not seen Specht's manuscript before publication.

At the end of 1925 Werfel gave readings in some twenty German cities, mostly from three scenes of the unfinished *Paul Among the Jews*. On occasion he read all of *Juarez and Maximilian*. He was present at the successful world premiere of Alban Berg's *Wozzeck* in Berlin in mid-December. In 1922 Alma had helped Berg, a friend of many years, to finance his own publication of a piano score of excerpts from his opera. Werfel had yet another reason for feeling close to the composer: in May 1925 Alban Berg had visited Prague and fallen passionately in love with Werfel's sister, Hanna von Fuchs-Robetin.

Werfel stayed in Berlin until the beginning of February, attending rehearsals of *Juarez and Maximilian*. Max Reinhardt was now presenting the play to a Berlin audience. Werfel's friend from his schooldays, Ernst Deutsch, played the part of the Mexican general Porfirio Díaz; they saw a lot of each other during these weeks, meeting with Willy Haas, spending time in an artists' tavern, the Black Tomcat, reminiscing about the old days, imitating their professors, and laughing to the point of tears. Werfel's favorite and most successful impersonation was that of Karl Kyovsky, their homeroom teacher at the Stefansgymnasium.

Juarez was a big hit in Berlin as well, running more than fifty performances; in addition, in January 1926 it received the coveted Grillparzer Prize from the Vienna Academy of Arts and Sciences. In March Werfel attended the extremely successful world premiere of his adaptation of *La Forza del Destino* in Dresden—it seemed as if everything he had put his hand to in the last two or three years was gaining him ever greater recognition and fame. Yet his self-doubts did not vanish after these triumphs.

Back in Breitenstein he devoted himself exclusively to *Paul Among the Jews*, after a hiatus of six months. He wrote to Arthur Schnitzler at the beginning of June that he was working on his play "without concentration and pretty much in despair." "I revise scenes, characters, words, but do not achieve any clarity. Is it possible to paint a picture anew when the colors have dried? And it's much worse if the feelings have dried up. And yet it is a subject that closes up, time and again, and then opens up new depths." He went back to reading the source material and made notes about what elements of suspense, characters, and scenes were still missing from the first two drafts, for instance, "the human element of the Paul character," as he remarked in his notebook. He also felt that Paul's acceptance of Christ and the Resurrection had to be made more central, the cowardly outrages perpetrated by the Roman occupation troops more vivid. At this time, one of Paul's reasons for his rejection of the Torah was, according to Werfel: "[It] is my death sentence, and I am obliged to read it, every day, every hour. But who can love his own death sentence?"

"Second draft of *Paul* gotten rid of, June 1926" was his note on completion of the third manuscript. "Gotten rid of"—thus a play he had almost consigned to the desk drawer and had completed only at the urging and encouragement of a few friends like Hofmannsthal and Schnitzler. After many revisions in both galley and page proofs, the play came out in late August, published by Paul Zsolnay Verlag. "This is not a depiction of religion," Werfel says in an afterword, "but of the people who have to suffer it. . . . Nothing else is shown here except for the great tragic moment of Judaism. . . . No caprice. This is how it is! This is how it was!" A few weeks after the publication of the play, it began to be rumored that Franz Werfel had converted to Catholicism.

Sigmund Freud was extremely cool in his reaction to the play. He wrote Werfel a letter that set forth his reservations. The two had met briefly in September 1926, and Werfel had given Freud a copy of *Paul Among the Jews*. He now penned a desperate defense of his position, saying that contrary to Freud's assumption, his intention had not been to glorify Christianity but to write the play "as a Jew" to whom the "catastrophic moment" when Paul parted ways with Judaism seemed a particularly tragic and hence interesting subject. "My intention was only to describe *that* moment, the cause of endless consequences, the decisive point at which *both* possibilities still existed."

Freud surprised Werfel by replying to his reply, and Werfel wrote back to the "deeply revered Herr Professor," begging him to "throw away these lines unread," without a qualm, should the continuation of their debate cause the great man's "rightful wrath." A passage in the afterword to the play, one that Freud had found particularly offensive, suddenly seemed "unbecoming" to Werfel himself, who said that the "unpleasantly arrogant tone of those words" was now "doubly embarrassing" to him. However, it was not true that he was attached to a "pious child's faith," as Freud had conjectured. "May I confess to you," he wrote (a confession that did not entirely correspond with the facts), "that I grew up in an areligious milieu, never suffered from scruples and religious emotional catastrophes as long as I can remember, did not have to outgrow cult residua, and lived until I was almost twenty in a state of indifferent atheism." Apart from that, he entirely agreed with Freud's definition that God was really nothing but an "exonerating fantasy" of mankind. Nevertheless, he had to admit "that I do suffer a great deal from these exonerating fantasies, particularly of the metaphysical sort. . . . When I say that I 'suffer' from them, that is a lie, because the feeling of pleasure that accompanies them is indescribable." Then, a little fearfully: "Now I have revealed myself to you, most revered Herr Professor, as an incurable mystic and illusionist." On the other hand, Werfel said, Freud's work often impressed him "with a . . . demonic power. . . . It is the power that otherwise emanates only from truly great works of art! . . . As Aristotle the logician became a fore-father of the church, Freud will become the forefather of the time and—religion—to come!"

Stefan Zweig, in thanking Werfel for sending him *Paul Among the Jews*, expressed his utmost approval. He not only regarded the piece as a work of genius and predicted its great success on the stage but also felt that it proved once again that Werfel really was the only author of this generation who already had an entire oeuvre to present to the world.

In any case, his popularity reached another high point in 1926. The German journal *Die schöne Literatur* had polled its readers on their favorite contemporary German-language author, and Franz Werfel received the great majority of votes, many more than Gerhart Haupt-mann, Stefan Zweig, or Rainer Maria Rilke. That summer he was the talk of the town in New York after *Goat Song* premiered there in English translation. In response to great public interest, the Theatre Guild arranged several Sunday afternoons of lectures and discussions about the play, and these were attended by audiences of more than two thousand people. In the fall the founding members of the Prussian Academy of Arts and Sciences—among them Heinrich and Thomas Mann, Arthur Schnitzler, and Jakob Wassermann—bestowed member ship on Franz Werfel.

With the completion of *Paul Among the Jews*, Werfel's creative block seemed to have passed. He now devoted himself with renewed energy to a whole series of simultaneous projects. In collaboration with the musicologist Paul Stefan, he prepared an edition of Verdi's letters, prefaced by a long essay, "A Portrait of Giuseppe Verdi" ("Ein Bildnis Giuseppe Verdis"). He started a large-scale prose text, *Pogrom*, dealing with the question of the assimilation of the Jews, but it remained a fragment. The first draft of a new play was completed: *The Kingdom of God in Bohemia* (*Das Reich Gottes in Böhmen*) was to deal with the Hussite wars of the fifteenth century. In addition, Werfel was working on a long novella that he finished in October 1926. *The Man Who Conquered Death* (*Der Tod des Kleinbürgers*) was based on the lives of Alma Mahler's caretakers at Breitenstein, the Gubsches and their assistant Klara. In letters to Alma and in his diary he had often noted the peculiarities and eccentricities of those three, particularly the mendacity and meanness of Klara, Frau Gubsch's sister. When Werfel returned from his trip to the Near East in the spring of 1925, he was informed of the death of old Herr Gubsch after a long illness in a Vienna hospital. The idea of creating a literary memorial to the Gubsches, those incarnations of the

Austrian ethos, may have occurred to him even then. Werfel placed his novella about the former doorman Karl Fiala in the Vienna of postwar misery and inflation. Fiala has an insurance policy that will provide for his family after his death as long as he lives past sixty-five. Two weeks before that date, Fiala becomes seriously ill. Providing his physicians with "a genuine case, almost a sensation," he valiantly struggles with death until he has survived his sixty-fifth birthday by forty-eight hours. "His insides were now only *one* wound, *one* raging suppurative focus. . . . Then the figure collapses, a pile of bones."

Werfel described Austrian petit-bourgeois existence with remarkably loving empathy. Beyond that, he strove for a profound analysis of the social injustices that made it possible, for instance, for the novella's hero, Fiala the proud doorman, to be dismissed from his post before he reached retirement age. Werfel combined his memory of socialist ideals with concepts provided by his friend Dr. Julius Tandler, the Viennese city councillor who had made extensive proposals for social change to the authorities, aiming at a reorganization of the city's entire public welfare system.

Free of the stylistic floridity of *Verdi* in its concentration on a vivid description of the milieu in which Fiala and his family live, Werfel's novella is a remarkable work of prose that will stand the test of time as a compellingly candid portrait of a truncated Austria at that moment of its post–World War I history.

"I can still see it quite clearly: it was in Cologne, I was about eighteen, so it must have been at the end of 1925. Werfel came and gave a reading at a matinée at the city theater. He read for more than two hours, Juarez and Maximilian, *without a break, it was incredible!" Hans Mayer is reminiscing. A professor of literary history for many years, first at the University of Leipzig and later in Hanover, this cultural philosopher now lives in Tübingen. His home by the Neckar is quite close to Hölderlin's tower.*

"Maybe one-sixth of the seats of the big Cologne theater were occupied. It was quite dark, and there was a table with a lamp—and then appeared this small, fat fellow, Werfel, but he had the voice of a giant. I remember the end of the reading in particular—that's where everything falls apart. Maximilian has been executed, and from backstage there comes the shout of the people: 'Juarez!' And how Werfel read that 'Juarez!' The victor! . . . Of course his distortions of history showed; you could sense the dramaturgic elements clattering away. But at the end the audience was totally enchanted. Werfel was a tremendous reader. Apart from Thomas Mann, there have really been only three writers who were able to read their own works so magnificently: Kraus, Canetti, and Werfel.

"A few years later, perhaps in 1927, he gave another reading in Cologne, but

this time to a packed house in town. He read The Man Who Conquered Death, *one of his masterpieces. Not too long ago I was talking to Canetti, whose views of Werfel are quite ambivalent but at the same time very precise—I told him that the novella made an indelible impression on me and that it is, to my mind, the best thing by Werfel that I know. Canetti's face lit up, and he said, 'I'm so pleased to hear you say that—it's what I expected you to say.' Then he pointed out, correctly, that* The Man Who Conquered Death *wouldn't exist without its model, Tolstoy's* Death of Ivan Ilyich. *'But,' he added, 'Werfel's novella is really his own, and it's not run-of-the-mill.' Canetti has the greatest respect for Werfel as a propagandist for Verdi. It was Werfel who made operas like* La Forza del Destino *and* Don Carlos *part of the permanent repertory of the world's great opera houses.* Simon Boccanegra *too, of course. He was a powerful force in the Verdi renaissance. On the other hand, Werfel always regarded Verdi's absolute masterpiece—that's* Falstaff, *of course—as less important than works such as* Forza del Destino, *an opera that's just a string of ideas, 'notions.' And that was because Werfel himself was still a believer in the romantic theory of 'inspired ideas'—that's why he makes Verdi's wonderful idea of an opera based on* Othello *the centerpiece of his Verdi novel.*

"*But for Verdi, the 'idea' was always just one constructive element, which he took as a starting point for the work as a whole. Werfel never knew how to be economical with his ideas; he used them, so to speak,* raw. *'The task of a writer consists in being able to* make *something out of an idea,' Thomas Mann said. But it was just that 'making' that Werfel never quite managed. Well, of course he didn't work on the intellectual, rational level that Thomas Mann or, in a different way, Robert Musil did. Werfel had endless ideas—far too many; if Musil had had as many, he would have finished* The Man Without Qualities! *Werfel just doesn't always have the constructive creative power. While it is true that most of his works have a genuine idea, they're then inflated, instead of being realized as slim novellas.* Class Reunion [Der Abituriententag], *for instance, written in 1927, could have been a truly charming story if Werfel had let it be only forty pages long. That's why* The Man Who Conquered Death *is so successful—he didn't try to make a novel out of it. He was really successful in the* small *forms.*

"*For Werfel, the decisive things were the emotional aspect, the romantic idea, the lyrical substance—the power of language. He did have a language of his own! Unlike Stefan Zweig, who is simply an intolerably poor writer. Zweig blows himself up, he inflates ideas that he doesn't even have. Whereas Werfel is prodigal with his ideas but often doesn't know how to make anything out of them. He was an infinitely greater natural talent than Musil, but Musil is the infinitely more interesting writer. I think I know what Werfel lacked: he hardly ever questioned himself. He could be a Marxist, he could be an anarchist or a conservative, he could be a Catholic—it was all interchangeable, it all depended on the moment's whim, idea, emotion. That is where Karl Kraus's evil eye did, after all, see the truth: while writing was a necessity for Werfel, while he had the urge to express,* what *he then wrote—the actual message—was totally interchangeable. Werfel pulled himself under, time and again. That was a talent of a great writer who destroyed himself.*

"On the other hand, someone who wrote The Man Who Conquered Death, *and a few very, very beautiful poems, and* The Forty Days of Musa Dagh, *and also another book that I don't regard as highly as Ernst Bloch did, the* Verdi*—Bloch considered it a masterpiece!—well, he has to be an important writer. And he is part of my youth. . . . I grew up with expressionism, expressionism was the experience that formed me; how could it be otherwise?"*

Barbara, or Reality

I N RAPALLO, NOT far from Genoa, Gerhart Hauptmann owned a splendid villa. Encouraged by Alma, Werfel and Hauptmann had met in
recent years, and they held each other in mutual esteem. Werfel even
imitated Hauptmann's sartorial style to some extent: he often appeared in plus-fours and high-buttoned waistcoats similar to those
affected by the distinguished German dramatist, and they both wore
their hair long, like a flowing mane.

In January 1927 Werfel and Alma Mahler met Hauptmann in Santa
Margherita Ligure, a village close to Rapallo. On his recommendation,
they had taken rooms at Santa Margherita's most luxurious hotel, the
Imperial Palace, which Werfel found very congenial. It was surrounded by a magnificent park with palm trees and flowers even in
winter; the spacious rooms had balconies with views over Portofino Bay.
As soon as they arrived, Werfel decided to stay awhile and get some
writing under way.

Alma picked the most appropriate suite for her lover and then
proceeded to Nervi, a nearby health spa, leaving Werfel to his work. He
was planning the completion of a cycle of novellas that had begun with
The Man Who Conquered Death. Childhood memories cropped up in
these tales, puppet theater plays, summer vacations in the Salzkammergut, the last years at school. *Poor People* (*Kleine Verhältnisse*) described the erotic tension between an eleven-year-old boy, Hugo, and
his nanny, Erna Tappert (who came from "poor people"). The story
was based on Werfel's happy memories of his governess Erna Tschepper, who had once lived on Mariengasse in Prague, hired to relieve
Barbara Šimůnková. Franz had liked her very much, but his mother
fired her when she became pregnant.

In the novella *The House of Mourning*, Werfel resurrected his last two
years at the Stefansgymnasium, specifically those nights when he and

some classmates made the rounds of Prague's nightclubs—Franz regaling the world with loud arias—and frequently visited the notorious brothel Gogo on Gamsgasse. He projected some of his own experiences in the Salon Goldschmied onto the year 1914 and the summer night on which word of the assassination of the heir to the Austrian throne reached Prague. The story, an extended metaphor for the downfall of the Austro-Hungarian Empire, also presents Werfel's ideas about the kinship between Judaism and Christianity, embodied in Max Stein, a Jewish brothelkeeper who believes in Jesus.

This period of preoccupation with childhood and youth culminated in a novel whose first draft Werfel also began in Santa Margherita while still working on the cycle of novellas: *Class Reunion: A Story of Youthful Guilt.* His Berlin reunion with Willy Haas and Ernst Deutsch in early 1926 may have inspired the story of a group of students in Prague fond of the same kinds of adventures that Werfel, Haas, Deutsch, Kornfeld, and Janowitz enjoyed—frequent absences from school, visits to nightspots, spiritualist séances, garden parties given by wealthy Prague German families. Surrounded by her numerous admirers, even Werfel's first love, tennis enthusiast Mitzi Glaser, puts in an appearance. "To be in love with her," we read in *Class Reunion,* "was fashionable. . . . This fashion had made particular, deeply painful inroads in my heart. Encounters with Marianne gave me palpitations and slight cases of vertigo."

Werfel's teacher Karl Kyovsky was rendered lovingly and often verbatim, and other professors of the Stefansgymnasium came back to life in the story. Even his own earliest attempts to write poetry became part of the novel's subject matter, but Werfel divided himself between two contrasting characters, both of whom write poems, plays, and fiction: the Jew Franz Adler, a young genius (who also shares some traits with Paul Kornfeld and Ernst Popper), and the Christian Ernst Sebastian, a sadistic sophisticate. The novel is framed by the twenty-fifth anniversary celebration of the graduation of Sebastian's class. Sebastian, now an examining magistrate, stays awake all night remembering the sin of his youth that had the gravest consequences: he undermined the position of the precocious young poet Adler, the best student in the class, and systematically tried to destroy his already sickly classmate both psychologically and physically. It was a battle for survival, a duel—to a considerable degree, one between Judaism and Christianity—and Adler emerged as the moral victor.

Once again Werfel was engaging the subject matter that had become a leitmotiv in his life: the emancipation of Christianity from Judaism.

* * *

In mid-July 1927, after Werfel had returned to Austria, thousands of workers staged a protest in Vienna against a court decision they considered unjust. The city's police chief, Johann Schober, hunted the demonstrators down like rabbits: the police shot and killed ninety people in bitter street battles, and there were more than two hundred casualties. At the high point of the melee, the city's Palace of Justice burned to its foundations. The events gave rise to vehement political arguments between Franz Werfel and Alma Mahler. Alma regarded the people's unrest and the general strike as Moscow-inspired and said that communism and socialism were now showing their true colors. Werfel, on the other hand, tried to defend the cause of the protesters, investigated facts, and ended by sympathizing with the workers up to a point. He was horrified by Alma's opinion that the doomed republic could be saved only by the unification of Austria and Germany. While they had had frequent and similar disagreements during their first decade together, Werfel had never been quite so upset by Alma's political outlook as he was now.

It was not a productive summer. Werfel worked mainly on editing a large selection of his poems of the past twenty years, in which he included a small number of new poems written since 1923, the year of *Incantations.* In his afterword to the book, which was the first volume in Werfel's Collected Works to be published by Zsolnay, he stated, "As I leaf through the beginning of this book, my own words seem to me as if they came not from another time, but from another life; especially those I love best."

At the end of 1927, after an extended stay in Venice, Werfel and Alma returned to the Imperial Palace Hotel in Santa Margherita. They met Gerhart Hauptmann and his wife again and celebrated New Year's Eve with them. In early January there were several champagne parties at the Hauptmanns' in Rapallo, during which the two writers often read from their works. Hauptmann once read his essay "Jehovah" ("Jehova"), which had certain anti-Semitic overtones. The slightly intoxicated Werfel heckled him so much that he had to stop.

After finishing *Class Reunion* Werfel spent months without a new project, and once again his state of indecision troubled him. "I feel at home with myself as if I were merely a tenant," he wrote in a notebook at the beginning of 1928. At the age of thirty-seven, without any apparent need, he made his will and named Alma Mahler his sole heir. The will also asked her never to publish posthumously anything of his that didn't come up to the level of his better writings. He also told her to give his "parents and sisters . . . those mementoes that she would be asked for."

Intense preoccupation with his own past and the reliving of memories of childhood and youth may have given rise to thoughts of death, and they may also have sparked reminiscences of war and his soldiering days. Werfel found himself contemplating literary projects based on this segment of his life—as well as his experiences as a supporter of the Red Guard. He had recognized his literary facility with autobiographical material while working on the cycle of novellas and the *roman à clef* *Class Reunion*. His approach to the continuation of his autobiography would remain much the same.

Then came the idea to use the Catholicism of his nanny Barbara Šimůnková, her innocence and capacity for love, as the main motive force of his new narrative. It excited Werfel's imagination. In the character of Bábi—now past seventy, she was still living in his parents' household on Mariengasse—he felt he had discovered a heroine to inspire his work with a protective and guiding hand. Thus began his most ambitious project to date, the novel *The Pure in Heart* (*Barbara oder Die Frömmigkeit*).

Divided into four sections, called "life-fragments," the book followed the German tradition of the *Entwicklungsroman*, a novel charting the spiritual growth of its protagonist, in describing the life story of Ferdinand R, a ship's doctor. Ferdinand, thirty-six years old, endowed with "a very intense and exceptional power of visual memory," stands one night on the foredeck of a luxury liner on its way to Africa: "The doctor, staring at the horizon, stood quietly leaning out over the handrail." Within a few seconds, his entire life passes before his mind's eye: "Ferdinand's mind still holds a reality which dates from his very earliest years. . . . He can feel himself quite clearly, for instance, lying back in a white perambulator, being wheeled down the broad main avenue of a public park. . . . Barbara's huge face looms down on Ferdinand. And with her face the insidious scent of wild cherry, which pierces and envelops her hair."

Ferdinand R experiences the war in eastern Galicia as an army telephone operator, then participates in the Viennese revolution between the Ringstrasse and the "netherworld" of the Café Central as a fighting comrade of a Red Guard. Time and again the biography of the fictional character R parallels that of the author W, although there are some rather trashy, purely fictional scenes concerning the parents of the adolescent. Barbara—Werfel calls her "Guardian of Sleep" and the one who comes "to awaken the living fire"—often recedes into the background but remains the most important figure in Ferdinand's life, "the sheltering image of his childhood," a symbol of Christian virtue and his invisible guide in all of life's decisions.

In *Class Reunion* Werfel divided his own characteristics between Adler, the Jew, and Sebastian, the Christian. He now lent autobiographical traits to the ship's doctor, R, a Christian, and his best friend Alfred Engländer, the rebellious scion of a wealthy Jewish family of textile manufacturers, who believes in Jesus but does not want to be baptized. He preaches the final reconciliation between Judaism and Christianity, and repeatedly states that he is "a Jew in the flesh and a Christian in spirit, like the apostle Paul—whom I know as I do myself."

In the third life-fragment, all the figures of bohemian Vienna have their counterparts in Werfel's own coffeehouse acquaintances between 1917 and 1920. The reporter Ronald Weiss, Ferdinand's comrade in the war and later the founder of Vienna's Red Guard, is clearly modeled on Egon Erwin Kisch. It is Weiss who during the last year of the war introduces Ferdinand to the Café Central on Herrengasse and to its circle of friends, including Gebhardt, anarchist psychoanalyst and sexual theorist—an unmistakable portrait of Otto Gross. The newspaper publisher Basil is kin to Franz Blei; his friend Hedda Aschermann corresponds to the writer Gina Kranz (later Kaus), and the wealthy Aschermann to her adoptive father Josef Kranz. The painter Stechler is Albert Paris Gütersloh; the panhandling poet Gottfried Krasny is a pseudonym for the poet Otfried Krzyzanowski, whose death by starvation and subsequent burial in Vienna's Central Cemetery are described exactly as they happened in real life.

Within the framework of the third life-fragment, Werfel also describes, with remarkable sarcastic distance, the events of the November revolution in Vienna. This time, it seems, he manages to do what he had already tried to do in *Goat Song*—dismiss his participation in the revolt and his espousal of communist ideals as youthful blindness, a folly he regrets now, ten years later, as an acclaimed Austrian author. The erstwhile anarchist had become a disillusioned socialist, and the socialist has turned into a propagandist of Roman Catholicism— hardly identical anymore with the poet of *The Friend of the World*, the creator of *Mirror Man* and *Goat Song*.

Nevertheless, the atmosphere of the collapse and self-inflicted dissolution of the Hapsburg monarchy had rarely been described in a more gripping fashion. Rare, too, was Werfel's compelling picture of the Vienna of 1918 in *The Pure in Heart*. His photographic eye and remarkable memory resurrected post–World War I Vienna and cast a clear and harsh light on Austria's postwar despair.

The novel was written in Breitenstein, Vienna, and Santa Margherita. Between February and May 1929, Werfel hardly left the Imperial Palace Hotel. He worked mostly at night, drinking endless cups of strong black coffee and surrounding himself with a dense cloud of cigar and cigarette smoke.

At the end of June, after his return to Vienna, Werfel completed the first draft of *The Pure in Heart*. Only a few days later he carried out a decision that would have been quite apposite for his fictional character Alfred Engländer: on June 27, 1929, he abandoned the faith of his forefathers and, in an official act affirmed under oath, he resigned from the Jewish community. He did not take this step just to be faithful to his literary model: ten years had passed since he had first expressed his desire to marry Alma Mahler, and now she had finally acquiesced to his repeated pleas. Shortly before her fiftieth birthday, she declared her willingness to marry Werfel, but on one condition—he would have to leave the Jewish faith before the marriage, even if he could not see his way to convert to Christianity (even in this respect he resembled Alfred Engländer and Max Stein).

Franz Werfel and Alma Mahler's civil wedding took place on July 8, 1929. Alma's decision had been influenced in large part by the wishes of her fourteen-year-old daughter Manon Gropius: her mother's lover now became, at long last, her legitimate stepfather. Only a few weeks after the wedding, Alma noted in her diary that she felt constrained by this new marriage, to an even greater degree than she had feared before the wedding.

In this summer of 1929 Werfel appeared years older. Hugo von Hofmannsthal's sudden death at the age of fifty-five had affected him greatly: "Now we have lost one of the very last *poets*—in the sacred, classical sense—we had in this world," he wrote in his eulogy. "He was a seraph, a messenger of alien powers in our midst. His timelessly youthful appearance confirmed that. In the twenty years that I knew him, not a single feature changed in his beautiful face."

After completing the second draft of *The Pure in Heart*, the Werfels went back to the Ligurian coast, first to Nervi, then to Santa Margherita. While Werfel spent an evening at the opera in Genoa, Alma approached a young woman in the dining room of the Imperial Palace who struck her as *simpatica* and who had attracted her attention for some time. As the young woman's husband was away that evening, Alma invited her to her drawing room, where she plied her guest with large quantities of Benedictine, her own favorite drink. Young Mrs. Tina Orchard told Alma her life story. She had been born in Naples, the daughter of an extremely strict father who had had to spend time in jail after the bankruptcy of his firm; she spoke of her great love for her brothers and sisters, and of Mr. Orchard, a British citizen who had come to the rescue and brought about a happy ending to the family drama by marrying Tina.

Alma sensed material for a novel in the story. As soon as Werfel returned to the hotel that night, she told him about it, and that same

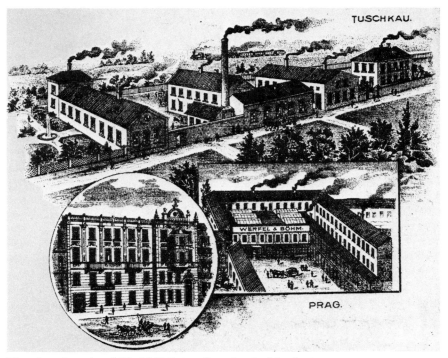

The glove factories of Werfel & Böhm (letterhead of the firm)

Werfel's birthplace, Reitergasse 11, Prague

Later residence of the Werfel family, Mariengasse 41, Prague

The graduate, 1909

First love: Maria Glaser

1910

Ca. 1918

The second sister: Mizzi Rieser, née Marianne Werfel.

Dispatch rider Franz Werfel on the East Galician front, 1916–17

Gertrud Spirk

Haus Mahler, Alma Mahler's villa in Breitenstein

The lovers

Haus Mahler, Breitenstein

Manon Gropius (right, with her father, the architect Walter Gropius)

The lovers in Trahütten, Styria, ca. 1920–21

Alma Mahler-Werfel, Franz Werfel, Anna Moll, Carl Moll, ca. 1930

Hundredth birthday of Franz Werfel's grandfather Bernhard Kussi, Pilsen, 1932

Casa Mahler, Venice

In Venice, ca. 1924

In Santa Margherita, ca. 1928

Ca. 1926

In Santa Margherita, ca. 1929

Alma Mahler-Werfel with her daughter Anna, ca. 1930

Anna Mahler and her mother,
ca. 1928

Hotel Südbahn, Semmering: Franz Werfel, Frau Hauptmann, two unidentified men, Ernst Lothar, Alma Mahler-Werfel, Gerhart Hauptmann, Adrienne Gessner

Franz Werfel and Gerhart Hauptmann in front of the Hotel Südbahn, Semmering, ca. 1930

Franz Werfel and Alban Berg, Santa Margherita, ca. 1928–29

Hugo von Hofmannsthal shortly before his death, Breitenstein, 1929

Franz Werfel in Florence, May 1933

Arthur Schnitzler, summer 1930

Alma Mahler-Werfel and Franz Werfel during their trip to America, 1936

Alma Mahler-Werfel and Franz Werfel, ca. 1937

The tower room in Sanary-sur-Mer today

*The tower in Sanary-sur-Mer, where the Werfels spent
most of 1938–40*

Bernadette Soubirous of Lourdes

The house at 610 North Bedford Drive, Beverly Hills, California, into which the Werfels moved in the fall of 1942

Last photograph of Franz Werfel, summer 1945

The grieving widow

night the two of them elaborated the outline of a tale of a Neapolitan family. Werfel went on inventing subplots, auxiliary characters, and complications into the wee hours. During the following days he asked Mrs. Orchard numerous questions about her family, asked for detailed descriptions of her brothers and sisters, and so forth—but Tina had become more cautious; she was no longer as forthcoming as she had been that first evening. Nevertheless, Werfel had the basic outline for his next novel. It even had a working title: *Die Geschwister von Neapel* (eventually published in English under the title *The Pascarella Family*).

In the fall of 1929, while the Werfel's were still in Italy, *The Pure in Heart* was published, and like *Verdi*, it sold extremely well. The first printing was fifty thousand copies, considerably more than any previous Werfel book.

Reviewers called the novel a classic and its creator a genius of the epic mode, praising *The Pure in Heart* not only as the high point of his oeuvre to date but indeed as a masterpiece of Tolstoyan dimensions. But there were others who called Werfel a bore and a cliché-monger whose work was devoid of both style and form. Heinz Liepmann, the critic of the Berlin *Weltbühne,* recommended that the author be sent to Canada or Siberia to lose his smugness and operatic floridity in the Arctic cold.

In *Die Fackel,* Karl Kraus quoted a few fairly random passages from the third life-fragment to demonstrate why Werfel "should be chased off Mount Olympus with a wet rag." Although he admitted to having read only a single chapter of the *roman à clef,* he called it simply "popular garbage."

Jewish critics were dismayed by Werfel's deep sympathy for Catholicism and accused him—without knowing about his separation from the religious community—of desertion.

Even Willy Haas joined the chorus of negative reaction, up to a point. In his journal *Die literarische Welt,* he called *The Pure in Heart* a noble and wonderful monument to love, but also pointed out the flaws of the eight-hundred-page novel; they could have been remedied so very easily that he, Haas, was reluctant to so much as mention them.

For years, Ernst Polak had been Werfel's editor. In the case of *The Pure in Heart,* he missed a number of grammatical errors and gross breaches of style; the extremely short fourth life-fragment, which deals with Ferdinand R's medical training and his farewell from Barbara, had turned out very badly and destroyed the novel's dramatic structure.

Soon after the publication of the book, a reporter asked Egon Erwin Kisch whether he felt offended by the portrait of Ronald Weiss, who was clearly modeled after him. Not at all, Kisch replied: no question about it, it had been at least partly his fault that Werfel, whose close friend he had been many years ago, had joined the Red Guard and become involved in the chaotic events of the November revolution—exactly as the novel described it. Furthermore, Kisch said, his friend had a stupendous memory: there were instances of dialogue in *The Pure in Heart* that had taken place ten or more years ago but were rendered with such accuracy that one might think Werfel had somehow managed to record them on phonograph discs.

"Hedda Aschermann" is what Werfel called Gina Kranz, his friend from the Café Central days, in The Pure in Heart. *"A radiant, . . . expensively dressed woman" and easy on the eye as well. "She really possessed some cultivation which, with masculine instinct, she displayed to the best advantage." The adopted daughter of the Viennese tycoon Josef Kranz lived in a splendid mansion. "Thus Hedda, who did not want to part with either, had begun to lead an intricate double life between Aschermann's splendors and the café."*

In 1920, at the age of twenty-six, Gina Kranz married the writer Otto Kaus. She then wrote and published, under the name Gina Kaus, numerous novels—such as Catherine the Great (Katharina die Grosse), *a fictional biography of the Russian empress—as well as plays and later, as an immigrant, successful scripts for Hollywood studios. For more than forty years she lived in Los Angeles, in a large Brentwood bungalow surrounded by tall eucalyptus trees and a neglected garden. But this is not where I find her: I am driving down a wide boulevard toward the Pacific Ocean; a few weeks before her ninetieth birthday, Gina Kaus has been moved to a nursing home in Santa Monica.*

"Get me out of here!" is her greeting from the wheelchair. "This is a terrible place! You have to promise that you'll get me out of here. You see, my housekeeper has been waiting for me to die for years. Because I was stupid enough to make her my heiress. This time she just picked some silly little thing as an excuse to have me brought here. I just happened to stumble at home, and before I know it, I'm here. To make me hurry up and die."

A young nurse in a dazzlingly white uniform pushes the wheelchair out onto the patio, past rooms with half-open doors. Motionless bodies lie on their beds, their heads shrunk down to the skull. Outside, in the shade of wide palm leaves, Gina Kaus starts reminiscing: "Franz Blei and I—it's true what Werfel says in The Pure in Heart, *we were the closest of friends. I have to admit I never cared that much for the book, nor for Werfel either, really. But Blei: he truly was an amusing, genuinely witty, incredibly cultivated man. He knew everything. By heart. My adopted father hired him as his private secretary; that's how he got to Vienna from the provinces. And in no time at all he became the focus of the literary café crowd in the Central and the Herrenhof. And such a nice man! He really had an abundance of good manners. And that was rare.*

"No: my experiences with Werfel were not so pleasant. You see, I had this

pied-à-terre on Boltzmanngasse, because I really couldn't stand that Kranz mansion in the long run. So I told Kranz, Listen, I have to rent some place to keep my thousands of books. And he agreed. It was a really nice, large studio apartment, and that's where we had the editorial office of the journal Summa. *Two of the rooms had a view of a park with wonderful trees and monks walking around in it. Well, when* Summa *folded after four issues, and Werfel was really poor back then, I said to him, 'Let's rent this space together. You need a place to live, I need a studio. In the daytime, you're working at the Military Press Bureau—but I won't use it all that much anyway.' But I must say that Werfel really behaved abominably: he never paid his share, not even half the rent. Well, I can see that; he simply thought that I could afford it better than he could. But I even paid for his maid; you see, he* lived *there, Alma came to visit, there were sheets to be laundered, and so on—but Werfel never paid dear old Frau Reisinger anything! And I couldn't really believe he was* that *poor. That was too much, I couldn't swallow that."*

In a meeting room, two clergymen are trying to get a group of wheelchair patients to join in on some hymns, but after various futile attempts they simply choose "God Bless America." "I implore you," Gina Kaus says again, while the choral voices ring out in the background, "please see to it that I get out of here! Well, sometimes when my adopted father was out of town, I would invite my favorite people in the Central to this tremendous mansion, the so-called Villa Kranz. We made a lot of music, as I remember. Blei played the piano. And Werfel sang Verdi arias—that was really very nice . . . and it went on until late, late into the night. You know, that Werfel, he sang with love!"

Gina Kaus is pushed back to her room, and two nurses help her into bed. Talking under her breath so as not to disturb her roommate, she continues: "I think that Werfel really had only one true friend, and that was Ernst Polak. Musil, Broch, and others did not care for him at all. At least, I can't remember one memorable conversation between Werfel and Musil, even though Musil— whom I revere as an author—came to the Herrenhof every day. I think Karl Kraus liked Werfel at first, but he just couldn't stand anyone who rose to such prominence. He could stand Brecht, to a certain extent—Brecht best of all. I myself liked Kraus a great deal; there was a time when we saw each other every day. And often until five in the morning: Kraus could talk endlessly. But then we had a big argument, in the thirties, when he started praising that right-wing Austrian militia, the Heimwehr, because he saw it as a possible antidote to Hitler. And it was the end of our friendship. The last thing he said to me was, 'I know you can't stand me! I know it.' And I didn't contradict him. Goodness, I think I'm remembering all these things for the first time."

Her small, deeply wrinkled face rests almost motionless on the large white pillows. She whispers, "Please don't forget what I asked you to do. Promise? . . . Now! Wait a minute! Don't leave yet. Please, give me a good- bye kiss."

Hohe Warte

A T THE BEGINNING of 1930, the Werfels went on their second journey to the Near East, first to Egypt, as in 1925, and then on to Palestine. In contrast to their impressions on the first visit, Palestine now seemed much less barren, even livable: Alma liked Jerusalem so much that she toyed with the idea of acquiring a house there. While Werfel still did not identify with Zionism, he felt the greatest respect for the Jewish reconstruction of Palestine and acknowledged its utopian vision. He also had more sympathy for Jewish national consciousness than before. Arab nationalists had perpetrated a massacre of Jewish settlers in the summer of 1929, and Werfel realized that the Jews would have to arm themselves against future pogroms. Nevertheless, his main sympathies lay with the pacifist organization Brith Shalom, which worked for reconciliation with the Arab neighbors. Werfel's idealistic world view simply could not accept that the two nations would remain in a perpetual state of war.

After their arrival in Egypt, Werfel suffered from a recurring slight fever in the evenings. A physician in Jerusalem reassured him that it was just a mild case of malaria, and there was no reason to abandon his plan to travel on to Syria and Lebanon. The Werfels went to Damascus, accompanied by a heavily armed tourist guide as protection against roving bandits in the Syrian desert. A group of these did, indeed, cross their route but only observed them from a distance before riding on.

The guide took the Werfels through Damascus, a decayed, sad, and dirty city, showing them, among other sights, a carpet-weaving establishment. Around the numerous looms, they saw many crippled and emaciated children and youths who seemed to be staring vacantly. When Werfel asked about these pitiful creatures, the owner of the establishment told him that he had taken them in a number of years ago, to save them from death by starvation: they were orphans, children of Armenian Christians. Between 1915 and 1917 more than a million people had become the victims of a massacre of unimaginable dimensions—ordered by the Young Turk regime of the time, an ally of Germany in World War I. While serving in the Military Press Bureau, Werfel had repeatedly heard about the genocide committed against Armenians, but it took this personal confrontation with Armenian orphans to transform the abstract number of casualties into a horrifying reality.

That encounter at the carpet weavers' was one he could not forget: on the subsequent way stations of their journey, in Baalbek, Beirut, Acre, and Haifa, he wrote down what the man in Damascus had told him. He tried everywhere to find out more about the fate of the Armenians and looked for survivors who would be able to tell him more about the atrocities. Thus he heard about a community of some five thousand Armenians who had armed themselves and retired to the so-called Mountain of Moses, Musa Dagh, and there defended themselves against superior Turkish forces. Not only were these courageous people able to hold their positions, they also inflicted considerable casualties on the enemy. When they had used up all their ammunition and supplies, so Werfel was told, a French warship sighted them on the mountain, as if by a miracle, and the French marines came to their rescue.

After his return to Austria, Werfel visited the French ambassador to Vienna, Count Bertrand Clauzel, and asked if he would help him obtain official documents on the Armenian genocide. Werfel had decided to devote a literary work to this event, the greatest organized mass murder in the history of mankind up to that time, and to create a lasting memorial to its victims. Clauzel was able to provide Werfel with large amounts of material, including French investigative protocols on the atrocities committed by the Young Turk government and statements given by survivors of the massacres—among these, documents on the heroic freedom fight of a group of rebels on Musa Dagh.

Before turning to his time-consuming research for a novel about the fate of the Armenians, Werfel first devoted himself to another subject entirely. The play *The Kingdom of God in Bohemia* was based on a sketch made in the summer of 1926: a historical tragedy, it described the religiously inspired, antifeudal struggle of revolutionary Hussites, the Taborites, against the high nobility of Bohemia. Werfel completed the first version of this drama of civil strife in only five weeks in the spring of 1930. According to his own words, his intention was not to produce a historical genre painting but to clarify an ancient struggle between fundamentally different views of the world—the recurrent overthrow of one dominant ideology by another. "Everywhere, and in every epoch, people have tried to establish a 'Kingdom of God in Bohemia,'" Werfel stated in a newspaper interview. "We always see the impetuous new . . . trying to supplant the conservative and complacent element. That is the battle humanity has fought innumerable times, and in which . . . time and again the immovable and static has maintained itself and the dynamic has perished." He quite consciously refused to take sides for either the revolutionary forces or those of reaction: "That is not the dramatist's business."

The characters of this "tragedy of a leader" used the language of the twentieth century: Werfel was not interested in historical realism. Nevertheless, they were reminiscent of characters in plays by Raimund or Grillparzer, dramas the young Werfel had once loved. When he was fourteen, the smell of dust that wafted into the audience from the stage of the Neue Deutsche Theater in Prague was the most wonderful odor he could imagine. *Juarez and Maximilian, Paul Among the Jews,* and finally *The Kingdom of God in Bohemia,* written when Werfel was forty, provide clear evidence of his nostalgia for the theater of the nineteenth century.

There was nothing in this world of which he was so sure, he wrote to Kurt Wolff in March 1930, "as that . . . *The Friend of the World* and *The Pure in Heart* are one and the same." Certainly he had not changed into another person in the course of the years, as so many were now claiming publicly. The reason for Werfel's letter to his former publisher was an urgent plea to do more for the work of his youth: "I find it . . . very hard to accept that *our* volumes don't deserve at least a modest existence." This state of affairs was even more deplorable considering that Wolff had to be regarded as "*the literary instrument of the last poetic movement*" that Germany had known. Admittedly, he wrote, "the shape of the world . . . has changed so considerably that only a future time will be able to do justice to the generation to which we both belong." Wolff's reply must have had a sobering effect on Werfel: he informed his erstwhile favorite author that he had to close down his publishing operation because he had not been able, for some time now, to achieve even nominal sales. Wolff said that he had paid for the enterprise with his "life's blood," both materially and psychologically, and that he was now living quietly on the outskirts of Berlin, slowly recuperating from the hardships of the last years.

While he was still working on the play about the Hussites, Werfel made his first visit to the Armenian monastery of the Mekhitarists in Vienna and met Archbishop Mesrop Habozian. He told the archbishop about his project to write a long novel about the heroic fight of the rebels of Musa Dagh, which was by now fairly well delineated. The cleric strongly encouraged Werfel in his plan and put the monastery's large library at his disposal. Werfel began his research there in June 1930. He first read the comprehensive reports of the German pastor Johannes Lepsius, who had pleaded for the Armenian people with the highest Turkish authorities and had also tried to pressure the German government into threatening Turkey with abrogating their military alliance if the genocide was not stopped.

Werfel went on to read the eyewitness accounts of the priest Dikran Andreasian and descriptions of the terrain around Musa Dagh on the Gulf of Alexandretta; he studied the flora and fauna of the region, made lists of names of Armenian notables, sketched first drafts of a possible plot line. He even thought he had found a name for his hero: Grigor Bagratian.

Franz Werfel's fortieth birthday coincided with the elections for the fifth German Reichstag in September 1930. The results of these elections were closely watched in Austria; they marked a clear swing to the right. The National Socialist German Workers' Party, under its leader Adolf Hitler, received over 18 percent of the votes, and the number of its seats in the Reichstag increased from 12 to 107. The Nazis were now the second strongest party in Germany, after the Social Democrats. Werfel, in Vienna to discuss the staging of *The Kingdom of God in Bohemia,* was not intimidated by the anti-Semitic atmosphere in the neighboring country: talking to a reporter from a Vienna daily, he openly admitted his origins and even stated that the "notion that I have left Judaism" was "quite incorrect." Actually, from the standpoint of rabbinical law, his decision to leave the community of worship was little more than a trifle: in the eyes of God, Werfel would have remained a Jew even if he had converted to an alien faith; thus his official resignation from the Jewish congregation, staged to please Alma, was really quite meaningless. "Religion as such is one of my main preoccupations, now even in my work," Werfel went on to say. "I believe I would be happiest in a world that . . . comes closest to the period of primitive Christianity. Then, Jewish and Catholic ethics were joined in one wonderful idea."

During the rehearsals for the world premiere of *The Kingdom of God* at Vienna's Burgtheater, which lasted for weeks and in which Werfel often participated, there were violent disagreements between him and the director, Albert Heine, who turned a deaf ear to all Werfel's suggestions for changes and drove him to despair. After the opening night, at the end of 1930, some critics did indeed criticize the author for failing to take a clear point of view, and Werfel was extremely hurt by this accusation. But there were very positive responses as well: Werfel's friends Raoul Auernheimer and Felix Salten wrote rhapsodic raves and attested to the incontrovertible success of a play they felt was Franz Werfel's "strongest" to date. A few weeks later, Arthur Schnitzler, Egon Friedell, and the Werfels talked together about what could be done to secure the Nobel Prize for Franz in the very near future.

Early in 1931 he returned, for the first time in more than a year, to Santa Margherita. Staying at the Imperial Palace, he began to write that "Neapolitan story" he owed to Alma's curiosity and Mrs. Orchard's tale. He made Tina the heroine of the book, calling her Grazia. Her five brothers and sisters, and her father, a widowed banker whom he christened Domenico Pascarella, all had their counterparts in reality.

While he was working on *The Pascarella Family*, Werfel felt haunted by the feeling that he was taking dictation—not only because he was retracing Tina Orchard's life story but because he sensed, behind every character and event, a second level, a kind of superreality. From the tale told by a chance acquaintance, Werfel derived a poetic metaphor for the crumbling of the patriarchal world order and male dominance.

"The waters of a story," Werfel wrote in his working notes, "run together and carry the author along on their ever rising surface." A surface that reflected, once again, many autobiographical images, among them Werfel's former difficult relationship with his own father. Placido, Grazia's brother, is a philosophical dreamer who wants to become a writer. Like young Franz, who had tried to convince his father that he did not want to follow in his footsteps, Placido has to withstand Don Domenico's rages: "Ever since [Father] has had a suspicion of my writing, he has hated me," the young poet complains. The annual opera festival that Domenico and his children attend regularly calls to mind Werfel's experience in Prague.

Alongside this novel, Werfel wrote a lecture to be given at the Viennese Cultural Alliance in the spring of 1931. Entitled "Art and Conscience" ("Kunst und Gewissen"), it was intended as a warning against the blind glorification of technological progress and the "suppression of human inwardness" that Werfel thought had been going on since the end of World War I in both the Soviet Union and the United States. This growing spiritual crisis, he feared, could also be seen in the "hysterical howls and cheers for a Third Reich." Only a recovery of what was "wondrous" in man could save him from the threat of worldwide brutalization, and as an antidote Werfel proposed a revolution of the spirit: "For the world can live only in the name of the miraculous."

In the novel about Grazia and her family, there are only hints of this fear of a dehumanization of society. Werfel did recognize that Italian Fascism was threatening individual liberties, but in the novel he did not condemn its inhumanity: the "new Italian"—and this was probably due to Alma's influence—seemed to him both "handsome" and "strong of will," and his "verve" really concealed "a shyness or uncertainty" that could surround even a Fascist government prefect of Naples "with a sympathetic aura." Benito Mussolini had been in power since 1924, and Werfel witnessed annual parades of the Italian blackshirts. It is hard to believe that he could not see their kinship with the howling and cheering hordes that had been marching through the streets of Germany and Austria for years.

During her husband's absence from Vienna, Alma Mahler-Werfel prepared for a big move: at the beginning of the year, the couple had acquired a luxurious villa at Hohe Warte, in Vienna's nineteenth district, built by the famous architect Josef Hoffmann. The purchase of the ostentatious building on Steinfeldgasse had been largely financed by Werfel—in recent years, since Paul Zsolnay had become his publisher, the novels and plays had brought in substantial royalties. (The connection between Werfel and his publisher had become even closer since Paul Zsolnay had married Alma's daughter Anna Mahler in 1930 and had thus become Werfel's stepson-in-law.) But Rudolf Werfel also assisted his son in the purchase of the palatial dwelling at Hohe Warte by contributing 40,000 Austrian schillings.

The house, which stood in a large garden, was in the immediate vicinity of Carl Moll's villa, and thus Alma became a neighbor of her mother and stepfather. Steinfeldgasse was in Döbling, high above the noise and dirt of the metropolis, with views of the hills of Kobenzl and Kahlenberg and the vineyards on their slopes. The interior of the Ast Villa, so called for its previous owner, the civil engineer Eduard Ast, was well suited to Alma but hardly to Franz Werfel: three sumptuously furnished floors, twenty-eight rooms partly done in marble. In the salon of this mansion, Alma placed glass showcases containing scores by Gustav Mahler and the original manuscript of Anton Bruckner's Third Symphony. Paintings by Emil Schindler, Hans Makart, Edvard Munch, and Oskar Kokoschka adorned the walls, and Auguste Rodin's bust of Mahler was prominently installed in the entrance hall. Alma had designed the top floor to serve as a spacious working studio for her husband, but he hesitated to move in. The entire ambience struck him as alien and uncomfortable. The bohemian Werfel did not enjoy looking down on Vienna from this height, while Alma considered such elevation her due.

Neither friends nor enemies of the Werfels had any doubts about the true reason for this move. Alma needed the baronial building in order to continue her famous salon and her large parties on the grandest possible level. At long last she had vanquished her friend Berta Zuckerkandl in the struggle for social status—her house at Hohe Warte was now considered one of the best addresses in Vienna.

On his return from Santa Margherita, Werfel did not move into the Ast Villa but went to Breitenstein to work on the final version of *The Pascarella Family* through the summer of 1931, chain-smoking and drinking black coffee in his modest wooden mansard studio. He loved the story of Domenico Pascarella and his six children more than he did any of his previous books; he was not only satisfied with its linguistic form but felt that the novel as a whole was as close to perfect as he could make it.

When the book came out in the fall, it was a hit of the now customary kind: the first printing sold out quickly, and the book was well received by its readers, whereas the critics were lukewarm. He received congratulatory telegrams and letters from admirers, and numerous journalists asked for interviews.

Two years earlier, when they had first met Mrs. Orchard, the Werfels had taken a mutual vow never to reveal the source of *Pascarella*. Werfel now said publicly that the Neapolitan story had "approached" him sometime last winter: "I think we should call my book a fairy tale." He said that the novel—he had felt this every moment while writing it—had come into existence as if some secret source had "whispered" it into his ear. "The characters assumed a dictatorial life of their own and chose their own paths." Nevertheless, his conscience prompted him to make a small concession to the truth: "The first seed of this idea," he told a Viennese reporter, "came to me in an anecdote told by a lady of my acquaintance."

The Werfel villa at Hohe Warte became the scene of magnificent parties, a meeting place of writers, theater people, painters, politicians, philosophers. Alma Mahler-Werfel was a famous hostess with the special knack of introducing people to each other who might otherwise not have met, at least not easily. She devised her guest lists for success. Egon Friedell, Carl Zuckmayer, Ödön von Horváth, and Hermann Broch participated in these festivities—which often continued into the early morning hours—as did Ernst Bloch, Elias Canetti, Franz Theodor Csokor, Fritz Wotruba, Arnold Schoenberg, Alban Berg, and Bruno Walter. On her way home after one of these soirées, Arthur Schnitzler's mistress, the writer Clara Katharina Pollaczek, burst into tears: the lavish circumstances of the Werfels had aroused her envy, and she blamed herself *and* her lover for not having achieved a similar level of luxury.

Ever since the suicide of his eighteen-year-old daughter Lily in the summer of 1928, Schnitzler had been a shadow of his former self. He died on October 21, 1931, not long after his seventieth birthday, of a cerebral hemorrhage. At the Berlin Volksbühne theater Werfel delivered a eulogy for his revered friend "who had not given a damn for the . . . honors bestowed by whoever was in power." Werfel stressed that it would be absolutely wrong to regard Schnitzler's oeuvre as outdated: on the contrary, the nonfashionable, timeless quality of his writing would carry his influence beyond his own day. Schnitzler himself must have realized this when he decreed that certain writings "could only be published thirty, in some cases, fifty years after his demise. . . . The author was certain that, when he died, his work and personality would go on living and exerting their power in distant times. And if he, the old, tenacious skeptic, believed it so firmly, then we need have no qualms if we believe it too."

Starting out in Berlin in the fall of 1931, Werfel went on an extended reading tour that took him to Basel, Zurich, Munster, and Cologne. After his lecture "Art and Conscience" in the East Prussian industrial town of Insterburg, he had to flee the hall in a hail of catcalls and whistles, inadequately protected by police. The audience, mostly students, interpreted Werfel's call for a return to spiritual values as Jewish-communist propaganda.

He stayed briefly at Hohe Warte after his return but soon retired to Breitenstein. He paid a visit to Gerhart Hauptmann, who had come to spend the end of the year in the Südbahnhotel on the Semmering, and he collaborated with Lothar Wallerstein, an opera director, on the translation of Verdi's *Don Carlos,* which Verdi had based on Friedrich Schiller's play about Philip II of Spain. "I have to admit," Werfel said in an interview published in a Viennese daily, "that these ten years in the service of Verdi's oeuvre and its rediscovery constitute a great sacrifice, as they have taken up most of my working hours. But I offer this sacrifice because I regard the enrichment of the world by the inexhaustible music of the Italian master as an increment of happiness in these dark days."

He was also preoccupied with a very different idea, although it too was closely related to the disturbing developments in world events: four or five times a year, he wanted to write position papers on political questions of the day and have them distributed by Zsolnay as low-priced pamphlets. The publisher, however, was skeptical: polemical writings might be harmful to the image of the great author. Although Werfel insisted he did not really intend to be polemical, Zsolnay did not agree to the project.

Werfel gave a lecture in March 1932 at the Vienna Cultural Alliance that had political undertones: "Can Mankind Survive Without Religion?" ("Kann die Menschheit ohne Religion leben?"). It was a sequel to "Art and Conscience," given the previous year, and it presented Catholicism, the philosophy of Thomas Aquinas in particular, as the true road to salvation in an era poisoned by communism and Nazism: "This world that calls itself civilized can heal itself spiritually only if it finds its way back to a genuine form of Christianity." This was a conviction, he pointed out, to which he felt entitled by "ancient ties of blood and nature, precisely because I am a Jew." One should not be content with the "spiritual surrogates" that the spirit of the times had produced "in a hundred variants," but one had to listen to "the divine" within oneself: "And once the empty secular belief has been lost, it is possible to advance into one's own inmost self." Only then could the "perception of the divine" permeate everyday life "step by step."

Werfel went to Pilsen in April 1932, to participate in a large family reunion celebrating the one-hundredth birthday of his maternal grandfather, the mill owner Bernhard Kussi. Franz asked the old man, who had been born only a few weeks after Goethe's death, which single event in the course of his life had left the greatest impression. After hesitating for a moment, Kussi told his grandson that the most memorable event of his life had been the abolition of serfdom in czarist Russia in 1861.

"Not to take life for granted!" "Always believe in miracles!" "Meditate about the soul's salvation!" These were notebook entries Werfel made on a trip through Italy, shortly after his visit with the centenarian. He often felt like "a newcomer from the beyond"—and he firmly resolved to record, from now on, "every second" of his life as consciously and accurately as if he were "a guest from distant centuries."

The palazzo facing the magnificent Basilica dei Frari in the San Polo district of Venice, purchased by Alma Mahler in 1922, still stands. Its surrounding walls, the entry portal, the small garden with its palms and lemon trees, the townhouse itself—all of it has remained practically unchanged.

In Santa Margherita, the massive white edifice of the luxurious Imperial Palace Hotel towers above Portofino Bay. I stand in the same hotel park that Franz Werfel liked so much, sixty years ago, and look up at the grand suite with its wide balcony, on the second floor, where Werfel first stayed in 1927 and to which he returned many times.

At Elisabethstrasse 22, in the first district of Vienna, I look for Alma Mahler's former apartment. On the fourth floor, I ask a tenant for help. "Of course I know where Werfel used to live with his Alma," she says. "Right here, above me. I saw the two of them many times when I came here to visit my grandparents. Werfel wrote The Pure in Heart *up there, and our concierge used to tell us that she was the model for the main character. Did you know that? That wasn't true, you say? But I heard it from her own lips. She was a lady, let me tell you, that concierge of ours; she was a delight! Well, why don't you go on upstairs, the Frau Doktor who lives there enjoys unannounced visitors."*

The elderly heiress of a Salzburg brewery guides me patiently through the rooms of her large, high-ceilinged apartment. Here Alma Mahler lived first with Oskar Kokoschka, then with Walter Gropius, and finally with Franz Werfel. "In this room," the old lady tells me, "Gustav Mahler had his piano. This was where he worked. And he had one of those washstands, he never used a bathroom. And there, in that room, catty-corner from this one, Alma used to have her orgies with Werfel, and I'm sure Mahler was aware of them." When I venture the remark that Frau Mahler did not move into this apartment until 1914 and did not meet Franz Werfel until 1917, six years after Gustav Mahler's death, the lady of the house is indignant: "Nonsense! You see, I heard that from our concierge—she's dead now, God rest her soul—she was there when it all happened, and I'm sure she told me the truth. No doubt about it!"

On Hohe Warte, only a few steps from the terminal of tram line 37, stands the Ast Villa, onetime mansion of the Werfels. A policeman is doing sentry duty in front of the entry gate, a submachine gun strapped to his shoulder. The white-and-green flag of the kingdom of Saudi Arabia flaps in front of the bulletproof windows of the building, now the residence of His Excellency the Saudi Arabian ambassador to Austria.

As we walk through splendid salons and reception rooms, bedrooms and bathrooms, the petite Filipino maid tells me about her homeland, about the hardships of her extended family, to whom she sends most of her earnings. In the hallways hang garish paintings bought in department stores: sunsets, moor landscapes, horses. In the great salon where once Alma Mahler received her guests and paintings by Munch, Makart, and Kokoschka adorned the walls, there are now huge color photographs of King Fahd of Saudi Arabia and Prince Abdullah, commander of the National Guard. Precious swords hang on the marble walls. The glass cases that formerly contained Gustav Mahler's scores now display Arab necklaces, gilded knives, turquoise vases, and other knick-knacks received as gifts from numerous statesmen.

The fourth floor, once the studio space Werfel never really liked, was destroyed by a bomb a few weeks before the end of World War II. The reconstructed floor has been divided into several guest rooms—unfurnished except for one containing an exercise bicycle.

I look down into the large, flowering garden in which Manon Gropius sometimes fed the deer that ventured here from the surrounding forests. The small pond is unchanged; Manon's pet turtles used to walk its stone rim. From the other side of the top story, I have a view of the vineyards of Kobenzl and Kahlenberg, of the nearby St. Michael's Church and the former Jewish orphanage right next to it. I tell the maid that the poet Werfel used to enjoy this view from his desk. She says that she feels so terribly lonely here in Vienna and asks me to come back soon to tell her more about that stranger who used to live and make up stories here, so very long ago.

The Forty Days of Musa Dagh

I N THE SPRING of 1932, during Werfel's absence from Austria, the country was in a state of political turmoil: after the resignation of Chancellor Karl Buresch, Austria was governed by a right-wing coalition under the former minister of agriculture, Engelbert Dollfuss. His attempt to create a nonpartisan government had failed. Two months later, at the end of July, Germany elected its sixth Reichstag, with the Nazis emerging as the strongest party by far; their ringleader, however, had no say in the formation of a government. And during those days, Franz Werfel—now back in Breitenstein—began the first draft of his great novel about the Armenians, whose title was to be *The Forty Days of Musa Dagh*.

Gabriel Bagradian—Werfel's final version of his hero's name—returns to his native home at the foot of Musa Dagh after more than twenty years spent in a state of "total assimilation" in Paris. He has married Juliette, a Frenchwoman; his son Stephan has received a French education. Their visit to Yoghonoluk, to take care of some family matters, is meant to be short—but during their stay, World War I breaks out and the Bagradians are trapped.

Turkey's Islamic Young Turk government distrusts its Armenian-Christian citizens, especially after the outbreak of the war, and accuses them of fomenting rebellion and entering into secret agreements with foreign enemies. This is the historical background to Bagradian's story. These suspicions were sufficient reason for Enver Pasha, Talaat Bey, and Mustafa Kemal to impose the death sentence on more than two million people. This death sentence was camouflaged by terms such as "deportation" and "resettlement" in order to reassure the victims that they were merely part of a large-scale relocation operation. In reality, Istanbul had ordered all the regional presidents to exterminate the entire Armenian population of Turkey, with the exception of a few inhabitants of the large cities.

Over a million men, women, and children became the victims of the first genocide in history ordered by a government and executed according to official plans. The Turks moved the people rounded up in western Anatolia, Cilicia, and northern Syria into so-called concentration camps. Many died of exhaustion on long forced marches through the desert; others were beaten to death, shot, burned, drowned—or simply starved to death.

The deportation orders were ignored only by the inhabitants of a few small communities at the foot of Musa Dagh: some five thousand people moved onto the high plateau of the Mountain of Moses, bringing with them their cattle and their most important belongings. They were ready to die in battle rather than be led as defenseless victims to the slaughter.

Dikran Andreasian, an eyewitness whose account Werfel used in his novel, gave the duration of the siege as twenty-four days, while other documents mention thirty-six days. Werfel's choice, forty days, called up biblical associations: the flood lasted forty days and nights; Moses spent forty days and nights on Mount Sinai; Israel's time in the wilderness was forty years.

The rebels appoint Gabriel Bagradian their leader, and he takes his people to the Mountain of Moses. Like Moses, his biblical model, he is an outsider in his own land who will not be granted the sight of the Promised Land in the company of his people. Like Moses, who is granted only a glimpse of the land of Israel from the top of Mount Nebo before he dies, Bagradian dies on the summit of Mount Musa while his eyes witness the miracle of the rescue of his people.

Werfel made use of even the smallest details he learned in two years of research. In addition to eyewitness reports, collected primarily by the German pastor Dr. Johannes Lepsius, he integrated into his novel data on Armenian children's games, crafts, architecture, agriculture, and clothing.

In *The Pure in Heart*, Werfel's passionate interest in military matters had helped to impart great authenticity to the chapters dealing with World War I; now he meant to describe with absolute credibility the scenes when the Turkish army confronted the Armenian rebels. Ernst Polak researched administrative and jurisdictional matters about the Armenians for his friend and also sent Milan Dubrovic, then a young journalist, to the geographical records of the national library in Vienna, to research weather conditions in Anatolia in the summer of 1915—the amount of recorded precipitation, the direction of the prevailing winds.

*   *   *

Werfel worked on the novel almost continuously until mid-November 1932, interrupting it only for a lecture tour. In Amsterdam he lectured on Verdi and then traveled to several German cities, where mostly he read "Interlude of the Gods," a completed chapter from *Musa Dagh,* which portrays a conference between Johannes Lepsius and the Turkish minister of war, Enver Pasha. Lepsius, the German pastor, had become one of the novel's main characters, and Werfel had taken, almost verbatim, Lepsius's documentary report on his dramatic failure to convince the pasha to put an end to the extermination of the Armenian people.

At the beginning of his readings, Werfel introduced his project for a novel to the audience—in cities that in those very weeks became arenas of extreme radicalization as hordes of SA (Storm Troops) and SS (Elite Guard) organized their almost daily, bloody street battles. *The Forty Days of Musa Dagh,* Werfel explained, was not, as one might suppose, about something that happened in the remote past; rather, it dealt with the fact that "in our own day, one of the oldest and most venerable peoples of the world has been destroyed, murdered, almost exterminated"—and not by "warlike enemies but by their own countrymen." He said that the Armenians had been the first nation to accept Christianity as their official religion, but the nationalism of the Young Turks had made them commit "one of the most insane atrocities in the history of mankind."

In early December 1932 the Werfels were visiting the northern Silesian town of Breslau on the same day Adolf Hitler held one of his demonstrations there. In the new Reichstag elections, a month earlier, the Nazis had once again emerged as the strongest party but had lost votes and were still excluded from the government. That evening, while Werfel went to deliver his lecture "Art and Conscience," Alma stayed in the hotel, hoping to catch at least a glimpse of Hitler. After a long wait—Werfel had given his lecture and returned to the hotel—the party leader entered the hotel lobby. Timidly hiding behind the back of an SS man, Alma looked into the "clasping" eyes of a *"frightened youth,"* as she noted in her diary. To her surprise, Hitler did not seem the least bit pompous—unlike, say, Mussolini. When she asked Werfel's opinion of Hitler, he replied, "Unfortunately, not all that bad."

A few weeks later, on January 30, 1933, Hitler was charged with forming a viable government and sworn in as chancellor of the Reich by President Hindenburg. After his appointment the National Socialists implemented their long-laid plans to take control little by little until all power was in their hands. Werfel was in Santa Margherita at that time, totally immersed in his work on *Musa Dagh* and hardly paying any attention to the political upheavals. The Reichstag building in Berlin burned at the end of February, a wave of arrests swept across all of Germany, and the Reichstag elections of March 5, 1933, secured the National Socialists more than 44 percent of the vote. Now he was no longer able to close his eyes to reality. "The terrible events in Germany" were making it impossible for him to "concentrate on anything," as he noted in the margin and on the backs of pages of his *Musa Dagh* manuscript. He was "spiritually exhausted" and proceeded sentence by sentence "only with difficulty." "Perhaps I should even change the plot!"

Heinrich Mann, president of the Prussian Academy of Literature, had been one of the signatories of a manifesto published in early February 1933, urging the Socialist and Communist parties to join in a united front against the threat of a final takeover by Hitler. As a result, some members of the academy forced Mann to resign even before the March 5 elections. One week after the fatal elections, all members of the Academy of Literature received a circular initiated, formulated, and classified as "confidential" by Gottfried Benn, in which they were asked to let the new board of the academy know whether they were willing, in view of the "changed historical situation," to remain in the service of the parent organization, the Academy of Arts and Sciences. Should the response be positive, the circular stated, this would entail a simultaneous renunciation of any public political stance or action directed against the new government. What was more, this declaration of loyalty would oblige the signatories to cooperate in a "national-cultural" sense.

Of the twenty-seven members of the literary section, nine replied to this circular with a "no"—among them Alfred Döblin, Thomas Mann, and Jakob Wassermann. Ricarda Huch vehemently rejected the demand for a declaration of loyalty, saying that she was not willing to relinquish her right to express her opinions freely. She announced her resignation from the academy and expressed her condemnation of actions already taken by the new government, such as the defamation of dissidents and the state-sanctioned rabble-rousing propaganda against Jews.

Franz Werfel, however, signed the declaration of loyalty to the new ruling powers, having sent a telegraphic request for the appropriate form on March 19. Perhaps his major reason for taking this step was his desire not to jeopardize the future sales of *Musa Dagh:* if he were stripped of academy membership, the epic about the Armenians might be banned altogether, especially since it was directed against the inhumanity of nationalist fanaticism. Like so many others, Werfel did not expect the sinister charade staged by Hitler, Göring, and Goebbels to last very long, and thus underestimated the consequences of his action.

In a letter he wrote from Santa Margherita to his parents in Prague, there was not a word mentioning his declaration of loyalty. He excused his lengthy silence by saying that he was totally immersed in his work, writing eight to ten hours a day, and that he had completed three-quarters of the first draft of *Musa Dagh* on the Ligurian coast. "It may well be my major work," he wrote, adding that the book had "acquired symbolic timeliness because of events: oppression, destruction of minorities by nationalism." He admitted that the political changes in Germany were deeply depressing but said that he would rather devote all his strength to work than fritter it away in "empty cries of woe." "What will happen, will happen. Probably not all that much." He was reliving the fate of the Armenians, and this gave him a "different perspective." As in Italy, the German variety of fascism would probably and slowly "consolidate itself . . . until nobody talks about it anymore." After a period of steady advancement, the Jews would now suffer a setback, he could at least see that coming, "but perhaps it will be only a brief setback." In any case, he had only "the best of news" about the sales of his books; in Germany they had not "diminished by a single copy."

Only a few weeks later, Franz Werfel's works were being burned on bonfires. German students, acting in unison with hordes of Storm Troopers, had removed the works of some 130 authors from private, university, and lending libraries, from bookshops and publishers' sales rooms. On May 10, 1933, at the end of four weeks of this large-scale action "against the un-German spirit," the book burnings took place in the centers of all German university towns. They were accompanied by energetic incendiary speeches and patriotic songs and marches performed by SA and SS bands. The students' "fighting units" flung into the flames the works of Sigmund Freud and Karl Marx, Alfred Kerr and Egon Erwin Kisch, Arthur Schnitzler and Stefan Zweig, along with *Mirror Man* and *Goat Song*, *Class Reunion* and *The Pascarella Family*, *Juarez and Maximilian* and *Paul Among the Jews*.

Two days before the book burnings, Werfel had received a registered letter from Max von Schillings, the new president of the Prussian Academy of Arts and Sciences, informing him that, according to the principles now in force in the state, he could no longer be regarded as a member of the literary section. On March 23, 1933, the Reichstag had passed an enabling law that gave Hitler the power to govern for the next four years without any parliamentary interference. After the Reichstag Fire, the German Reich began establishing so-called concentration camps for thousands of political internees. Jewish citizens were systematically removed from leading positions in cultural life and the civil service, and a nationwide boycott of Jewish businesses was proclaimed.

"An idea conceived in fifteen minutes, how to get rid of H[itler]." So begins a diary entry of spring 1933, noteworthy as a demonstration of how amazingly reactionary and naive Werfel could be. His idea was that a papal bull be sent to the German bishops, pointing out that "the persecution of the Jews" would only make them persist "in their error" and thus postpone "the kingdom of God." A congress of German nobility should be held in Regensburg to demand the return of Kaiser Wilhelm and Crown Prince Otto von Hapsburg to the throne. Along with the idea that President Roosevelt should send a telegram to Hindenburg to avoid further reprisals or—and this was not implausible— that a militant organization should be formed "to protect endangered world democracy and freedom," there were more absurd notions: "Kempinsky and similar eating establishments to introduce open free lunches on future boycott days, only for Christians. . . . And 44 other ideas that I won't write down."

In mid-May 1933 Werfel participated in a music festival in Florence, giving the Verdi lecture he had previously delivered in Amsterdam. His knack for turning off worries of a political nature and focusing on subjects that seemed to matter the most to him is truly surprising: a photograph taken during the Maggio Florentino shows a jovial and high-spirited Signor Werfel. He then returned to Breitenstein to complete the first draft of *Musa Dagh*.

True, he felt most abandoned and lonely in this moment of the "*last battle* with a monstrous world," as he wrote from the Haus Mahler to his "sweet, sweet life," but on the other hand it pleased him greatly that Johannes Hollnsteiner was with Alma, as he had "a great, great deal of love" for "*genuine* and *serious* priests." Hollnsteiner was a Catholic professor of theology and a close confidant of Cardinal Innitzer, archbishop of Vienna. During Werfel's months away in Santa Margherita, Alma had entered into an intimate relationship with this slender, bespectacled man of the cloth who now visited the house at Hohe Warte almost daily. When Werfel, rarely enough, spent any time at Steinfeldgasse 2, he was certainly not unaware of the somewhat bizarre love story unfolding between his wife and the thirty-eight-year-old theologian, but he was able to contain his jealousy: he did not begrudge the fifty-four-year-old Alma this late passion.

At the end of May he completed the first draft of *The Forty Days of Musa Dagh*. Almost immediately, and while still in Breitenstein, he embarked on the second draft of this work, which had grown into his largest and stylistically most convincing literary accomplishment to date. Now he discussed the individual chapters with his friend Ernst Polak, who warned him against modeling such characters as the priest Ter Haigasun; or Krikor, the apothecary; or the wild deserter Kilikian;

or the schoolmaster Oskanian after the Jews they had both known in Prague. Polak advised him to mask the characteristics of these Armenian personalities a little more, and after some hesitation Werfel agreed.

He tried to avoid the kind of black-and-white narrative in which the Armenians would be given only positive attributes, the Turks nothing but negative ones. In marginalia to his manuscript, he frequently reminded himself: "Don't be *polemical* about the Turks. . . . Enver [Pasha] has to be right in some instances." The novel stressed the existence of dissident Turkish intellectuals and Islamic clergy who deeply regretted the turn of political events in their country and loathed their government. Thus a doctor from Istanbul told Pastor Lepsius that the majority of the Turkish nation did not at all support the intrigues of Enver Pasha, Talaat Bey, and Mustafa Kemal.

Before *Musa Dagh* went to the printers, Werfel wrote a third and a fourth draft, revising some passages of the three books into which the novel was divided—"Coming Events," "The Struggle of the Weak," "Disaster, Rescue, The End"—as many as eight times. It was like climbing a mountain, he told Alma, and every time he had the sense that he had reached a high point, the next one beckoned, "and yet the summit seems ever farther away." Nevertheless, he was optimistic, and the second volume would be "a thousand times more exciting than the first." He worked daily from ten in the morning until one A.M., felt periodically ill and exhausted, and subjected his constitution to further wear and tear by excessive smoking of cigars and cigarettes. "Nicotine is my bane," he said in one of his letters of lamentation to Alma.

After finally completing the novel, Werfel started worrying about his publisher's possible lack of interest in it, as he told his wife in a November letter from Prague. He felt that Paul Zsolnay would hardly be able to consider the "Chimborazo of a work" with the empathy and understanding it required. He also expected Zsolnay to print a far smaller first edition than originally planned, due to possible cancellations of German prepublication orders. "*I really don't have any party on my side in this world.*" He went on to say that he felt betrayed by Zsolnay—after all, the name Werfel had earned the house not only "a lot of money" during the ten years of its existence but also "its only honorable recognition."

Toward the end of 1933 anti-Semitic slogans proliferated on billboards and walls in Prague. Rudolf Werfel was afraid that this rabble-rousing would grow more intense even in Czechoslovakia. In the German Reich, in yet another Reichstag election, the Nazis won 92 percent of the popular vote. Werfel's sister Mizzi arrived from Zurich to visit her parents, and Franz had a violent political disagreement with her. Ferdinand Rieser, Mizzi's husband, had been the director of the

Zurich Schauspielhaus since 1926 and was responsible for the theater's repertory, together with his very ambitious wife. Mizzi now wanted to present only plays that were directed against Hitler's Germany and Nazi cultural policies. This caused her brother to fly into a rage: under no circumstances, insisted Werfel, was the theater to be misused as a political arena.

The Forty Days of Musa Dagh appeared at the end of November 1933. In Austria and Switzerland the reading public received the novel with practically unanimous acclaim. By contrast, official reaction in Germany was negative and vitriolic: even the least sensitive reader had to understand the parallels between Young Turk nationalism and Nazi ideology. Even though no publicity for the book was permitted within the boundaries of the Reich, German booksellers sold all the copies they had ordered. That it was at all possible to market a work by the "burned author" Werfel was one of the contradictions that prevailed during those first months after Hitler's rise to power.

On the initiative of Joseph Goebbels's Propaganda Ministry, the Reich Association of German Writers had been founded in the summer of 1933, under the aegis of the so-called Reich Chamber for Literature. In the fall of 1933, all German writers were called on to register with this new association, whose members had to be "of German blood" and politically acceptable. In December 1933, shortly after the publication of Musa Dagh, Werfel wrote to the association's general directorate in Berlin, applying for "membership in this Reich Association." Once again, as with the earlier declaration of loyalty, his first concern may have been the dissemination of Musa Dagh in Germany; nevertheless, it is hard to imagine how he could possibly have hoped to be accepted by the association.

"Please note that I am a Czechoslovak citizen," he wrote in the petition (which, of course, was never answered), "and a resident of Vienna. At the same time, I wish to declare that I have always kept my distance from any political organization or activity. As a member of the German minority in Czechoslovakia"—he could not resist this reference to his pro-German airs—"resident in Austria, I am subject to the laws and regulations of these states." Should these data "not appear sufficient" for his acceptance, he asked the directorate to obtain further information from Frau Grete von Urbanitzky and Dr. Hanns Martin Elster, who had both declared themselves willing to "vouch for" him. Both these writers were long-time supporters of Nazism. Soon after Hitler's rise to power, Dr. Elster had been appointed to the Civil Service Press Bureau, and not long thereafter he became editor of the NS-Beamtenzeitung, the newspaper published for the civil service.

At a press conference organized by Hungarian journalists, Werfel—

who had come to Budapest to give his Verdi lecture at the Innerstädter Theater—stated his views on recent events in the Third Reich. He compared the political upheavals of the present to religious disagreements during the Thirty Years' War: then, he said, the Catholic Mediterranean principle collided with the Nordic neopagan, and now the unbounded will to power of the Nazis could start a new war over Christianity. He did not mention any immediate danger to the Jews but repeated his—by now well-known—opinion that he did not find Bolshevism a viable alternative and that he rejected that dictatorial and hopelessly antiquated way of governing as strongly as he rejected the German variety of fascism.

Werfel spent the end of the year 1933 in Rüschlikon, near Zurich, as the guest of his sister Mizzi. He went to Italy early in 1934 to begin work on a new project. After accompanying Alma to Venice, he went to Santa Margherita by himself. This time the town seemed dismal to him, which was probably due to the absence of tourists and particularly poor weather: it rained incessantly, for days and weeks. Financial considerations prevented him from taking his spacious favorite room; he had to be content with the cheapest accommodations in the Imperial Palace.

Gerhart Hauptmann, whom he met frequently, seemed intent on proving his anti-Nazi attitude to his friend. Hauptmann assured him of his total rejection of the currently dominant German world view, adding that it caused him personal pain. He said that he had not identified with the new wielders of power for even a moment, although Hitler had assured him of his veneration and Goebbels had wanted to appoint him councillor of state. "In spite of all that," Werfel wrote to Alma, "(in contrast to Strauss, Furtwängler, etc.), he said no. For the rest, he tacks along, as befits his noncombative nature, trying to avoid all risks. . . . I get the impression (as so often with him) of a deep-seated indecisiveness and dependence on mood." Werfel could hardly have bettered this as a description of his *own* attitude during those fateful months after Hitler's ascension to power.

In the meantime there were moves afoot to have *The Forty Days of Musa Dagh* banned in Germany. Among others, a Turkish journalist and author appealed to the German authorities for an official determination that the novel was an insult and act of aggression against Turkey, a country that had been Germany's ally during World War I.

In early February 1934, two months after the novel was published, it was indeed confiscated and prohibited nationwide, according to paragraph 7 of the Reich's presidential ordinance for the protection of the German people. The official proclamation claimed that the book was of a nature liable to endanger public order and safety. The decision was

met with loud approval by the German press, brought into line by the
Nazis. "In the so-called best years of my life and after working without
pause, I now stand on the ruins of myself," Franz Werfel wrote to his
mother-in-law, Anna Moll, from Santa Margherita. "In Germany I have
been deleted from the book, and the books, of the living, and since I
am, after all, a German author, I am now suspended in empty space."

In dense fog, the vaporetto—*with me as its only passenger—arrives at the
terminal: San Lazzaro, Isola degli Armeni. Father Beszdikian, whose grandfather fought on Musa Dagh, lives in the great Venetian monastery of the
Mekhitarist congregation. At the time, his mother was seven years old; now
eighty, she lives close to her son in the city on the lagoon.*

*"My mother's father was one of those heroic men who died fighting the Turkish
soldiers," Beszdikian tells me. He is a strong, tall, priestly figure in his late
forties, his beard neatly trimmed and whitish gray. "He has a hero's tomb now, on
top of Mount Musa. My grandfather even appears in Franz Werfel's book! He is
the man who lies on a rock and holds out until the last cartridge. And my mother
was one of the maybe five hundred girls, and of the four thousand survivors
altogether, who made that stand on the mountain. She can tell you all about it
herself one day; she is not feeling well right now, but we'll go and see her when
you come to Venice again."*

*The priest, who wears a black robe down to his ankles, tells me about his
childhood. He was born in Vakifli, at the foot of Musa Dagh. After the end of
World War I the region was under a French mandate, and many of the
survivors of the tragedy decided to return to their old homeland from Egyptian,
Syrian, and Lebanese refugee camps. "But later, not long after I was born,"
Beszdikian continues, "the French had to cede the territory back to the Turks,
and all those families had to flee again, mine among them. They settled in Anjar,
near Beirut, in the Bekaa valley, where they have stayed to this day. As a result of
the Lebanese war of 1982, the area is now under Syrian occupation. The
Syrian forces are stationed very prominently in the Armenian settlements—they
know Israel won't attack them there, since the Armenians are friends with the
Jews because of the historical similarities of our fates. The similarities between
the two people, the Armenians and the Jews, existed even before the incredible
Holocaust: there is a legend, for instance, according to which the people living
around Musa Dagh were descendants of an Israelite tribe."*

*We tour the large library of the monastery. It shelters precious documents of
the spiritual history of the Armenian people, including very early handwritten
copies of the Bible and prayer books from the second and third centuries A.D.
Young men in black robes pass us in silence; they come here from the countries of
the Armenian diaspora to learn the language and the script so they can become
priests. "Did you know that Moses Der-Kaloustian, who was Franz Werfel's
model for his hero Gabriel Bagradian, died only a month ago, at the age of*

ninety-nine?" Beszdikian goes on: "But a French wife, like Bagradian's unfaithful Juliette—they would never have accepted that around Yoghonoluk, that was purely a product of Werfel's imagination. In the provincial world of the villages around Musa Dagh, it would have been impossible for them to pick an 'assimilated' man like that for their leader!"

The priest takes down a large tome from one of the library's tall shelves: the thousand-page book describes in meticulous detail all the historical events on the Mountain of Moses and traces the lives of many survivors and their descendants. "In the Viennese monastery of the Mekhitarists, where Werfel did his research under the guidance and encouragement of Abbot Habozian," Beszdikian translates from the reference work, "he met a pastor by the name of Katshazan who had survived the weeks on Musa Dagh. And he pointed out various small mistakes to Werfel. But Werfel replied, 'My goal is not to give an absolutely exact historical account of what happened but to create an epic work.'" Beszdikian turns the pages. "Here: in this section, he discusses the particular dialect spoken in the Musa Dagh region, which is quite different from classical Armenian. Or here: the description of a feast we celebrate every year, worldwide, to remind ourselves of the heroic weeks on Musa Dagh— always in September, we make a big lamb stew, because that was practically our daily fare up there on the mountain."

Father Beszdikian excuses himself for a moment; he has to change clothes for a visit to the city. He returns a little later in street clothes, wearing dark sunglasses despite the foggy winter weather. In his left hand he carries a slim briefcase with a gold-colored combination lock. We walk down a few stone steps beside the vacant pier of the island of San Lazzaro. A black Venetian boat is waiting for us, and a cross-eyed ferryman, kin to the Charon of myth, steers the boat across the lagoon. I have trouble retaining my balance on the narrow, swaying floorboards of the vessel.

"The Armenian people find it incomprehensible that the government of Turkey to this day *refuses to admit that it ever committed that genocide!" Beszdikian says. We are slowly approaching the Lido. "I do condemn the Armenian terrorist acts of recent years, but all they want to achieve is* one *thing: to have Turkey admit to the world at large that it committed those atrocities of 1915–17. Not only were Turkish officials busy trying to get Werfel's novel suppressed in the thirties, they have also stopped MGM from making a film of the novel. Turkish diplomats and high government officials have managed to thwart the project time and again. You have to understand one thing: Franz Werfel is* the national hero of the Armenian people. *He wrote our national epic. His great book is a kind of consolation to us—no, not a consolation, there is no such thing, but it is of eminent importance to us that this book exists. It guarantees—and any Armenian anywhere in the world, in Los Angeles, in Paris, in Jerusalem, or in Beirut, will confirm what I say—it guarantees that it can never be forgotten, never, what happened to our people!"*

Bad Tidings

FOUR DAYS OF civil strife in February 1934 transformed the Republic of Austria under Chancellor Engelbert Dollfuss into a clerical-fascist dictatorship. The Austrian army, in concert with Prince Starhemberg's fascist Heimwehr militia, put down a workers' rebellion: at least three hundred people were killed, at least eight hundred wounded. The government (Chancellor Dollfuss had disbanded Parliament in March 1933) declared martial law, dissolved the labor unions, and banned the Social Democratic Party.

Karl-Marx-Hof, the citadel of proletarian resistance, was situated in the immediate vicinity of the Werfels' villa, where Alma and her daughter Manon were staying, and battles were raging right outside on Steinfeldgasse. Kurt von Schuschnigg, minister of justice and education, a friend of Alma Mahler-Werfel's and Johannes Hollnsteiner's, invited Alma to come and stay with him for the duration of the troubles. She thanked him but declined, maintaining her position at Hohe Warte.

Due to the general strike, telephone communications between Santa Margherita and Vienna were interrupted for days. Franz Werfel was tormented by worries that something had happened to his wife and stepdaughter. "Bolshevism is the worst, that's for sure," he wrote to Alma after "the days of trembling" were finally over. "But the next worst," he added, was the radicalism of the right, which he considered a kind of Bolshevism of the petite bourgeoisie. He said he was hardly able to breathe anymore in this world of brute force and "enslavement of the individual." It seemed as if Adolf Hitler, the true beneficiary of the Austrian crisis, had a "lucky star." Werfel wrote that the history of mankind seemed to him, to an ever increasing degree, a "dark intervention of the supernatural in the natural." After all, even Attila, king of the Huns, was just a "belching savage," yet at the same time he had

148

been "God's scourge." After Dollfuss's brutal suppression of the rebellion with the use of heavy artillery, Austria's outraged workers would now join the Nazis in ever greater numbers, and the Dollfuss government faced the future "covered in blood." Hitler (and in this respect he had acted like a *"true man of the people"*) had at least seen to it that there were new organizations ready to accept the workers after the dissolution of the old unions. Dollfuss, on the other hand, had left the proletariat in a state of rage and grief. *"Nevertheless, one has to declare one's instant and unqualified support for Dollfuss."* Only a truly strong Austrian government would be able to prevent a takeover attempt by the Nazis.

The political events in Austria, the situation in the Third Reich, the ban of *The Forty Days of Musa Dagh,* and the hate campaign mounted by the German press against him and his works—all these plunged Werfel into deep depression during the winter weeks of 1934. He found it very hard to work with any concentration. He hoped that the world would come to an end *"radically, quickly, and definitively,"* as he wrote to an employee of Zsolnay Verlag. "Then we're rid of it. (I smell war.)" The only pleasing news Werfel received in these dark days came from Hollywood: Metro-Goldwyn-Mayer had acquired the rights to *The Forty Days of Musa Dagh,* and this coup brightened Werfel's mood a little. The twenty thousand dollars MGM paid for the option eased his increasingly acute financial worries, at least for now. In his Santa Margherita hotel room, he pulled himself together to work on a commission he had accepted at the end of 1933 but had not yet done anything about.

Meyer W. Weisgal, an American theatrical producer born in Poland, was the initiator of this project. In the fall of the preceding year, Weisgal had traveled to Paris and Salzburg in order to enlist Max Reinhardt, now in exile from Germany, in the production of a biblical drama. This era of an imminent threat to the Jewish people, Weisgal felt, called for a theatrically effective adaptation and retelling of the Old Testament. Weisgal wanted to premiere the play in New York and then send it on a worldwide tour, and he was hoping that the famous director would be willing to stage it. Reinhardt turned down the offer, but Weisgal insisted and kept insisting until he finally softened, telling the impresario that he would on some suitable occasion discuss the project with his friend Franz Werfel, who just might be interested in the creation of such an oratorio (Weisgal was thinking of vocal and orchestral interludes).

Reinhardt found to his surprise that Werfel was indeed interested in Weisgal's proposal. Werfel's plan was to use the Books of Moses, Kings, and the Prophets without adding a single word of his own, except for a modest framing device. He intended to cut and rearrange dramatically only in those places where the laws of the stage demanded quick transitions and emphases. He did not, however, find the work easy. It was "a terrible affliction," he told his wife in a letter. "I find anything truly creative a hundred times easier. . . . It's a grotesque idea to think that these gigantic world tragedies, of Jacob, Joseph and his brothers, Moses, could be thrown together in a hurry. *Something in me really resists the idea.* I'm still not certain if I want to take it on." In any case, he was "back at one of the greatest tasks, fraught with the greatest responsibility" of his life.

The frame action, a brief prelude, was to take place in a small synagogue where a venerable old rabbi tells his frightened flock— fleeing from a pogrom—the story of Israel, from Abraham up to the prophet Jeremiah. "I would have forgotten you long ago, congregation of my birth," whispers one of the persecuted people, no doubt reflecting Werfel's own feelings about Jewry. "I would not have returned here if the crowd outside hadn't recognized my face." And the thirteen-year-old son of this alienated man asks his father, "Why are they persecuting us? Why have you never spoken out? Why have I not known anything?"

Werfel had finished about half of the biblical play's first draft by early April 1934. He went to visit his wife in Venice, then traveled with her to Milan and back to Vienna in the middle of the month. There they received word by telephone that Manon, who had wanted to stay on in Venice, was suddenly very ill. Alma took a plane to Venice the next morning, and Werfel, Anna Mahler, and Paul Zsolnay followed her on the afternoon plane. A rapidly convened council of physicians immediately decided on a spinal tap and made the frightening diagnosis that the eighteen-year-old had fallen victim to polio. A polio epidemic in Venice had been kept secret by Italy's censored newspapers, and the virus had attacked Manon Gropius.

After only two days paralysis set in in her legs and soon thereafter in her whole body. Manon was taken to Vienna, in an ambulance railway carriage provided by the Austrian government. She was unable to leave her bed and was in great pain for several months. Now and again she was able to distract herself by memorizing long theatrical parts. Her passion for the theater had become more pronounced in recent times, and before her illness she had frequently expressed the wish to attend the Max Reinhardt Seminar in Vienna to be trained as an actress.

Anxiety about his stepdaughter overshadowed Werfel's work on the biblical drama, but he finished the first draft in the spring of 1934. He visited Max Reinhardt in Leopoldskron Castle in Salzburg and recited *The Eternal Road* (*Der Weg der Verheissung*) to him. Kurt Weill was present as well. Reinhardt wanted to commission him to write the songs and orchestral parts of the oratorio.

Meyer Weisgal, too, had come from New York to attend this reading, but he seemed rather disappointed by the first version of the play. He felt particularly doubtful about the end, in which a messianic, Christ-like figure appears out of the smoking ruins of the Temple to speak words of consolation to the people of Israel. With that for a finale, it would be difficult to persuade the Jewish community of New York to lend its financial support to the gigantic project, the impresario warned. Weisgal asked Werfel to try to avoid Christian associations in his next version of *The Eternal Road*.

In the summer of 1934, while Werfel was working on the second version, Austrian Nazis staged an abortive coup d'état in Vienna. Chancellor Dollfuss was assassinated, but the government crisis the German planners had hoped for did not occur. Although he declined the offer at first, Kurt von Schuschnigg, until then the minister of justice and education, became chancellor and continued on the domi-nant clerical-authoritarian course set by his predecessor.

Franz Werfel expressed his approval of Schuschnigg's appointment in a Viennese weekly, saying that the personality of the new chancellor, in addition to his qualities as a statesman and politician, included "three of the noblest human values: religious depth, incorruptible spirituality, great artistic talent and education"—thus a "trinity" that personified the "God-given *harmony of the Austrian character*. . . . What a gift of fate, and hopeful fate for Austria, that it has found, on the very edge of the abyss, this distinguished and *firm hand to guide it*."

But even in the summer of 1934, Werfel seemed not to have fully realized the dangers that truly lurked in the Nazi abyss: at the end of August, after he had finished the second version of the Bible play, he wrote to the theater critic Julius Bab that although his new work had been written primarily with an American audience in mind, he would regard himself happy if he could "have his say" in Germany with a play that served "Israel and the Bible."

Alma Mahler-Werfel's parties in the festive marble-clad rooms and in the great garden of the villa on Hohe Warte continued unabated. Up to two hundred guests often greeted the dawn here, and the closest friends were served breakfast. After Schuschnigg's appointment to the chancellorship, Alma invited increasing numbers of ministers, highly placed civil servants, and diplomats, introducing them to representa-tives of cultural life, in the hope that such connections might be useful to both sides. Schuschnigg himself, who liked Werfel's work, was a frequent guest at these soirées, being an old admirer of Anna Mahler's and hoping to see her there.

Franz Werfel withdrew more and more from this hectic social life.

During the last few years, the tumult about his literary success and his person had become a little too intense, and the speed with which political reality was changing a little too rapid. He was forty-four years old and needed time to collect himself, to find himself again; a quarter-century had passed since he had recited a few poems—breathless with excitement—to Max Brod from what was to become the collection *The Friend of the World*. Now, in 1934, Brod turned fifty, and Werfel's fame had surpassed that of his erstwhile mentor by far. Ten years ago, his friend Franz Kafka had died; in an elegiac letter to Kafka's confidant, Dr. Robert Klopstock, Werfel wrote at the end of 1934 that he had always regarded Kafka as a "messenger from the King . . . who, tragically, had been given too great a share of the supernatural. Franz Kafka is one who was sent down to us, one of the great elect. . . . I was always aware of that distance between him and myself, a mere poet."

Werfel spent the beginning of 1935 mostly by himself and in quiet circumstances. He rented a large hotel room in Baden, near Vienna, and wrote—for the first time in years—only poems. In this time of private crisis, memories of childhood offered security and shelter: "When I fetch childhood / Strange and intact, / I do not think it is like coal / Long since burned out, long since consumed. / Where the child's ghosts are nesting / I go as my own echo / Eternally to the Piarists / Somewhere in God's universe."

A physician had told him a while earlier that there was no hope of recovery for his stepdaughter Manon and that he had to be prepared for the worst. During February and March 1935 he wrote many poems about death. At the end of March he received the news of the death of his nanny Barbara Šimůnková: at the age of eighty, she had passed away in the Prague hospital of the Sisters of St. Elizabeth. "Please wait," Werfel called out after her, "until I, stricken with silence and coldness, / Come once more to say thanks to you." And in the poem "The Transfigured Maid" ("Die verklärte Magd") he wrote: "So heavy a final burden you carried / And faded away so lightly, so lightly, / Now you live again, vivid / Within me, you guardian of the dawn. / I walk through the park of my childhood / . . . In a glory of consolation / Walk as I once did, holding your hand."

Manon Gropius died on April 22, 1935. Her funeral, at the Grinzing cemetery, degenerated into a social occasion that everybody wanted to attend. The upper crust of Vienna crowded around the open grave-side, at which not Manon's stepfather but Johannes Hollnsteiner spoke the eulogy. Werfel experienced the days before Manon's death as "the most difficult time" of his life, and he wrote, on the last page of a notebook he kept during those weeks; "I started this in 1932 when everything was still going well, and I was not yet marked by deep wounds."

Soon after Manon's funeral, the Werfels and Anna Mahler embarked on a grand tour of Italy. A desperate attempt to find distraction, it took them first to Rome and Florence and finally to Viareggio, where they met up with Kurt von Schuschnigg. In a state limousine provided by Benito Mussolini, they made day trips to various places, including Giacomo Puccini's home by a small Tuscan lake. As the palazzo in Venice was so closely connected with memories of Manon, Alma wanted to sell it as soon as possible, and the Casa Mahler ceased to exist as their household before the end of that summer.

In mid-July 1935, after Chancellor Schuschnigg had returned to Austria, he and his wife were involved in a serious automobile accident. Herma von Shuschnigg was killed instantly, while her husband suffered only slight injuries. "A charming, delicate woman was taken from us by some unfathomable decision," Franz Werfel wrote in the *Wiener Sonn- und Montagszeitung* "How often must Herma von Schuschnigg have trembled for the life of her husband in the past months . . . the life of this extraordinary and pure man, who . . . out of selfless love for the fatherland . . . shouldered the burden . . . Who knows whether, in the mysterious net of fate and determination, this death does not have the significance of a sacrifice?" Despite this "terrible blow of fate," Chancellor Schuschnigg was now obliged to show "no weakness." "Austrian humanity, the very thing he himself, the spiritual, sensitive, steadfast man, personifies to such a high degree . . . has to be preserved and fostered for the salvation of Europe."

The opponents of the regime reacted to Werfel's eulogy with wild indignation. While all opposition newspapers had been banned within the borders of Austria, the German-language socialist *Arbeiterzeitung* published in Czechoslovakia was able to express its rage to its fullest extent, saying that Franz Werfel had celebrated the leader of Austrian fascism as an "incarnation of humanity," while victims of the dictatorship were on hunger strikes and were abused daily in prison. The paper said that Werfel, in his toadying, had proved to be one of the lowest of scribblers.

Meyer Weisgal had meanwhile succeeded in finding a great number of Jewish backers in New York for his oratorio. The world premiere of *The Eternal Road* was originally planned for February 1935, in a tent designed along the lines of the Old Testament tabernacle, 120 feet tall and seating 5,000 spectators. Production costs, however, soon exceeded

Weisgal's budget, and the first night was postponed until the end of the year. Weisgal rented the Manhattan Opera House, a theater that had stood empty for years, and rehearsals were set to begin in September.

"I'm not exaggerating," Werfel explained to a journalist who interviewed him about his biblical play in Salzburg's Café Bazar, "when I say that this will be the creation of an entirely new stage concept, one that has never been tried before." To give an idea of the special nature of *The Eternal Road,* Werfel mentioned that the production would require seventy solo musicians, a ninety-piece orchestra, and about a thousand extras.

Before Max Reinhardt left for the United States, Werfel sent him the final version of the play, which incorporated ideas from the conversations they had had in Salzburg. "I have tried to fulfill all your wishes," he said in the covering letter. "The great scene in the last part and the end have been modified the way you wanted." The messianic figure that had displeased Weisgal was now, in Werfel's final version, "the Angel of the Last Days"—but he said that its definitive designation, "to avoid all possible objections," would have to be chosen during rehearsals or shortly before the first performance.

At the beginning of November 1935, the Werfels set sail for New York to attend the world premiere of *The Eternal Road.* This was Franz Werfel's first visit to the United States, but he did not arrive there unknown: in the fall of the previous year, *The Forty Days of Musa Dagh* had appeared in English translation and had been selected by the Book-of-the-Month Club as its most important new book. It was number one on the best-seller list for many weeks, and 150,000 copies of the American edition had been sold. The fact that it had been banned by the Nazis no doubt contributed to its success.

Armenians living in exile in New York invited their idol, the author of their national epic, to one gala dinner after another. Werfel had never been feted so lavishly; he was even called "a friend God has sent" to the Armenian people, who had succeeded like no one before him in plumbing the depths of the Armenian soul.

In the meantime the Manhattan Opera House was being totally rebuilt for *The Eternal Road.* The work devoured large amounts of money and transformed the auditorium as well as the stage into a permanent construction site. Soon it became obvious that the first night could not take place as planned. Weisgal and Reinhardt agreed to postpone it until February 1936. Werfel decided to stay in New York until then: he liked the metropolis and its chaotic liveliness.

The Werfels stayed at the St. Regis, near Central Park, making frequent visits to the opera and the theaters. They met artists, scholars, and scientists, among them Albert Einstein, who offered his personal assistance in raising funds for the *Eternal Road* project. Speaking to a Jewish audience in New York, Werfel said that he had not for a moment felt like a stranger in the United States, "but here, among you, I feel at home in a deeper sense." He had not needed "Herr Hitler" to discover his Jewishness, he assured his audience. It was true that he had grown up in an assimilated milieu and had at times become quite estranged from the faith of his fathers, but "through suffering and recognition" his Jewishness had grown very strong over the years. He believed that he "could no longer be expelled . . . from this Jewishness, not by Christians or even by Jews."

In a Jewish environment, far away from the recently proclaimed Nuremberg race laws and just as far from the influence of the anti-Semitic café atmosphere of Vienna, taken to the bosom of New York intellectuals, Werfel finally spoke out about the "new persecution" afflicting Jewry, hastening to express, almost proudly, his conviction "that Israel cannot be destroyed by any persecution."

The Werfels' stay in America was overshadowed by another death: in December of this year of grief, 1935, their friend and confidant Alban Berg had died of blood poisoning. The composer was only fifty years old at the time of his death; his last work, a violin concerto completed in the summer of 1935, had been dedicated to Manon Gropius—"To the memory of an angel."

The rehearsals of *The Eternal Road* had to be broken off in their final stages, in early February 1936, and the opening postponed indefinitely. About $400,000 had been spent on the production, and Weisgal's funds were exhausted. Hundreds of people—actors, extras, dancers, musicians—became unemployed; the producer, whose private life had long since fallen apart in this extended disaster, had to start raising funds again. At least another $175,000 was needed to stage the play. Rehearsals would probably not be resumed before the fall of 1936.

The Werfels returned to Europe on the luxury liner SS *Champlain*. When they arrived in Paris from Le Havre, they were received by a large and excited crowd at the Gare du Nord: these were exiled Armenians, and, like their brothers and sisters in New York, they celebrated Werfel as their national hero for days on end. One of the numerous dinners given in his honor was graced by the presence of the French rear admiral Dartige du Fournet, who, as the commander of the flagship *Jeanne d'Arc*, had led the rescue operation off the coast of the Musa Dagh range and saved the lives of more than four thousand men, women, and children.

In early March 1936 the Werfels returned to Hohe Warte, to "a Vienna that was like a cemetery." He was trying to "find his way back into life here," Werfel wrote to Rudolf Kommer, Max Reinhardt's secretary, who had stayed in New York. And he added, "Funnily enough, despite all the bad experiences and disappointments there, I feel a kind of homesickness for New York."

Not far from Leopoldskron Castle in Salzburg, once the residence of Max Reinhardt, lies Klesheim Castle, surrounded by extensive parklands. At the end of a wide gravel road, tucked away in a dale, is the small castle of Hoyos, home of Max Reinhardt's son Gottfried Reinhardt. The screenwriter, director, and movie producer is a massive, ponderous man who divides his time between Salzburg and Los Angeles. Following the stream of his memories, he strides back and forth in his large study.

"My father was very fond of Werfel, and he directed many of his plays. I can still remember Juarez *in detail," Gottfried Reinhardt tells me. His voice is nasal and rasping; the floorboards creak under his feet. "In Vienna and Berlin,* Juarez *was one of my father's very best productions ever. I think he really loved that play. The last play he ever directed in Vienna was also one of Werfel's:* One Night (In einer Nacht). *That was in 1937, at the Josefstadt Theater. Then, of course, he directed* The Eternal Road *in New York—a grotesque business! Meyer Weisgal had read in the paper that Max Reinhardt had been expelled from Germany, and he immediately sent my father a telegram: 'If Hitler doesn't need you, I do!' During the World Exposition of 1933 in Chicago, Weisgal had put on a small biblical show in the so-called Palestinian Pavilion, and now he wanted something similar, only on a much larger scale. He kept knocking on my father's door, but Max didn't want to have anything to do with it. In private, he was an observant Jew; he even fasted on Yom Kippur, but at the same time he was a completely assimilated German. And he wore those blinkers that kept him from seeing what things were really like. It took him years to grasp the fact that he was regarded as a Jew and an immigrant,* politically. *Anyway, Max Reinhardt tried to keep his distance from the Jewish question for as long as possible. Probably not least because his father-in-law, Hugo Thimig had always been an anti-Semite. (My father married Helene Thimig after he divorced my mother.) We often had big arguments, my father and I, about his suppressed Jewishness—I couldn't stand his attitude. After he turned Weisgal down, I wrote to him from New York that he had made a great mistake. If he had any future at all, it would be in America. 'You must be insane,' I wrote to him, 'not to accept Weisgal's offer to direct this play, here in this city with three million Jews.' And I received a rather disgruntled reply: 'Don't be childish, I'm not going to deny my Jewishness—but I can't put on a biblical variety show! Not even Cecil B. DeMille could get me to do that!'*

"After prolonged vacillation, he asked Werfel to think it over. In some demonic way, he had managed to pick someone who would try to create a biblical play that was as un-Jewish as possible. So he proposed a playwright who was fundamentally a pious Catholic; a composer who was a Communist—Kurt Weill had collaborated with Brecht: one could hardly imagine a greater contrast than that between Brecht and Werfel—and finally, a stage designer of genius who was a notorious anti-Semite: Norman Bel Geddes.

"But my father underestimated Weisgal's tremendous energy. In New York practically every Jew had to pay a kind of head tax to make it possible to stage this monstrosity. Then, when Werfel came to Salzburg with his first version of The Eternal Road, it was really a tremendous blow for Weisgal to realize that the author of the play felt and wrote like a Catholic! So Weisgal tried to convert Werfel back to Judaism, in a crash course, as it were—I can just imagine what it must have been like!

"Then, when my father came to New York in the fall of 1935 to start rehearsals, it turned out that the stage designer had omitted the synagogue, where the rabbi is consoling his congregation. Mr. Bel Geddes wasn't interested in it, and the two had awful arguments. Werfel, who had also come to New York, said, 'My play is being ruined here!' But where to put the little synagogue? There was no room left on the stage. Someone suggested the orchestra pit, but Kurt Weill protested. 'If you take the orchestra away, I quit!' But that's where they finally put it, and the musicians had to sit in a separate room—which created enormous problems of synchronization between onstage events and orchestral music.

"Indescribable things happened during those rehearsals. The whole theater had to be rebuilt—the front boxes were torn down, new dressing rooms had to be constructed. While tunneling into the bedrock under Manhattan, workers accidentally drilled into a spring, so all the rooms below the stage were flooded. And that was just one of the more harmless incidents!

"When the play was performed at long last—the first night was in January 1937—the audience witnessed a splendid and seamless production, up to the intermission. In the fourth and final act, everything fell apart and the whole thing ended in chaos. My father, Weisgal, and the hundreds of people involved were preparing themselves for terrible reviews. But that night, when the first morning papers appeared, almost all the reviews were raves! The Eternal Road was praised to the heavens. What had happened, of course, was that many critics had left during the intermission to meet their deadline and hadn't witnessed the catastrophic last part. Well, no one ever got to see that fourth act again—it was simply cut.

"The production ran for five or six months, steadily losing money, even though the Manhattan Opera House was sold out every night. But Weisgal lost thousands of dollars every week: in the two top balconies, there was a rebellion every night because no one up there was able to see the synagogue scene down in *the orchestra pit. Many members of the audience asked for their money back. The entire production became so costly that it was a catastrophe for my father: people held him personally responsible for the enormous losses. I suppose he had had the right intuition at first, when he refused to have anything to do with the project."*

Jeremiad

Y

ESTERDAY, LATE AT night, after I finished the introductory and transitional notes for the American edition of my novellas, to be called *Twilight of a World,* I lay down with the unpleasant feeling of having no inspired idea, no real vision for a new work, and having to suffer through a time of painful idleness," Franz Werfel wrote in his notebook in late April 1936. A short while earlier, he had joined Alma and Johannes Hollnsteiner in Ticino, at the Muralto Park Hotel near Locarno. He had been suffering for months from this "work void," as he called his uninspired state. While his wife had helped him in previous years in the search for new subjects and ideas, she was now almost exclusively engaged with the theologian Hollnsteiner and *his* world of thought—she had even encouraged Hollnsteiner to write a book.

"I thought of the legends that I had started writing the previous tragic summer after Mutzi's [Manon Gropius's] death," the note continues. Under the title "The Intercessor of the Dead," ("Die Fürbitterin der Toten"), Werfel then wrote an outline of the life of the "miraculous virgin Christina von Trugen," a saint who had lived in Holland in the twelfth century. However, he decided, that same day and after eighteen pages of manuscript, that he did not want to proceed with this material "for the time being"—mainly because he was reluctant to "make the story of a saint who is still being venerated . . . the subject of nonauthentic inventions of my own epic." But one day later, on May 1, Werfel had an idea: "True, many things within me are warning me not to undertake such a boundless, dangerous, and probably thankless task. But my head started hammering and spinning away. The plan would be to write a novel on the prophets, the proclaimers of God, probably an epic on the prophet Jeremiah, as it is the most suitable in terms of drama and event. So I went to a bookshop to buy a copy of the Bible. I opened it absentmindedly. To the page: 'The Book of Jeremiah.' "

In the weeks that followed, first in Muralto, then in Bad Ischl, an Austrian spa, Werfel started making notes for this major novel. He immersed himself in works on Jewish history and the life story of the prophet Jeremiah, and once again, as he had while working on *Paul Among the Jews*, read Bible and Talmud commentaries. He studied the history of Babylon and old Egyptian writings, the Egyptian Book of the Dead in particular. Mapping out sequences of events, he outlined individual characters and invented a frame story, as he had in the case of *The Pure in Heart*. A member of a group of English tourists, a writer by the name of Clayton Jeeves, becomes haunted by insistent déjà vu experiences on the site of the first two temples of the Jews in Jerusalem. "Now it's here again, that feeling. *I have lived through this once before....* Here the novel of the Jerusalem of the prophets begins. It ends, after perhaps a thousand pages, with Mr. Jeeves's realization . . . that his fear of the Dejavue [*sic*] was really unfounded." Nevertheless, it was Werfel's plan to have Jeeves experience the entire, fascinating, story of the life and sufferings of Jeremiah in just a few seconds. "Even if this'll only be a 'frame,' the workmanship of that frame has to be so surprising and tight that even the astute reader won't be able to slip away."

Werfel already saw one of the novel's supplementary characters "during my very first moment of concentration." He is a friend of Jeremiah's, not a prophet but a "penetrator of God" who is convinced that "there is no salvation"—the closer you get to God, the more dangerous the chasms opening up in front of the seeker. Franz Kafka was the model for this tall young man "with a low forehead and burning eyes."

He wrote to Max Brod from Bad Ischl that he was "living" inside a great new epic work, trying his hand at a subject that he would "probably fail" to master. At the end of June 1936 he went back to Breitenstein, where he continued work on the first draft of the novel. He spent the whole summer in Haus Mahler, often writing for ten hours at a stretch and producing hundreds of manuscript pages in a matter of weeks. A deeply Jewish book with profound insight into the history of Israel, it was permeated by great love for the Jewish people. It also replied to all those critics who had, for years now, blamed him for his silence on the subject of Nazism and for his Christian sympathies. Its language possessed a power Werfel had rarely managed before, with the exception of *The Forty Days of Musa Dagh*. Jeremiah's flight from God, his descent into the Egyptian world of the dead, his ascension to Babylonian astral spheres, his final resignation and acceptance of the prophet's fate imposed on him by God—all these scenes are among the most compelling in all of Werfel's work. At the same time, he managed to make the novel into a coded call for resistance, with the figure of Jeremiah a symbol of those able to resist and question the might of the state and the smugness of the mighty.

While the novel on the prophet was taking shape, Karl Kraus died in Vienna at the age of sixty-two, without ever having reached a reconciliation with Werfel. Adolf Hitler and Kurt von Schuschnigg signed an agreement in which the Third Reich acknowledged the sovereignty of the state of Austria; in return, Schuschnigg promised an amnesty for jailed Austrian Nazis and declared himself willing to accept into future cabinets politicians of German nationalist persuasion.

In mid-July there was a military coup in Spain, in the wake of the assassination of Carlo Sotelo, a leader of the monarchists. The coup was soon followed by the outbreak of civil war. Werfel's sympathies were with the lawfully elected, leftist government of Spain, but Alma sided with the rebels, militarily supported by both Hitler and Mussolini and led by Francisco Franco. While the Spanish Civil War raged on with increasing heat, the Werfels, too, had almost daily and extremely vehement fights over their political convictions, which were drifting ever further apart.

"Title still undecided," Werfel noted on the title page of the first draft of the Jeremiah novel, completed in Baden near Vienna in mid-November 1936. *"The Harbinger of the Lord??? The Terrible Voice??? The Eternal Hunter??? The Gold Refiner???"* Werfel's epic ends with the destruction of Solomon's Temple by Nebuchadnezzar and the deportation of the Jewish people to fifty years of exile in Babylon. Jeremiah has prophesied this apocalypse to the people of Israel, but they have not heeded him. Now the prophet follows the punished people into exile. As a final consolation, Werfel lets God speak to His messenger: "Look upon the sign I send to thee in the midst of these abominations, so that thou mayest live! Thou hast suffered so that thou wilt be mine, and I, thine. Your victory groweth from defeat to defeat, so that ye may live!"

With his Jeremiah novel, clearly written against Alma's wishes and as a polemic against Johannes Hollnsteiner's philosophy, Werfel himself was trying to be a warning voice, more consciously so as he proceeded, in a time whose everyday political realities impressed him as deeply ominous. He feared that a new apocalypse would take place if the excited and propagandized masses of Europe could not reach a point of calm and reflection. A modern Nebuchadnezzar, Adolf Hitler, could unleash it, and its consequences could be more horrifying than the destruction of Jerusalem in 586 B.C., even more fateful than those of World War I.

While he was working on the second draft of his novel, in the spring of 1937, Werfel received the highest Austrian decoration for achievement in the arts and sciences, on Kurt von Schuschnigg's initiative. The chancellor visited "his" poet laureate regularly at Hohe Warte and liked to hear him read poems, not only Werfel's own but also the German classics. Occasionally he even discussed political matters, and both

Werfel and Alma repeatedly encouraged him in his decision to resist pressure from Hitler's Germany as much as possible. In spite of his fears of catastrophe—yet naively confident that the Third Reich would not interfere with a "strong" Austria—Werfel went on enjoying his role as a favored child of the Austro-fascist corporate state.

At the end of April 1937, a few days before the destruction of the Basque capital of Guernica by German fighter-bomber planes of the Condor Legion, Werfel completed the second draft of his novel and gave it the final title: *Hearken Unto the Voice* (*Höret die Stimme*). His quarrels with Alma over their contrary attitudes toward the Spanish Civil War had escalated to the point of marital crisis: Werfel retreated to Zurich, to his sister Marianne Rieser, while Alma contemplated the sale of the villa at Hohe Warte. She said that she regarded it as a "house of misfortune" in any case, and besides, her husband had never liked to work there. The Werfels agreed to rent out the mansion for the summer, and Alma started packing their possessions into countless crates. In the middle of June they threw a kind of farewell garden party that continued into an evening of new wine and song, to which they had once more invited the so-called elite of Viennese society, members of the nobility, tycoons, politicians, and artists.

Werfel attended the International PEN Congress in Paris on June 21–24. Lion Feuchtwanger, who had emigrated from Germany into exile in southern France years earlier, gave a short speech in which he attacked the reign of terror instituted by the Nazis. Werfel, who spoke immediately after Feuchtwanger, attacked the latter because of his trip to the Soviet Union, where the writer had been received by Joseph Stalin; he accused Feuchtwanger of condemning Hitler's Germany in the *Pariser Tageszeitung* while deliberately not saying a word about the atrocities committed by the Bolsheviks. Despite this vehement difference of opinion, the two writers became friends during the days of the congress and enjoyed their impassioned political-philosophical arguments.

At the same congress, Werfel's American publisher, Ben Huebsch, introduced his author to James Joyce: they celebrated the meeting at Fouquet's on the Champs-Elysées and discovered, at a late hour, the one thing they truly had in common—a passion for Italian opera. Joyce, who had once wanted to become an opera singer, performed one Verdi aria after another. The later it got, and the more deserted the restaurant, the louder they sang. Joyce's son joined in to form a trio.

Invited by the League of Nations' organization for intellectual cooperation, Werfel gave a speech in Paris on the subject of the conference, "The Future of Literature" ("Die Zukunft der Literatur"), in which he advocated the establishment of a "World Academy of Writers and Thinkers" that would voice its opposition to the current widespread "barbarization of life." Like the Christian synods, this academy would provide an antidote to the "thundering avalanche of propaganda" and thus become an "essential organ for peace." The delegates rejected Werfel's naive proposal almost unanimously.

"After I had been working for an average of twelve hours a day, every day, for fourteen months to complete my major epic *Hearken Unto the Voice*," Werfel told a newspaper reporter in October 1937, "I was so utterly exhausted that I had actually decided not to start anything new and to avoid anything that could possibly inspire me to do so." But no later than July, when he was back in Breitenstein, he was plotting a verse drama about civil war, set in no particular period, to be called *Our House* (*Unser Haus*). But that project was set aside when he happened to read a newspaper item "taken from the British press" that engaged his imagination so actively that he could see his "newest dramatic piece like an apparition." "All thoughts of rest were then forgotten; it literally forced me to my desk."

In a few summer weeks in 1937 Werfel produced an embarrassingly bad play, *One Night*, the drama of a triangle between Felizitas, her husband Eduard, a landowner, and Gabriel, the love of Felizitas's youth and also an old friend of Eduard's. The landowner's jealousy culminates in the murder of his rival, but the latter is only in a state of suspended animation and returns to new life on Halloween night.

Each of the play's characters corresponded to a fundamental concept in the philosophy of Thomas Aquinas's *Summa Theologica*, much admired by Werfel. Virtue, Good, and Evil were reflected and personified. Elements from Werfel's one-act play *The Visit from Elysium*, written when he was only twenty, resurfaced twenty-seven years later: the former Hedwig corresponds to the desirable Felizitas; Lukas, the returnee from the land of the dead, to Gabriel, the man in suspended animation; and the gross and violent civil servant of the first play to Eduard, the crude owner of the castle. Tensions and scenes of jealousy that had taken place between Alma Mahler, Walter Gropius, and Franz Werfel were also woven into the play: as had been the case with Alma and her lover, music is the particular element that unites Felizitas and Gabriel. After all these years, the trauma of the death of their son reappears: we are told that Felizitas's only child died a few hours after its birth.

Max Reinhardt, who had returned from the *Eternal Road* disaster in New York for a short stay in Europe, immediately started rehearsals for the world premiere of *One Night* at the Josefstadt Theater. Werfel was a frequent participant in the rehearsals but did not always agree with the director and had to prevent him from indulging in overly melodramatic notions. The play opened in early October 1937, with Helene

Thimig, Attila Hörbiger, and Anton Edthofer in the main parts. It was an instant success. The reviewers, it is true, concentrated mainly on the reception given in the theater's gala rooms by its director, Ernst Lothar, and his wife, Adrienne Gessner. In addition to Chancellor Schuschnigg and many of his cabinet ministers, diplomats, and heads of departments, the guests also included Deputy Police Chief Johann Presser, the same man who in November 1918, then only a lowly commissioner, had interrogated Franz Werfel and threatened him with expulsion from Austria.

With this opening and the simultaneous publication of the Jeremiah novel, Werfel's fame within Austria's borders reached its zenith. Nevertheless the poet laureate now asked himself with increasing urgency whether he should not leave the country, in view of the threat of a Nazi coup. That question hung in the air at a reunion dinner at the Franziskanerkeller in Vienna with his former publisher Kurt Wolff, in November 1937. Besides Wolff and his wife, who had emigrated from Germany in 1933, the orchestra conductor Wilhelm Furtwängler was also present but seemed restrained and did not say much. At any rate it was courageous of Furtwängler to appear publicly in the company of such a renowned Jewish writer: any of the waiters could have been a spy. Werfel's extreme nervousness was contagious, although Alma was apparently untouched by the oppressive atmosphere and talked optimistically about her good relations with the archbishop of Vienna, Cardinal Innitzer, and Chancellor Schuschnigg. She said that she wouldn't dream of emigrating; Vienna was her home and would remain so. There was no question of her leaving all her possessions and fleeing the country.

"Of Man's True Happiness" ("Von der reinsten Glückseligkeit des Menschen") was the title of a lecture Werfel gave in early December 1937 to the Austrian section of the League of Nations in Vienna. He lamented the fact that art had been condemned to a life in the catacombs, because only by a rediscovery of the true values—the "visionary nature" of art—could mankind awaken from its present "nightmare." "The neobarbaric fanaticism of the hate-fed masses" could be neutralized only by means of a conscious remembering of the cultures of antiquity. The enjoyment of art was not only a pastime, *Zeitvertreib*, but, as he said he had found out for himself, "Art is the opposite. . . . It is a *Todvertreib*, a way of banishing death."

My mobile home is parked in Beverly Glen Canyon in Los Angeles, on a slight incline—the bed tilts, my feet lie lower than my head. The heat of the morning sun and the chirping of the cicadas wake me up, and I take a short walk uphill to

Anna Mahler's modest, slightly sagging frame house. Here, on bumpy dead-end Oletha Lane, the sculptor has created most of her works of the last three decades; many of them populate a concrete surface at the bottom of a steep orange grove, like mysterious alien organisms.

"I had a hard time falling asleep last night. I had nightmares after all the matters we've been talking about," Anna says as we sit down to breakfast in her kitchen. "All those suppressed and forgotten things reemerge. Why don't we give the memories a rest for a few days?" But when I agree, she immediately goes on: "When my mother first met Werfel, her political orientation wasn't all that far to the right. That only came about with her resistance to Werfel, when he returned to her after his escapades during the revolution in Vienna. After that, they kept having political arguments, but even those only really came to a head during the Spanish Civil War. The daily battles between Werfel and Mammi (every year I spent a couple of weeks on the Semmering and witnessed quite a few) were horrible, and Alma kept growing stronger, Werfel, weaker. You see, she had worked out a very clever strategy: she never tried any new arguments but simply repeated the same opinions over and over again. Werfel kept trying new arguments. It was stupid of him to try to convince her. Then, after hours of embittered yelling, he lost his patience and ran out of the house, still seething, while Alma proceeded to attend to entirely different matters with the greatest composure, paying no attention to the fight they had had. He would come back, still upset, not relaxed in the least, and would start roaring again. Alma, fresh and in a good mood, received him graciously, as if she had won the argument. That was her strength: she didn't really take the political disagreements seriously, while Werfel was ready to shed his heart's blood over them. She used these quarrels against him. Werfel and I would commiserate in whispers behind closed doors. And the Spanish Civil War lasted for such a long time! I often met Werfel in Vienna, in one of the less-crowded coffeehouses. He would call and ask me to come and meet him. Back then, I was way over to the left in my political views. And he would tell me, every time, that he couldn't stand living with Alma anymore and wanted a total separation. He was really ready to leave her. But he didn't have the strength to do it. He went back to her every time. His weakness, his tendency always to give in—those were the negative aspects of his character. He submitted to Alma, quite consciously. It wasn't good for either one of them— a lot of the time she really treated him as if she were his governess."

"Did you tell him that Alma was a fervent supporter of Franco in the Civil War?" Albrecht Joseph calls out from an adjacent room. "And the affair with Hollnsteiner? That she rented a small apartment for him and herself—with Werfel's money? Where she served champagne and caviar to her lover?"

"Well, that gossip's not that important," Anna says. "But I have to admit that Hollnsteiner was to some extent responsible for Alma's reactionary politics. She was really infatuated with him, probably mostly because he was a priest, and the cardinal's right-hand man, and yet she had managed to seduce him. Yes, Werfel

demonstrated his nobility and native wisdom in that affair: even though he knew about it—of course he did—he tolerated it without saying a word."

"One of Alma's rules of life," adds Albrecht, who has joined us at the kitchen table, *"was 'Whoever needs help does not deserve it!' And another one of her maxims—borrowed from Nietzsche, if I'm not mistaken—was 'If someone falls, give him a kick in the ass while he's down!' "*

"Mammi used to say, 'I know everybody at first glance.' But she didn't even know me. *Much later, she confessed to me, 'If I had known you as I know you now, I wouldn't have treated you so miserably.' That really shocked me—because it showed that she had done it consciously, all those years. For instance, when I received the Grand Prix de Sculpture at the Paris World Exposition in 1937, she hardly acknowledged it. She didn't treat Manon any differently, really—she never recognized her uniqueness. Everything that she (and Werfel, too) later wrote about Mutzi was essentially dishonest and dictated by their bad conscience. Alma decided, 'Manon, you'll study Italian and become a teacher of Italian.' But Mutzi had extraordinary theatrical talent—her greatest desire was to become an actress."*

"Forgive me for interrupting," says Albrecht, *"but I just remembered a story from the thirties in Bad Ischl, when I was working on a film script with Rudolf Forster. One morning, to my surprise, I ran into Werfel on a bridge there, and he told me about his Jeremiah novel. He had just gotten started on it. He was grinning like a schoolboy playing hooky: he said that Alma had wanted him to work in Vienna or in Breitenstein, but that he had preferred to retire here, to the Salzkammergut. That same night I was sitting at a table in some inn, and I heard this voice behind me: 'All right—a week without any results, that's reasonable. Even two weeks. But almost* three *weeks without a line?!' It was, of course, Alma. Next morning I ran into Werfel again, on the same bridge. Now he looked sad. He sighed and said, 'No more good times. My wife has arrived from Vienna. She'll take me back there tonight.' "*

"I'll tell you more another time," says Anna Mahler. *"We have to take a break for a couple of days. It's too strenuous for me, digging in the past like this. I can't sleep at night. Next time I'll tell you about the catastrophic year 1938. But not today, not today."*

1938

Early in 1938 the Werfels spent a few vacation weeks on the Mediterranean island of Capri, staying in a suite at the Hotel Morgano & Tiberio Palace. "I've been rushed and abstracted," Werfel wrote to Stefan Zweig at the end of January, "and then really ill, for weeks. Only here in Capri am I beginning to come back to myself." He wrote numerous poems: one of them was called "The Friend of the World Does Not Know How to Grow Older" ("Der Weltfreund versteht nicht zu altern"). He was also planning a collection of his essays since 1915 and wrote a prophetic new essay, "Thoughts on Tomorrow's War" ("Betrachtung über den Krieg von morgen"). The impending world war, whose advent Werfel no longer doubted, would not be an unequivocal "national war," as the last one had been, but "a comprehensive civil war across national fronts." While in 1914, when World War I broke out, certain conventions were still observed, at least in principle, and despite all the cruelty there still was some respect for international law, the second time around only the law of strength would prevail and, by means of broadcast propaganda, spread across all countries, across all boundaries. "If no miracle happens, the white nations will be buried not only in a hail of projectiles but in the ashen rain of lies."

The Werfels made several visits to nearby Naples and excursions to the countryside around it. They met Tina Orchard again, the heroine of *The Pascarella Family*, whose husband—"Arthur Campbell" in the novel—had died not long before. Werfel now met Tina's family for the first time and immediately made notes of scenes and dialogues for a possible sequel to his favorite book. He drafted a couple of chapters, "Placido Visits the Sibyl" ("Placido bei der Sibylle"), "The Keening Bell" ("Die schrillende Glocke")—the latter intended as the projected climax, a description of the death of Tina's sister Annunziata. He also wanted to introduce, as a new main character, nine-year-old

Franca, one of Mrs. Orchard's nieces, whose "wild imagination" had enchanted him.

On February 12, 1938, while the Werfels were still in Capri, Adolf Hitler and Kurt von Schuschnigg met at very short notice for talks at Obersalzberg, near Berchtesgaden. Hitler insisted on the unconditional fulfillment of the agreements made in July 1936 concerning the immediate release of all imprisoned Nazis and demanded more evidence of a pro-German policy on the part of the Austrian government: the Hitler salute was to be legalized, the swastika flag declared nonsubversive. To prevent Hitler from making good his threat of sending troops into Austria, Schuschnigg accepted the ultimatum.

Even though Alma at first wanted to go back to Vienna immediately in order to get a clearer picture of the situation, she let another two weeks go by in Naples before her departure. These were two weeks of indecision, two weeks of fear for Austria's independence, during which the Werfels distracted themselves from their anxiety by visiting the Teatro San Carlo, the opera house of Naples, almost every night.

Werfel found it unusually difficult to part from Alma and needed days to recover his psychological equilibrium. Soon after her departure, he wrote to her that, without her, he *truly felt like a man with only one arm and one leg.*" His longing was as great as it had not been since the early days of their relationship. At first Alma had only reassuring news to report from Vienna, where there was a general upsurge of hope after an optimistic speech by Schuschnigg to Parliament.

Disturbed by the noise of neighbors behind the thin walls of the Hotel Morgano & Tiberio Palace, Werfel dedicated himself, with his customary intensity and sharply raised consumption of nicotine, to a new play, *The Lost Mother, or The Foundling of an Evil Time* (*Die verlorene Mutter oder Der Findling einer schlimmen Zeit*). The play centered on the fate of a young man who, after twenty years of aimless wandering, meets his mother, whom he had believed dead. The project, Werfel thought, was rather like a popular "romantic horror" story, and he was afraid—to an unusual degree—of "sounding the wrong notes," as he confided to Alma in a letter. He was fully aware of "the dangers of sentimentality and trashiness" inherent in the subject, yet he could not desist and completed the first act as if under some compulsion. With this play, "a classical drama disguised as a modern comedy," he was aiming for a big theatrical hit, but, on the other hand—as he openly admitted to Alma—there just wasn't any other idea he found urgent enough.

Alma advised him to get started on the sequel to *The Pascarella Family*, but Werfel did not feel like taking that advice: "I can't get going on the second *Pascarella* novel for a while yet. With me, an *incubation period* is

1938

essential. Something has to be generated *unconsciously* before it appears clearly in the mind. . . . I am an *anachronism* in an age of *machers* who can get to work as soon as they have a subject. Without inspiration and inner heat, I am *less talented* than those types. My associations don't start moving until the emotion is there." Besides, the *Pascarella II* idea was not suitable for the United States, as the first novel had not appeared there. And it was from the United States that the author who had been banned in Germany expected his salvation: "There just is no other *real* help for us except success in America!"

At the beginning of the year, the Jeremiah novel, *Hearken Unto the Voice*, had been published by Viking Press in New York, and Ben Huebsch sent a telegram saying that prepublication orders and first reviews had been most encouraging. At first Werfel did not want to believe in an American success for his epic on the prophets: although he thought the book "the weightiest and most complex of all of mine," he did not assume "that this *untam* [Yiddish-Viennese word for someone hounded by bad luck, an awkward person; here it refers to the prophet Jeremiah], the most grandiose in all of history, would achieve a posthumous success."

In Austria, the political situation was moving toward a flashpoint. Chancellor Schuschnigg found himself the target of ever more aggressive polemics from Berlin. "The Nazis' new wave of attack" was being treated by the Austrian government, as Werfel feared, with excessively "great fear and kid gloves." In his opinion Schuschnigg should have "called for an instant plebiscite" immediately upon his return from his talks with Hitler. It took the Austrian chancellor until March 9 to see his way to that decision: he called upon the Austrian people to decide their own fate on March 13. If the majority would vote for the Anschluss of Austria to the German Reich, Schuschnigg (who was counting on an overwhelming show of support for the sovereignty of the Austrian state) would respect it. Word of the referendum triggered hectic reactions in Berlin: German troops were massed on the border with Austria, and Schuschnigg was asked to postpone the referendum and, finally, to resign. On March 11 the chancellor of Austria did resign, declaring in his last radio speech that he was yielding to force. The following night, a National Socialist government was proclaimed under the leadership of Arthur Seyss-Inquart. On the morning of March 12, the German Wehrmacht marched into Austria, greeted with jubilation by most of the populace. The Austrian army joined the German troops, and Adolf Hitler's dream of joining his homeland to the German Reich had come true. Hitler entered Vienna in triumph on March 15, feted by hundreds of thousands who lined the main streets of the city.

"This Sunday, March 13, my heart is almost breaking with pain, even though Austria is not my homeland," Werfel wrote in his Capri diary. "O house in Breitenstein, where I worked for twenty years, shall I never see you again?" An attack of angina accompanied by a high fever had been "divine succor"—thanks to "feverish somnolence," he had experienced "these abominable days that are now forcing me for the third time since '33 into a new epoch of life" only "as if through a veil." And he wrote, on the last page of the first act of *The Lost Mother,* "The Finis Austriae renders this piece a fragment."

Alma fled Vienna, going first to Prague with her daughter Anna, then on to Milan, where she was reunited with a despairing Franz Werfel. They then went to Zurich, where Werfel's sister Marianne Rieser had invited them to stay in her villa in Rüschlikon. Little by little, the extent of the catastrophe became apparent to Werfel: more deeply shocking news arrived from Austria every day. Two days after Hitler's entry into Vienna, Werfel's friend Egon Friedell had taken his life by throwing himself out of the window of his apartment. Kurt von Schuschnigg had been arrested immediately. Csokor, Zuckmayer, Horváth, and most other members of Werfel's circle of friends left Austria within hours; all who began their flight too late were captured and disappeared into prisons and concentration camps. In Vienna alone, 67,000 people were arrested in the first few days after Hitler's entry. Because of his loyalty to Schuschnigg, Johannes Hollnsteiner was deported to Dachau as a political prisoner. Vienna's Jewish quarter in the second district became the scene of pogromlike atrocities committed by the Storm Troopers and their cohorts. Throughout the city and the whole country, open season had been declared overnight on all Jewish men, women, and children.

Soon after the completed Anschluss, the Viennese dailies, duly brought into line, wrote about the "Werfel" (a wordplay on *Würfel,* or die) being cast: now that the "Jewish charade" was over, thank God, even that Jew from Prague, Schuschnigg's favorite, Franz Werfel, with his arrogant aristocratic crowd of admirers, would "never rise again" in Greater Germany.

Werfel had fallen into a state of absolute indecisiveness and spiritual paralysis. In April he wrote to Kurt Wolff saying that he had now spent three weeks in Zurich "without having made a definite decision for the future." In the meantime, on the tenth of the month, a well-organized referendum had been held under Nazi auspices: 99.7 percent of the Austrians said yes to the Anschluss of the "Ostmark" (as Austria was now called) to the German Reich.

In the Rieser household, there were tensions between Alma and her sister-in-law Marianne, not least due to Alma's frequent anti-Semitic remarks. After attending to basic passport formalities, the Werfels left Switzerland at the end of April and went first to Paris; then, a week later, via Amsterdam to London. "It really doesn't matter to us *what* happens and *where* we live," Werfel had written to Alma as recently as early March. "We are at home everywhere." But now, after the catastrophe, after the loss of the working studio in Breitenstein and the villa at Hohe Warte, the search for a new home proved to be a painful and demeaning reality.

In mid-May, Gottfried Bermann Fischer visited Werfel in a London hotel. The son-in-law of the publisher Samuel Fischer had become the director of S. Fischer Verlag in 1934 but had to emigrate from Berlin to Vienna in 1936 and then flee Austria in the days of the Anschluss. He was now staying in Stockholm, hoping to be able to establish Bermann-Fischer Verlag there. He had come to England to persuade Werfel to sign a publishing contract: after the coup in Vienna, Werfel's relationship with Paul Zsolnay Verlag seemed unclear, and there had been no communication between the author and his publisher, who was still in Vienna. At the time Werfel had no plans for an extended work, but he agreed with every point of Fischer's proposal, which guaranteed him a monthly income.

Werfel liked London much better than he had expected and tried to persuade his wife to choose the city as their place of exile: he felt that Anna Mahler's decision to establish her new home there was an additional reason. Alma, however, absolutely refused to remain in Great Britain and insisted on going back to France.

In Paris the Werfels took lodgings in a small but comfortable hotel close to the Madeleine, the Opera, and the Gare St. Lazare. At the beginning of June 1938 the Royal-Madeleine, on rue Pasquier, became their new home. They met fellow exiles every day, in the streets, cafés, and restaurants; the city was teeming with émigrés. Often fighting with each other, these people who had fled persecution in Germany and Austria—monarchists and communists, Schuschnigg supporters and socialists—often shared the smallest spaces and anxiously waited for what else this, the most difficult time in their lives, would bring.

On June 1, the day the Werfels arrived in Paris, their friend Ödön von Horváth died in an unusually absurd manner: during a violent storm, he was killed by a heavy branch from a shattered chestnut tree on the Champs-Elysées. "I have seen the face of a dead man," Werfel noted in his diary. "It was in the hospital mortuary. A terrible cellar. . . . Exhausted by the brooding heat of the summer's day, the mourners crowded into that narrow and bare cellar space. They were mostly writers, refugees, exiles, people without hope in a strange land. . . . In all of their faces there was so much pain, so much distraction and destruction, that everyone seemed to shrink back from the rest. . . . If it didn't sound so horrible, one might say that, among all these yellow and greenish gray faces who had gathered to mourn him, [Horváth] looked like the healthiest, handsomest one."

The burial took place in the cemetery of the Parisian suburb of St. Ouen. Here, too, the writers in French exile foregathered: Werfel, Joseph Roth, Carl Zuckmayer, Walter Mehring, and others. The brief eulogies were drowned out by trains thundering past the cemetery. All his life, Horváth had liked trains, and now his grave lay in the immediate vicinity of railroad tracks: every train that left the Gare du Nord passed by it.

In mid-June, Werfel moved away from the humid heat of the metropolis to the suburb of St. Germain-en-Laye, about twenty minutes by train from the center of Paris. He had felt quite ill and weak for several days, and hoped to recuperate from what he suspected to be nicotine poisoning. In the hotel Pavillon Henri IV, an annex to the building in which Louis XIV was born, he took a very large room with a fine view across the Seine and the outskirts of Paris: he could spot the tip of the Eiffel Tower on the horizon. The hotel was near the Château St. Germain, where in 1919 an Austrian delegation had signed the peace conditions set by the Allies, sealing the dissolution of the Austro-Hungarian Empire and the fragmentation of Central Europe.

Werfel took daily walks in the large park of the château and the even larger oak forest that surrounded it, and slowly recovered from the physical and psychological ordeals of the last weeks and months. Alma was meanwhile traveling in the South of France, looking for a better place for both of them. She liked the climate of this region, which is similar to that of the Ligurian coast, and thought it would be better for Werfel's health and work to gain more distance from the excitements and strains of Paris. Her choice was the small fishing town of Sanary-sur-Mer, near Marseilles, where painters, writers, and philosophers who had left Germany since 1933 had already established a kind of artists' colony in exile. The first to arrive in St. Cyr, right next to Sanary, had been the art historian Julius Meier-Graefe; Heinrich and Thomas Mann, René Schickele, Lion Feuchtwanger, Bertolt Brecht, Ernst Bloch, Arthur Koestler, and others followed. After a brief search, Alma, assisted by her friend Anne Marie Meier-Graefe, the art historian's wife, located what she felt was a suitable place: an old Saracen tower with a little garden behind it, situated high above Sanary. Le Moulin Gris towered above the lovely bay like a lighthouse.

"I feel more ill than ever," Werfel wrote in his diary on July 1, 1938, in St. Germain. "My head feels as if it were full of water. It threatens to explode from interior pressure." A hastily summoned physician diagnosed a mild heart attack. Alma left Sanary immediately and had Werfel transported from St. Germain to Paris. During the next few days he suffered from weakness, acute fear of death, nausea, and depression. Every few hours he was given injections to lower his extremely high blood pressure. "My God, what is going to happen?!" he wrote, but he recovered more quickly than expected, due to Alma's energy and self-sacrifice.

Four weeks after the attack, the Werfels moved to Sanary-sur-Mer on the Côte d'Azur. Werfel particularly liked the circular room on the second floor of Le Moulin Gris. It had twelve large windows that rattled in the wind, and Werfel loved the view of the open sea from his desk. He began to have hopes for the future again as he wrote sketches and short dramatic texts as well as poems, among them "Ballad of Illness" ("Ballade von der Krankheit") and a poem against Hitler, "The Greatest Man of All Time," ("Der grösste Mann aller Zeiten"). The events of two of the dramatic sketches, "The Physician of Vienna" ("Der Arzt von Wien") and "The Actress" ("Die Schauspielerin"), take place on the day the German army entered Austria.

"When I manage to get some work done, which I do now and then," Werfel wrote to his father-in-law, Carl Moll, "I still feel the great fundamental problems of mankind as ever, but desperately little politics and partisan rage and hatred, even though there are many who expect those feelings from me now." Moll, influenced by his daughter Maria and her husband, the lawyer Dr. Richard Eberstaller, had been a Nazi sympathizer long before the Anschluss but nevertheless kept up his close friendship with Werfel. In the meantime, the villa on Steinfeldgasse and the house in Breitenstein had become the property of the Molls and the Eberstallers; the onetime Haus Mahler had been festively decorated with swastika flags and renamed Haus Eberstaller. "The enemy can hurt my freedom of choice and my creature comforts, but he can't hurt me where I *truly* exist, he can't even *reach* me there," Werfel claimed in his letter to Moll. "Even when I try to assist him in the endeavor, he does not manage to intrude into my creative realm. In my true thoughts and talents, he does not exist."

A few days after his forty-eighth birthday, Franz Werfel began a big new project. Despite his protestations to Carl Moll that he did not want to deal with political questions, he now planned a novel trilogy in which he would expose the Nazi terror. His first title for it was *Illness That Leads to Life* (*Krankheit, die zum Leben führt*). It was the story of Cella Bodenheim, a half-Jewish young woman who must leave Austria after the Anschluss and lead the life of an emigrant, first in Paris, then in New York. "*Danger:* echoes of *Musa Dagh*" reads one of his first notes for the novel. "Avoid the word *Jew* if possible." But Cella's father, the Jewish lawyer Hans Bodenheim, became—perhaps against Werfel's original intention—the real protagonist of the first part of the trilogy.

Werfel chose Burgenland, the easternmost province of Austria, as the main setting for the novel. He liked the harsh, flat landscape around Lake Neusiedler, liked Eisenstadt and the vineyard villages along the Hungarian border. But what had once seemed light and joyful now seemed ominous and dark, enveloped in a mood of wintry grief—not a region of peace, not a land of security.

With great precision, Werfel described all layers of Austrian society, from the unemployed to the aristocrats to the clerics, from teenagers inflamed by Nazism to dreamwalking old monarchists to assimilated Jews; he drew the milieu of Austria between the fall of 1937 and the spring of 1938 in concise, unsentimental language that made the work read, in places, like a documentary: "Suddenly, the mass of people was ready, the operatic chorus of a first night in history. Now it broke loose, the song of murder that consists of only two notes: *Sieg Heil! Sieg Heil! Sieg Heil!* Like the braying of an automatic donkey as big as a mountain! Like a Stone Age war cry, mechanized in the Industrial Age." And he characterized, with all the incisiveness he could muster, the kind of people who had sold their souls to Nazism: "There was, in the faces of these men, a grandiose emptiness and absence from self, the likes of which had probably never existed before in the course of history. . . . They lived as cleanly, precisely, without thought, without conscience as motors. They were only waiting to be turned on or off. . . . Robots."

The Munich Pact between England, France, and Germany, signed at the end of September 1938, permitted Hitler to annex the Sudetenland—"a high point of horror and shame!" as Werfel noted after he heard that the western region of Czechoslovakia, mostly settled by German-speaking Czechs, would become the next victim of Germany's policy of expansion. "I feel more for Bohemia than I would ever have suspected." The danger of a world war loomed large in Europe. At this time, Werfel contacted the Czech consul in Marseilles to inform him that he wanted to put himself at the disposal of the Beneš government in whatever capacity it saw fit and was now waiting in Sanary to hear whether he would be entrusted with a task and what it would be.

Werfel's response to the German annexation of the Sudetenland in October was a series of short essays that aggressively insisted on the sovereignty of the state of Czechoslovakia and declared solidarity with the Czech people. These were published in exile newspapers in Paris and London. "Just drops in the bucket," as Werfel admitted to his parents, who were visiting their daughter Marianne in Zurich. As soon as his new novel had reached "a certain point . . . that secures the book," he would, he assured his parents, come to visit them. He told them that he and Alma had applied for a visa to the United States but that they intended to emigrate only when "political necessity arrives at the door-step." Life in France was "charming and cheap," and working conditions in his sanctuary, Sanary, were "incomparable." Financially, too, the Werfels seemed to be in good shape, at least for the time being: Alma had received royalties for Gustav Mahler's works from the composers' association in Vienna, and *Juarez and Maximilian* was to be made into a Hollywood movie the following year—the contract with Warner Brothers was almost ready to sign.

Kristallnacht in Germany, November 9, 1938, was the most violent pogrom since Hitler had assumed power: synagogues, Jewish shops, department stores, and private buildings were burned down, destroyed, and plundered, and more than a hundred Jews were murdered—scenes beside which the events described in Werfel's Cella novel seemed relatively tame. Now Werfel felt that the timely, straightforward subject matter of the planned trilogy had been overtaken by the latest political events and the almost unimaginable atrocities of everyday reality. He began to feel doubtful about the project and even toyed with the idea of abandoning it.

He reacted to Kristallnacht by writing a commentary, "Israel's Gift to Humanity" ("Das Geschenk Israels an die Menschheit"), for the Paris émigré publication *Das Neue Tage-Buch*. In it he emphasized the important contributions Jews had made to cultural and spiritual developments in world history, and their great range from Moses to Kafka, Jesus to Freud, Marx to Mahler. "A dark commandment," he noted, "compels this people without a country and without a language, to make a gift to others of all it owns of its life of the spirit and not to keep anything back for itself. Once again Israel is on the road, its bundle on its back and no valid passport in its pocket. Frightened, it appears among the good nations that still allow it entry (for how long?) and raises its hands."

Werfel's reunion with his parents took place at the end of November in Rüschlikon. His sister Hanna had come from Prague to join them. In a deeply anxious mood, the family discussed whether they should stay in Europe and wait to see if Hitler's expansionist urge would be satisfied after the annexation of the Sudetenland, averting the danger of another world war. The eighty-year-old Rudolf Werfel pleaded for immediate emigration to America. "Papa tortures me with his whining: 'Save your lives, you and Alma,'" Werfel wrote to his wife. "He imagines that the Gestapo will shoot us if we stay in Europe." Werfel's father gave his son five thousand dollars to tide him over during the initial period in the United States. The poor state of Rudolf Werfel's health, his alarming fragility, caused his son to fear that his father could not stand up to the hardships of emigration.

He himself felt much better than he had in the summer months but had to observe a strict diet and totally refrain from smoking. "I hope I'll be 'normal' again soon," he wrote to Alma, who was now in London: after receiving the news of her mother's death, she had gone to stay with her daughter Anna. Werfel tried to console his wife and assured her that he was in love with her "as on the first day and again and again with new powers and from new sources."

He went to Paris in mid-December to sign the contract for *Juarez*. Shooting of John Huston's adaptation of the play, under the direction of William Dieterle, who as an actor had worked for Max Reinhardt, was to begin in the new year. Werfel was paid $3,500, and this made him feel quite confident. A few days before the new year he wrote to Gottfried Bermann Fischer, "The new year stands before us. Very sphinxlike. Can it get worse than '38?? Possibly! Nevertheless, and for no sensible reason, I am curiously optimistic in my premonitions."

In the mayor's office of Sanary-sur-Mer, the little town on the Côte d'Azur, the names Franz Werfel and Alma Mahler ring no bells. The helpful officials turn the pages of numerous hefty folios and check hundreds of yellowed index cards but are unable to discover any reference to the Werfels' ever having lived there. Even Le Moulin Gris, their erstwhile residence, is not known here. A young police officer gives me advice: "You should visit Monsieur Bartholomé Rotget. He'll be able to help you. He knows everything about the Germans who were here before the war."

My way to the Rue de la Harmonie at the edge of town takes me down a palm-lined promenade past the small fishing port. The cafés with their big outdoor terraces still bear the same names as when Sanary became the center of German literature in exile: Le Marine, La Nautique, Le Lyon. Even the Hôtel de la Tour is still there, the first stop for most of the emigrants before they found a place to stay in Sanary and its environs.

Orchids are the passion of Monsieur Rotget, a sinewy elderly gentleman and former Foreign Legionnaire who fought in Indochina in the 1950s. He knows every precious flowering species of orchid, at least by name. "And my second passion is the history of Sanary, especially the years of German emigration to the South of France. I know every little cottage where the German writers lived. Today, no one here even mentions those people anymore. The names Thomas Mann, Lion Feuchtwanger, Franz Werfel don't mean anything here. In the official history of the town, A Thousand Years of Sanary, *you won't find one word about the refugees."*

M. *Rotget drives me to the villa where Lion Feuchtwanger lived from 1933 until his arrest in 1939. "You know, Ludwig Marcuse once said, 'Sanary was the capital of German literature!' But no one here pays any attention to that. There was no hostility back then; people were just totally indifferent to those writers. And it's still that way." We are standing in front of the high fence of the splendid villa Valmer, where Feuchtwanger wrote his antifascist novel* The Oppermanns (Die Geschwister Oppermann) *and worked on the sequel to his historical novel* Josephus. *"This house and its garden were the most important gathering place of those exiled writers," M. Rotget says. "Every newcomer showed up here first, and then they would come back—there were regular weekly meetings—to exchange ideas, to discuss crises. See over there? That terrace was where it all took place."*

We cross a grove of cedars rustling in the breeze and, after a steep climb, reach the top of the hill and the villa La Tranquille, a building surrounded by cacti, cypresses, and wild brambles. "Thomas Mann stayed here at the beginning of his exile, in 1933. But that house had to be rebuilt after the war: the Nazis dynamited a number of buildings up here to get a clear line of fire. You see, they expected the Allies to land nearby, in Marseilles or Toulon. And where do you think those German soldiers who destroyed everything up here were quartered? In Le Moulin Gris, quite close by."

The round three-story tower stands on the edge of a steep cliff, high above Sanary Bay, facing the chapel Notre-Dame-de-Pitié. A small plaque affixed to the wall of the Saracen tower reminds us that the painter J. G. Darragnès (1886–1950) resided here for a while. It is an unassuming building with a flat, slightly tilted roof. It is now inhabited by Monsieur and Madame Romans from Lyons. The lively lady of the house takes me on a tour: first the kitchen on the ground floor, then the other tiny rooms. She is surprised by my interest in an author of whom she has never heard. "I know that Parmelin, the writer, used to live here after the war. She told me that a writer by the name of Fecktwanger, something like that, had rented the tower before the war. So that wasn't right? Well, there you are, that's how history gets written, with people making things up based on erroneous information."

In the Werfels' former bedroom, on the second floor of the tower, M. Romans is reclining on a couch. He rises with difficulty, gray of skin and beard, very tall but emaciated and stooped; he stands there while his wife chatters animatedly, hears that a writer called Franz Werfel once lived here and wrote novels on the top floor. M. Romans acknowledges it all with some incomprehensible phrase and lies back down on the couch.

A narrow circular staircase takes me to the top, to Werfel's round workroom, a space he enjoyed a great deal; it even consoled him a little for the loss of the Haus Mahler in Breitenstein—the loss of his mansard studio with the rough wooden walls and a view, over the top of a tall beech tree, of the Rax and Schneeberg peaks. Nine of the twelve windows have been bricked up since the war; the three remaining have a view that extends to the horizon over the open sea. A bright room in the sky, on the edge of a precipitous coastline. The wall is crumbling. Today only a rickety table, a narrow bed, and two broken lamps stand on the stone floor.

Heaven and Hell

Y ET ANOTHER INFERNAL outrage!" Franz Werfel noted in mid-March 1939. "Prague occupied by the *boches!* Hanna waited too long." Now Prague, Bohemia, and Moravia had become German protectorates, and the city of Werfel's birth had been incorporated into Adolf Hitler's Third Reich. His sister's family was in mortal danger, as was Willy Haas, who years ago had moved back to Prague from Berlin and now found himself trapped in his native city. Werfel, who in the meantime had been appointed honorary president of the Austrian PEN Club in exile, immediately sent a telegram to British PEN asking them to invite Haas to London on some urgent pretext.

Two weeks later the ever increasing pace of political events made it impossible for Werfel to continue work on his trilogy about the half-Jewish pianist Cella Bodenheim. Not long before, he had told his publisher G. B. Fischer that the book's first draft would be about eight hundred pages long and represent a kind of *Musa Dagh* of the past twelve months, "powered" by his personal sense of having lost his homeland.

His main concern at this time was to see that Hanna, her husband, and their children managed to get out of Prague, and the Fuchs-Robetins arrived in Switzerland at the end of April 1939, safe and sound. Werfel traveled to meet them, and the whole family was reunited in Rüschlikon. "Alma and I still haven't decided . . . whether to stay in France or go on to America (perhaps as soon as May 3)," Werfel wrote to Fischer from Rüschlikon. But he managed to change his wife's mind: they would emigrate, but only if there was absolutely no other choice or if war broke out.

"Perhaps I can slip in a smaller book (a simple, human-interest subject, something I'm good at) that I could finish by Christmas," he wrote to his publisher after abandoning the Cella novel. In early May, in the round room of Le Moulin Gris, he started writing this new book, *The Story of a Maid* (*Geschichte einer Magd*), based on an idea Alma had given him. It had been years since Alma last influenced her husband's choice of subject matter, but, having seen how hard he had taken what he considered the failure of the Cella project, she now suggested to him the true story of Agnes Hvizd, a woman who had been Alma's cook for many years. She had served in the household in Gustav Mahler's lifetime and left her post only after the Werfels moved to Hohe Warte. She died in 1933, at the age of seventy-two.

For many years Agnes had sent all her savings to a nephew, in the firm belief that the young man was getting a theological education and would one day—when he had become a priest and his generous aunt had passed on—secure her a good place in heaven by means of his daily prayers. The young scoundrel misused the funds provided by his benefactress, neither going to divinity school nor even contemplating the priesthood. When Agnes finally realized the deception, her world collapsed, and she only recovered a little from the shock after making a pilgrimage to Rome and taking part in a group audience with Pope Pius XI.

Werfel wrote the story of Agnes Hvizd with great pleasure and enthusiasm, a welcome change from the daily struggle with the Cella project. In a few days he completed several chapters. He was suddenly feeling much stronger and healthier; the new book, *Embezzled Heaven* (*Der veruntreute Himmel*), was not going to be just a "stopgap," he assured G. B. Fischer, "but a fully valid Christmas present."

The tale of the cook Teta Linek, as she is called in the novel, is intertwined with another narrative consisting of thinly disguised autobiographical elements. Theo, the other protagonist of *Embezzled Heaven*, is an exiled writer who reminisces about his stay in the country house of "the Argans," patrons of the arts. While Austria was still free, Theo had retired there in order to recuperate from the strain caused by an abandoned work (an obvious reference to *Cella*). "I feel my exile as a summons to renewal. . . . Yet I will not deny the sadness by which I am seized at this moment as I think of the house at Grafenegg and the room there which I called my own." Grafenegg in the Mountains of the Dead was a simple disguise for Breitenstein on the Semmering Pass, and the furnishings, scents, and colors of the wood-paneled house, the parties and celebrations, all correspond to Werfel's favorite place and its own history of the past twenty years.

The first version of *Embezzled Heaven* was completed as early as June 1939. Werfel told his publisher that he didn't usually believe in his work while it was still in progress, but this time seemed to be an exception, and his prognosis for the book was quite optimistic: what had been merely a "primitive attempt" in the commercially successful *The Man Who Conquered Death* had been "polyphonally elaborated" in this book. Teta, the heroine, a soul sister to Barbara, had to be regarded as "an exemplary instance of simple popular Catholic piety." While he was working on the second draft, he informed Fischer that he considered this "story of a maid . . . one of the best books" he had ever written.

One of the first people to whom he gave the finished manuscript was his friend and editor of many years, Ernst Polak, who was now living in exile in London. "Remember, I wrote the novel twice in about ten weeks," Werfel told Polak by way of apologizing for possible stylistic or dramatic shortcomings. "Surely this *Embezzled Heaven* is one of my most architectonic books. . . . The narrative is modeled, to a certain extent, on the musical fugue. . . . The subject: death and the hereafter." In any case, he had "taken endless pains" in the construction of the book.

Werfel also asked his friends Lion Feuchtwanger and René Schickele for their opinions of the book before it went to press, and both predicted enduring success and even confirmed that *Embezzled Heaven* was the best work Werfel had ever produced in this genre. Fischer had asked his author to choose another title, but after exchanging several letters they agreed to keep the original one. Werfel suggested that the publisher use thick paper and a large typeface for the first edition, saying that his readers were used to books of from eight hundred to a thousand pages, and it was important to avoid the impression that this was only a marginal or "stopgap" work.

The Werfels led a lively social life with their friends and fellow exiles in Sanary. Walter Hasenclever lived nearby, in Cagnes-sur-Mer; Ludwig Marcuse, Robert Neumann, and Arnold Zweig belonged to their circle of friends, and almost daily Werfel met the journalist Wilhelm Herzog, the communist writer and physician Friedrich Wolf, and Lion Feuchtwanger in the cafés and on the beach promenades. They talked mostly about the extremely precarious and—for every one of them—life-threatening political situation. Werfel and Feuchtwanger had regular arguments, during which Werfel became tremendously excited while Feuchtwanger always remained calm and unshakably certain of his convictions.

On August 22, one day before the signing of the Nazi-Soviet Pact, Hitler ordered the Wehrmacht to march into Poland on September 1. He had commanded his "Death's Head" units to "send any man, woman, and child of Polish origin and language to their deaths." Only by physically destroying the adversary would it be possible to gain the *Lebensraum* Germany so badly needed. When voices were heard saying that genocide might further damage the already bad reputation of the German Reich abroad, the Führer replied that only a little less than twenty-five years after the extermination of the Armenian people, no one in the world was talking about the Turkish government's actions.

After Hitler's attack on Poland, France and Britain declared war on Germany. Instantly, German-speaking immigrants in France were regarded as undesirable aliens, possible spies, members of a fifth column, or Bolshevik fomenters of unrest. House searches and arrests in the streets became daily events. In the vicinity of the Sanary courthouse, Franz Werfel was stopped by a burly policeman who shouted that the author surely wrote his poems and novels mainly for the proletariat. "No," replied the intimidated Werfel, "I write them for everybody." He was verbally and in some cases even physically abused on the street by local people.

During an interrogation in nearby La Seyne, he was afraid he might faint from fear; the investigating official was slowly turning the pages of blacklists, but it turned out that the summons had been issued by mistake. "But I'm still quite ill from it," Werfel wrote in his diary. "At the end of the interrogation, Alma showed the commissioner my picture in the magazine *Match* with the caption 'Un des plus grands écrivains contemporains' ['One of the greatest contemporary authors']. We take that picture everywhere. It's really comical."

In mid-September, Werfel volunteered for the Czechoslovak Legion. Should he be fit for service (which was hardly to be expected), he regarded it as his patriotic duty, he informed the Czech consulate in Marseilles, to bear arms against the Nazi regime or at least to perform clerical duties behind the lines.

"The Hitler gang will be destroyed; no doubt about it." With these words he encouraged both himself and Fischer. "Perhaps we'll all be permitted to enjoy a modest future." But a new edict from the French government declared that all males of German origin who were not past fifty would be put in a French internment camp, at least temporarily. Uncertain whether he, as a German from Prague, would be counted as a member of this group, Werfel spent days and nights of fear and despair in Le Moulin Gris.

In the course of the summer, before the outbreak of war, Rudolf and Albine Werfel, Hanna, and her husband, Herbert von Fuchs-Robetin, had moved from Zurich to Vichy in central France, a step they now bitterly regretted. To make matters worse, Franz Werfel's eighty-two-year-old father had recently suffered a stroke and seemed to be declining rapidly. At the end of October Werfel at last succeeded in obtaining a travel permit, a *sauf conduit*, which allowed him to visit his family for at least a few days.

In early December, Werfel reported to the draft board of the Czechoslovak Legion and was examined by a regimental physician. "I wouldn't have believed it possible that I would once more stand in front of the yardstick of a draft board," he wrote to his mother in Vichy. "I had to laugh at myself in my Adamic nakedness. It is all like a grotesque dream." However, and by no means surprisingly, the regimental physician declared Werfel unfit for military service.

Urged on by Alma, Wilhelm Herzog started a campaign to award Franz Werfel the Nobel Prize for Literature in the coming year, on his fiftieth birthday. At the end of 1939, Herzog organized a petition and asked former Nobel Prize winners and members of the most highly respected academies of the arts and sciences to support it; it was his intention to present the entire list to the Nobel Committee in Stockholm. One of the first to respond to Herzog's initiative was Thomas Mann, who said that while he certainly admired Werfel's work, he had already voted for Hermann Hesse, whose prospects looked better to him, since Hesse belonged to a "higher German tradition."

After an extended stay in Paris and another visit to his parents in Vichy, Werfel started work in February 1940 on a "tricky little marital story." He warned his publisher that it was "something I have never tried before" and at the same time announced that upon completion of this novella he would turn to his true "favorite idea," the sequel to *The Pascarella Family.* He had "really wonderful plans" for this big novel.

The marital story, *April in October (Eine blassblaue Frauenschrift)*, dealt with Leonidas, a prominent civil servant, and his wife, Amelie; like *Cella,* it reflected the tragedy of Austria, the Anschluss to the German Reich. The greatest fear in Leonidas's life is his "relationship with a Jewess eighteen years earlier, at the beginning of his marriage," Werfel noted in his sketchbook. "Convinced there is a child, his only son . . ." Vera Wormser, the author of the letter in pale blue handwriting that plunges Leonidas into violent conflicts of conscience, is the most positive Jewish character in Werfel's oeuvre, aside from his portrayal of the prophet Jeremiah. Werfel's Jewish characters usually have a degree of self-contempt and are depicted with kindly, compassionate forbearance (for example, the convert Kompert in *Embezzled Heaven*) for their supposed crudity, lack of sensitivity, and pushiness, but Vera Wormser is very different than that cliché: her aristocratic, forgiving behavior places her far above the Austrian civil servant Leonidas, who starts his social climb by marrying a wealthy woman.

German troops occupied Denmark and Norway in April 1940. In a brief radio address, Werfel spoke to his Norwegian listeners: "The treacherously attacked land has fallen prey to the bandit. Now Norway lies in chains. No! Only Norway's hands are shackled. Norway's soul is free." The French writer Jules Romains, since 1936 president of PEN International, asked Werfel to write six more speeches against Nazi Germany to be used by French radio as counterpropaganda. On May 10, the Wehrmacht marched into Belgium, the Netherlands, and Luxembourg. An attack on France was expected any day, and the propaganda assignment was dropped.

At the Hôtel Royal-Madeleine in Paris the Werfels lived in constant fear of bombing raids: nine hundred civilians had perished in a German raid on Rotterdam. The alarm was sounded practically every night; all hotel guests had to leave their rooms and spend several hours in the cellar. All of France was in tumult, and tens of thousands of immigrants with their very particular fear of a German invasion wanted to leave what had been their sanctuary as quickly as possible.

The French authorities required all men and women between the ages of fifteen and seventy-five who had been born within the territory of the new Greater Germany to register immediately so they could be interned at a later date. Once more Franz visited his mortally ill father, who now scolded him fiercely for not having emigrated to America two years earlier, when it would still have been relatively easy, instead of hoping to escape now, when it was really too late: both Franz's and Alma's U.S. visas had expired.

Lion Feuchtwanger, Friedrich Wolf, and Walter Hasenclever had already been interned in the French camp of Les Milles near Aix-en-Provence when the Werfels arrived in Sanary at the end of May, for only a few days, to dissolve the household at Le Moulin Gris in great haste. They spent the next two weeks at consulates in Marseilles, desperately trying to obtain new immigration papers for the United States.

When Hitler marched into France in early June 1940, meeting very little military resistance and taking Paris on June 14, Werfel immediately wanted to make a run for Spain, even without valid visas. After an odyssey with many mishaps, many journeys in taxicabs, limousines, and trains, the Werfels finally reached Bordeaux, in a state of almost total exhaustion. They lost all their luggage on this journey, including valuable original manuscripts and their remaining wardrobe.

Shortly before their arrival Bordeaux had been badly bombed by the Germans, and chaos reigned everywhere. The French government under Premier Paul Reynaud, which had fled there from Paris, announced its resignation. The city was an armed camp, with soldiers and civilians, refugees from the northern regions of the country, entering it in a steady stream. After the aged Marshal Pétain had taken over the reins of government and Germany had presented its first armistice agreement, things calmed down for a while. For the Werfels, this was a signal to continue their flight without delay.

Biarritz, Bayonne, Hendaye, and St. Jean-de-Luz were the next way stations. Time and again they had to spend great amounts of money to hire automobiles and drivers, and to pay for gasoline. The refugees encountered the same scene everywhere: thousands of desperate people were laying siege to the Spanish and Portuguese consulates, hoping to receive visas to freedom.

The German forces were closing in, and a Portuguese consul in St. Jean-de-Luz was rumored to be providing every émigré with valid papers without complications. When Franz Werfel finally arrived at this assumed savior's door, he was told that the consul had gone mad a few days before and tossed a great number of the passports at his disposal into the sea.

After France signed the armistice agreement, three-fifths of the country came under German occupation. German soldiers advanced as far as Hendaye, reaching the township on the Spanish border on the same day as the Werfels. For the first time since they had left Sanary, Franz Werfel lost his composure and had a nervous breakdown. In the internment camp of Les Milles, some five hundred kilometers east of Hendaye, Walter Hasenclever took his own life with an overdose of Veronal to avoid falling into the hands of the Gestapo.

Werfel calmed down after Vicky von Kahler, his friend from Prague days, managed to obtain some fuel and a taxi. The Werfels and the Kahlers pressed on—they had met briefly and accidentally once before on this journey, in Biarritz—and after an extremely difficult drive reached Orthez, which looked like a ghost town: it had been designated a border crossing town of the occupied zone. In Pau, the capital of the Pyrenees, where they arrived at dawn the following day, the refugees learned that Lourdes, the shrine town, was the only place for miles around in which it might just be possible to find lodgings in the midst of all the chaos and collapse. They rented another automobile for the remaining thirty kilometers and arrived in Lourdes on June 27, 1940. Though the town had about three hundred hotels, they were at first unable to get a room. Even Lourdes—world-famous for the visions of the Virgin seen there by Bernadette Soubirous, a miller's daughter—was terribly overcrowded. After a search, Alma found a place for them: the proprietress of the Hôtel Vatican decided to move a young couple out of their tiny room, and, for the first time since their departure from Marseilles a little less than a fortnight before, the Werfels were able to relax for a short while.

They had come to Lourdes chiefly to obtain new safe-conducts for a return to Marseilles, having abandoned their plan to flee to Spain without valid papers. Only in Marseilles, the Werfels thought, would it still be possible for them to get the necessary visas. They sent a number of telegrams to the United States, urgently pleading for help. One of these was addressed to the American Guild for German Cultural Freedom, an organization founded by the journalist Prince Hubertus Löwenstein, who had emigrated to America.

The German Reich demanded a more stringent internment policy from the Pétain government: the arrest of all citizens of the Greater German Reich without exception. Every former Austrian, Czech, or Pole could be arrested, taken to French internment camps, and handed over to the Gestapo on demand. In mid-July 1940 numerous foreign newspapers (such as the *New York Post,* on its front page) reported that, according to BBC broadcasts, the famed author Franz Werfel had been shot and killed while trying to escape the Nazis.

After Vichy became the capital city of the new French government, Werfel's parents left and moved to Bergerac, a sad little provincial town about ninety kilometers east of Bordeaux. They went to a clinic in Bergerac that had been recommended to them, where the mortally ill Rudolf Werfel was put under observation and his wife was able to stay with him. In the meantime, Hanna and her family had managed to get out of France, even though her parents at first did not know where they were. "It is for all of us an unspeakably terrible situation," Werfel wrote to his mother from Lourdes. "But what I find *most* terrible of all is that even Papa and you haven't been spared this." He said he was considering a return to Sanary if his efforts to obtain exit papers in Marseilles once again proved unsuccessful.

Soon the Werfels were given a larger room in the Hôtel Vatican, and Werfel was able to work again for the first time in months. He completed the final draft of his novella *April in October.* During the five weeks of his stay in Lourdes he returned time and again to the center of the shrine, the massive and ugly Basilica of the Immaculate Conception and the grotto at Massabielle, where the Virgin Mary was said to have appeared to the fourteen-year-old Bernadette Soubirous and where, in 1858, the holy spring, whose water had saved the lives of many incurably ill people, had materialized. Millions of pilgrims from all over the world arrived there every year, many of them ailing, seriously ill, or at death's door. In wheelchairs and on stretchers, they were taken to the grotto, and hundreds of bedridden pilgrims often celebrated mass in the open air. The large expanse on the banks of the Gave was then transformed into a sea of dark blue blankets and spume-white habits of the numerous priests.

Alma obtained books about the Lourdes miracle, and from these Werfel learned that the Church had not, in fact, accepted Bernadette's visions at first but, on the contrary, had tried to suppress them by all available means. When the girl insisted that the wondrous lady had appeared to her seventeen times and spoken to her intelligibly every time, the Soubirous family was accused of trying to enrich itself by inventing this story. All threats from clerical and governmental authorities were in vain: the miller's daughter stuck to her story, and she and her family were simply carted off to jail.

Werfel often drank from the spring, hoping for a miracle—the miracle of escape from the enemy, of finding his way out of this desperate, infernal situation and reaching the free world, the United States.

When the police gave the Werfels new safe-conducts to Marseilles in early August 1940, Werfel visited the grotto one more time to make a kind of vow: if his escape to the United States was successful and he survived this intense emotional and physical trial, he would first of all write a book in honor of the sainted Bernadette Soubirous.

In Marseilles the Werfels stayed at the Hôtel Louvre & Paix on the Canebière, the wide main street leading from the railroad station to the old port. The city was like a witches' cauldron. thousands of emigrants congregated here to besiege the consulates. Any country at all, as long as it could be counted among those of the free world—be it China or Argentina, Brazil or India—was now a desirable land of exile.

Marseilles was not yet part of occupied France, but even here there were numerous Gestapo agents and German officers. Some of them even stayed in the Hôtel Louvre & Paix. The Werfels had registered under a false name after making friends with the desk clerk, Monsieur Martin, who could be relied on to warn them of any immediate danger.

The personal intervention of Cordell Hull, the American secretary of state, led to a sudden improvement of the Werfels' situation, only a few days after their arrival in Marseilles: they received transit visas for Spain and Portugal as well as visitors' visas for the United States. Now all they needed were French exit visas, and Werfel addressed an urgent appeal to the influential writer Louis Gillet, a member of the Académie Française: "Nous sommes dans une *situation terrible*—nous sommes quasi prisonniers. . . . Si vous avez une possibilité: Aidez-nous!"

Werfel told his parents that the chances of salvation had improved considerably. "Now only the *visa de sortie* [exit visa] is a problem." However, he found it "incredibly hard to leave the country knowing that you are still here." Then he qualified his optimism: "No one knows if it

will be possible to get out. . . . It's all made worse by the perpetual
rumors that keep one awake at night. We all feel godforsaken." At the
beginning of August the Czech Embassy had informed Werfel that his
name was at the top of a blacklist of intellectuals and artists that France
was absolutely obliged to hand over to the Germans.

In the middle of August, a decisive and even miraculous turn of
events brought to Marseilles a young American Quaker who immediately came to visit the Werfels in their cozy room at the Hôtel Louvre
& Paix: Varian Fry, a courageous idealist, had been sent to France on a
secret mission by a group of European immigrants and independent
American citizens, First Lady Eleanor Roosevelt among them. The
Emergency Rescue Committee's goal was to save endangered scientists,
artists, and intellectuals from the clutches of the Vichy police and the
Gestapo, and bring them to the United States.

"You *must* save us!" Werfel implored the unknown rescuer at their
first meeting, and Alma celebrated Fry's arrival by opening a bottle of
champagne. That evening Fry promised to get the Werfels out of the
country illegally, without exit papers: it was his plan to smuggle them
and Heinrich Mann, his wife Nelly, and nephew Golo, as well as the
Feuchtwangers, to North Africa in a small boat. A short while earlier,
Lion Feuchtwanger had been freed from the San Nicola camp near
Nîmes by the American consul Harry Bingham. He was now in Marseilles. This successful rescue had been initiated by Feuchtwanger's
wife, Marta.

"So now we're forced to make decisions," Werfel wrote to his mother.
"You may not hear anything about us for a while. But don't worry!" The
small vessel chartered by Varian Fry was being stocked with provisions
in the port of Marseilles when members of an Italian armistice commission became suspicious and confiscated the boat, causing the plan to
be aborted. Now Fry decided to take his group on a train from Cerbère
across the Spanish border; this was a risky venture, but his desperate
protégés agreed to it without hesitation.

Franz Werfel's fiftieth birthday was celebrated in a large restaurant at
the port, in nervous anticipation of things to come. The guest of honor
looked years older, marked by the anxieties and strains of exile and the
heart attack of the summer of 1938, from which he had never really
fully recovered.

The next day, the eve of their departure from Marseilles, Werfel
burned the manuscripts of his anti-Nazi essays of the past years in the
fireplace of their hotel room. In the early hours of September 12, 1940,
the refugee group met Varian Fry at the St. Charles railway station. The
Feuchtwangers remained in Marseilles for the time being because it was
rumored that Spanish customs officials were no longer allowing state-

less persons across the border. Feuchtwanger, no longer a German citizen, did not want to endanger his friends by his presence, and Fry promised to escort him and his wife to Spain and Portugal a little later.

The Werfels now had twelve pieces of luggage: the suitcases that had been lost on the trip to Bordeaux—containing, among other things, the uncompleted *Cella*, a few scores by Gustav Mahler, and the score of Anton Bruckner's Third Symphony—had reappeared intact in the meantime. The refugee group, consisting of the Werfels and Heinrich, Nelly, and Golo Mann, accompanied by Fry and his colleague, Dick Ball, now traveled via Narbonne and Perpignan to Cerbère, where they arrived late that evening. French border officials refused to let them go on to Spain without the proper exit visas. Although some customs officials were known to have let refugees cross the border on occasion without valid documents, luck was against them that night of September 12–13, 1940.

Ball had to leave the refugees' passports with a border official. He tried to persuade the man to let his five protégés through, and showed up again the next morning. The official assured him that if he was alone in the office in the afternoon when the train left for Port Bou, he would let the group pass; on that very day, however, a particularly conscientious superior would also be on duty and would certainly double-check each one of his decisions. Hence, he urgently advised Ball to drop this plan and send the two women and three men across the border mountains on foot. Better today than tomorrow, the official said: the next day might bring new regulations issued by the Vichy regime, obliging customs officials to detain every refugee.

Fry and Ball were afraid that both Werfel and the seventy-year-old Heinrich Mann might not be up to the strenuous hike; however, they had no choice but to attempt it. The Werfels left all their luggage with Fry, who, as an American citizen, would have no difficulty boarding the train to Port Bou. They would carry only the essentials; Alma concealed her jewelry and their remaining cash in her clothing.

In the blazing noonday sun, they set out on their perilous march, escorted by Dick Ball. They were following a steep goat path. Driven by terror of falling into the hands of French *gardes mobiles* and the Gestapo, Franz Werfel, drenched in sweat, climbed from one ledge to the next, stumbled through thornbushes, and dragged himself onward.

This difficult ascent must have given him a sense of déjà vu, of the fulfillment of a vision, a prophecy: in 1917, while he was still serving on the East Galician front, he had written the play fragment *Stockleinen*, whose main character was a dictator in a brown uniform. After he has usurped power and installed his brutal regime, many of his opponents try to flee the country. In the second act of the play, Martin, a young laborer, describes the dismal failure of his own attempt to escape: "There were many thousands who wanted to cross the border, the best of the people among them. . . . One stop before the customs station, everybody got off, and the people ran forward on all sides as if to cheat death of each second! No exodus ever compared with this for terror and hope of salvation. As soon as the border posts came into view, an exhausted and terrifying shout of joy burst from the throats of the panting, running band. A mad wave threw itself with closed eyes against the fence. Then it broke. Everyone had to turn back. The roads on the other side had been chained off, the rails had been torn up, a ring of men blocked the way into the valley and the hills. No one would be able to cross. They were the stricken people in the desert, as they reeled back, aged, sere, in rags, covered with dust. The directorate had canceled all trains, by way of revenge. Our friends had disappeared. . . . No one will survive this without being swallowed up."

In about two hours, the Werfels reached the top of Mount Rumpissa, an altitude of seven hundred meters. They had left the rest of the group far behind, and Alma suggested that they go on alone; it would be better in any case to cross the border as a couple and not as part of a group of five or six. They could see a small Spanish customs station immediately below them. When the exhausted Werfels arrived there, the officials thought they were hikers unfamiliar with the terrain and escorted them part of the way, leading them—and the Werfels did not realize this—back toward the French border. To their horror, some of the feared French *gardes mobiles* appeared shortly thereafter but let them go on their way, indeed warning them to make a right turn, not a left, at a fork in the path on top of the mountain, in order to reach the right border post.

Just before the Spanish border they met up again with Heinrich, Nelly, and Golo Mann. In front of the customs officials they all acted as if they knew each other only casually. Alma gave the border policemen generous tips and cigarettes. During the Spanish Civil War, these Catalan gendarmes had fought on the Loyalist side against Franco, and they were sympathetic to antifascists everywhere (among whose number, in these circumstances, Frau Mahler was only too happy to be counted). They let the refugees cross the border without further difficulties.

When they finally reached the small town of Port Bou, after a strenuous descent, in a state of absolute mental and physical exhaustion, they had to submit to yet another grilling, hand over their travel documents yet again, and wait anxiously in a shabby customs station until their passports were returned. After this trial—the last for now—they had achieved what still seemed impossible the previous day: they had escaped from hell. For the first time in three months, since Hitler's invasion of France, Franz Werfel felt free again. He had been saved.

THOMAS MANN—that is all it says on the small brass plate by the entrance to a villa in Kilchberg, near Zurich. This is where the great novelist lived until his death in August 1955. His son, the writer, historian, and critic Golo Mann, now resides in the house on Alte Landstrasse. I ring the doorbell several times, but nobody answers. After ambling aimlessly through the alleys of Kilchberg, I return once more and attack the bell.

"I have one or two visitors every day, announced and unannounced," says Golo Mann, leading me into a large, very light living room with a view of the Lake of Zurich, "and they all ask me questions about Thomas Mann, about Katia, Heinrich, Erika, Elisabeth, Klaus Mann . . ."

Professor Mann fills his pipe, whispers soothing words to his large black Labrador, and gently lowers himself into memory: "In her autobiography Alma really gave a pretty accurate account of our mad crossing of the Pyrenees. However, she does make one unfounded claim: that Nelly Mann insisted in Cerbère that we shouldn't undertake the ascent on Friday the thirteenth, as this was definitely an unlucky day. It was of course Franz Werfel who cried out in despair, 'No! Let us wait until tomorrow! Let's not go on the thirteenth!' But Alma managed to talk him out of that superstition. The ascent itself was pretty strenuous—for Heinrich Mann and Werfel in particular. Alma managed surprisingly well.

"When the worst was over and we were in Spain, that's when I really made friends with Franz Werfel. We traveled first from Port Bou to Barcelona, then took the night train to Madrid. We were standing there in the corridor of the train, watching the countryside go by in the bright moonlight. We talked about poetry in general and about his poems in particular. I mentioned his 'Song of Parents' ['Elternlied'] and he asked me, 'You know it?' I even had it memorized, because I really liked his poetry very much. He got excited, opened the door to his compartment, and shouted, 'Alma! It's amazing! Golo knows all my poems by heart!'

"In Madrid we took lodgings in a modest hotel. We were given special permission to stay five days. One night we complained to the concierge about all the cumbersome bureaucracy and especially the fact that we had to have our permits validated every day. He started shouting at us, 'Ne vous plaignez pas! Don't complain! Especially not you, you're all Reds!' And when Alma went to the office of the state-owned Spanish airline for tickets to Lisbon, she saw pictures of Hitler, Mussolini, and Franco on the wall and was so horrified she screamed out loud.

"From Madrid we went on to Lisbon, where we had to wait fourteen days for the departure of our Greek steamship, Nea Hellas. Once Werfel and I visited a

large and very handsome exhibition in Lisbon about the ship in which Vasco da Gama had gone on his voyages. The Portuguese were really proud of that show. It got late; we went to the railway station to take the train back to Estoril and our hotel. We missed it, went into a tavern, had a drink or two, and missed the second train, the one that left at midnight. Werfel was mortified: he was afraid that Alma would make a scene, the way she used to. And he seemed so visibly overstressed in his excitement that it seems to me he was suffering from an acute heart condition even then.

"Our ship was terribly overcrowded, the crossing to New York quite unpleasant. I spent my time socializing with the Manns and the Werfels, back and forth. From New York, the Werfels soon went on to Los Angeles, to 'German California.' Later, in the spring of 1941, my father and I also moved there. T.M. really liked Werfel a great deal: he found him very amusing and loved to listen to him singing Verdi arias. My father didn't think much of Werfel's work—he liked the man much better than the author. About The Song of Bernadette, *which Werfel wrote shortly after his arrival in America, T.M. once said, 'A well-made bad book.' But his kindness, sweetness, his utterly good nature and capacity for friendship—those were the qualities my father and I valued greatly. At first T.M. was in a financially precarious position in the States, but when his Joseph novel became a selection of the Book-of-the-Month Club, he received an immediate payment of twenty thousand dollars. And how did Werfel react? He was flushed with joy! There wasn't a trace of envy in the man! He himself went from one success to the next. You mustn't forget that: Werfel was always successful. Occasionally he would jokingly call himself a 'novel manufacturer.' Right after* Bernadette *he wanted to write a big novel about the Mormons—a life of their founder, Joseph Smith—but Alma talked him out of that one: 'Franzl,' she said, 'don't you become a village crucifix carver!' He abandoned the idea. From the very beginning, Alma would provide him with material, but she would also censor subjects he came up with.*

"As for his essays, one could well be of two minds about those; they probably aren't as substantial as his narrative works. They're rather uneven in their subject matter as well. Werfel once said to me, 'Since I've been living in America, I find it so hard to pick a subject.' A very characteristic statement from him. Just think, for instance, of T.M. in regard to that: when and where would my father ever have had trouble 'picking a subject'?! He knew, even as a young man, what he would have to write in his lifetime, come what may. Just think about the Joseph trilogy: it took him almost twenty years to write." After a protracted silence, Golo Mann adds, "I really liked Werfel very much—and I owe him a great deal. He once said to me, 'You're a writer, right? You should write a lot more.' I've never forgotten that."

"I'm an American"

N OW, HAVING ALMOST reached the Statue of Liberty, I embrace and fervently kiss you," Franz Werfel wrote in mid-October 1940, still on board the steamer *Nea Hellas*. The letter was addressed to his parents, who had not had any news from him since the end of August. "Now America lies before us, an entirely unknown continent. I hope that it will be favorably disposed toward me. Indications are that I'll be received with friendship." His parents' situation caused him great anxiety. "Do you have enough to eat? Are you able to . . . provide Papa with the diet he needs?" He and his sister Mizzi would try everything in their power to rescue their parents soon. Marianne Rieser was now living in New York; Hanna and her family had ended up in London. "Tomorrow, Mizzerl and I will discuss all that needs to be done."

On the morning of October 13, exactly one month after the Werfels crossed the Pyrenees, the *Nea Hellas* docked at the Fourth Street pier in Hoboken, New Jersey. Numerous writers, journalists, and intellectuals, whose escape stories often surpassed the Werfels' in terms of hardship, were among those saved; relatives, friends, and reporters now greeted them on the pier. Marianne Rieser and her husband, and Brigitte and Gottfried Bermann Fischer, who also had emigrated to America a short time before, were waiting for the Werfels; Thomas Mann had come to meet his son and his brother. An improvised press conference was held on the pier. Heinrich Mann, Alfred Polgar, and Franz Werfel were asked about the details of their escape, but Werfel did not oblige: he explained to the disappointed journalists that details of his escape might endanger those still trapped in France waiting to be saved. When he was asked about his plans for the near future, he replied, "To have a little peace."

In their small suite at the St. Moritz Hotel on Central Park South, with a view over the park, the Werfels surrounded themselves, from the very beginning of their stay in New York, with admirers, acquaintances, and friends, mostly émigrés like themselves. They saw the Feucht-wangers and Zuckmayers again, this autumn of 1940, and got together with Anton Kuh and Hermann Broch, Franz Blei, Count Richard Coudenhove-Kalergi, Otto von Hapsburg, and Alfred Döblin. On each one of these occasions Werfel would tell the story of his escape, calling it "the flight from Marseilles to Marseilles." He described the weeks of mortal fear as an absurd but not at all comical farce, embroidering certain details with care, making both himself and his audience laugh until they cried. He told them about a night spent in a vacant brothel in Bordeaux and about meeting with a banker from Stuttgart, Stefan Jacobowicz, a fellow guest at the Hôtel Vatican in Lourdes: this man had told them his own escape story. In the company of another fugi-tive, an anti-Semitic Polish officer, this Jacobowicz had crossed France in a rattletrap automobile although neither one of them really knew how to drive, with many narrow escapes from advancing German troops.

"We're doing *wonderfully* here," Franz informed his parents, "even though we pay for our happiness with a bad conscience." A few days after their arrival, the American edition of *Embezzled Heaven* had been published and become an instant best-seller. It had been selected by the Book-of-the-Month Club, and within a week Viking Press sold over 150,000 copies. "My latest book . . . is a hit," he wrote to his parents. "For the time being, this good fortune has freed us from all worries. I regard my success and fame here as *undeserved;* most of the others are in poor shape and have to fight hard for their livelihood, with little hope."

During his first weeks in the United States, instead of relaxing as he had planned, Werfel charged from one meeting or reception to the next, speaking at fund-raising dinners and writing essays. *Aufbau* pub-lished his article "Our Road Goes On" ("Unser Weg geht weiter"), a passionate appeal to the Jewish people to recognize World War II as the "greatest and most dangerous moment" in the history of Israel, one that demanded, from each and every one of its members, determina-tion and readiness to fight: in this "most terrible religious war of all time," the enemy's goal was "the complete extermination of the Jewish spirit on this planet," and it was now imperative for all democratic forces to make a concerted effort to save the Jews. According to Werfel's thesis, Israel's destruction would cause "the Christian churches [to] fade into empty shadows and oblivion," and the entire civilization to subside to the lowest level of its history. Thus all of mankind's political as well as spiri-tual fate depended on the existence of Israel: Werfel said that the recog-nition of this link made him "shiver to the roots of my being."

Werfel regularly sent food packages to his parents from New York. His sister Mizzi even toyed with the idea of traveling to France in order to escort their parents personally from Bergerac via Spain and Portugal to the United States. "But that is just fantasy," Werfel admitted to them.

In and around Los Angeles, along the Pacific Coast, many German-speaking émigrés began to settle within easy reach of each other, establishing a colony once again, like the one in Sanary-sur-Mer. The refugees were attracted there by the mild climate, California's easygoing ways, and not least the great movie studios. Hollywood had already put a number of German authors under contract, encouraging them to hope for financial security for the duration of their life in exile.

Thomas Mann was planning a move to Los Angeles, as was his brother Heinrich. The writers Alfred Döblin, Bertolt Brecht, and Lion Feuchtwanger moved there, and Ludwig Marcuse, Arnold Schoenberg, Erich Wolfgang Korngold, and Max Reinhardt were already established residents. Ernst Deutsch, whom Werfel knew from his schooldays, had settled in the movie metropolis with his wife, Anuschka.

"Before Christmas we'll probably move to *California*," Werfel told his parents. Alma asked two friends, Venetian antique dealers who had moved their business to Los Angeles in the 1930s, to look for a suitable dwelling. The couple, Mr. and Mrs. Loewi, soon found the right place, a small house in the Hollywood hills, high above the largest urban sprawl in the world. They furnished it lovingly with all the basics and told the Werfels in mid-December 1940 that all was ready for their move to Los Angeles. The Loewis had even found a butler for the Werfels, a young German operetta tenor who had left his touring ensemble and remained in America.

One day before the end of the year, the Werfels moved into their new house at 6900 Los Tilos Road, a very narrow, winding street in the Outpost district. The warm air was fragrant with orange, acacia, and oleander blossoms; there were fruit trees and rosebushes in their own garden as well as in the opulent gardens of their neighbors. In the evenings, natural acoustics permitted them to enjoy concerts and performances of operas and operettas—their house sat on a slope immediately above the Hollywood Bowl and its "Music Under the Stars."

Their butler, August Hess, chauffeured his employers through the endless city in a roomy Oldsmobile and ran all their errands. Franz Werfel thought he had found paradise. It was spring in the middle of winter, things greened and flowered in every season, the ocean was nearby, and in less than an hour's drive one could reach sandy deserts and snowcapped mountains. "The Riviera is just trash compared to this," Werfel wrote to his parents in his first impressions of California. He was quite overwhelmed by American comforts: "You push a button, and it gets warm in ten seconds." Every room, even the servant's, had its own bathroom. And food was delivered to the house "almost ready to eat." The climate was "so marvelous" that he "felt ten years younger" and had no circulatory problems whatsoever. "If only I could get you here! I would give years of my life for that."

The High Song of Bernadette (Das hohe Lied von Bernadette) was the title of the first version of the Lourdes novel on which he started work in mid-January 1941 in the house on Los Tilos. On the voyage from Lisbon to New York, Werfel had written in his notebook: "Almost decided on Bernadette"—clearly not as certain about the undertaking as he later claimed in his preface, when he called the book "the fulfilment of a vow."

Georg Moenius, a German priest whom the Werfels knew from Europe and who now shared their exile in California, advised Werfel on all theological questions and provided him with pertinent literature, such as a work by the French canon Joseph Belleney, *Our Holy Shepherdess Bernadette* on which Werfel based much of his own text.

He worked as intensely and happily as he once had in Breitenstein and later in the round room at Sanary, devoting himself to the novel eight hours a day, every day. At first he did not believe that the book would be a commercial success: Protestant America would hardly be interested in a Catholic miracle, a subject that was doomed to seem quite irrelevant in the midst of a world war. Ben Huebsch, Werfel's American publisher, shared his misgivings; he, too, was convinced that the story of Bernadette Soubirous would not do well but nevertheless declared himself willing to publish it, since all of Werfel's other books had come out under his imprint, Viking Press.

During the months of work on *Bernadette,* Werfel continued his efforts to get his parents to the United States. Varian Fry was involved in the project and had already found an ambulance in which Rudolf and Albine Werfel were to be taken from Bergerac to Lisbon. But Fry was worried that Werfel's aged father would not be physically strong enough for the hardships of the journey. "I want you to know," Franz wrote to his mother, "that all of us are pondering, day and night, what would be best for you and how we should arrange it all. . . . I would give my right hand if we could spare you all that." If he weren't so well known, he would immediately take the plane back and try to save them in person. "I notice, with great envy, that many people here have managed to bring their parents over, among them people in their eighties."

In mid-March 1941, NBC broadcast a radio interview with Werfel in its program series "I'm an American." Every week a well-known European immigrant who had applied for American citizenship appeared in the studio to be interviewed by a prominent official on behalf of the Immigration and Naturalization Service in Los Angeles. Werfel's move to the United States was a great gain for the cultural life of the country, stated his interviewer, W. A. Carmichael. Werfel replied that the United States was "more than a country and a people. It is a huge continent and a unique amalgam of strong races. Its size, its freedom, its way of life overwhelm me." He thus wanted to become a U.S. citizen "not only out of necessity but out of a recognition of this greatness." "Many years ago" he had "in a few essays" expressed his "firm belief that America has been called to defend, victoriously, the eternal values, the Christian values against Satan's *Blitzkrieg*. America will be the radiant phoenix that rises triumphantly from the world conflagration. . . . If ever a Christian has seen into the furthest depths of the Antichrist's treacherous heart, it is President Roosevelt. And as long as this champion of God lives and acts, he will not permit the entire globe to fall into the hands of the murderers of humanity."

A few days after that broadcast, on March 22, 1941, Werfel crossed the border between Mexico and Arizona near the small town of Nogales: he had to reenter the United States as an immigrant after the expiration of his visitor's visa so that he would be able to apply for citizenship.

In May, after working for four months, Werfel completed the first draft of his life of Bernadette. "I have dared to sing the song of Bernadette," he said in the preface, "although I am not a Catholic but a Jew." He had been encouraged in his endeavor by a "far older and far more unconscious vow" than the one made in Lourdes: "Even in the days when I wrote my first verses I vowed that I would evermore and everywhere in all I wrote magnify the divine mystery and the holiness of man."

Departing from his usual practice, Werfel dictated the second draft of the novel. His secretary was Albrecht Joseph, a literary historian and former theatrical director, recommended to him by the writer and fellow immigrant Bruno Frank. In the summer of 1941, as German troops marched into the Soviet Union, at first proceeding speedily and victoriously toward the interior, Werfel finished his Lourdes book, dedicating it "To the memory of my stepdaughter Manon." Now he announced the novel to G. B. Fischer as the story of a "true genius of a girl." "In a certain sense Bernadette is a personification of the magical powers that do not die out in humanity, any more than poetry does." He confessed to his sister Hanna, now living in London, that he had worked harder on this novel than on anything else in his life. He said that he had been laboring on the huge book day and night for the past months, "bringing it into being by means of daily, hourly self-mortification." To get on in the United States, one had to work three times as hard as in Europe. "I've agreed to a terrifying lecture tour in the fall. I'm frightened. My English isn't first-rate yet."

In the meantime Werfel's parents in Marseilles had been waiting for several weeks for their Portuguese visas in order to board the ship *Serpa Pinto,* scheduled to sail from Lisbon to New York in September 1941. "Mr. Fry cabled that Papa is getting weaker and that the doctor thinks he'll soon be unable to travel," Werfel wrote to Hanna, adding that there was an acute food shortage in Marseilles. "That our poor parents, after a life of calm and security, are subjected to this horrifying trial . . . is an inconceivable torment to me. . . . Perhaps there will be a miracle." On July 31, 1941, ten days after his son had wished for a miracle, Rudolf Werfel gave up the struggle for survival—in Marseilles, a few weeks before his eighty-third birthday.

Werfel's grief for his father was now mingled with the fear that his seventy-year-old mother might not be able to cope with the flight from France by herself, but he soon received the reassuring news that Albine Werfel was already in Portugal and would shortly arrive in New York. Franz was able to embrace his mother at the end of September, after more than a year of ceaseless anxiety about her survival. He stayed for some time on the East Coast, living with Alma, at his favorite hotel, the St. Moritz on Central Park South, and helped his mother to the best of his ability to recover from the shock of her husband's death and to feel somewhat at home in the United States. Alma started up her salon again in their hotel suite; as if she were back in Vienna, she entertained Austrian princes and princesses, politicians and artists, happy once again to see herself as a social focus but nevertheless subjecting her husband to bitter recriminations: only because of him did she have to leave her beloved Austria; by herself she could have remained at Hohe Warte in happy security and freedom from worry. Franz's Jewishness was the reason she had lost her homeland—which she now glorified from afar. Only because of Werfel was she forced to live a deplorable life in exile, in a country lacking culture and spirituality. Helpless and miserable, the target of these attacks endured the rages of his wife. There was only one escape route from Alma's bad temper: work.

While busy looking for a New York apartment for his mother, he prepared himself for the lecture tour that would take him to several states, among them Nebraska, Missouri, and Texas. Like an actor studying his part, Werfel now learned his lecture on belief in God, originally written in 1932, which he retitled "Can We Live Without Faith in God?" ("Können wir ohne Gottesglauben leben?") Before setting out, he gave a couple of interviews and said in one of them that he was now familiar with both the East and West coasts of the United States, and had arrived at the conclusion that the American nation was "relatively without hatred." He had rediscovered the feeling of "sunshine" that he had experienced as a boy in the wonderful poems of Walt Whitman. While Europe and Asia were becoming increasingly godless, the ideals of religion and morality were evidently preserved in America, and he assumed that after the war the United States would have to shoulder the responsibility of initiating a moral renewal of the rest of the world.

In December 1941, immediately after the Japanese attack on Pearl Harbor and the subsequent declaration of war against Japan, and Germany's declaration of war against the United States, the German edition of *The Song of Bernadette* was published by Bermann-Fischer Verlag in Stockholm, with simultaneous publications in French, Spanish, Portuguese, Swedish, and Hungarian. The American edition was scheduled for the spring of 1942. After Werfel had finished "the difficult task of proofreading the translation," he wrote from Los Angeles to his mother, who had stayed in New York, "People here . . . feel directly threatened by the Japanese, but I think that is nonsense. Some are leaving the coast." Even Alma, who "always expects the worst," was considering a move inland, perhaps to Denver or Colorado Springs. "For my part . . . I'd rather stay here." Admittedly, economic survival would become increasingly difficult for Europeans: "American nationalism is in full flower, and one will have to work hard and with deliberation if one wants to stay on top. One can sense it particularly here, in the movie city. . . . The hardest year in American history has just begun."

The previous fall Werfel had received a very depressing letter from Stefan Zweig in which his friend told him about his nervous breakdown: the pain caused by the loss of his language and of his identity had driven him to the verge of despair. Zweig had since settled in the Brazilian city of Petropolis and now, in another letter, enthused about the magical beauty of his new refuge, praising the landscape that surrounded him. He seemed to have come through the crisis and even invited Werfel to visit him the following summer. He felt that Werfel would find Brazil far more stimulating than Hollywood. But Werfel would never make the trip to South America: at the end of February 1942, Stefan Zweig and his wife Lotte committed suicide. "It is appalling! He wrote us desperate letters, but unfortunately I didn't really take them seriously," Werfel wrote to his mother. At a memorial service in a Los Angeles synagogue, Werfel stressed that he found Zweig's suicide particularly hard to comprehend because his friend had handed the archenemy a triumph: German newspapers celebrated the exile's decision to die "like the sinking of a British cruiser." Nevertheless, Werfel went on to say, Zweig's suicide was evidence of "a secret greatness" behind which lay an unfathomable mystery. "Later generations will judge the tragedy of those poets and writers who have been exiled from their language to cower, like Ahasuerian beggars, before the threshold of an alien grammar and culture." In one of his last letters to Werfel, Zweig had said that whenever he heard about bombing raids and collapsing buildings, he himself collapsed along with them. "His death proves that those words were truly not exaggerated. . . . No, he sensed, he *knew* that things would and must become worse from one day to the next."

As he had feared, Werfel's financial position deteriorated after America's entry into the war. The Book-of-the-Month Club showed no interest in *Bernadette,* and that depressed its chances on the movie market. No producer or studio made an offer. In this sudden crisis, Werfel tried to refurbish some older works for Hollywood: thus *April in October* was turned into a treatment and made the rounds of the studios. The director Robert Siodmak showed some interest in the project, but nothing came of it.

Werfel's best friend in Los Angeles, apart from his Piarist schoolmate Ernst Deutsch, was the Viennese writer Friedrich Torberg, whom he had known slightly in the Café Herrenhof days; back then, he had rather avoided Torberg because of the latter's admiration for Karl Kraus. They had met in Estoril while fleeing Europe, and Torberg had been living in Hollywood since the previous fall. Werfel recognized him as an equal and a kindred spirit. Thirty-four years old, Torberg was full of humor, a spiritual product of Imperial Vienna. Werfel opened up to him without reservation: only Willy Haas and Ernst Polak had ever been as close to him as this new friend. At least in a small way, Torberg provided Werfel with the sense of familiarity and coffeehouse atmosphere that the latter missed so much in his exile. When they were together, the hard fate of exile, of being cut off from the cultural life of Austria, did not seem quite so tragic as before.

In the spring of 1942, Werfel and Torberg collaborated on a "film story" based on the life of Zorah Pasha, the sultan's daughter. It was a blood-and-thunder subject, one that Werfel had made a note of as long ago as 1925 on his trip to Egypt. They produced a detailed treatment, "The Love and Hatred of Zorah Pasha." To make this rather embarrassing dime-store stuff look a little more interesting, Werfel wrote a brief foreword in which he claimed to have written a first draft of this work in Europe but to have lost it on his flight through France, Spain, and Portugal.

About six weeks before the publication date of *The Song of Bernadette*, the Book-of-the-Month Club made a surprise decision to select the novel after all and to recommend it to its members in July as the most important new book on the American market. Viking Press printed a first edition of 200,000 copies, and Ben Huebsch's initial skepticism instantly turned to boundless optimism. "Now the chances for a movie are much better," Werfel wrote to his mother. "Negotiations are going on constantly."

The Song of Bernadette was published on May 11, 1942. Three weeks later it had climbed to fourth place on the best-seller list, and Viking was printing another 100,000 copies. In June, *Bernadette* overtook John Steinbeck's war novel *Bombs Away* and became the best-selling book in the country, retaining that position for several months. It was an almost unimaginable success, a kind of restitution of justice after book burnings, exile from the homeland, and life-endangering flight; a justice, it is true, that had not been evident in the fates of his fellow writers in exile who, almost without exception, lived at subsistence level. Werfel's present triumph was not only the greatest success story of his life, but *The Song of Bernadette* became one of the greatest hits in American publishing history.

The mass-media furor reached its peak in June 1942: major newspapers published long features on the book and the miracle of Lourdes, radio conversations with Werfel were broadcast nationally, and he was snowed under with requests for interviews. In the midst of all the excitement, Ben Huebsch asked him to come to New York, where Werfel was passed from one press conference and party to the next.

It was a triumphal procession, observed by many of Werfel's fellow exiles with astonishment. They indulged in—often public—wisecracks about the mawkish legend of a saint and assumed that the author could not really be naive enough to believe in this Catholic fairy tale, accusing him of only pretending to do so. Werfel's visit to the East Coast was also overshadowed by the flare-up of an old family antagonism, one that caused him deep concern and depressed him for a long time. Mizzi Rieser had written a play, *Eugenia,* which she tried to have produced on Broadway. She expected her brother, with his connections, to get her a theater contract—perhaps to suggest the play to Max Reinhardt. After Werfel had sent *Eugenia* to the New York Theatre Guild and received a firm rejection, he made no further attempts to place it. Mizzi subsequently wrote a highly accusatory letter to her brother, a kind of farewell message, and Werfel was very hurt by it. He replied that Mizzi had "really ruined" his stay in New York: his sister and his brother-in-law Ferdinand were talking "about my wife and myself in the most malicious manner. . . . In company, Ferdi refers to Alma only as 'die Mahler,' which certainly does not degrade her but is a deliberate insult to me. Strangers tell me about your orgies of abuse of Alma. You are fond of claiming that I am one person in my writing and another in my life—thus a liar. And now the last straw! Not even my worst enemies would dare to invent what you are proposing: that I owe my successes to 'protection and connections.' And that the Book-of-the-Month Club picked my *Bernadette* only because we are friends with Harry S[c]herman [founder and president of the Book-of-the-Month Club]." Besides, Mizzi was vastly overestimating her brother's influence: "As we know, here in America money is everything. In local theater jargon, a play is called a 'property'—and rightly so. The money people alone decide if it will be produced or not. . . . We live . . . in an alien world with its own laws, one not easily mastered. I too would die of starvation here if my reputation didn't date back twenty years. . . . A hundred recognized European artists, among them a few true geniuses, . . . are subsisting on alms and handouts."

Mizzi Rieser replied that as an artist she felt oppressed by her brother, and as a human being simply ignored. Werfel responded by trying to provide a psychological analysis of his relationship with his sister: even as a child, she had always felt rejected and mistreated. Mizzi's present "emotional turning away," however, dated back to about 1936, in his opinion: Alma's anti-Semitic remarks, which then had "burned . . . like vermouth" on the "wounds" of the Riesers, had caused this real rift between sister and brother. "And since Ferdi . . . was Alma's enemy from the beginning, you soon had a collection of bitter injuries, which you ascribed to Alma. Thus Hitler had thrown his torch between us too. . . . Thus I had married an anti-Semite (an ancient conflict situation in Jewish families)." He did, however, readily admit to Mizzi that Alma's anti-Semitism had caused him "a hundred bitter hours" in the twenty-five years of their relationship.

Upon his return to Los Angeles in July 1942, Werfel continued the correspondence with his sister. "Only once have I ever met someone," he wrote to her, whose attitude had been similar to hers: "Karl Kraus. . . . To climb into each other's psyches is not courage, not fighting spirit, but one of the intellectual ills of the past epoch. It is one of the roots of Nazism. I would be very happy if we wanted to understand each other instead of trying to 'see through' each other."

After his sister had accused him of moving too close to a *Christian* world view over the past years, Werfel wrote a kind of afterword to their disagreement: "To me . . . Catholicism is nothing but the only *spiritual system* that still exists in the flat desert of materialism. But the Jews don't have enough imagination to realize that, once Christianity is finished, they will be as superfluous in the world as the Poles or Bulgarians."

At this time, late July 1942, sales of the American edition of *The Song of Bernadette* had reached 400,000 copies.

"During the war years, my friends and I practically lived from one news broadcast to the next," says Albrecht Joseph, steering his rattletrap Dodge through Beverly Glen Canyon and on to the San Fernando Valley to do his weekly shopping at a supermarket. "Because of the nine-hour time difference between California and Europe, the most important news from the battlefronts came in the middle of the night. That was when we could hear what new catastrophes had taken place over there. To while away the time until the midnight news, a group of us would often meet in the evening and play games. The most popular one was charades, where you had to mime an animal or a plant or a quotation from world literature—whatever—and the others had to guess what it was. We all did it, even Thomas Mann, who was otherwise rather reticent. And it really got quite grotesque sometimes—we were all fit to be tied. What wouldn't I give to have a documentary movie of those days!

"One evening we were gathered in Bruno Frank's house. Our host, a gigantic man with broad shoulders and the head of a Roman emperor, was crawling on the floor on all fours, acting a mouse. Suddenly the door opened and Werfel and Alma stood there, having just arrived from France via New York. Years later, Werfel told me that this sight counted among the strangest moments of his life, even after all the tumultuous events of his emigration.

"A few months later I started working for Werfel. He dictated his novel The Song of Bernadette *to me. I went to his little house in the Hollywood hills. Alma's piano was on the ground floor, but the bedrooms were below that because the house was built on a steep slope. So there was this narrow spiral staircase down into Werfel's little room with its whitewashed walls, a narrow bed, a wardrobe, a desk, and two chairs. I sat at the typewriter and Werfel dictated from eight school composition books with black covers. He wrote everything in long-hand, mostly in that kind of notebook. 'When I was a boy, they forced me to practice writing in these things,' he once said to me, 'and ever since, it's been my sweet revenge to write whatever I want to write in them!'*

"Right at the beginning of our work on Bernadette *he told me, 'If something doesn't seem convincing to you, please let me know.' But there really wasn't*

much to complain about. If there is anything wrong with the book, it is perhaps only that it's written too smoothly, almost like a tourist guide. Sometimes he would look at me as if to say; Do you like that or not? But I rarely had any objections. There was no friction at all in our work together. After work Alma used to call me to her room and say, 'Don't act like a Jew. Sit down and have a little glass of schnapps.' I reminded her repeatedly that wine drinking was part of Jewish ritual and that there had been at least two Jewish alcoholics in Vienna: one of them her friend Egon Friedell; the other, Joseph Roth, who had drunk himself to death. But rational argument never stood a chance with Alma. Her dogma was that Jews were inferior to Aryans, and that was that. When we talked, Alma never mentioned Werfel's writing. It would have been only natural for her to ask how the novel was coming along and whether I liked it. Nothing. Not a word. I don't think that Alma was too interested in what he was doing. She mostly just talked about what a criminal Roosevelt was and how Hitler was really a very intelligent person. There were other émigrés in L.A. with similarly bizarre views of the Germans—Fritz Kortner, for instance, or Arnold Schoenberg. This was still before Stalingrad, of course. They were visiting the Werfels when I was there and saying, 'But of course the Germans will win the war. They have that discipline, and they're much smarter than the Americans!'

"Alma loved a fight. One morning, when I came to work on Bernadette, *I walked right into one. This one, like so many before, was about the war news from Europe, which had again been particularly depressing. And again, Alma took the view that those German victories were not at all surprising, as they were all supermen, Hitler included. Werfel did not want to let her get away with that nonsense, but Alma didn't give an inch until Werfel slapped my shoulder and said, 'Come on, let's go down and work on* Bernadette.' *Then he stopped halfway down the spiral staircase, turned to look at me, and sighed. 'What do you do with a woman like that?' It sounds almost good-natured, but there wasn't a trace of humor in his voice. He felt really desperate. I tried to say something, but he just shook his head and said, 'One mustn't forget, she is an old woman.'*

"The Werfels' living room was a frequent meeting place for Jewish émigrés— Ernst Deutsch and his wife, Torberg, Bruno Frank, Leonhard Frank, Kortner, Schoenberg, the Korngolds, and many more. Alma loved to insult or provoke this group. Even though she herself had just escaped from Nazi terror, she stated one afternoon, at one of her tea parties, that one should not condemn on principle everything the Nazis did; some of their actions were, indeed, laudable. When one of the guests countered that the single fact of the concentration camps was enough to drive one insane, she replied, 'Oh, come on, those horror propaganda stories, they're all made up by émigrés like you! One of my good friends, a head nurse, assured me that there is excellent medical care in the camps and that the Red Cross looks after the prisoners very conscientiously.' And suddenly Werfel leaped *out of his chair, his face turned* purple, *his eyes bulged. I had never seen him like that. I wouldn't have thought it possible that he could*

get so furious—basically, he was a very gentle and sweet person. But this was like the thundering of an Old Testament prophet! He had lost all control over himself. And all of us knew how weak his heart was, and that an outburst like that could be lethal. Everybody wanted to get out of there as fast as possible, but then again, everybody knew that it was impossible to leave Werfel alone with her. There was talk about this and that. Small talk. And Alma seemed quite unmoved. She was probably just thinking that her childish husband had once again misbehaved like a naughty child."

Dance of Death

Ａbout eighty miles north of Los Angeles on the Pacific coast, surrounded by citrus groves, lies Santa Barbara, possibly the most beautiful town in California. Cyrill Fischer, a Catholic clergyman whom Werfel had known in Vienna and whom he held in great esteem, had retired to the Old Mission there, a large monastery of the Franciscan order, in the beginning of the 1940s. Werfel visited Father Cyrill frequently and came to regard Santa Barbara as an ideal refuge for undisturbed work, far from the big city, as Breitenstein and Santa Margherita had been. At the end of June 1942 he moved into a bungalow by the ocean, part of the luxurious Biltmore Hotel.

He told his sister Hanna that he was now living "in a charming Spanish-style hotel." "Paradise—balmy, cool—orgies of flowers— swimming pool with stunningly beautiful girls at whom I stare with one eye while the other peruses Scheeben's 'Secret of Predestination.' "

He wrote a new play in ten days, *Jacobowsky and the Colonel*, (*Jacobowsky und der Oberst*), subtitled "The Comedy of a Tragedy" ("Komödie einer Tragödie"). He combined experiences of his own flight from Marseilles to Marseilles with the rich collection of anecdotes of the Stuttgart banker S. L. Jacobowicz, his next-door neighbor in Lourdes. These were the stories he had "performed" those past months, over and over, the way an actor presents his favorite part. He had done so the previous fall at a dinner party given by Max Reinhardt, and Reinhardt's son Gottfried had suggested that Werfel turn the stories into a play: he sensed that this might be the break for which his father had been waiting for years—to have a hit on Broadway. At first Werfel had rejected Gottfried Reinhardt's idea, saying that the subject was not right for a work bearing his name, and Alma Mahler also voiced her vehement opposition to such a play. Gottfried Reinhardt then asked Werfel for permission to adapt his stories for the stage, promising his friend a fifty-percent share in the proceeds and persuading the successful American playwright S. N. Behrman to be his coauthor. After a few weeks, when the two had completed the first act of their play, they received a letter from Werfel in which he told them that he had changed his mind and decided to write the play himself after all. Reinhardt and Behrman reacted angrily and told Werfel that they would take him to court if he did not compensate them for their loss.

Working on the play in Santa Barbara, Werfel sent completed scenes to Albrecht Joseph in Los Angeles to be typed, and at the end of August 1942 he sent the finished manuscript to the New York Theatre Guild. He had decided that, with this new play, he would achieve a breakthrough on the American stage similar to the one he had managed with *The Song of Bernadette* in the American book market. Viking Press had now sold almost half a million copies of the novel, and demand for it was still rising. "This development, . . . which no one really anticipated," he wrote to sister Hanna, "is another miracle of Lourdes, and I accept it with humility and gladness." He had realized, he told Hanna, that he would have to write "commercially viable things for the Americans" in order to survive in the United States.

In the meantime, *The Song of Bernadette* had been sold to 20th Century–Fox. Werfel's agent, George Marton, a native of Budapest, had conducted protracted negotiations and secured the uncommonly large sum of $125,000 for the movie rights. Werfel's simple imagery and his tendency to treat his subjects in a somewhat florid style—in *Bernadette* it becomes almost sentimental—were well suited to the demands of the dream factory. Ever since *Verdi, The Pascarella Family,* and *Juarez and Maximilian,* his work had seemed compatible with Hollywood's needs. If a massive Turkish intervention had not finally prevented MGM from realizing its projected movie version of *The Forty Days of Musa Dagh,* that, too, would surely have broken box-office records.

The Jacobowsky play was finished. Werfel turned to a new project, undoubtedly with an eye to its commercial potential: he wanted to write "a big Jewish novel." "Mostly we hear about the fate of the émigrés," he wrote to Hanna, "but I want to describe one who stayed at home. An honest silk manufacturer who packs his family off to America but thinks that he still has time. . . . And so he proceeds to his doom, step by step, down to the Yellow Star and Poland. The strange apotheosis and purification of the man, in the midst of the massacres in Poland, is the climax of the book. An ordinary Jew, a nothing and a nobody, with a shop on Rothenturmstrasse or Obstmarkt" (both shopping areas in Vienna).

For decades Werfel had preached, in always new variations, the inseparability of Jewish and Christian religious thought. After his sensational success with *The Song of Bernadette*, however, he was no longer identified with the Jewish cause. In order to tone down his purely Catholic image a little, he had finally decided to write *Jacobowsky and the Colonel*, and a similar motivation probably led him to plan a Jewish novel. Its working title was *The One Who Stayed* (*Der Zurückgebliebene*). He also considered it a kind of sequel to *Musa Dagh*—ten years after Werfel had called the atrocities committed by the Young Turk nationalists the most barbarous cruelty in human history, he realized that the German race madness surpassed the murders instigated by Enver Pasha and his cohorts by far. It is also possible that he conceived *The One Who Stayed* as a defense against his wife's attitude: Alma was still dismissing the news of the German slaughter of the Jews as "atrocity propaganda."

How much Americans already regarded Franz Werfel as a *Catholic* author was evident from the fact that Church authorities kept urging him to convert: there were rumors that he had converted long ago, and in the fall of 1942 Archbishop Rummel of New Orleans wrote to ask him whether he had become a Catholic or not. In his reply to Rummel, Werfel said that while he regarded Catholicism as the "purest force sent by God to this earth . . . to combat the evils of materialism and atheism," the current extremely cruel persecution of the Jews prevented him from "escaping the flock of the persecuted" at this time. Besides, as long as there were anti-Semitic Christians, the baptized Jew would in any case remain "a figure who is not entirely welcome and also somewhat intrusive." Nevertheless, Werfel assured the archbishop, he would "not stop writing books such as *The Song of Bernadette*" and would take every opportunity "to praise the glory of the supernatural."

Six years earlier, in his notebook for *Hearken Unto the Voice*, he had remarked, "Even for a Jew who regards Jesus Christ as the true, historically realized messiah, baptism and conversion are not satisfactory. . . . The Jew cannot be 'cured' by baptism and faith. . . . No matter how much of a believer in Christ [a Jew] may be as an individual, he is as tragically barred from being a Christian as he is from being a German or a Russian."

On the other hand, in a letter Werfel wrote (at roughly the same time as the letter to Archbishop Rummel) to Rudolf Kommer, the confidant and assistant of Max Reinhardt, he said, "I bow my head before your dear grandfather Simon Kornblüh, whose benevolent eyes become piercing at the sight of your ham sandwiches and my *Bernadette*." A short time before, Kommer had presented Werfel with an "announcement of victory" that had relieved the latter of "a shade" of his own "Jewish sense of guilt"—Kommer told him about promising efforts by

American Zionists (led by Chaim Weizmann and David Ben-Gurion) to bring about a Jewish "commonwealth" in Palestine. According to Werfel himself, the afternoon he received the news was "one of the proudest" of his life. Thirty years after his impassioned debates with Max Brod about the foundation of a Jewish state in Palestine, three decades after his vehement rejection of a new Jewish land in the Israel of the Bible, the exiled, persecuted, and burned poet had made his peace with Zionism.

Kommer had received the Jacobowsky play with enthusiasm, and Werfel told him that he had basically "dashed it off for fun" in only ten days but that he believed that the characters had "a certain charm." He considered the antithetical relationship between Jacobowsky and the Colonel "symbolic" and hoped "that the comic horror in the background of all the scenes—a Raimund fairy tale of the greatest collapse in world history"—would be effective in a successful production. The New York Theatre Guild had meanwhile read the play but insisted on making an American adaptation before even considering a Broadway production. Humiliating as this was to Werfel, he accepted: a theatrical success seemed worth any price, even that of agreeing to an American coauthor. "But—but—here comes the big worry!" he wrote to Kommer. "Just as with *Eternal Road,* the whole thing is vitiated by a lack of clarity from the start. . . . And now the conflicts begin to bloom. . . . The Reinhardts, father and son, are treating me in an entirely incomprehensible manner. They don't recognize this opportunity." He realized that his play needed "an American adaptation," but not "some patchwork at the hands of strangers who are ignorant of this material and could destroy its charm."

At the end of September 1942 the Werfels moved from the Hollywood hills to far more prestigious Beverly Hills. With the money made by *Bernadette* they purchased a roomy bungalow with a large and beautiful garden on Santa Monica Boulevard and North Bedford Drive, diagonally across from the Church of the Good Shepherd. Even in Venice and Sanary, Werfel's domiciles had been situated close to Catholic houses of worship—the Basilica dei Frari or Notre-Dame-de-Pitié.

This move brought the Werfels closer to their friends and acquaintances. Their immediate neighbor was the conductor Bruno Walter; Ernst and Anuschka Deutsch and Bruno Frank and his wife lived nearby. Erich Maria Remarque was a frequent visitor, as were the Slezaks, Schoenbergs, Korngolds, Friedrich Torberg, and Lion Feuchtwanger. Alma's closest friends in Los Angeles were Gustave O. Arlt and his wife, Gusti. Arlt was a professor of German literature at the University of California; some claimed that Alma loved those two particularly because of their "Aryan" background and the fact that this American couple was not entirely opposed to National Socialism.

Thomas Mann was also a frequent visitor to the house on Bedford Drive. He would sometimes read from the latest chapters of the final volume in his tetralogy *Joseph and His Brothers.* Werfel would act out scenes from *Jacobowsky and the Colonel,* playing all the parts.

The Werfels spent the turn of the year 1942–43 in New York. Franz wanted to see his mother, who was now living at the Langdon, an apartment house, and feeling lonely and friendless in the foreign metropolis. She saw hardly anyone except her daughter Mizzi and a female companion. Alma, on the other hand, held her obligatory salon at the St. Moritz, receiving her numerous friends who lived in the East.

Meanwhile, Archbishop Rummel of New Orleans had released to the press certain passages from Werfel's letter, which were quoted out of context and thus highly ambiguous. *Time* magazine printed these quotations and created the impression that the author of *The Song of Bernadette* was a wholehearted believer in Catholicism. This in turn triggered a flood of letters to the editor, asking Werfel ever new variations of the same question: Why was he taking a public stand for the Catholic Church, with all its anti-Semitism, but none against the persecution of the Jews that was raging in Europe?

In November 1942 Russian forces surrounded some 250,000 German troops of the Sixth Army at Stalingrad. Shortly before that, Allied forces had landed in North Africa, and the war took its first decisive turn against Hitler's Germany. Werfel had seen it coming six months earlier, writing to his mother that he could see "the beginning of a new time" and that he was certain "that our scale is rising higher in the balance from day to day. . . . We will soon see a requital whose like has rarely been seen by mankind." Werfel, however, was heard to make a strange remark at a dinner party in New York—the Sixth Army had already surrendered—to a circle of friends: "Children, let's not go overboard. This peace will be so far 'left' that you won't believe your eyes and ears!" Thomas Mann, who was present, was outraged by his friend's statement and even noted in his diary that he had considered it *improper* to have such things uttered in his presence.

At the beginning of 1943 Werfel worked on the American adaptation of *Jacobowsky and the Colonel* with Clifford Odets, who had been recommended to him as a coauthor by the Theatre Guild. After some weeks of collaboration, Werfel was at the end of his tether and wrote to his agent George Marton that he kept trying to "convey the European misery of France to an American deaf-mute by means of sign language" but seriously doubted whether anything would come of the project. On top of it all, Werfel was being harassed by S. L. Jacobowicz, the banker from Stuttgart, who was now also living in American exile and had heard about the comedy. Jacobowicz warned Werfel that if he did not receive adequate compensation for his indirect assistance in the creation of the play, he would be compelled to take Werfel to court. In the meantime Gottfried Reinhardt and S. N. Behrman had followed up on their threat and sued Werfel. Alma Mahler wrote to her friend Friedrich Torberg in California that her husband was surrounded by "vultures" in New York. In the spring of 1943, after his return to Los Angeles, Werfel received Clifford Odets's final version of the *Jacobowsky* adaptation and rejected it as a silly, sentimental distortion of his original. One of the typical changes made by Odets had Jacobowsky flee through France with a portable gramophone on which he played Mozart records while the Gestapo was stalking him in the bushes. The Theatre Guild now suggested another adapter, the actor and producer Jed Harris, who had presented plays by Ibsen and Strindberg in New York. However, when Werfel reacted to this suggestion without enthusiasm, things came to a halt and the adaptation of the "comedy of a tragedy" stalled for months. At this point the ill-fated project had caused Werfel more trouble and strain than any other in his writing life.

"I am not really one who believes in dreams." That is the first sentence of a text Franz Werfel began in May 1943. The night before Palm Sunday he had a dream that "overwhelmed" him with its "inexplicable vividness" and seemed quite distinct from all his previous dreams. The dream continued all night like "installments" of a "novel serialized in a newspaper." Werfel felt "disembodied in the most uncanny way," a phenomenon that gave him a "sense of well-being" he had never experienced before. Even two weeks later, the memory of that feeling of happiness was so vivid that Werfel was compelled to "get over my reluctance to work and pick up the pen."

That "reluctance to work" must have been one of the reasons why he had, in the meantime, abandoned the project of a big Jewish novel, *The One Who Stayed*, at precisely the time when a few rebels began their desperate fight in the Warsaw Ghetto, actively resisting deportation and certain death—not unlike Gabriel Bagradian and his five thousand Armenian countrymen.

In only six days, the hotel bungalow of the Biltmore in Santa Barbara witnessed the creation of more than five chapters of the new work, simply titled *A Short Visit to the Distant Future* (*Kurzer Besuch in ferner Zukunft*). Werfel himself did not yet know what would become of it. To friends he referred to it as a "travel novel," but also noted *Behind Time's Back* (*Hinterm Rücken der Zeit*) as a possible title. He let himself become ever more deeply enveloped by the very curious atmosphere of the book, which was unlike anything he had ever written before, by a chain of events that took place in the year 101943, in the Eleventh Cosmic Capital Year of Virgo, on an entirely leveled globe that had been ravaged by numerous wars and was now overgrown by gray grass, most of its inhabitants living underground.

"F.W.," the novel's hero, is summoned by spiritualist means to a wedding in the city of "California," as a kind of amusement for the newlyweds. Disembodied at first, F.W. is met by his former schoolmate B.H., who is to serve as his guide (Vergil to his Dante) through the "Astromental world." B.H.—the initials barely conceal the identity of Willy Haas, Werfel's closest friend since childhood—has lived through several reincarnations while F.W. has lain buried in California without being born again. B.H. can therefore tell the newcomer all about the most important events of the past one hundred millennia, including a solar catastrophe that destroyed all birds and increased the distance between Earth and the sun. Most of mankind now lives below the surface, eating pastel-colored essences. People live for two hundred years or longer, and locomotion is achieved by means of a "travel-puzzle." " 'When we travel,' " B.H. explains, " 'we do not move toward our objective, but we move our objective toward us.' " Only two ideas have remained unchanged in the course of the small eternity F.W. has missed: the Catholic Church and Orthodox Judaism. "Two antitheses," as Werfel wrote, "that had to fight to a finish because they were in reality two identities."

After F.W.'s astral body has changed back into the stocky male figure that once bore the name Franz Werfel, wearing the tailcoat in which he had been carried to his grave in California, B.H. presents the visitor to the newlyweds' kindly and amused host family. The lady of the house immediately asks him if he was a cowboy or a goldhunter in the California of a hundred thousand years ago. F.W. replies, "No, Madame. . . . Neither as a cowboy nor as a goldhunter; not even in the movies, but simply as a refugee."

The very first chapters of the "travel story" indicated the course the novel would take. Werfel fused the abstruse reality of the year 101943 with detailed reminiscences of the turn of the century, of his childhood and youth in Prague, of experiences in both world wars and in exile in Europe and California. A kind of summary of Werfel's life and work was the most important theme threading through the novel, giving it the aspect of a half-disguised autobiography.

The novel also made numerous allusions to works of literature that

Werfel had valued in the course of his life. In addition to Dante's *Divine Comedy,* Pliny's fantastic tale *Another World,* illustrated by the gifted French graphic artist Grandville, and *Gulliver's Travels* by Jonathan Swift were particularly inspiring. Thus, Gulliver's experiences with the inhabitants of Laputa, their strange foodstuffs, and their love of astronomy are clear precursors of Werfel's Astromental society in the Eleventh Cosmic Capital Year of Virgo. Even stylistically Werfel followed Swift closely, addressing the reader directly and combining autobiographical disclosures with the various adventures of his hero.

Werfel was aware that he was writing a completely nonpolitical novel. His narrator comments: "I confess and acknowledge: my time is short and I am wasting it unscrupulously. I have not forgotten that I, too, am persecuted. Nor have I become too deaf to hear the roar of the bombers, ... the death rattle of the mortally wounded.... The monstrous reality ... constrict[s] my throat by day and night.... Of course I am neglecting my duty. But this reality does not leave me even enough breath for an echoing groan to the cry of torment." While it had been his initial plan to dedicate a book to "the ravished, the tortured, the massacred"—by which Werfel undoubtedly meant the abandoned novel about the simple Jewish silk manufacturer—he had been sent, one night when he was searching for a perfect pen, on a "voyage of exploration" which he now wanted to write down instead.

"In only a few days," Werfel told G. B. Fischer at the end of May 1943, he had produced "one-fifth to one-fourth" of a new novel. "Superstition" prevented him from revealing the content of the work, but he was willing to say that it was "something entirely unexpected."

At this time, science fiction was not yet truly established as a popular genre with a wide readership. Apart from H. G. Wells's utopian novels and Aldous Huxley's *Brave New World,* published in 1932, fictional visions of the future were rarely published anywhere outside the American magazine *Amazing Stories* or, on a far lower level, in the comics. Werfel's "travel novel" has to be regarded as one of the pioneering works in the field.

In Beverly Hills, Werfel had to set his "travel novel" aside to complete yet another version of the *Jacobowsky* adaptation, this time in collaboration with Jed Harris, the Theatre Guild's candidate. Though it was as difficult for him to accept Harris's suggestions as those made months earlier by Clifford Odets, his ambition to have a Broadway hit made him fight on, with a certain amount of bitterness and determination. He returned to the Biltmore and, during a heat wave, rewrote *Jacobowsky and the Colonel* for the third time, according to Harris's specifi-

cations. "I have *squeezed out* everything to the last drop," he wrote to
Albrecht Joseph, asking him to pass this on to Jed Harris, "but I have
not *put in* anything that isn't there. This is all I can do, as the author of
this comedy." Exhausted and dissatisfied, he mailed the manuscript
back to the Theatre Guild, but all his efforts seemed to have been in
vain: the Guild did not even acknowledge receipt.

During these weeks, Werfel corresponded with Max Brod, who had
been living in Palestine since 1939 and had informed Werfel of the
death of his wife. "It moved me greatly to see your handwriting after so
many years of separation," Werfel wrote to his friend. He told him
about *Jacobowsky* and sadly noted, "Now that the worst seems to be over
and one hopes to see the end of the war, my feelings of loss and grief
are growing stronger by the minute. . . . Will we ever find each other
again?"

News of the successful Allied landing on Sicily brought him some
comfort. Throughout Italy, popular opinion suddenly turned against
Mussolini, who was deposed at the end of July 1943. Radio Rome
proclaimed the end of Fascism.

Werfel tried to take his mind off the disappointing *Jacobowsky* affair
by frequently visiting the set of *The Song of Bernadette* on the 20th
Century–Fox lot. If he had, as a young man (quite unlike Franz Kafka),
been inclined to look down on the cinema, he now became a movie
enthusiast, frequently attended glamorous gala premieres, and knew
many stars personally, among them his particular favorite, Edward G.
Robinson. They made him feel as shy and reverential as he had felt
about the famous actors and singers who came to the May Festival at the
Neue Deutsche Theater. Jennifer Jones, still an unknown, played the
title role. The screenplay was by George Seaton. It had been rewritten
several times; Werfel had found the first version too mawkish and
rejected it. The producer was William Perlberg; the director, Henry
King, one of the most esteemed movie directors of his day.

At the end of August 1943, back in his hotel bungalow in Santa
Barbara, Werfel wrote his first poems in a long time, free-verse works
he intended to collect and publish under the title *Word of Life on Earth*
(*Kunde vom irdischen Leben*). "Lyric poetry (a term I detest) is a jealous
goddess," he had written a year earlier to the writer Rudolf Voigt. "She
does not tolerate novels, novellas, and plays by her side." As in the
"travel novel," memories of the Prague years resurfaced in these new
poems, as in the "Ballad of the Winter Frost" ("Ballade vom Win-
terfrost"), which resurrected Gunner Werfel's year of volunteer service.
The actress Maria Immisch, a guest at the Prague festival, whom he
had once adored, suddenly arose from his memory: "In the year five,
when I was fifteen / They were celebrating the great Schiller year. / I

saw her as the heroine of famous plays. / Even today my heart is full of gratitude. / The city park was in full leaf."

On the eve of Werfel's fifty-third birthday, the University of California at Los Angeles conferred an honorary doctorate on him. Gustave Arlt and other prominent academics had taken the initiative to obtain the honor, which was quite unusual for an émigré. Two years after his death, Rudolf Werfel's dream had come true: his unruly heir had received his doctorate. Hanna Fuchs-Robetin wrote that their father would have been at least as pleased by this honor as by the German defeats in Stalingrad and North Africa.

Two days after Werfel's birthday, Friedrich Torberg paid his customary afternoon visit to the house on Bedford Drive. The friends chatted amicably while Werfel smoked one of his strong Havanas. Soon after Torberg left, in the early hours of September 13, 1943—on the second anniversary of his crossing of the Pyrenees—Werfel had a severe heart attack, far more dangerous than the one in 1938. He complained of fear of death and intense pain. The doctors prescribed digitalis. For weeks, life-threatening lung embolisms kept recurring, a series of near-death events that gave the patient the feeling that he and the "F.W." in *Star of the Unborn* who had been buried in California A.D. 1943 were one and the same.

In what seemed a premonition of things to come, Werfel had written on the back of a Biltmore Hotel menu, two weeks before the heart attack: "In reality, the curse of illness reveals a double intention. It invites us to hell or to heaven. It either delivers the human being soulless into the hands of matter, or it frees his sanctity by offering up his ego as a sacrifice and letting it become ever more transparent until the moment of death."

Max Reinhardt's sudden death at the end of October 1943 was yet another severe blow: one of the homeless, like himself, had become a victim of exile. The most important man in the German-language theater of the twentieth century had never been able to gain a real foothold in the United States, especially not after the *Eternal Road* debacle in 1936–37.

Bouts of fever, great difficulty in breathing, and fear of suffocation now marked Werfel's days and nights, while the weakness of his heart caused his lungs to congest. Anguished, he asked the friendly priests at the Old Mission of Santa Barbara to say daily prayers for him. He was confined to bed in his bright room on Bedford Drive, attended by his wife and Friedrich Torberg. An oxygen tank had been installed beside his bed, and he sometimes used it for hours to assist his breathing. He told Alma that he was in "the birth pangs of death" and sat up in bed one day in mid-December to write a poem, "Dance of Death" ("Totentanz"). "Death swung me around in a dance. / At first, I did not miss a step. / In the dance of death, I did step out / Until he speeded up the tempo. / . . . But suddenly he dropped his prey / And in the alphabet of the First Silence / *He* spoke only two words: Not today!"

A few days after Christmas, Hollywood witnessed the festive and vastly successful world premiere of *The Song of Bernadette*—America's first great Catholic movie. Werfel was unable to attend the gala event, but he listened to a live radio broadcast reporting the arrival of illustrious guests at the Cathay Circle Theater. A million copies of the novel had been sold by now; the U.S. government purchased fifty thousand for the army. The San Francisco *Herald Examiner* was running the novel as a daily comic strip. A manufacturer in Alabama had come up with a soap statuette of Bernadette Soubirous that was marketed all over the country. There was a hit song on the radio, "The Song of Bernadette," and the famous illustrator Norman Rockwell produced a large, endlessly reproduced portrait of Jennifer Jones as Bernadette.

In the meantime, S. N. Behrman, the original co-initiator of the idea to turn the flight from Marseilles to Marseilles into a play, had written yet another version of *Jacobowsky and the Colonel*. His version, never approved by Werfel, was based on the version by Clifford Odets that Werfel despised. At the beginning of 1944, a young director, Elia Kazan, was already rehearsing the play—this, too, without Werfel's consent. Werfel now spent hours on the telephone to Lawrence Langner of the Theatre Guild, trying desperately to avert the worst. He protested against the melodramatic watering-down and sentimentalization of his play, and the daily excitement put an additional strain on his extremely unstable condition. Numerous, often page-long telegrams attest to his worries and rage. He told Langner that if he weren't so ill, he would have no trouble convincing everybody that he was right. He was particularly distressed that Behrman decided to cut his favorite scene, in which the refugees meet Francis of Assisi and the Wandering Jew riding a tandem bicycle. "I implore you," Werfel cabled Behrman in his less than idiomatic English, "not to reject every thing for what I am fighting with perhaps the last heartpower I have." And a few days later, in a telegram: "I beg you on my knees to restitute the end of scene IV."

While the first previews of the comedy were presented in New Haven, Boston, and Philadelphia, Werfel kept on protesting, still without success. "I am depressed to death because I feel helpless," he cabled Lawrence Langner, who replied laconically that Werfel's contract with the Theatre Guild clearly assigned the latter the right of final decisions.

Werfel clung to one last hope: to see his own original version of the play, in Gustave Arlt's translation, in the bookshops as soon as possible, so that every member of the theater audience could form his or her own opinion about it.

The Broadway premiere of *Jacobowsky and the Colonel* took place in mid-March 1944 at the Martin Beck Theater. The "comedy of a tragedy" now had the misleading tag "Original play by Franz Werfel, American play based on same by S. N. Behrman." The New York critics reacted mostly with praise, some even with enthusiasm; they wrote that Werfel's own contribution to the play remained unclear, although some reviewers did assume that at least the two main characters, the Jew and the anti-Semitic officer—both of whom were generally regarded as theatrically effective and original—owed their existence to Franz Werfel. The production relied heavily on the Viennese-born actor Oscar Karlweis in the part of Jacobowsky, and the critics hailed him as an exciting talent, perfectly cast. None of this consoled Werfel, who remained more hurt and angry than ever before in his life. He even considered a lawsuit against the Theatre Guild, but a few days after the first night it became apparent that the play would indeed be a hit, and Werfel gave up the idea. All the excitement about the ill-starred enterprise threatened to deprive him of his last reserves of strength.

In the spring of 1944, while he was still convalescing and mostly confined to his bed, he slowly recovered from his disappointment over the *Jacobowsky* affair. He read a great deal, including the works of Sinclair Lewis and Ernest Hemingway and, above all, Thomas Wolfe, his favorite American author. The "travel story" begun the previous year gradually started preoccupying him again; while Alma played Bach sonatas on the newly purchased Steinway or the radio blared musical programs sponsored by the California Gas Company, which often included fine recordings of Verdi arias, Werfel called up the spirits of memory. He searched for images of childhood and youth, moments of his days as a soldier, editor, and bohemian, in order to weave them into the narrative when he took up work on the utopian novel again. His thoughts circled most often around Willy Haas, who had found refuge in a Himalayan village in northern India; he reviewed their walks along the hillsides around Prague, their arguments in the coffeehouses, their first erotic adventures. He asked himself which moment of his life had been the most important, concluding that it was midsummer 1918, when Alma hemorrhaged and their son was born prematurely, after which he had to endure weeks of anxiety over the survival of mother and child. It was his intention to include this crucial event in his novel.

The gigantic work soon took shape in his mind. He told a reporter that this "travel story"—provided he managed to complete it—would be his very best and most important book. The journalist noticed that Werfel kept toying with an unlit cigar: since the doctors had strictly forbidden smoking, he wanted at least to touch and play with the beloved object.

Gulliver's Restaurant in Marina del Rey is close to the yacht harbor of Los Angeles. The walls of the entirely windowless restaurant have been decorated with famous episodes from Jonathan Swift's "travel story," and the waiters and waitresses, most of them out-of-work actors and actresses, wear costumes of the early eighteenth century. The furnishings are imitations of the same period. Hidden in a booth is Gustave O. Arlt, eighty-eight years old. This is the favorite haunt of the former chairman of the Department of German Literature of the University of California at Los Angeles. "My acquaintance and later friendship with the Werfels really started right after they came to the West Coast," says the sturdy old man. "We became particularly close in those last years before his death. While Werfel was writing his 'travel story' in Santa Barbara, I was translating the manuscript into English and often collaborated with him. I think it is his most important book—and he was very enthusiastic about it himself. Did you know that the title of the novel, Star of the Unborn, *was my idea? Werfel had chosen a quotation from Diodorus, another travel writer, for an epigraph: it says that it is the poet's task to seek out and describe the creatures of myth and fable, even the unborn on their star. That's how we hit upon the idea to call the book* Star of the Unborn. *Next to* Class Reunion *and* The Pure in Heart, Star *is the most reliable source of information on Werfel's childhood. There's a lot of autobiographical material in it, more or less disguised. I never asked Werfel any indiscreet questions, but sometimes he seemed ready to divulge personal things—and then often spoke of Willy Haas, in the most loving way, insisting that Haas had been the dearest friend he'd ever had.*

"In those final years, Werfel always wore very expensive suits. He had them tailored in Beverly Hills at the London Shop on Rodeo Drive; the store is still there, by the way. But never mind how expensive the pinstripe may have been, it always looked as if it didn't belong to its owner: both the coats and the pants always looked baggy and wrinkled, immediately. And he was always covered with food stains and cigar ashes. 'He smudges so easily,' they used to say about Werfel. And he smoked incessantly: cigars, cigarettes, pipes, sometimes all three at once, placed in different parts of his study. (He used the same method with his glasses: he had countless pairs that he left here or there, so that he'd always have some at hand without having to look for them.) After the severe heart attack in September 1943, he had to stop smoking, of course; he was lying in bed and asked August, their butler, to light a cigar and sit down next to him and blow the smoke at him. He was like a mischievous schoolboy all his life. August Hess was a

failed opera tenor from Germany, around forty, homosexual, and a jack-of-all-trades in the Werfel household: cook, chauffeur, servant. And extremely loyal. He hated animals. For instance, the turtle that the Werfels had brought back from an excursion to the Mojave Desert and that they took with them everywhere, for years, even to the St. Moritz in New York and to the Biltmore in Santa Barbara: it was allowed to do anything it wanted, including flooding the back seat of the Oldsmobile with its urine—Alma just loved such little contretemps. But one day the turtle disappeared. And August was the strongest suspect. A high-pedigree Irish setter and a Siamese cat didn't fare much better in the Werfel household; August saw to it that they left after a very short time.

"Here's a totally different image I just remembered: the day Werfel and Alma passed their exams for U.S. citizenship—it must have been in 1944. I went with them to the courthouse in downtown Los Angeles. They were both sweating blood, they were so nervous. They were questioned separately about American history and government. 'What is the name of the current president of the United States?' was one of the questions. Or: 'Who are the senators for California?' Of course they didn't have any trouble at all.

"Or our automobile trip at the height of the summer of 1941—Werfel had just heard that his father had died. The four of us drove to Yosemite Park and stayed at the Ahwanee Hotel. Werfel mostly sat on the big veranda and wrote and wrote, hot as it was. Alma left one of her countless bottles of Benedictine liqueur—she consumed one a day—sitting in the sun, and it heated up until it exploded and covered everything with its sweet, sticky contents, including Werfel's notes.

"In the middle of meals, when we went to restaurants—Romanoff's in Beverly Hills was one of Werfel's favorite places—he would suddenly jump up and run out into the street, looking for a newsboy to get the latest edition of the paper. 'I have to see the evening papers!' he'd shout. He was that eager to have the latest news about his beloved Europe; he was deeply attached to it, he had to read the latest dispatches from the fronts. August had to run out for the papers several times a day.

"When Werfel and Alma quarreled, it was really only about politics. And how Werfel could yell! He was the choleric-sanguine type. But sometimes he yelled at Alma just because she was really hard of hearing. And he found that very irritating. Especially since she did nothing to correct it; she was much too vain to get a hearing aid.

"But they were unanimous about the question of how Werfel should be buried. They talked about that quite often, especially after that serious heart attack. I often heard him say to Alma, 'Now, you won't have them bury me as a Jew, will you?!' And he was really serious about it. You know, he lived in this curious mix of Judaism and Christianity—he was absolutely convinced of the 'permanence' of the Jewish people, as he discusses it in Star of the Unborn. *But at the same time he felt deeply attached to the Catholic fathers, such as the sophisticated Jesuit*

Georg Moenius, who published an anti-Nazi journal and was one of his best friends during his years in California. Moenius was more a politician than a man of the cloth. And the Franciscan monk Cyrill Fischer, who lived in Santa Barbara, a mild and lovable man who never mastered the English language—discussions with him were particularly important to Werfel while he wrote his 'travel novel.' You'll find them reproduced in Star, in the conversations between F.W. and the Grand Bishop. Fischer died in May 1944 of cancer of the liver—another severe blow to Werfel. I accompanied him many times to the Old Mission in Santa Barbara, where he spent most of his time in the beautiful library or visiting the fathers he knew there. I remember one Saturday when we went there and practically all the Franciscan monks were sitting in front of a television set watching a football game—I've never forgotten that."

A waitress in a red Gulliver outfit brings Professor Arlt a huge half-bloody T-bone steak. "Did you know," Arlt continues without breaking stride, "that Alma published Star of the Unborn after Werfel's death in an arbitrarily cut version? Well, she even published Mahler's symphonies, after his death, in abbreviated versions—she believed that Mahler's 'long-windedness' was detrimental to his popularity! (It's true that Werfel often admitted to being a bit too verbose, like Victor Hugo, Balzac, or Dostoyevsky.) You do look surprised about Alma's editorial interventions in Werfel's work. You have to understand one more thing: after Werfel's death, Alma talked much more often about Mahler and Kokoschka than about her 'man-child' Franzl. I always felt that she never loved the man Werfel as much as his fame and genius. If Werfel hadn't been a genius, Alma certainly wouldn't have been interested in him."

"The Book Must Be Finished"

MARLENE DIETRICH, A good friend of the Werfels, commissioned Carroll Righter, then America's best-known astrologer, to cast Franz Werfel's horoscope in the spring of 1944. The only information she gave Righter was that the person in question had been born in Prague during the night of September 10–11, 1890. Righter's prognostications extended up to August 1946 and stressed, above all, the unknown subject's extremely precarious state of health: particular caution was to be exercised until November 1944—until then, upsets of any kind would have to be avoided. Unfortunately, it seemed that this Virgo had a tendency to get upset by mere trivialities. The fall of 1944, Righter prophesied, initiated a period of powerful inspiration of, as it were, a visionary nature—never before, the popular stargazer noted, had he seen a chart like this: the man to whom it applied had to be an extremely idealistic and at the same time magnanimous person, and what was more, there was no doubt that he was a genius.

Werfel remained in bed during the spring of 1944. Nevertheless, urged by his American publisher Ben Huebsch, he decided to publish a collection of thoughts and ideas on ethical and religious questions, under the title "Theologumena." He gathered sketches and fragments from his desk drawers and old notebooks, some of them dating back to 1914, when Werfel first considered an essay to be called "On the Subject of Theodicy" ("Zum Thema Theodizee"). He also wanted to incorporate a large number of aphorisms and epigrams he had jotted down during his months of illness. He began to dictate these short texts, which spanned a period of thirty years, to Albrecht Joseph in the latter part of March. Modeled on Pascal's *Pensées* and Novalis's *Fragments*, they failed to match either, not even reaching Werfel's own customary level. "What would Israel be without the Church? And what would the Church be without Israel?" Next to this typical credo, Werfel also tried to express his own rather abstruse sense of Jewishness, which ascribed the guilt of persecution to its victims: "It is one of Israel's strangest transgressions that by means of its nature and form of being, it calls forth ... from Christians, ... the sin of anti-Semitism, which leads to its own destruction." He also did not hesitate to defame the expressionist ideals of his youth: there had never been, he now claimed, "a more devastating, insolent, sarcastic, satanic arrogance" than that of the "avant-garde artists and radical intellectuals" among whom he had to count himself. He concluded, "While amusing and shocking a few Philistines, we, otherwise unnoticed, stoked the fires of the hell in which mankind is roasting now."

Sitting up in bed dictating "Theologumena," Werfel (along with his doctors) believed that he had gotten over the worst. However, he suffered another coronary occlusion in mid-May and had to spend further weeks and months in bed. Not until the height of summer was he gradually able to lead a more normal life, nine months after the first major attack in September 1943. He went on his first, still very cautious walks and spent hours sitting in the garden. However, he wanted to pick up his work on *Star of the Unborn* as soon as possible, and to that end he moved back to Santa Barbara in July. Even then, Alma did not go with him, but he was accompanied by his private physician, Dr. Spinak, who lived with him from that time on. Dr. Spinak, a native Austrian, outwardly resembled Franz Schubert and hence bore the nickname "Schwammerl" (Little Mushroom), borrowed from R. H. Bartsch's famous fictional biography of Schubert. A few days after the two had moved into a bungalow on the grounds of Werfel's favorite hotel, the Biltmore, it was taken over by the American military. Werfel and Spinak had to move into Santa Barbara itself, where they rented a cottage on the spacious grounds of Hotel El Mirasol.

Despite his mortal illness, Werfel returned to his task with familiar intensity, working on the creation of a world that was taking on increasingly bizarre and fairy-tale forms. It was populated by Foreignfeelers and Geoarchons, Starrovers and Chronosophers, Marvelers and Animators. The year before, he had simply told Gottfried Bermann Fischer that he was trying "something quite unexpected"; now he wrote that he was working on a novel set "in the most remote future," which was "a kind of fantastic travel book, but also the story of souls, hearts, and love." "Pretty strange ..."

Strange, indeed, this *Star of the Unborn*, dictated by a powerful imagination. It was, among other things, Werfel's vision of America's future, a warning to the United States of the 1940s not to underestimate the risks of overdoing its technology and to put a halt to the displacement of nature by increasing automation, if it did not wish to subject its descendants to an entirely artificial and inhumane world. To this threatening aberration of mankind Werfel opposed the concept of the Jungle, zones of natural simplicity that the Astromentals of the year 101943 regard as "swinish hubbub." This Jungle resembles the Europe of the early twentieth century—its atmosphere is also a bit reminiscent of *Goat Song:* Jungle people are still busy herding cattle and tilling the soil, and their Slavic features are those of Albanian peasants. "The Jungle people not only had to plow, sow, and reap, they also had to spin and weave. In short, they had to labor." Not only their work but also their dwellings distinguish the Jungle folk from the Astromentals: they are still living in houses aboveground. "What a horrible thought," says one Astromental to his visitor F.W., "that humans live in such boxes, and on the surface, at that." And another companion blusters, "You can't call those creatures humans."

The inevitable happens, "the calamity [that] proves to be the turning point of Astromental history." War breaks out between the Astromentals and their enemies, the Jungle people. The combatants deploy their "trans-shadow-disintegrators" everywhere, and suddenly the book resembles a run-of-the-mill dime novel, not unlike the Flash Gordon comic strips of the late thirties and the sci-fi movies (among other B productions) that flooded the American market in the forties. Werfel had seen quite a few of these: in Santa Barbara, where there were few other distractions from work, he often went to the movies in the evening, picking them at random and enjoying even those of little artistic merit.

To Werfel's own amazement, work on the first draft of the novel proceeded apace, and he took breaks from writing only on weekends. These were spent in Beverly Hills with his wife. During the week, he talked to Alma three or four times daily on the telephone, reporting on the steady progress of the book.

By fall, he felt considerably better than he had at the beginning of the year, although he had not "returned to the old me," as he wrote his sister Mizzi; they were now on more or less friendly terms again. "I now take daily walks of a couple of hundred strides, very slowly, like a ghostly replica of those decrepit old Jews in Prague's city park. . . . Amusingly enough, one does not get used to dying. . . . It is particularly amusing if, while engaged in that serious activity, one doesn't really feel grown-up (much less, old) as I do." He also told Mizzi that the "travel novel" had in the meantime changed "from a little children's stroll to the conquest of a glacier." He said that his scientific education was quite insufficient for this work, which was why he had to spend his evenings "learning many things from books written in English, to be able to fantasize with impunity in the daytime."

His new novel was a "humorous-cosmic-mystical world poem, in a mix that has not been attempted before": thus Werfel praised *Star of the Unborn* to his American publisher, Ben Huebsch, while expressing far more pessimistic views to Friedrich Torberg—who had, to Werfel's great regret, moved to New York: "I'm working, sluggishly and with a bad conscience, on my great big novel of the future. Sometimes it makes me want to puke. You see, I don't really know if what I am doing is good." In addition, the work was becoming far too voluminous and demanding: "Hardly able to breathe again, and back in the soup!" (Werfel himself often referred to his big novels as "Wild West stories"— in his own view, only the poems were entirely serious work.)

Around the turn of the year 1944–45, Werfel began the third part of this mammoth novel, the episode of the Wintergarden, in which F.W. goes to the interior of the planet Earth and learns about the future people's burial rites: after very long lives, the Astromentals voluntarily move into a region where they are immersed in "retrogenetic humus" and slowly transformed back to their embryonic state and finally planted in an immeasurably large field, ending up as daisies. In contrast to his comic-strip treatment of a futuristic world war, Werfel's Wintergarden passage is one of the most brilliant creations of his oeuvre. The certainty of mortal illness permitted him experiments and stylistic and thematic risk taking he would not even have considered only a year earlier.

Philosophical Library published Werfel's volume *Between Heaven and Earth* at the end of 1944. In addition to "Theologumena" (spelled "Theologoumena" in this edition), it contained three of his lectures from the thirties: "Realism and Inwardness" (originally titled "Art and Conscience"), "Can We Live Without Faith in God?" and "Of Man's True Happiness." The American public's reaction to this publication of the famous best-selling author's ruminations was lukewarm. Jewish reviewers went so far as to brand "Theologumena" as anti-Semitic; Werfel's opponents found his insistent flirtation with the Catholic Church impossible to explain. On the other hand, there were critics from the ranks of the Dominicans and the Jesuits who attacked him just as vehemently: they considered the section "On Christ and Israel" a total failure.

Max Brod wrote a letter in response to his friend's collection of aphorisms and noted that it repeated the same arguments that had once alienated them from each other in Prague. Unlike Werfel, Brod was not at all ready to accept Jesus of Nazareth as the messiah but regarded him as a rabbinical figure, one less important than, say, Hillel,

Maimonides, or the Ba'al Shem Tov. Furthermore, he could not comprehend how Werfel was able to urge the people of Israel to join a church whose absolute failure in every respect had been obvious for centuries. Once again Werfel defined his position: he wrote back saying that he regarded the life of Jesus as "the decisive event in Jewish history.... Without the effect of Christianity, Judaism would never have survived."

Werfel also told Brod about the extremely precarious state of his health: he wrote that his heart had "cracked" and that he now lived in constant fear of "cardiac asthma and emphysema." Everything had become "extremely tiring," and he was particularly exhausted by speaking, "more ... than by anything else." It was his fervent wish to once more "walk about in the city park" in Prague with Brod, "arguing as we once did so terribly long ago," but he did not expect "ever to do that again." Werfel reported that *Star of the Unborn* threatened to become a thousand-page opus: "I fear that I have fallen for a monstrous mélange of philosophy and entertainment." In his salutation, he embraced his friend—"in the old fidelity of youth"—and uttered this hope: "Perhaps God will permit us to see each other once more in this crazy world.... I myself cannot make any plans."

In Europe this was the time of the decisive battles to defeat Hitler's Germany. In January 1945 the Ardennes offensive, the Third Reich's last great push, had failed, and Allied air raids on Berlin and Dresden killed tens of thousands of civilians. The Americans crossed the Rhine at the beginning of March, and, only a little later, the Red Army advanced toward Berlin and Vienna. By mid-April, Vienna was firmly in Russian hands. Only a few hours before the Soviet troops entered the city, Alma's stepfather, Carl Moll, committed suicide, together with his daughter Maria and her husband, Richard Eberstaller. Those three had believed in Hitler's "final victory" to the end.

The Allies liberated the survivors of the concentration camps and revealed the unimaginable extent of systematic mass murder; pictures of infernal cruelty were seen around the world, unveiling the greatest crime in human history. At Auschwitz-Birkenau alone, more than two million people had been killed in the gas chambers. The survivors looked like breathing skeletons, living corpses, not unlike those saved at Musa Dagh, about whom a British naval officer in Werfel's novel comments: "It seemed to me that I had not seen human beings, only eyes."

The news came fast and furious: Mussolini shot. Hitler commits suicide. Germany surrenders unconditionally. Werfel and Alma were already toying with the idea of going to Europe as soon as possible, planning a visit to Rome, which had remained almost unharmed, as their first stop. "The defeat of Germany," Werfel wrote in a German-language New York daily, ". . . is a fact that has no like in world history." Germany's collapse was unmatched by "the defeat of Carthage, or even the greatest of military catastrophes." It was an event that would make the Germans conscious of having been "possessed by a spirit from hell." The only road now open to the German people was one of "inward purification from the most atrocious crimes imaginable."

He expressed similar sentiments in a message, "To the German People" ("An das deutsche Volk"), that was cabled to Europe by the U.S. Office of War Information to be printed in German-language newspapers: "Germans, do you know what happened, what you were guilty of and accomplices to, in the years of our Lord 1933 to 1945? Do you know that Germans killed millions and millions of peaceable, harmless, innocent Europeans with methods that would make the Devil himself blush for shame?" These atrocities were committed by a horde of individual criminals; they were supported by the community of the German people. "In this terrible hour of trial," the Germans could find help only by casting their minds back to their "saints and great masters." "Only they can relieve you of your shame."

His work on *Star of the Unborn* was overwhelming Werfel. He sent a continuous stream of manuscript pages to Los Angeles, to his new secretary, the former Viennese theater director and scholar William W. Melnitz (Albrecht Joseph had, in the meantime, taken a job as a film editor), and only after the book was almost a thousand typewritten pages long, in the middle of June 1945, did he allow himself a few days of rest. When his friends Ernst and Anuschka Deutsch pleaded with him to slow down a little and not to return to Santa Barbara yet, he replied, "The book must be finished—before I am."

He confessed to Friedrich Torberg in a letter of June 18 that he broke into a "sweat of anxiety and embarrassment" when he thought of the "impossible adventure that is this book"—a book that wanted to prove "that things will be much worse in a hundred thousand years than they are now, mainly because things will be so much better." He was also afraid that "partisans of all camps"—"Muscovites to Catholics, and all in between"—would, after the publication of the novel, punish him for his basic political attitude and "hang [him] upside down like Mussolini." He subjected himself to upsets and strains, although he was only kept alive "by the grace of foxglove"—a reference to the drug digitalis, which his doctors continued to administer to him.

In the summer of 1945, in Santa Barbara, Werfel wrote the final chapters of *Star of the Unborn* and asked his "sweet, only beloved Alma" to forgive him for his long absence. After three days and nights in the future world of the year 101943, F.W. asks the Great Bishop to let him return home, to the place where he had actually lived before his death in the twentieth century: "at the corner of Bedford Drive and April 1943." Accompanied by Io-Squirt, whom he had met in the "Lamasery of the Chronosophers" and in whom he had subsequently recognized an incarnation of his own son, Martin Johannes, F.W. leaves the utopia of the Astromentals. "My entire being was light, bright, airy joy, the very memory of which brings tears to my eyes," says the narrator. And he strides past the mischievous, smiling gaze of his son Io-Squirt, "until I knew nothing more." Below these last words of the twenty-sixth chapter, Franz Werfel wrote: "17 August 1945. Sta Barbara."

"Fat Man" and "Little Boy" were the loving nicknames the American military had given the two uranium bombs that wiped out Hiroshima and Nagasaki on August 6 and August 8, 1945. The utopian reality of the Atomic Age had already begun.

Werfel planned a final, twenty-seventh chapter *"in which is concealed an epilogue that is also an apology,"* but he decided to return to Beverly Hills first for about a week in order to get a little rest from the strains of recent months. Only a few hours before his departure he wrote to Friedrich Torberg that he had now finished the third and last part of his "travel novel"—"a ride across Lake Constance, physically and emotionally and spiritually, but I hope I won't have to share the fate of that rider."

It was an unusually hot midsummer afternoon. August Hess drove Werfel to Los Angeles, to North Bedford Drive, where the exhausted author immediately took to his bed. A general practitioner from the neighborhood made a house call—his personal physician, Dr. Spinak, had taken a few days' leave. Werfel complained of feeling weak and unwell, and the doctor gave him an injection for his heart. He also prescribed a morphine injection, to be administered that evening. During the night Werfel suffered a severe attack and was convinced that he was about to die. Early in the morning, however, the danger seemed to have passed, and a group of consulting physicians ordered strict bed rest. Werfel had a fever, for no discernible reason. He was upset and angered by the thought that he would not be able to write the epilogue to *Star of the Unborn.* There was an owl sitting in a tree just outside his window, and it seemed to fix him with its gaze, day and night. Werfel perceived its presence as an omen of death.

Around this time Werfel received a letter from his friend Johannes Urzidil. The Prague-born writer, who had been living in New York since 1941, congratulated Werfel on the "Theologumena," saying that they corresponded closely to his own world view: he was the son of a

Christian father and a Jewish mother. With great nostalgia prompted by the end of the war, he reminded both Werfel and himself of the Prague of yesteryear, their conversations in the Arco, Edison, and Continental cafés, and their visits to less reputable establishments. He reminisced about a city that would never again be as it had been—a magical construct inhabited by a mix of Austrian nobility, Czechs, Germans, and Jews. Urzidil noted that the nobility had been wiped out by World War I and the Jews by World War II; the Czechs were now busy eliminating the German element so that henceforth they would be in sole possession of the "golden city." The Prague of their childhood and youth was gone forever.

One week after his return to Beverly Hills from Santa Barbara, Werfel felt considerably better. He was allowed to get up and spent time at his desk, editing a selection of his favorite poems from the years 1908–45 to be published in German by a small press in California. The conductor Bruno Walter, a neighbor, came by on a Saturday evening to pick up the Werfels for a drive to town. Before they left, Walter sat down at the piano and started playing a melody from Bedřich Smetana's *Bartered Bride*. Werfel, who loved that particular Czech opera, rushed from his room and belted out the aria in question, even taking a few exuberant dance steps. Then the friends spent a convivial evening in Werfel's favorite restaurant, Romanoff's, exchanging gossip, reminiscences, and anecdotes.

The following morning Werfel, in a good mood and feeling exceptionally well, discussed the projected trip to Europe with Alma. First of all, he wanted to see his sister Hanna again as soon as possible—she was still living in London—but he also wanted to visit Prague and Vienna, Venice and Rome. The doctors advised strongly against air travel but regarded a sea voyage as relatively safe.

In response to a commission from the United Nations, which had been established as the successor to the League of Nations, Werfel wrote a piece that Sunday, "A Greeting to Salzburg" ("Gruss an Salzburg"), in which he pondered Austria's political future. The city of Salzburg was now part of the American zone of occupation, and there were plans to reestablish it as a center for the arts. "Would it not be an idea with great potential," Werfel suggested, "for the United Nations to depoliticize all of Austria and to guarantee her economic existence in order to establish, on her sacred soil, a paradise of national reconciliation, a perennial fair at which all compete by offering the best gifts they have?"

In the early evening, while Alma was receiving visitors, Werfel was again sitting at his desk editing that selection of favorite poems from almost forty years. He was just working on "The Conductor" ("Der

Dirigent"), written in 1938, when his heart stopped beating, a few minutes before 6:00 P.M., on August 26, 1945. Franz Werfel slipped from his swivel chair to the floor.

"Even in Vienna, Werfel often told me, 'I don't know whether dear Alma is my greatest joy or my greatest disaster,'" Anna Mahler says. "I think it was in Santa Barbara that he really disengaged himself from her psychologically. Yes—there, in the last years of his life, while Star of the Unborn *was created, he freed himself from her oppression. But she probably had a final victory over him after his death: there are persistent rumors that she and her friend, Father Georg Moenius, performed something called a 'baptism by desire.' Nothing was more important to her than to see that her Franzl didn't go to meet God as a Jew."*

"Alma asked me," says Albrecht Joseph, "to reserve seats for the most prominent mourners, in the chapel of the Pierce Brothers' Mortuary; when I went back to pick her up and told her, 'Come, Alma, it's time, we have to—,' she said, 'I'm not going.' 'What do you mean, you're not going?' 'I never *go to those things!' And then, when all the mourners had gathered, the entire republic in exile of German-language literature, we just sat there and waited and waited for the ceremony to begin. Bruno Walter played some Bach, played a Schubert sonata; Lotte Lehmann sang several songs by Schubert twice. Everybody thought we were waiting for Alma. But we were really waiting for Father Georg Moenius; he was going to deliver the eulogy. By the way, it was he who had delivered Karl Kraus's eulogy in Vienna, eight years earlier. When he finally appeared, there were whispers that he was late because Alma had rewritten his entire speech. Moenius stressed that he was not speaking on this sorrowful day as a Catholic clergyman, but as a friend of Franz Werfel. He went on to claim that in the Astromental world of* Star of the Unborn *the old enemies Werfel and Kraus would now shake hands and be reconciled. He made a special point of the explicitly Catholic tendency of most of Werfel's work—and then went on to say, to the amazement of the congregation, that while it was true that the deceased had never joined the Church formally, by being baptized, he had, however, been on the way there when death called him away. The Church, he said, recognized not only the customary baptism by water but also baptism by blood and, further, the so-called baptism by desire, which applied to all those who had desired baptism but had not received it in their lifetime. Moenius's speech raised eyebrows: why was he discussing the different varieties of baptism in a eulogy for his friend Werfel? Naturally, the rumor that Alma and Moenius had indeed baptized Werfel after his death spread like wildfire, but both of them denied it until their dying day."*

"When Werfel died I was still living in London," says Anna, "and it was I who had to tell his sister Hanna the news that her beloved brother had died. And she had this fit of rage, the most tremendous I've ever seen anyone have. And the main target of that rage was God. That God had been able to do this *to her!*

Although she had kept her vow and stopped smoking! God had done this to her! An awful scene. Hanna was thrashing about on her bed. For her, the worst thing was, of course, that she hadn't been able to see Franz one more time, now that the war was over at long last.

"I myself came to the United States years later, in 1950, when Mammi was no longer living in California but in a small apartment in New York. And every time I visited her, she would say at least twice, 'If Mahler walked in that door now, I'd go with him immediately!' One thing is true, of course: Alma didn't grow any more with Werfel. She had a strong personality. She was much stronger than he. She needed someone like Mahler to put up enough resistance. With Kokoschka, there was a kind of balance, and that was good for her. Yet she sent him off to war. And Hollnsteiner? When he visited America once, after the war, Alma refused even to see him. When she was eighty-five—that was in 1964, shortly before she died—Alma told me a dream that haunted her: Franz Werfel had come walking down the stairs in the hallway of a building and had passed her without a word, without even looking at her, even though he almost brushed by her as he kept on descending those stairs. It hurt her terribly that he had pretended she didn't exist. She pondered and pondered why that had happened; and then, three days later, she told me, 'I've got it! I'm sure there's another woman behind it all!' "

After my final visit to Anna Mahler and Albrecht Joseph, I return once more to the university library basement in Los Angeles that houses most of Franz Werfel's literary estate. For weeks the boxes have been piling up on my desk, and I have been going through letters and jottings, notebooks and diaries. Once more I pick up the original manuscript of the "travel novel"—and find, between two of its pages, some dried flowers that Alma had given her husband for good luck more than forty years before, when he resumed work on Star of the Unborn *in the middle of summer 1944.*

In an Italian notebook from the year 1932, I find some hastily scribbled sentences that read like a premonition of Star of the Unborn. *It seems to me that these words contain Franz Werfel's credo, the leitmotiv of his oeuvre: "Sometimes I have such a strange feeling in the area of my heart. Be conscious of every second—something says to me—write down everything, if possible. After all, you are not from and of this world but a visitor from distant, ancient centuries."*

Box 34 contains a plaster cast of Werfel's right hand. The fingers are thick and short, the thumb uncommonly wide; there is an ugly signet ring. I find a package wrapped in black velvet and open it carefully. It is a moment that could well be in Star of the Unborn. *I see Franz Werfel's death mask in yellow-white plaster—here, in the fluorescent light, deep down under the earth of California. I stare at the calm and gentle features for a long time; then, lightly, I touch the very high, deeply wrinkled forehead. I touch the eyebrows, the strong nose, thick lips, double chin. I run my fingertips over the closed eyelids. Until now I have never realized how much life can emanate from such a mask. Then I quickly wrap it in its velvet covering and close the lid of Box 34.*

Another large collection of Franz Werfel's papers is preserved on the East Coast, in Philadelphia. It was brought together by his friend and editor of many years, Professor Adolf D. Klarmann, who was a teacher of German language and literature in this city. The attic of the library of the University of Pennsylvania— again, a windowless room, lit by fluorescent lights and air-conditioned, not underground this time but high above the campus—is the last way station on my quest for the story of Franz Werfel's life.

My excavations uncover a bluish metal case for eyeglasses, lined with a red fabric with Franz Werfel's name stamped on it in gold letters; the extremely powerful lenses lie there surrounded by their frame, which has disintegrated into dozens of yellow splinters, as if a thousand years had passed since the death of their owner. Next to a travel alarm clock, notepaper, and calling cards (with the legend DR. H. C. FRANZ WERFEL*), I find one of his numerous cigar holders. Even today, after forty years, the smell of smoke and ashes from Werfel's fat Havana cigars lingers on the small, brownish object.*

I read, in a typescript by Willy Haas: "Franz Werfel surely knew my address in the small village in the Himalayas, and there was a post office in that village. But he never wrote to me. Now and again, rarely enough, I received a letter from his wife, Alma, in her gigantic Gothic letters, three lines of them per page. I wrote to her, 'Of course I cherish your letters just as much as I do those from Franz, but I can't understand why he hasn't written to me for years.' I received my answer a couple of months later, as usual. Alma wrote, 'You'll find out why when you read Franz's posthumous novel.' I received the posthumous novel, Star of the Unborn, *a year later. I read a couple of pages and had to stop, because I had realized something that I found impossible to imagine: it appeared that Franz Werfel, in the last years of his life, had been thinking about me more than about any other person in the world. He had written a novel about our friendship. I had to overcome a slight state of shock before I was able to read on, with flushed cheeks, day and night, in my little room at the edge of the jungle. Outside, hyenas were laughing, jackals howling. There were many dozens of people in this novel, but really only two characters: Franz and myself, and for more than seven hundred pages we conducted a conversation we had conducted hundreds of times, more or less, as boys, a conversation without end."*

I turn the pages of a thin school notebook with a black-and-white checkered cover. It is dated 1918 and bears the inscription SECRET DIARY. *On the first page I read: "Whosoever happens to come upon this book is* implored to close it *again—no noble eye will want to read private disclosures that are not meant for the* public—nor for itself. Even a mother's eye will desist here." *This little secret book—after some hesitation, I disregard Werfel's plea—contains diary entries from the summer of 1918, the time when Alma gave birth to Martin Johannes. There are no surprises in the text: Frau Mahler-Werfel had made her husband's most intimate notations public a long time ago, incorporating them verbatim in her autobiography,* Mein Leben, *published in 1960.*

Adolf D. Klarmann's own notes, essays, and university lectures on Werfel's life and work are also preserved here in the library attic. Immediately after the death of his idol, Klarmann interviewed Werfel's friends and relatives, his mother, his sisters, Kurt Wolff, and Friedrich Torberg. Alma confided to him in October 1945 that her husband had been baptized very soon after his death; thanks to the efforts of the Jesuit Georg Moenius and the archbishop of Los Angeles, a so-called baptism by desire had been performed. This was a secret that Professor Klarmann had to keep to himself under all circumstances. Alma's devoted admirer underscored the word secret *twice and kept that promise all his life.*

"Of course Werfel was not *baptized," Alma lied to her friend Friedrich Torberg, who had not been able to rid himself of his suspicions ten years after Werfel's death. "I could have had an* emergency *baptism when I found him— but I would* never *have* dared *to do that!" she insisted. "Werfel was accessible to* all *true mysticism, but he would have told me, in* one *word, if he had wanted* that. *He told me once while he was working on* Star of the Unborn *that he wanted to be buried that way, interdenominationally. And there were no symbols, no Talmud, no Cross. He was provisionally placed in a mausoleum (as you know), because I* wanted *him to have a grave of honor. But since the gentlemen of Vienna are now punishing me for my Jewish interrelations . . ."*

Alma Mahler had her man-child buried in tails and a silk shirt, just the way Werfel had described his burial in California soil. "I had probably been buried in this ceremonial costume," he says in Star of the Unborn, *"more than a hundred thousand years ago, and even then this tailcoat had been . . . nearly twenty years old. . . . My fingernails gleamed and even showed a rosy tint; the California mortician had had me manicured." However, only thirty years after his death, in July 1975, Franz Werfel's mortal remains—in clear disregard of his last will but in accordance with Alma Mahler's (she, too, was now buried in Vienna)—were exhumed from the soil of Hollywood's Rosedale Mortuary & Cemetery, packed in a wooden crate, and sent on a regular TWA flight to the former capital of the Austro-Hungarian Empire. The shipping label read:* PLEASE HANDLE CAREFULLY, *and the crate was addressed to the Palais Wilczek, the location of the Austrian Society for Literature. This palace in Vienna's Inner City stands at one end of Herrengasse, only a few steps from the two places that were home to Franz Werfel during his time in Vienna: the Central and Herrenhof cafés.*

The director of the Austrian Society for Literature was able, at the very last moment, to prevent the delivery of the wooden crate from Hollywood—ulti-

mately destined for an honorary grave in Vienna's Central Cemetery—to the rather plush offices of the society. He rushed out to the airport. In his presence, the gentlemen of the Austrian Customs Service opened the top of the crate. For seconds, deeply shocked, the director stared down at some whitish bone fragments tightly wrapped in a sheet of plastic.

Chronology

1890   Born September 10, the son of Rudolf and Albine Werfel (*née* Kussi).

1896   Attends private elementary school of the Piarist order.

1900   Enters the Royal and Imperial German Gymnasium in the New Town of Prague.

1903   Bar mitzvah, Maisel synagogue, Prague.

1904   Transfers to the Royal and Imperial German Gymnasium, Stefansgasse; goes to the Neue Deutsche Theater, attends May Festival with performances by Enrico Caruso.

1905   First poems; in love with Maria Glaser.

1908   First meeting with Max Brod; on February 23, FW's poem "The Gardens of the City" appears in *Die Zeit*, Vienna; spiritualist séances.

1909   Graduates; friendship with Max Brod and Franz Kafka; Café Arco; audits lectures at the Karlsuniversität.

1910   From October, works for the shipping agency Brasch & Rothenstein; *The Visit from Elysium.*

1911   Hamburg; poems from *The Friend of the World* previewed in *Die Fackel*, edited by Karl Kraus; *The Friend of the World* published mid-December by Axel Juncker in Berlin; from October, military service as a one-year volunteer at Hradčany Castle.

1912   Prague; one-year volunteer service; writes *The Temptation* on maneuvers; from October, an editor at Kurt Wolff Verlag, Leipzig.

1913   Leipzig; Malcesine on Lake Garda; *We Are;* meets Rainer Maria Rilke in Hellerau; begins translation of *The Trojan Women;* gives numerous readings; first quarrel with Karl Kraus.

1914   Leipzig; readings; meetings with Martin Buber; called up for service at the beginning of the war but soon discharged.

1915   Called up again, posted to Bozen; discharged once again; injured in Bozen; unfit for military service; called up again in September: Elbe

Kostelec and Trebnitz; first meets Gertrud Spirk; discharged again; *Each Other* published; *The Trojan Women* published.

1916 Prague; called up again in May: Elbe Kostelec; quarrel with Karl Kraus worsens; sent to the front in eastern Galicia; Hodóv; serves as a messenger, never in the trenches; writes numerous polemical essays.

1917 On the front, Hodóv and Jeziema; *Stockleinen;* August: transfer to Vienna, Military Press Bureau; first meets Alma Maria Mahler-Gropius in mid-November.

1918 Military Press Bureau sponsors trip to Switzerland; lectures, readings; FW accused of antiwar propaganda, trip interrupted; continues work in press office; relationship with Alma Mahler grows more intimate; birth of his and Alma's son Martin Carl Johannes; *The Midday Goddess;* end of the war, revolt in Vienna, FW participates in the storming of Parliament, sympathizes with Red Guard.

1919 Begins writing *Mirror Man* in Breitenstein am Semmering; death of son, Martin Johannes; *The Last Judgment* appears; *Not the Murderer.*

1920 *Mirror Man;* works on *Goat Song.*

1921 Reading tour through Germany; mid-October: world premiere of *Mirror Man.*

1922 Mid-March: world premiere of *Goat Song* in Vienna; Venice; writes *Schweiger;* first notes for *Verdi: A Novel of the Opera;* quarrels with Franz Kafka over *Schweiger.*

1923 Venice; Alma Mahler purchases the palazzo Casa Mahler; FW works on *Verdi;* mostly in Breitenstein.

1924 *Verdi* appears; Kafka dies, June 3; from July, FW works in Breitenstein on *Juarez and Maximilian;* leaves Kurt Wolff Verlag, goes to Paul Zsolnay Verlag.

1925 January and February; trip to Near East; summer: begins work on *Paul Among the Jews;* translates Verdi's *Forza del Destino* with Alma.

1926 April: resumes work on *Paul;* first draft of *The Kingdom of God in Bohemia;* meets Sigmund Freud, corresponds with him about *Paul;* autumn: writes *The Man Who Conquered Death.*

1927 Hotel Imperial, Santa Margherita Ligure; novella cycle: *Poor People, Severio's Secret, Estrangement; The House of Mourning;* begins work on *Class Reunion.*

1928 Santa Margherita, Vienna, Breitenstein; begins work on *The Pure in Heart.*

1929 Santa Margherita; continues work on *The Pure in Heart;* July 6: marriage to Alma Mahler; July 15: death of Hugo von Hofmannsthal; idea for *The Pascarella Family,* conceived in Santa Margherita; new German version of Verdi's *Simon Boccanegra.*

1930 January, February: second trip to Near East; idea for *The Forty Days of*

Musa Dagh, works on *The Kingdom of God in Bohemia,* premiere in December at the Burgtheater, Vienna.

1931   Santa Margherita; writes *The Pascarella Family;* continues in Breitenstein; October 21: death of Arthur Schnitzler.

1932   Breitenstein, Venice; begins work on *The Forty Days of Musa Dagh;* new German version of Verdi's *Don Carlos.*

1933   January: Hitler rises to power in Germany; FW works in Santa Margherita on *The Forty Days of Musa Dagh;* March: signs declaration of loyalty; May 10: book burnings in Germany; expelled from Prussian Academy of the Arts; November: *Musa Dagh* published; December: tries to become a member of the Reich Association of German Writers.

1934   *The Forty Days of Musa Dagh* banned in Germany; FW in Venice and Santa Margherita; February: unrest in Vienna, FW not there; works in Santa Margherita on *The Eternal Road;* July 25: Dollfuss murdered, Schuschnigg (friend of FW's and Alma Mahler-Werfel's) chancellor as of July 30; Manon Gropius contracts polio.

1935   *Eternal Road* collaboration with Max Reinhardt and Kurt Weill; writes poems; April 22: death of Manon Gropius; sale of Casa Mahler; November: trip to New York; December 24: death of Alban Berg; volume of poems *Sleep and Awakening (Schlaf und Erwachen)* published.

1936   New York until mid-February, via Paris to Vienna; Locarno; idea for Jeremiah novel; summer: works on *Hearken Unto the Voice* in Breitenstein; outbreak of Spanish Civil War.

1937   Finishes *Hearken Unto the Voice;* writes *One Night;* Breitenstein, Vienna.

1938   Capri; FW not in Vienna when Hitler occupies Austria in mid-March; Milan, Zurich, Paris, Amsterdam, London, Paris; St.-Germain-en-Laye; first heart attack; Sanary-sur-Mer, begins work on *Cella, or Those Who Overcome;* back and forth between Sanary and Paris; after the Anschluss, Gottfried Bermann Fischer (Stockholm) becomes FW's new publisher.

1939   St. Germain-en-Laye; abandons *Cella;* Sanary; works on *Embezzled Heaven;* outbreak of World War II.

1940   Sanary; *April in October;* Paris; flight; Lourdes, Marseilles; crosses Pyrenees on foot; Barcelona, Madrid, Lisbon; October 13: arrival in New York; end of December: move to Los Angeles.

1941   *The Song of Bernadette;* Hollywood; July 31: death of Rudolf Werfel in Marseilles.

1942   New York, Los Angeles; *The Song of Bernadette* becomes a best-seller; Santa Barbara; works on *Jacobowsky and the Colonel;* quarrels with sister Marianne Rieser; friendship with Friedrich Torberg.

1943 New York; Los Angeles; *Jacobowsky and the Colonel;* Santa Barbara;
     begins *Star of the Unborn;* June: honorary doctorate from UCLA;
     September 12: severe heart attack; December 14: another severe
     heart attack; unable to work.

1944 Los Angeles; mostly unable to work until the summer; dictates
     "Theologumena"; from July, in Santa Barbara, works on *Star of the
     Unborn; Between Heaven and Earth* published.

1945 Santa Barbara and Los Angeles: works on *Star of the Unborn;* finishes
     the book in August, only a few days before his death on August 26.

Notes

The following abbreviations have been used for works by Werfel (see Bibliography), or for sources and archives containing material on Werfel.

ADK notes	Unpublished notes on conversations with Alma Mahler-Werfel, Werfel's sisters (Hanna von Fuchs-Robetin and Marianne Rieser), and others, conducted shortly after Werfel's death by Adolf D. Klarmann, his friend and editor of many years (Alma Mahler-Werfel Collection, Van Pelt Library, University of Pennsylvania, Philadelphia)
DA	*Der Abituriententag*
DB	Deutsche Bibliothek, Frankfurt am Main
DD	*Die Dramen*
DL	Deutsches Literaturarchiv, Schiller-Nationalmuseum, Marbach am Neckar
DlW	*Das lyrische Werk*
EzW	*Erzählungen aus zwei Welten*
FK letters	Author's correspondence with Dr. František Kafka of Prague
FW/Mahler	Correspondence between Werfel and Alma Mahler-Werfel (Franz Werfel Collection, Department of Special Collections, Research Library of the University of California at Los Angeles)
FW/Spirk	Correspondence between Werfel and Gertrud Spirk (Deutsches Literaturarchiv, Schiller-Nationalmuseum, Marbach am Neckar)
GBF	Letters from Werfel to Gottfried Bermann Fischer (in the possession of the recipient)
KW Archive	Kurt Wolff Archive, Beineke Rare Books Library, Yale University, New Haven
MD conversations	Author's conversations with Professor Milan Dubrovic of Vienna

M-W Coll.   Alma Mahler-Werfel Collection, Van Pelt Library, University of Pennsylvania, Philadelphia
SU   *Stern der Ungeborenen*
UCLA   Franz Werfel Collection, Department of Special Collections, Research Library of the University of California at Los Angeles
ZOU   *Zwischen Oben und Unten* (1975)
Zsolnay Archive   Archive of Paul Zsolnay Verlag, Vienna

Also abbreviated are six works of secondary literature that were of major importance for this biography.

SL   Max Brod, *Streitbares Leben: Autobiographie 1884–1968* (Frankfurt am Main: Insel Verlag, 1979)
Foltin   Lore B. Foltin, *Franz Werfel* (Stuttgart: J. B. Metzlersche Verlagsbuchhandlung, 1972)
Haas   Willy Haas, *Die literarische Welt: Lebenserinnerungen* (Munich: Paul List Verlag, 1957)
DRM   Adolf D. Klarmann, Introduction to *Das Reich der Mitte,* a Franz Werfel reader (Graz: Stiasny-Bücherei, 1961)
ML   Alma Mahler-Werfel, *Mein Leben* (Frankfurt am Main: S. Fischer Verlag, 1960)
BeV   Kurt Wolff, *Briefwechsel eines Verlegers 1911–1963,* ed. Bernhard Zeller and Ellen Otten (Frankfurt am Main: Verlag Heinrich Scheffler, 1966)

CITY PARK

3   *violent rainstorms: Prager Tagblatt,* issues for early September 1890.
3   *Franz Viktor Werfel:* Birth certificate, M-W Coll.
3   *Rudolf and Albine Werfel:* Rudolf Werfel (September 21, 1858–July 31, 1941) and Albine Werfel, *née* Kussi (March 10, 1870–1964?) were married on December 15, 1889 (ADK notes, FK letters; see also FW's own statements in "Autobiographische Skizze," *ZOU,* pp. 701ff.
3   *Reitergasse 11:* ADK notes, FK letters.
4   *Barbara Šimůnková:* The full name of FW's nanny is given in ADK notes. Her dates of birth and death (August 21, 1854–March 23, 1935) were researched by Dr. Kafka, FK letters.
4   *"Maschina! Maschina!":* ADK notes.
4   *to mass . . . to construct an altar.* Adolf D. Klarmann, "Das Weltbild Franz Werfels," in *Wissenschaft und Weltbild* (Vienna: Herold Verlag, 1954), pp. 35ff.
4   *Father Janko:* ADK notes. These also mention Albine Werfel's apocryphal anecdote that Father Janko repeatedly exhorted Rudolf Werfel *not* to convert to Christianity.
4   *the light . . . of candles:* FW, "Erguss und Beichte," *ZOU,* pp. 690ff.
4   *In the playgrounds:* See Haas, p. 11; and see his unpublished lecture "Der junge Werfel: Erinnerungen von Willy Haas," M-W Coll.

4 *Kakitz . . . the "chair lady":* See FW's poem "Der dicke Mann im Spiegel," *DlW*, pp. 19f., and Johannes Urzidil, *Prager Triptychon* (Munich: Langen Müller Verlag, 1960), p. 13.

5 *the private elementary school of the Piarist order:* "Piarists, bad Christians!" was a taunting cry addressed to the children who went to that school. See Peter Demetz, *René Rilkes Prager Jahre* (Düsseldorf: Eugen Diederichs Verlag, 1953), p. 34.

5 *most of the students:* Dr. Kafka (FK letters) managed to obtain exact details of FW's schooldays from the archives of Prague. According to these, FW went to the Piarist school from 1896 to 1900, to the Royal and Imperial German Gymnasium in the New Town from 1900 to 1903, and to the Royal and Imperial German Gymnasium on Stefangasse from 1904 to 1909. All of his school records have been preserved, as have the names of his teachers and classmates. The famous actor Ernst Deutsch was FW's schoolmate at the Piarists', as was the renowned graphic artist and illustrator Walter Trier, who was the son of a glove manufacturer too.

5 *in a whitewashed classroom:* See FW's poem "Der Kinderanzug," *DlW*, pp. 14f., and *SU*, pp. 286f.

5 *the birth of a sister, Hanna:* Johanna Werfel. Dr. Kafka (FK letters) gives her birthdate as July 11, 1894; other sources give 1896.

5 *a sickly child:* The main evidence for this comes from FW's school reports; he missed so many classes that he did not receive any grades for a semester. A letter to his aunt Emilie Böhm, one of his father's sisters, written between 1897 and 1899, during his time at the Piarist school, has been preserved (DL). As it is the earliest extant written document by FW, it is quoted here verbatim: "Dearest Aunt! On your birthday celebration today I send you many good wishes. May the dear Lord make my dear Auntie very happy and jolly, may he shower the dear aunt with his richest blessings, may he repay her many times over for all the good things she has done in her life! Ardent kisses from your nephew Franz."

6 *Marianne Amalia:* Born October 30, 1899 (FK letters).

6 *the Werfel family moved:* ADK notes.

6 *The business, which was expanding steadily:* Unpublished memoirs of František Kraus, Prague, M-W Coll.; see also the official letterhead of the firm Werfel & Böhm.

7 *anti-Semitic demonstrations:* On the entire complex of questions surrounding the relationships of Jews, Germans, and Czechs, and on the actions of the employees of the Werfel glove factory, see Christoph Stölzl, *Kafkas böses Böhmen: Zur Sozialgeschichte eines Prager Juden* (Munich: Edition text + kritik, 1975).

7 *King David's musicality:* FW, "Erguss und Beichte," *ZOU*, pp. 690ff.

7 *illustrated boys' magazine:* See FW's poem "An den guten Kameraden," in *DlW*, pp. 17f., and *Der Gute Kamerad*, volumes for 1899 to ca. 1907.

8 *While reading:* ADK notes.

8   *May Festival:* See May issues of *Prager Tagblatt* for any year during this period.

8   *Angelo Neumann:* See Willy Haas, "Werfels erster Lehrmeister," in *Die literarische Welt,* no. 26 (June 29, 1928); Haas says of Neumann (1838–1910), ". . . an old wandering comedian with Caesarian pretensions—the scintillating form, glossy with brillantine, hair tonic, and makeup, tightly corseted, both Napoleonic and sleazy, of old *Angelo Neumann!* . . . He is the true social ruler of this city. . . . Out of thin air, he constructs a society, salons, conversations, sophistication, even something like a social hierarchy. The center of this mirage of a society is the opera box; everything depends on it. And the center of that center is the May Festival, the great annual Italian *stagione* in May. Caruso comes to sing, and so do Battistini, Arimondi, Brombara, La Tetrazzini, La Hidalgo; Maestro Toscanini from Milan's Scala is the conductor. All Verdi's main works are performed. . . . An entire society literally constitutes itself around this musical event."

8   *the joy of expectation:* In a letter to his lover Gertrud Spirk dated November 16, 1916, FW wrote: "When, as a child, I was taken to the theater, I was always overwhelmed by great sadness during the first act because things kept moving on, there was no stopping them, and in a short while it would all be over. I always yearned terribly for the happiness of expectation in the mornings" (FW/Spirk).

8   *puppet theater:* ADK notes. See also FW's novella *Die Entfremdung, EzW,* vol. 2, pp. 67f., 88f.

8   *Georg Weber:* See FW, "Erguss und Beichte," *ZOU,* pp. 690ff. "Up to my fourteenth year, my only and most faithful friend was a Christian. He died of consumption at the age of eighteen" (p. 693).

8   *Franz Jarosy:* Ibid. FW refers to him only as "F.J."; the full name of this classmate was deduced from school documents provided by Dr. František Kafka.

9   *A very different theatrical event:* See Haas, p. 15, and *Prager Tagblatt,* June 1901.

9   *summer vacation:* See, for instance, *SU,* p. 76: "Ten weeks of summer vacation lie before me—an eternity of laziness, of curiosity, of physical pleasure and spiritual happiness: swimming in the lake, sailing, wild games with other boys, croquet tournaments, drives, outings, mountain climbing, picnics . . ."

10 *Franz was bar mitzvahed:* FK letters.

10 *the teeming crowds:* FW, "Erguss und Beichte," *ZOU,* pp. 690ff.

10 *these moments . . . he loved:* Ibid.

10 *The Werfel family moved again:* ADK notes. See also Haas, p. 18: "When one entered the wide, glossy-white corridors of the Werfels' apartment, there was always a smell of fresh lacquer or other ingredients of extremely genteel cleanliness."

10 *costly carpets . . . valuable paintings:* Interview with FW in *Green Sheet Journal,* Milwaukee, Wis. (March 17, 1944). See also FW's novella

Kleine Verhältnisse, EzW, vol. 2, pp. 238, 249. No doubt the description of the eleven-year-old Hugo's paternal home is largely based on the Werfel apartment at Mariengasse 41.

11 *Anna Wrtal . . . Erna Tschepper:* ADK notes. On Erna Tschepper, see also FW's *Kleine Verhältnisse, EzW,* vol. 2, where FW calls her Erna Tappert. Dr. Kafka discovered that Erna Tschepper was born on May 9, 1869, in Reichenberg; she was a Catholic and officially listed her profession as "governess" (FK letters).

11 *Franz cried for two nights:* FW in a 1917 letter to Gertrud Spirk: "I remember that I cried secretly for two nights after our *bonne* told me she would be leaving us. . . . One was still a member of the human race, then" (FW/Spirk).

CARUSO

13 *In May 1904:* The *Prager Tagblatt* for May 1904 gives extensive reports on festival performances and Caruso's triumphal visit.

13 *The arts . . . his passion for the theater:* "Autobiographische Skizze," *ZOU,* pp. 701ff.

13 *knew entire arias by heart:* ADK notes.

13 *Reclam pocket editions:* Ibid.

13 *Portraits . . . poetry: Ibid.*

14 *imitating adults:* Ibid.

14 *impersonation of the cantor.* Ibid.

14 *Stefansgymnasium:* FK letters. The change of schools may have been suggested by Rabbi Kisch, who taught at the Stefansgymnasium.

14 *The two often read secretly:* Haas, "Der junge Werfel," M-W Coll.

14 *Kyovsky wanted to know:* Haas, p. 14.

14 *Willy Haas was a daily visitor:* See the chapter "Geheimnisse des alten Prag" in ibid., pp. 18ff.

15 *Hugo Salus . . . "Graveyard in a Field":* FW notebook, UCLA.

15 *mini-dramas: DD,* vol. 2, p. 518.

15 *fountain . . . kitten:* ADK notes. See also "Die Katze," *ZOU,* pp. 815ff.

15 *regular soirees:* See Haas; and see his "Der junge Werfel," M-W Coll.

16 *Maria Glaser:* Author's conversation with Anuschka Deutsch, May 1983. The precise biographical data were researched by Dr. Kafka (FK letters).

16 *aesthetic Sunday afternoons:* Communication from Freda Morawetz, Maria Glaser's sister, to Dr. Kafka (FK letters).

16 *tennis court:* See *DA,* p. 175.

16 *"You gave me . . .":* From "Die Schöne und das peinliche Wort," *DlW,* p. 21.

16 *"You play with many . . .":* From "Der Getreue," ibid., p. 41.

16 *Dr. Holzner:* ADK notes.

16 *His mother kept trying:* Ibid.

16 *accompany him to the factory:* Unpublished memoirs of František Kraus, Prague, M-W Coll.

17 *Paul Kornfeld* (1889–1942): His diary from his schooldays is preserved in DL.
17 *playing hooky:* FK letters. In his seventh year of gymnasium, FW missed eighty hours, of which thirty-one were unexcused. See also *DA*.
17 *performances . . . guest performances: See Prager Tagblatt* for the years 1905–7.
17 *Maria Immisch:* See FW's "Sechs Setterime zu Ehren des Frühlings von Neunzehnhundertundfünf," *DlW*, p. 489.
17 *Schiller festival: Prager Tagblatt,* May 1905.
18 *Vienna daily* Die Zeit: The poem appeared in the Sunday literary supplement on February 23, 1908.
18 *nausea and palpitations:* See FW's *Die Versuchung* (1912), *DD*, vol. 1, p. 32.
18 *"Wilted ivy twines . . .":* From "Die Gärten der Stadt," *DlW*, p. 514. Willy Haas claims, in his published and unpublished memoirs, that he sent FW's poems to numerous newspaper editors, among them Camill Hoffmann of *Die Zeit*. In his autobiography, *Streitbares Leben*, Max Brod writes that it was *he* who sent an envelope stuffed with FW's poems to Hoffmann. In this connection, Brod quotes an undated letter from Haas in which the latter thanks him for doing this. Brod does mention that it was Haas who introduced nineteen-year-old FW to him, but at the time, the poem in question had long since appeared. Hence, it seems that Brod assumes unwarranted credit, unless he as well as Haas sent those poems to Camill Hoffmann. See Joachim Unseld, *Franz Kafka: Ein Schriftstellerleben* (Munich: Hanser Verlag, 1982), p. 18: "Brod's dating is imprecise. . . . In his memoirs, Brod projects later events onto earlier ones"—and possibly the reverse).
18 *nightclubs:* FK letters.
18 *The Gogo:* See FW, *Das Trauerhaus, EzW,* vol. 2, pp. 181ff.
19 *"Carousseau!":* Haas, p. 12.
20 *Brod began to participate: SL,* pp. 19ff; see also *DA,* pp. 152ff.
20 *one of his letters of invitation:* In DL.
20 *excursions to the outskirts of Prague: SL,* p. 23.
20 *Anuschka Deutsch:* I spoke with Frau Deutsch, the widow of the actor Ernst Deutsch, in May 1983; she died in 1984.

Café Arco

23 *Franz did not register:* FK letters. Apparently FW's name does not appear in the registrar's records of the university.
23 *philosophy and law lectures:* FW, "Autobiographische Skizze," *ZOU,* pp. 701ff.
23 *subscriptions . . . Pošta, the headwaiter:* See Hans Demetz, "Der Prager Dichterkreis oder die Arco-Nauten," *Tiroler Tageszeitung,* February 6, 1971.
23 *most of them young poets:* Otto Pick (1886–1940), Rudolf Fuchs (1890–1942), Johannes Urzidil (1896–1970), Oskar Baum (1883–1941), Ernst Polak (1886–1947).

23 *Once again Willy Haas was his adviser:* See Haas; and see his "Der junge Werfel," M-W Coll.

24 *"At the urging of Dr. Max Brod":* Unpublished letter from FW to Axel Juncker (1890–1952), dated July 28, 1910, in the possession of FW scholar Ruth Stadelmann. Thus, Brod's claim (*SL*, pp. 43ff.) that he himself sent the manuscript of *Der Weltfreund* (as the published book was called) to Axel Juncker Verlag is clearly untenable.

24 *he had been told to make a glove:* Author's conversation with Anna Mahler, who recalled that FW had told her this story several times.

24 *"newer and more mature" poems:* Unpublished letter from FW to Axel Juncker, Marienbad, August 20, 1910; in DL.

24 *went to Munich:* FW, "Zauberer Moissi," *ZOU*, pp. 417f.

24 *Pension Schröder:* FW to Axel Juncker, Hamburg, October 24, 1910; in Kasimir Edschnid, ed., *Briefe des Expressionismus*, p. 9.

25 *an entire bundle of bills of lading:* Anna Mahler's recollection, from conversations with FW about his youth. Richard Specht also gives credence to this story in his biography *Franz Werfel: Versuch einer Zeitspiegelung* (Vienna: Paul Zsolnay Verlag, 1926).

25 *to leave his post:* FW, "Autobiographische Skizze," *ZOU*, p. 702.

25 *"job = vice":* Unpublished notebook, Hamburg, 1910, UCLA.

25 *Max Brod then wrote Juncker:* SL, pp. 43ff. Brod claims that his correspondence with Juncker "went back and forth for a long time" (p. 45), but it cannot have taken place this way, since it is obvious from FW's letter to Juncker dated October, 24, 1910, that poet and publisher had already arrived at an agreement at this time. We cannot discount the possibility that FW and Juncker made an agreement entirely without Brod's intervention.

25 *"I would like to call it The Friend of the World":* FW to Axel Juncker, October 24, 1910.

25 *He wrote poems and short stories:* The unpublished 1910 Hamburg notebook (UCLA) mentions, among others, the titles "Der neue Tenor," "Eifersucht," "Der Liebhaber aus Taktgefühl," and "Seestadt." (On "Seestadt," see the description of contents in *EzW*, vol. 2, p. 391.)

25 *often talked ... on the telephone:* See FW's poem "Das interurbane Gespräch" in the collection *Wir sind, DlW*, p. 103.

25 *ran into Mitzi Glaser:* See the quotation from FW's 1910 Hamburg notebook in *ZOU*, p. 742. See also Adolf D. Klarmann, "Zu Werfels *Besuch aus dem Elysium*," in *Herder-Blätter*, facsimile edition on the seventieth birthday of Willy Haas (Hamburg: Freie Akademie der Künste, 1962). I was referred to Klarmann's text by Dr. František Kafka.

26 *one-act play,* The Visit from Elysium: *DD*, vol. 2, pp. 11ff.

26 *tennis, dancing school, and "the cosmos":* See Anton Kuh's *Prager Presse* review of the premiere in Vienna, October 10, 1917.

26 *walk through a cemetery:* FW, "Karl Kraus," *ZOU*, pp. 340f. Annie Kalmar, a famous actress adored by Kraus, had a long career in the Viennese theater.

26   *dreamed of the funeral:* Ibid.

26   *"All I need to be happy . . .":* Unpublished letter from FW to Karl Kraus,
       Hamburg, May 17, 1911; manuscript collection of the Vienna
       Stadtbibliothek.

26   *"The praise . . .":* Unpublished letter from FW to Karl Kraus, May 23,
       1911; manuscript collection of the Vienna Stadtbibliothek. Concern-
       ing Kraus's first letter to FW, FW had already written to him from
       Hamburg on April 6, 1911: "Most esteemed sir, Herr Haas has been
       kind enough to send you some of my poems. You were good enough to
       make notes on these with a view to a change. Please forgive me for
       putting yet another demand on your kindness by sending you some
       other things instead of the previous ones, about which I was not too
       sure myself. It would make me happy if this selection would be ac-
       cepted for *Die Fackel.* Finally, allow me, most esteemed sir, to assure
       you of my admiration and reverence. Yours gratefully, Werfel" (un-
       published letter, Vienna Stadtbibliothek). FW's romanticized descrip-
       tion of the chain of events in his portrait "Karl Kraus" is a distortion, as
       Kraus's first letter to FW was his reply to the April 6 letter.

26   *his year of voluntary service:* This was a privilege of those who had gradu-
       ated from a gymnasium; everyone else had to serve two to three years.
       The original of FW's military record is in the Vojensky historicky
       ustav-Archiv, Prague; a copy is in the Kriegsarchiv, Vienna.

27   *hours of solitary:* FW, "Autobiographische Skizze," *ZOU,* p. 702. On the
       atmosphere of the barracks and FW's volunteer year, see FW, "Die
       Stagione," *ZOU,* pp. 821ff.

27   *sympathetic to Czech irredentism:* ADK notes. Among other things, the
       irredentists encouraged Czech soldiers to respond to roll call not with
       the German *"Hier!"* but with the Czech *"Zdé!"*

27   *Max Brod read a few poems:* See Kurt Krolop, "Zur Geschichte und Vor-
       geschichte der Prager deutschen Literatur des 'expressionistischen
       Jahrzehnts,' " in Eduard Goldstücker, ed., *Weltfreunde: Konferenz über
       die Prager deutsche Literatur* (Prague: Academia, 1967), p. 47; see also
       SL, p. 36.

27   *someone far more significant:* Franz Kafka's diary entry for December 18,
       1911, contains this unpublished passage: "Max came from Berlin
       yesterday—in the *Berliner Tageblatt,* some *Fackel* person called him
       selfless because he had read the 'far more significant Werfel.' Max had
       to delete this sentence when he took the review to the *Prager Tagblatt*
       for them to reprint."

27   *Kraus . . . made a point:* "Who renders the world so lovable in his song
       provides the misanthrope with a happy moment" (*Die Fackel,* vol. 13,
       nos. 339–40, pp. 47–51).

27   *laudatory reviews:* See, for example, Berthold Viertel's review in *Der Strom,*
       the journal of the Vienna Volksbühne, August 1912: "When he is
       moved, he is not sentimental, his joy is infectious, his flights make you
       fly. Life becomes richer, more attractive, fanciful and at the same time

more concrete through these poems; there is a light sort of magic in them, grace, a gentle humor that never allows them to become too mundane or too young."

27 *Franz Kafka envied his friend:* Kafka's diary entry for December 18, 1911: "I hate Werfel, not because I envy him, but I envy him too. He is healthy, young, and rich; everything that I am not. Besides, gifted with a sense of music, he has done very good work early and easily, he has the happiest life behind him and before him, I work with weights I cannot get rid of, and I am entirely shut off from music" (Franz Kafka, *Diaries: 1910–1913,* ed. Max Brod, trans. Joseph Kresh [New York: Schocken Books, 1948], p. 182).

28 *Werfel expressed disappointment:* See Haas, p. 30.

28 *argument about Richard Wagner:* See *SL,* pp. 26f.

28 *a one-act play,* The Temptation: *DD,* vol. 1, pp. 25ff. "Written in one maneuver day 1912."

28 *His friends and admirers esteemed him:* See Johannes Urzidil, "Der Weltfreund: Erinnerungen an Franz Werfel," in the journal *Das Silberboot: Zetschrift für Literatur* (Vienna), 1946, pp. 45ff.: "We loved the young Werfel as perhaps only few poets have been loved by their circle of friends. When he recited from his poems . . . we listened to every word with the greatest anticipation, we were in a trance. He was, in the classical sense, the bard of his poetry. . . . He debated with enthusiasm, passion, and such powers of persuasion that one never knew how to contradict him in his presence. Responses and counterarguments came to mind later, but when one presented them to him, they just melted away."

28 *Dostoyevsky:* See *EzW,* vol. 3; in FW's short story "Weissenstein, the World Improver" ("Weissenstein, der Weltverbesserer"), we read: "On what evening, in what season, did we *not* discuss Dostoyevsky? He was the patron saint of our generation." The story, written in 1939, contains FW's reminiscences of Prague in 1911.

29 *"Today's Café Arco":* I owe the description of the Café Arco in its present state to Dr. Kafka (FK letters) and to Christoph Tölg of Vienna.

The Day of Judgment

30 *Brod praised his friend:* See *SL.* On the story of Kurt Wolff's relationship with FW and on the disputes between Wolff and Rowohlt, see Kurt Wolff, *Autoren, Bücher, Abenteuer* (Berlin: Verlag Klaus Wagenbach, 1969). It is apparent from ADK notes that it was Brod who took FW to Kurt Wolff; Wolff himself told Klarmann, "Max Brod brought Werfel to me."

31 *In two large cupboards:* FW/Spirk.

31 *Rudolf Werfel . . . gradually relented:* Rudolf Werfel to Kurt Wolff, unpublished letter in KW Archive. See also Wolff, *Autoren, Bücher, Abenteuer,* op. cit.

31 *threatened Axel Juncker:* On November 5, 1912, Rudolf Werfel wrote to

Axel Juncker: "If I am not in receipt of the agreed sum of M 300 for
the second edition by Wednesday noon, I will retain all proprietary
rights in the second edition and enforce these in a manner I deem
appropriate. You know very well that you do not have any right to a
third edition; quite apart from the fact that no agreement exists
between me, as the representative of my underage son, and yourself"
(KW Archive).

31   *long hair combed straight back:* I thank Helen Wolff, Kurt Wolff's widow,
for the description of FW in his Leipzig days. See also a radio talk by
Kurt Wolff on Norddeutscher Rundfunk, May 19, 1962: "[FW] sailed
down the streets, singing or humming Verdi arias, and did not notice
that people turned to stare at him, holding their foreheads."

31   *Sternheim ... Wedekind ... Lasker-Schüler:* See Kurt Pinthus, "Erinnerungen an Franz Werfel," in *Der Zeitgenosse: Literarische Portraits und
Kritiken,* Marbacher Schriften 4 (Marbach am Neckar: Deutsches Lit-
eraturarchiv in Schiller-Nationalmuseum, 1971), pp. 82–85. This volume was published on the occasion of Pinthus's eighty-fifth birthday,
on April 29, 1971.

31   *"The Season": ZOU,* pp. 821ff.

32   *His new friends:* Walter Hasenclever (1890–1940), Kurt Pinthus (1886–
1975).

32   *a decision was made:* See Pinthus, "Erinnerungen an Franz Werfel," op.
cit.

32   *published inexpensively:* The volumes of the Day of Judgment series cost
80 pfennigs.

32   *slightly confused ad: ZOU,* pp. 474f.

32   *first public reading:* See Krolop, "Zur Geschichte und Vorgeschichte der
Prager deutschen Literatur des 'expressionistischen Jahrzehnts,'" in
Weltfreunde, op. cit., p. 79, n. 80.

32   *renewed his friendship with Franz Kafka:* See, for example, Kafka to Felice
Bauer, December 12, 1912: "You know, Felice, Werfel is really miraculous; when I read his book *The Friend of the World* for the first time (I
had heard him recite poetry before that), I thought I was going off my
head with enthusiasm. The man has tremendous ability. . . . I have no
idea how to end, since this strange young man has come between us"
(*Letters to Felice,* ed. Erich Heller and Jürgen Born, trans. James Stern
and Elisabeth Duckworth [New York: Schocken Books, 1973], p. 102).
See also Kafka's diary entry for December 23, 1911: "All yesterday
morning my head was as if filled with mist from Werfel's poems. For a
moment I feared the enthusiasm would carry me along straight into
nonsense" (*Diaries: 1910–1913,* op. cit., p. 188); and Kafka to Felice
Bauer, February 1–2, 1913: "I spent the whole afternoon with Werfel,
the evening with Max [Brod]. . . . Werfel read to me some new poems;
again they undoubtedly spring from a tremendous personality. Astonishing how this kind of poem, carrying its inherent end in its beginning, rises with a continuous, inner, flowing development—how one

opens one's eyes while lying doubled up on the sofa. And the young man has grown handsome and reads with such ferocity (to the monotony of which I actually have some objections)! He knows by heart everything he has ever written, and his passion seems to set fire to the heavy body, the great chest, the round cheeks; and when reading aloud he looks as if he were about to tear himself to pieces" (*Letters to Felice*, pp. 178–79).

33   *Ballets Russes:* FW, "Wenn die Russen tanzen, wenn Battistini singt," *ZOU*, pp. 199f.

33   The Stoker ... The Metamorphosis *and* The Judgment: See Wolfgang Göbel, *Der Kurt Wolff Verlag 1913–1930: Expressionismus als verlegerische Aufgabe*, with a bibliography of Kurt Wolff Verlag and associated publishing houses, 1910–1930 (Frankfurt am Main: Buchhändler-Vereinigung, 1977), pp. 133, 253, 212.

33   *brought Karl Kraus to Kurt Wolff's attention:* See Wolff, *Autoren, Bücher, Abenteuer*, op. cit., pp. 77ff.

33   *While Wolff was away on vacation:* See *BeV*, p. 101.

33   *wrote the unknown poet:* FW to Georg Trakl, April 1913; in Wolfgang Schneditz, *Georg Trakl in Zeugnissen der Freunde* (Salzburg: Otto Müller Verlag, 1951), p. 52.

34   *Walt Whitman:* See the dissertation by Vincent Consentino, "Walt Whitman und die deutsche Literaturrevolution."

34   *At the publisher's expense:* ADK notes on a conversation with Kurt Wolff: "Here [i.e., in Malcesine] Werfel stayed with Hasenclever and wrote a large number of the *Each Other* [*Einander*] poems."

34   *huge bowls of asparagus:* FW/Spirk.

34   *"Jesus and the Carrion Road":* DlW, pp. 186ff.; the poem reflects the beautiful surroundings of Malcesine.

34   *a letter from ... Rilke:* See Foltin, p. 29; on Werfel's meeting with Rilke (1875–1926), see also FW, "Begegnungen mit Rilke," *ZOU*, pp. 418ff. FW's reply to Rilke is dated August 15, 1913 (M-W Coll.). On Rilke's view of Werfel, see his essay "Über den jungen Dichter," in Rainer Maria Rilke, *Sämtliche Werke*, vol. 11 (Frankfurt am Main: Insel Verlag, 1975), pp. 1046–55.

35   *Rilke had decided:* See Rilke's letter to Hofmannsthal, October 22, 1913: "I was truly ready to simply embrace this young person; but I realized immediately that this was quite impossible. . . . The Jew, the Jewboy, to be quite plain about it, wouldn't have bothered me so much, but I must also have become aware of his clearly Jewish attitude to his work. . . . in any case, an exceptional talent, firmly determined to create perfect things . . . only that there was, finally, this almost imperceptible alien quality to all of it, a smell as if of another species, something insurmountable" (Hugo von Hofmannsthal and Rainer Maria Rilke, *Briefwechsel 1899–1925* [Frankfurt am Main: Suhrkamp, 1978], pp. 77f.).

35   *Paul Claudel's play:* Paul Claudel (1868–1955) spent some time in Prague as the consul-general of France.

35   *"Jewboy":* See Rilke's letter to Princess Marie von Thurn und Taxis,
        October 21, 1913: "At Hellerau and Dresden I saw a lot of Franz
        Werfel. It was sad, 'a Jewboy' [Judenbub], said Sidie Nadherny (who
        had come from Janowitz, quite startled), and she was not entirely
        wrong" (Rainer Maria Rilke and Marie von Thurn und Taxis, *Brief-
        wechsel,* vol. 1 [Zurich: Niehaus und Rokitansky Verlag; Frankfurt am
        Main: Insel Verlag, 1951], p. 323; original in French and German).

35   *a simply unforgettable man:* In her diary for September 14, 1913, Sidonie
        Nádherný wrote: "K.K. has gotten into my blood, he makes me suffer.
        He pursued my inmost being like none other, he understood, like
        none other. I won't be able to do anything unless I forget him" (p. 49).

35   *The deeply offended Werfel:* See Karl Kraus, *Briefe an Sidonie Nádherný von
        Borutin 1913–1936,* vol. 1 (Munich: Kösel Verlag, 1974), pp. 127f.

35   *rumors:* Ibid., pp. 154, 201.

35   *Jakob Hegner:* Author, translator, publisher. Hegner (1882–1962) both
        translated and published Claudel's *Annunciation.*

36   *Hegner's suggestion:* See FW's letter to Rilke, end of February 1914: "I
        have translated the Euripides Hegner recommended to me in Helle-
        rau. It is a tremendous piece of theater" (M-W Coll.).

36   *Werfel's translation of* The Trojan Women: *DD,* vol. 1, pp. 41ff.

36   *introductory note:* Ibid., pp. 546ff.

36   *His world consisted of the writers and composers:* See FW, "Erguss und
        Beichte," *ZOU,* pp. 69off.

36   *Willy Haas . . . followed his friend to Leipzig:* Haas, pp. 38f.

37   *Karl Weissenstein:* See Haas; and see FW's short story "Weissenstein, der
        Weltverbesserer" (written in the emigration period), *EzW,* vol. 3, pp.
        59ff.

37   *a dramatic appeal to Kurt Wolff:* See Rudolf Werfel's letter, Prague, April 2,
        1914: "He [FW] holds you in much high regard that if *you could
        transmit my wish* that he get his doctorate in Leipzig, he would surely
        comply. In view of his successes as a poet and his talent, the completion
        of this task won't be too difficult for him. In two years, when he has
        achieved his doctorate, he can . . . aspire to a *professional* position
        commensurate with his talent. His unfettered way of life makes me
        very anxious . . . a way of life that is bound to have a negative effect on
        his health in the long run. Since you have known him, you have
        demonstrated so much friendly interest in him that I feel I may ask
        you . . . to influence Franz—who is now in his twenty-fourth year and
        thus almost grown up—and encourage him to adopt a normal way of
        life and point out to him the value of a professional position for his
        future, when he may want to establish a family of his own. Any—even
        the smallest—success you may achieve in this direction will earn you
        not only the knowledge of having done a good deed for a not inconsid-
        erable human being but also the warmest thanks of his anxious par-
        ents" (KW Archive).

37   *"From the coolness of your handshake":* FW to Karl Kraus, Prague, April 6,

1914 (manuscript collection of the Vienna Stadtbibliothek). See also Kraus, *Briefe an Sidonie Nádherný von Borutin,* op. cit., pp. 126f.

37 *Kraus asked his lady friend:* Kraus to Sidonie Nádherný, April 7, 1914: "Nothing but unpleasantness in Vienna. Today, this letter from Herr W. As we agreed, I gave him the cold shoulder in Prague, but I suppose that I have to answer it. . . . Or should I let it go? I'm in favor of answering. Pleased with the opportunity 'to forge the logical chain out of low deeds.' That letter voices the indignation of a sponge to whom the suggestion has been made that it can't hold water. Too disgusting!" (ibid., p. 27).

38 *In the next issue of* Die Fackel: No. 398 (April 21, 1914), p. 19: "In Prague, where they're all very talented, everyone has grown up with someone who writes poetry, and writes poetry himself, and the child virtuoso Werfel pollinates them all, so that poets are multiplying there like muskrats, growing lyric verses like these. . . ." Kraus goes on to quote poems by Hans Gerke and Max Brod that he considers particularly disastrous.

THE GOOD SOLDIER

40 *excused from active military duty:* See FW's military records, original in the Vojensky historicky ustav-Archiv, Prague; copy in the Kriegsarchiv, Vienna.

40 *a play,* Esther, Empress of Persia: *DD,* vol. 2, pp. 343ff.

40 *the dialogue* Euripides, or On the War: Cf. ibid., pp. 378ff.; see also p. 514. In later years FW found this text "ideologically vague, lacking the highest degree of responsibility to itself, childish, random, well intentioned, and poorly thought out." He indicated that it was never to be published.

41 *personal involvement of Kurt Wolff:* FW to Kurt Wolff, January 12, 1915: "Now I have the firm and happy conviction that any book of mine is a matter that can only come about through your love and participation." Elsewhere in the same letter: "Is it not at all possible for you to obtain some leave? Follow my example! I have been released, partly because I am considered a madman. The feeling you describe, of longing for the front—I know a variant of it. At first I suffered a great deal from such moral self-recriminations" (KW-Archive; published in *Briefe des Expressionismus,* op. cit., pp. 13f).

41 *Georg Heinrich Meyer:* See *BeV,* pp. xxviiiff.; on Meyer's "distance" to FW's works, see pp. 107f.

41 *to visit Martin Buber.* See Martin Buber, *Briefwechsel aus sieben Jahrzehnten,* vol. 1, *1897–1918,* (Heidelberg: Verlag Lambert Schneider, 1972), p. 361.

41 *a secret antimilitarist group:* See Specht, *Franz Werfel,* op. cit., p. 45: "Werfel . . . joined . . . such strong heads and hearts as Martin Buber, Gustav Landauer [1870–1919], and Max Scheler [1874–1928] in a secret group against the militaristic grimace of power." (It should be noted

that Max Scheler had published, only a few months before this time, a book that glorified war: *Der Genius des Krieges und der deutsche Krieg* [Berlin: Der Neue Geist Verlag, 1914].) See the unpublished letter from Buber to FW, February 12, 1915: "At the last meeting we divided up and discussed our separate areas of study; Scheler will deal mainly with the psychological, I myself with the ethical, and Landauer with the organizational aspect of our subject. Our next and probably most important meeting will take place next Friday the 26th at a quarter past four at Landauer's. . . . Will you be able to come? We all agreed that your presence would be particularly desirable at this time" (M-W Coll.).

41 *put in a personal appearance:* Unpublished letter from FW to G. H. Meyer, Bozen, April 19, 1915: "You have probably received my note from Vienna in which I told you that the Supreme Command of the army had sense enough to remove me from my responsibility-laden post to another where my nerves won't be under so much strain. I hope you are sharing my gladness about this, even though you are a proud German male" (KW Archive). Possibly FW or his family was acquainted with a high-ranking officer in the Supreme Command; it is hard to explain FW's transfer to Bozen otherwise.

41 *Werfel saw Karl Kraus:* See Kraus's letter to Sidonie Nádherný, April 14, 1915: ". . . *I* was brusque last Sunday in a clash with the poet W, who suddenly accosted me in a restaurant. At last I was able to take care of this old business. I was left holding a sponge. . . . All in all: pseudo-humanity, no better in contrition than in trespass. The case is a prime example of the need to protect oneself from the kind of talent that has mastered an entire register of beauty while being so ugly in itself" (Kraus, *Briefe an Sidonie Nádherný von Borutin,* op. cit., pp. 154f.). Kraus wrote this letter from Rome, but the incident described took place in Vienna.

42 *excursions into the Dolomites . . . following Dante's example:* FW, "Das Bozener Buch," *EzW,* vol. 2, pp. 389ff.

42 *"Dream of a New Hell":* *DlW,* pp. 547ff.

42 *severe injuries to both legs:* FW, "Das Bozener Buch," *EzW,* vol. 2, pp. 389f.

42 *As late as mid-June:* Unpublished letter from FW to G. H. Meyer, June 16, 1915: "I was quite ill in Bozen but was happy to return and feel much better now, even though I'm still unable to walk and limp along supported by canes" (KW Archive). In a later letter to Meyer (unpublished): "My state of health is still pretty much below zero. Supported by two canes, I limp through the flag-bedecked streets of Prague. Everybody wants to know whether the damage was done by infantry or artillery fire, and then listens with increasing disdain to my civilianly confessions" (KW Archive).

43 *most intensive publicity campaign:* See *BeV,* pp. xixf.

43 *Werfel consoled Meyer:* Unpublished letter from FW to Meyer, July 1915; KW Archive.

43   *engaged in vehement disputes:* See *SL,* pp. 56ff.

43   *Deeply disappointed:* A matter of gossip may have been an additional cause for the estrangement between Brod and Werfel. In ADK notes, Frau Mahler-Werfel mentions that Otto Pick tried to pit Werfel and Brod against each other by making them jealous.

43   *his novel* Tycho Brahe's Road to God: See *SL,* p. 53; the book was published in installments in *Die weissen Blätter,* January–June 1915, and in book form in 1916.

44   *Čabrinović:* See FW, "Cabrinowitsch," *EzW,* vol. 1, pp. 21ff.

44   *Gertrud Spirk:* See Foltin, p. 34. I owe all my information on FW's relationship with Gertrud Spirk to the lovers' correspondence, several hundred letters preserved in DL. Dr. Kafka (FK letters) provided Gertrud Spirk's date and place of birth: February 8, 1885, in Karlin, Karolinenthal. In 1930, she acquired a house at Palackého 147/75 in Prague and ran a fashion shop on the ground floor of that building. Gertrud Zach (*née* Spirk), a niece of Gertrud Spirk's, told me that her aunt's shop had been well known beyond the boundaries of Prague. Frau Zach reports the date of Gertrud Spirk's death as August 1967; she died in Vienna, and her grave is in Waidhofen an der Thaya in Lower Austria.

44   *mishap at the hairdresser's . . . chaotic life-style:* As reported by Gertrud Zach.

45   *heart attacks:* Unpublished letter from Willy Haas to Alma Mahler-Werfel and FW, 1943; M-W Coll.

45   *successful first night: The Trojan Women,* directed by Victor Barnowsky, premiered on April 22, 1916.

45   *congratulatory letter:* Kurt Wolff to FW, May 2, 1916, in *BeV,* pp. 109f.

45   *"extremely low spirits":* FW to Kurt Wolff, early May 1916, in *BeV,* pp. 111f.

45   *"The Blessed Elizabeth:"* DlW, pp. 194f.; See also FW's letter to Gertrud Spirk, postmarked September 6, 1916: "Back in Elb[e] Kost[elec] I wrote a poem and dedicated it to you. It's called 'The Blessed Elizabeth' and I think it begins, 'How she walks, the sister of / the fifth hour and the meadowlarks!' " (Jungk, *Das Franz Werfel Buch,* p. 386).

46   *"Man's Life": DD,* vol. 2, pp. 396ff.

46   *Days of worry:* See FW, *Barbara oder Die Frömmigkeit,* pp. 224ff.

46   *Hodóv, near Jezierna:* At the time, Hodóv had 1,200 inhabitants, Jeziema 4,700; both townships belonged to the judicial district of Zboróv, East Galicia (*Vollständiges Verzeichnis der Ortschaften der im Reichsrate vertretenen Königreiche und Länder,* 1880).

46   *Many of his superior officers:* These, as well as most other details of FW's service at the front, I owe to the unpublished FW/Spirk letters.

46   *telephone operator and dispatch rider:* Ibid.; See also FW, *Barbara,* e.g., pp. 262ff.

47   *he was writing . . . more regularly:* In Hodóv he wrote, among other things, the short prose pieces "Bauernstuben," "Die andere Seite," and "Geschichte von einem Hundefreund," a text directed against Karl Kraus (*EzW,* vol. 1, pp. 19f., 27f., 29ff.); "Der Berg des Beginns: Festkantate

mit Szene und Tanz" (*DD*, vol. 2, p. 412); and the polemical pieces "Brief an einen Staatsmann," "Substantiv und Verbum," and "Brief an Georg Davidsohn" (*ZOU*, pp. 210ff., 216ff., 577ff.).

47   *introduction to . . .* Silesian Songs: *ZOU*, pp. 476ff.

47   *"The Mission of Christianity": ZOU*, pp. 560ff.

48   *severe self-doubt:* FW/Spirk.

48   *"Elysian Matters, Melancholia: To Kurt Wolff": Die Fackel*, nos. 443–44, pp. 26–27. See also FW's poem against Karl Kraus, "Ein Denker," *DlW*, pp. 292ff.

48   *"Is this truly the language":* See FW, "Dorten," *ZOU*, pp. 559f.

49   *The telephone . . . sinister, hateful creature:* FW/Spirk. See also *Barbara*, p. 272: "Yet he recognized that his post, well behind the front line, was a gift of God and Captain Prechtl. Then the apparatus on the small table crowed again and fell into a long susurrus, like an insect that defends itself with a violent beating of wings against an enemy. . . . At any hour, day or night, whether Ferdinand was asleep or awake, the jealously humming creature called him to itself."

49   *tried to reassure Buber:* See FW to Martin Buber, January 31, 1917, in Buber, *Briefwechsel aus sieben Jahrzehnten*, op. cit., pp. 468f. In this connection, see also Max Brod to Buber, February 13, 1917: "First of all, you must not think that I have been trying or will ever try to force some kind of conversion on my friend Werfel. That would, of course, be folly. Since he has been at the front, I have tried to influence him by sending him suitable reading material. . . . I even avoided him when he was in Prague, because these debates always cause great strain and turmoil in me. He did, however, come to me and ask me to continue our discussion. Then, of course, I no longer avoided him, because I love Werfel *dearly*, and his mistakes, mostly due to a lopsided reading of Pascal, Kierkegaard, Strindberg, and other Christian authors, cause me pain. Quite apart from that, I do, of course, learn an incredible amount from him. . . . Thus, this is the state of the Werfel case: Werfel is not the sensitive, mimosalike type, like, for instance, my friend Franz Kafka (with whom I don't argue while being pleased to see how he is slowly and imperceptibly becoming more Jewish). Werfel is basically very robust and sensible. His entire life consists of argument. He argues incessantly, with everyone he meets" (ibid., pp. 472f.).

50   *"What I call Christianity":* Unpublished letter from FW to Buber, February 15, 1917; Martin Buber Archive, Jewish National and University Library, Jerusalem.

50   *every day he had survived:* FW in an unpublished letter to Alma Mahler: "Alma, I'm living here as I used to in the army years ago, where I would cut out every day I had survived from a calendar I had manufactured myself" (UCLA).

50   *Kraus printed Werfel's personal letter: Die Fackel*, nos. 445–53, pp. 133–47.

51   *"The Metaphysics of the Twist": ZOU*, pp. 581ff.

51   *Count Harry Kessler:* See Foltin, p. 35.

51 *Herbert von Fuchs-Robetin:* Born August 15, 1886, in Prague; died August 19, 1949, in Obergrünburg, Austria (FK letters).

51 *only twenty, and he regretted:* FW/Spirk.

52 *middle of March:* The wedding took place on March 21, 1917, in Prague (FK letters).

52 *Hanna helped him dress:* ADK notes. See also *SU,* pp. 51f., where FW participates in the Astromental wedding and is dressed the way he was for Hanna's wedding.

53 *a theatrical piece called* Stockleinen: This remarkable but until now largely ignored dramatic fragment can be found in *DD,* vol. 2, pp. 426ff.

54 *military archive:* Vienna Kriegsarchiv, Stiftsgasse 2, A-1070 Vienna.

54 *Schramm-Schiessl points out:* "Franz Werfel is an author with a strong reputation who has readers first of all in Germany and Switzerland but also in the Scandinavian countries and the Netherlands, and is therefore particularly suited for propaganda purposes. The lecture tour Werfel is to undertake is connected with the performance of his dramatic works *The Trojan Women* and *The Visit from Elysium* in Swiss theaters. The importance of Werfel is evidenced by the fact that, due to an initiative of the German Foreign Office, a German-Reich theater group is ready to perform the aforementioned works in Switzerland and Scandinavia. As can be seen from the enclosed superarbitration documents, Franz Werfel was repeatedly granted leave during the war by means of superarbitration, spent many months in the hospital, and was, during his time of active service, used solely as a telephone operator in the office of Regimental Command. Thus, since Franz Werfel's health does not permit him to serve as well in other military capacities as in his present assignment, . . . I request that . . . he be presently excused from reserve officers' school and permanently appointed to the Military Press Bureau. I take this opportunity to point out that there has been an increasing number of cases in recent times in which people who are eminently suited for intellectual propaganda service in the MPB have been removed from it, despite their inability to perform front-line service, and assigned duties that could just as well be undertaken by less intelligent persons" (Kriegsarchiv, Vienna).

ALMA MARIA MAHLER-GROPIUS

56 *safe haven for . . . writers:* See Foltin, *Franz Werfel,* p. 35; Peter Altenberg and FW were also living in adjoining rooms in the Graben Hotel on Dorotheergasse.

56 *Graben Hotel:* FW/Spirk.

56 *hardships of the last months:* FW/Spirk; the information on FW and Gertrud Spirk's relationship, and the details of FW's life in Vienna, were gleaned from this unpublished correspondence.

56 *One of these introductions:* See FW, "Vorbemerkung zu *Neue Bilderbogen und Soldatenlieder,*" *ZOU,* pp. 484ff.

57 *Kisch introduced the newcomer:* Egon Erwin Kisch (1885–1948; see the

roman à clef character Ronald Weiss in FW's *Barbara*); Otto Gross (1877–1920); Franz Blei (1871–1942), author, translator, and critic; Otfried Krzyzanowski (1891–1918).

57 *large room with high ceilings:* I owe the description of the Café Central to Werner J. Schweiger of Vienna, who was kind enough to provide me with a letter addressed to him by the author and screenwriter George Fröschel of Hollywood.

57 *spent the whole night:* MD conversations.

57 *end of September:* FW was in Dresden for the premiere (on September 20, 1917) of *The Trojan Women* and met Gustav Landauer and Walter Hasenclever there. At about the same time, FW staged his one-act play, *The Visit from Elysium* at the new Wiener Bühne theater as part of a Werfel matinée. The three actors performed so amateurishly that FW, who shared a box with friends in the sold-out house, had to laugh out loud (FW/Spirk).

58 *When Blei asked Alma Mahler:* See *ML,* pp. 85f., and Alma Mahler-Werfel's unpublished diary, M-W Coll.

58 *"The Seer": DlW,* pp. 160f.

58 *In mid-November:* From Alma Mahler-Werfel's unpublished diary, M-W Coll.

58 *"fat, bow-legged Jew":* Ibid.

59 *his socialist "affectation":* Alma Mahler was not alone in reacting negatively to FW's political views. A similar attitude can be seen in Arthur Schnitzler's 1917 diary. FW visited Arthur Schnitzler for the first time on August 15, 1917, probably in the company of Victor Barnowsky, a man of the theater. During dinner FW made disparaging remarks about Germany; according to Schnitzler, these were not well received, and FW became "muddled" and "started talking nonsense that none of us would accept. He struck me a little as an honest provincial who unsuspectingly sits down at a card table and suddenly notices to his dismay that he has joined a game of masters. When he got going on mysticism, I said, 'I draw the line at mysticism. As an author, I am a rationalist—and in political matters as well.' Despite all of that, he didn't strike me as a bad egg, and one could sense that he didn't 'really' mean what he said" (Arthur Schnitzler, *Tagebuch 1917–1919* [Vienna: Verlag der Österreichischen Akademie der Wissenschaften, 1985], p. 72). I owe the reference to Dr. P. M. Braunwarth of Vienna.

59 *"Imagine, yesterday":* FW/Spirk.

59 *In the presence of her husband:* See *ML.* In Alma Mahler-Werfel's unpublished diary (M-W Coll.) she also says about her meeting with FW: "How wonderful it is to be associated only with MINDS, how happy it makes me, who am touched by them. I thank *my* god on MY KNEES. ONLY PRESERVE THAT FOR ME, ONLY THAT!" (The claim made by Karen Monson in her biography *Alma Mahler: Muse to Genius* [Boston: Houghton Mifflin, 1983] that Alma did not write these diaries herself is untenable.)

59 *another official trip:* FW/Spirk.

60 *he boasted about his conquest:* MD conversations.

60 *found his wife rather frosty:* On Alma Mahler-Werfel's relationship with Walter Gropius, see *ML;* Karen Monson, *Alma Mahler,* op. cit.; and Reginald B. Isaacs *Walter Gropius: Der Mensch und sein Werk* (Berlin: Gehr, Mann, 1983).

60 *"Veni Creator Spiritus": DlW,* pp. 153f.

61 *"Homesickness, homesickness all the way":* FW/Mahler, January 18, 1918.

61 *the greatest public success:* Ibid.

61 *in the daily press:* See FW, "Report on my LECTURE TOUR IN SWITZER-LAND" (Kriegsarchiv, Vienna): "In one week, every newspaper in Zurich published articles of three, four, even six columns about me."

61 *twelve lectures in Switzerland:* Ibid.

61 *In Davos . . . a short speech:* FW, "Rede an die Arbeiter von Davos," *ZOU,* pp. 531ff.

62 *As soon as Werfel arrived back in Zurich:* FW, "Report on my LECTURE TOUR IN SWITZERLAND" (Kriegsarchiv, Vienna): "On March 20 the imperial military attaché in Zurich informed me of the Military Press Bureau's decision to discontinue my activities there and have me return to Vienna. As a consequence, I had to cancel four important readings scheduled for the last days of my stay, to wit, two evenings in Winterthur, one in Chur, and one in the Great Concert Hall (Tonhalle) in Zurich; the last-mentioned . . . was intended as an original and extraordinary experiment in which poetry of a modern bent was to be presented to an audience of a few thousand people. . . . In Vienna, I was immediately told by many sources about rumors according to which my lectures in Switzerland had displeased the Foreign Office, and I was even asked whether it was true that I had, as it were, been a fiasco. This notion . . . hurt and bothered me a great deal. . . . It is strange, indeed: important German papers . . . reported on my tour in Switzerland with highly laudatory articles, while there was not a single notice in any Austrian paper. . . . Be that as it may, and whatever I may be accused of, a pure consciousness of having worked for the glory of my fatherland allows me to deal with all attacks with equanimity."

62 *Hotel Bristol:* During these last months of World War I, FW lived at the Graben Hotel, the Hotel Bristol, and the Grand Hotel at Kärntnerring 9, in the immediate vicinity of the Bristol.

63 *Gina Kranz . . . found him an apartment:* FW/Spirk, and author's conversations with Gina Kranz Kaus (1894–1985) of Los Angeles. See also Gina Kaus, *Und was für ein Leben . . .* (Munich: Albrecht Knaus Verlag, 1979).

64 *sister Hanna gave birth to a son:* František Edvin, nicknamed Munzo by the family, born June 23, 1918 (FK letters).

64 *at the end of July: ML,* p. 94.

64 *Emmy Redlich:* According to Anna Mahler.

64 *in his "Secret Diary":* See *ML,* and FW, "Geheimes Tagebuch," *ZOU,*
    pp. 631ff. (original in M-W Coll.).

65 *Panic-stricken, he ran:* All details about Alma Mahler's hemorrhage are
    from FW, "Geheimes Tagebuch," as are the descriptions of the ensu-
    ing hours, days, and weeks.

66 *"to a frightening degree":* FW/Mahler.

66 *every time she had visitors:* Unpublished letters from Alma Mahler-Werfel
    to FW, M-W Coll.

67 *Gropius wrote to Werfel:* September 10, 1918, from Franzensbad: "Dear
    friend Werfel, I, the *absent* one, greet you who are *present.* Loving and
    healed of hate, I float above you; I suck your spirit into myself, I read
    your works and come ever closer to you. Thus will evil lose all its power
    over us. . . . I had to make my way through this chaos . . . in order to
    comprehend this incredible good fortune in its full extent, that the
    beloved, divine woman is *alive* and that our child [Apparently Alma
    was still leading Gropius to believe that while Werfel was her lover, the
    son was Gropius's] *lives,* that I myself *live.* Everything else pales into
    insignificance beside that . . . Our egos sink away the more we serve *her*
    who transfigures our life. *We have found our Messiah; she is* the fulfill-
    ment of what will place its seal upon the new world. *Love* in her very
    person has descended to me. You, Werfel, great poet and rediscoverer
    of the human heart, must immortalize this *singular* life in your best
    work, in such an inspiring manner and with such a burning heart that
    the distorted hatred will fall from all faces" (M-W Coll.).

67 *the play* The Midday Goddess: *DD,* vol. 1, pp. 91ff. In an unpublished
    letter to Alma Mahler written in the fall of 1918, FW writes: "My
    beloved eternal woman, I am not doing well at all. I do not know what
    you speak about with him [Walter Gropius], I do not know to what
    extent you are sacrificing me. I feel a great heavy homesickness for
    you. *All* my true vital feelings, my *thoughts* and *senses* are lost and
    exiled. . . . Whatever your doubts may be, I sense that I cannot endure
    life without you, that you are a great *strength of mine.* You know that
    yourself, very well; how else would I have succeeded in writing some-
    thing as lively as *The Midday Goddess!* It is a wonderful gift you have
    given me. *The second* divine gift. I believe that people will sense in it
    (despite all the hocus-pocus and sorcery) a living organism. That I
    received from you, Alma!" (FW/Mahler). In another unpublished
    letter to her from 1918, FW writes, "In my magical play I call you
    Mara. There, the I is missing from Maria, that sharp sound of the
    eternal virgin. . . . There, you are a pagan *Ur*-principle. . . . I love my
    homeland, I love you! You midday-midnight! Your body smells of the
    fragrance of the hearth on which creation is being cooked" (FW/
    Mahler).

68 *he was praying "to the gods":* KW Archive.

68 *Financial and contractual matters:* Unpublished letter from Rudolf Werfel
    to Kurt Wolff Verlag, KW Archive.

68 *Walter Gropius received a medical release:* See Isaacs, *Walter Gropius,* op. cit.
68 *talked things over: ML,* p. 117.
68 *I am visiting the sculptor:* Anna Mahler died on June 3, 1988.
69 *"Our cook":* Agnes Hvizd (1861–1933). I thank Dietmar Grieser of
    Vienna for the reference; See also Grieser, *Piroschka, Sorbas & Co.:*
    Schicksale der Weltliteratur (Munich: Langen Müller Verlag, 1978). FW
    immortalized her as "Teta Linek" in his 1939 novel *Der Veruntreute*
    Himmel. See also pp. 179–81. in this volume.

BREITENSTEIN AM SEMMERING

71 *"we are still too weak!":* See "Franz Werfel im November 1918: Bericht des
    Polizeikommissärs Dr. Johann Presser," in *Salzburger Nachrichten,* De-
    cember 29, 1973. On FW in November 1918, see especially Dr. Hans
    Hautmann's excellent study "Franz Werfel: *Barbara oder Die Fröm-*
    migkeit und die Revolution in Wien 1918," in *Österreich in Geschichte*
    und Literatur (Graz), vol. 15, 1971, pp. 469ff.
71 *In military barracks:* See also *Barbara,* "Third Life Fragment," pp. 289ff.
71 *he had other worries:* See "Franz Werfel im November 1918," op. cit.
72 *On November 12, 1918:* On the entire question of the November revolu-
    tion, see Hautmann, "Franz Werfel," op. cit., and FW's *Barbara.*
72 *On the morning of that historic day:* See *ML,* pp. 121f. FW's own view of
    events is found in a letter he wrote to his aunt Emilie Böhm in Prague
    in early 1919: "During the revolution in Vienna I became the target of
    much slander and persecution by the local press. Because I stood up
    for my convictions in public, I was called a protector of the so-called
    looters and arsonists. I'm sure you have read some of those things in
    the newspaper. In the end, it really doesn't matter, although it was
    irritating to be smeared that way" (M-W Coll.)
72 *daily visits to the Café Central:* I owe all the details on the Central and
    Herrenhof coffeehouses to my conversations with Professor Milan
    Dubrovic, who was a habitué of both establishments in younger years;
    see also Dubrovic, *Veruntreute Geschichte* (Vienna: Paul Zsolnay Verlag,
    1985).
73 *Ernst Polak:* See Hartmut Binder, "Ernst Polak—Literat ohne Werk," in
    Jahrbuch der deutschen Schiller-Gesellschaft, vol. 23 (Stuttgart, 1979),
    pp. 366–415.
73 *Milena Jesenská:* There is a biographical sketch of Franz Kafka's famous
    correspondent in the afterword of her collection *Feuilletons und Repor-*
    tagen 1920–1939 (Frankfurt am Main: Verlag Neue Kritik, 1984).
73 *worked as a maid:* All details on Milena Jesenská are from ibid.
73 *water on the brain:* See *ML;* FWs, "Geheimes Tagebuch," M-W Coll.; and
    the FW-Mahler correspondence.
74 *showed surprising empathy:* FW/Spirk.
74 *the child's condition:* Unpublished section of FW, "Geheimes Tagebuch,"
    M-W Coll.
74 *nightmarish dimensions:* In an unpublished 1917 letter to Gertrud Spirk,

written from the war front in eastern Galicia, FW describes a nightmare: "Children were playing on the steps. When I took a closer look,
one of the children was a genuine dwarf—not a cripple, but clearly an
evil fairy-tale creature. I think he had red hair on a hydrocephalic
head and legs extending up to his waist. Endlessly malevolent, this
dwarf tried to unknot the strange rope attached to the bit of my horse.
I grabbed him and tore him away a couple of times, but he went on
fiddling with the rope. Then I became terribly furious and grabbed
his neck with a disgustingly pleasurable feeling in my fingers. I
squeezed only a little, but then the dwarf lay there, and the children
were dancing around me and shouting, 'See, see, you murdered him' "
(FW/Spirk).

74 *she promised Walter Gropius:* See Isaacs, *Walter Gropius,* op. cit.

74 *never really loved anyone except Gustav Mahler:* Anna Mahler-Werfel's
unpublished diary, M-W Coll.

74 *the life of a hermit:* FW/Mahler; many of the details of FW's life in
Breitenstein have been gleaned from this correspondence.

74 *fantasy play* Mirror Man: *DD,* vol. 1. There are obvious Wagnerian influ-
ences on this play, sometimes an almost word-for-word convergence.
See, for example, *Parsifal* (Leipzig: Reclam, 1882), p. 59; a mirror also
plays an important role in *Parsifal.* I thank Dr. Lothar Huber of
Birkbeck College, London, for the reference.

75 *"Twice, Alma spent a week on the verge of suicide":* FW, "Geheimes Tagebuch," M-W Coll.

75 *"The Djinn": EzW,* vol. 1, pp. 63ff.

75 *"Play Yard": EzW,* vol. 1, pp. 131ff. FW wrote to Alma in an unpublished
letter: "Yesterday I finished a long dream–fairy tale replete with our
life. I don't know if it is a work of art. But it is full of that mysterious life
that lies behind us and so interwoven with a thousand things that I am
afraid to look at it now, and I wrote it with a feeling of anxiety as if
afraid of betraying myself. I am afraid to show it to you. It will cause
you pain. For me it was an enigmatic remembrance offering that I had
to bring" (FW/Mahler).

75 *Walter Gropius founded the Bauhaus:* See Isaacs, *Walter Gropius,* op. cit.

76 *the death of his . . . son:* FW wrote to Alma: "That the sweet, sacred Bubi is
no longer, I learned . . . before your telegram. My heart is still completely torn to pieces" (FW/Mahler).

76 *Titled* The Black Mass: *EzW,* vol. 1, pp. 79ff.

76 *She admitted:* See Alma Mahler-Werfel's unpublished diaries, M-W Coll.

76 *Alma wanted to revisit: ML,* pp. 133f.

76 Not the Murderer: *EzW,* vol. 1, pp. 163ff.

77 *"For God's sake, please": BeV,* p. 339.

77 *"The* Last Judgment *phase":* Ibid., p. 333.

77 *But he confessed to himself: ZOU,* p. 661. FW had started this "occasional
diary" in mid-October 1919, encouraged by Alma, but had made only
sporadic entries. See also the entry of October 27, 1919: "Reread

Turgenev's *First Love*—a masterpiece! The prose has some of my potential. But it is much truer than my *Murderer* novella, which has entirely unexperienced and yet nonobjective parts, such as the anarchist scenes. Construction!" (*ZOU*, p. 660).

77 *"Feeling of impotence": ZOU*, p. 658.

78 *Alma Mahler thought she knew:* The pertinent passage in her unpublished diary (M-W Coll.) reads: "He is often depressed and afraid of going mad. I do not fear mental aberrations but am, rather, worried about a softening of the brain in his case. He has surely laid waste to himself, to some degree, by insane masturbation up to the time he met me. From the tenth year of his life on, it took place daily, up to three times. That is why he is often tired and listless, and his cells are morbid. Why do the most wonderful examples of the human race persist in working on their own destruction? What this incredible poetic talent could have achieved if he hadn't wasted himself in such a horrendous manner!"

78 *Gina Kranz had evicted her tenant:* Author's conversations with Gina Kaus.

78 *Werfel went to Prague:* All details of FW's sojourn in Prague are from FW/Mahler.

79 *"In the city I'm no longer able": ZOU*, p. 664.

80 *Ernst Polak . . . told Werfel:* FW/Mahler.

80 *act of "irreverence":* FW/Mahler. The full text of FW's letter reads:

"Alma, this morning you have done the following to me, from which I still haven't quite recovered.

"At a time when I was full of anxiety about *Mirror Man,* you:

"first of all, *objectively deleted* things in my work, which is something *I* may do but which on your part is an act of irreverence, as these after all are lines, verses, work that one wants to regard as sacred even when they are not successful;

"second, you called Ehrenstein's manufactured talmudic prose better than mine, thus better than 'Play Yard' and so on;

"and third, you are right, and that is the worst thing of all."

80 *visions were not entirely unfounded:* See Isaacs, *Walter Gropius,* op. cit.: "[Alma Mahler's] first reaction to [Walter Gropius's] demand for a divorce had been an astonishing offer—she declared herself willing to spend the first half of every year with him and the second half with Franz Werfel. Walter Gropius immediately . . . rejected the strange proposal" (p. 225). "In ingratiating terms [Alma Mahler] wrote to him, her 'beloved Walter,' in November 1919 about her 'only wish' to be reunited with him: 'Since the fall . . . I have been straining to return totally to you. . . . Never have I considered what you call a *true* divorce—I come to you as a gift, and who knows what wonderful form we may be able to crystallize.' . . . [Alma] wrote a letter at the beginning of December [1919] in which she spoke of remorse and asked for sympathy: 'Love me—I deserve it *despite everything!* I am the guilty one . . . Leave me the possibility to come to you—when I long for

you. . . . Werfel visits, lives down in Breitenstein—works there. We are strictly separated by a vow. In the fall he wants to visit you for a while—if you want him to' " (pp. 237f.). See also FW's premonitory dream of Alma in *ZOU*, pp. 746ff.

80 *Max Reinhardt invited him:* FW/Mahler.

81 *To Walter Gropius's dismay:* "At the beginning of April 1920 Alma and Franz Werfel arrived in Berlin, went to cafés and theaters together, visited Max Reinhardt together. Now Walter Gropius's mother [Manon Gropius] no longer went along with her son's prettified versions of the affair: she wrote Alma an angry letter in which she accused her of infidelity" (Isaacs, *Walter Gropius*, op. cit., p. 240).

81 *beginning of May 1920: ML*, pp. 145ff.

"I Am Goat Song"

85 *publication of* The Last Judgment: See Hermann Hesse's review: "Werfel stands constantly between two poles, between chaos and form, between total surrender to the unconscious and sophisticated artistic delight in the personally shaped. Many have regarded, and still regard, him as a revolutionary and a destroyer of form. But one need only look at these songs to see this deep joy in giving form, even in the desire to find the character that deviates from the norm, to destroy the formal schema. . . . Time and again he closes his wise eyes, time and again he becomes a child, becomes unself-conscious, becomes pious, and time and again this piety turns into art for him, into word, into form, and he wakes up and throws it on the floor with a curse" (Hermann Hesse, *Eine Literaturgeschichte in Rezensionen und Aufsätzen* [Frankfurt am Main: Suhrkamp Verlag, 1975]; I thank Heiner Hesse of Ticino for the reference). After the publication of *The Last Judgment*, FW wrote to Alma in the fall of 1919: "I'm full of mistrust of myself. Want to produce something decisive, at long last. . . . It is terrible! I still haven't written my Op[us] I" (FW/Mahler).

85 *newspaper interview: ZOU*, pp. 591f.

85 *novel directed against Karl Kraus:* See FW's diaries, *ZOU*, pp. 667ff.: "The Relative. [*Der Verwandte*]. Idea for a novel."

85 *a play with literary symbolism:* Alma Mahler-Werfel describes the genesis of *Goat Song* in *ML:* "One day an elegant lady paid us a visit. This lady was very much against my attachment to Franz Werfel. She never really understood him, and like everybody else, she wanted to 'protect my good name.' Franz Werfel flew into a rage and went to lie down on the couch in my bedroom, while I sat there looking bored and enduring her not entirely inane conversation. After a while I went back to my room, but Franz Werfel seemed totally lost in thought, and I tiptoed out again. When the lady finally left, I found Franz Werfel in a greatly refreshed and pleasant mood. During the lady's visit he had come up with the idea for *Goat Song*. The 'repressed' had suddenly

become an event for him. He had seen the horrendous indigenous shape of the play clearly in his mind. . . . He went to the Semmering for a short while and wrote the whole play down as if it had been dictated to him by some unfathomable force" (pp. 141f.).

86 *called the project* Goat Song: *DD,* vol. 1, pp. 251–317. An unpublished letter to her daughter Sylvia from the painter Broncia Koller, the mother of Rupert Koller, whom Anna Mahler married in 1919, shows that FW made Anna the model for Stanja, the main female character: "Anna is Stanja, but Rupert, thank God, is no Mirko!" I thank E. Löcker for referring me to this correspondence.

86 *"the theme of our time":* In an unpublished letter of January 25, 1922, to the playwright Julius Berstl, FW writes: "In Berlin they are acceding to urgent demand and putting on scores of *Shakespeare plays.* Do you really believe that the public makes head or tail of the incredibly confused and vastly boring family history of *Richard III*—or of any of the other royal dramas or those inane and affected comedies? But Shakespeare is long dead, and the cities are teeming with culture vultures. *Goat Song* is much more lucid than your average royal drama, which really does not mean anything to anyone living today. *Goat Song* symbolizes the theme of *our* time, the *sense of destruction.*"

86 *divorced in Weimar:* "At last, on October 11, 1920, the divorce had become final. . . . To speed up . . . the proceedings, Walter Gropius had agreed that Alma would be the petitioner and he would assume the guilt. To this end, a marital transgression was carefully constructed. . . . It was a bizarre maneuver, even more so since Alma's marital infidelity was general knowledge. . . . For Walter Gropius, the separation from Alma was a deliverance" (Isaacs, *Walter Gropius,* op. cit., pp. 248f.).

86 *"Dramaturgy and Explication":* ZOU, pp. 222ff.

86 *"just a lot of barren verbiage":* Unpublished letter from FW to Kurt Wolff, KW Archive.

87 *Werfel and Alma traveled to Venice:* Unpublished letter from FW to Kurt Wolff, KW Archive.

87 *an extended reading tour:* The German tour, on which Alma Mahler accompanied FW in part, took him to Munich, Nuremberg, Düsseldorf, Berlin, and elsewhere.

87 *had become "unspeakably terrifying!":* Unpublished letter from FW to Kurt Wolff, KW Archive.

87 *"Autobiographical Note":* ZOU, pp. 701ff.

88 *When Werfel returned to Prague:* The unpublished FW/Mahler correspondence shows that he feared another world war after Karl I, the former emperor of Austria-Hungary, tried to seize power in Hungary: "Mobilization has been decreed and it almost got me, too. That idiot Karl and his . . . gang of criminals are calling up another world war."

88 *a "phantom":* See FW's reply to the question posed by a Prague newspaper, "Why have you left Prague?" (*ZOU,* p. 592): "My life instinct rebelled against Prague. For the non-Czech, it seems to me, this city is

unreal; for him it is a daydream that provides no experience, a paralyzing ghetto. . . . For the healthy, robust race that now rules the land,
Prague means life, capital, culture, culmination—the homeless one
understands the secret of the city better, at home and abroad."

88   *Robert Musil:* In his review Musil (1880–1942) wrote: "For years Werfel
has been struggling energetically for a deeper meaning; to my mind,
he conducts this struggle too cleverly, and not enough against himself—which may not prevent success from perhaps proving him right
this time" (Robert Musil, *Gesammelte Werke*, vol. 9 [Reinbek: Rowohlt
Verlag, 1978], p. 1561). See also Musil, *Der Mann ohne Eigenschaften*, in
ibid., vol. 3. The character Feuermaul is Franz Werfel, and Alma
Mahler is Frau Professor Drangsal. "The young poet Friedel Feuermaul—also known to his intimates as Pepi, as he was nostalgic for Old
Vienna and tried to look like the young Schubert—simply believed in
the mission of Austria, and he also believed in humanity. . . . Thus
Feuermaul was a busy young man, able to be quite vicious in the
struggle for advantage but wholly enamored of 'the human being'—
and as soon as he thought about humanity in general, he was quite
beside himself with frustrated kindness" (p. 1032).

88   *"My line of credit":* ZOU, p. 672.

89   *Alma Mahler visited:* According to Arthur Schnitzler's unpublished
diaries, which Peter Michael Braunwarth permitted me to see, Alma
told Schnitzler that Gropius was writing her letters in bad taste concerning their daughter Manon, in which he referred to the child as
"the fruit of my *Stamm* [stem, trunk, tribe]." Schnitzler notes that
Alma was sending these letters, with passages underlined in red, to
Werfel in Breitenstein (January 26, 1922).

89   *"All loneliness is illness":* From an unpublished FW notebook concerning
Schweiger, UCLA.

89   Schweiger: *DD*, vol. 1, pp. 319–83. It is interesting to look at this play
next to Robert Wiene's 1919 film *The Cabinet of Dr. Caligari:* the
screenplay for this expressionist film was written by Carl Mayer and
FW's former Stefansgymnasium classmate Hans Janowitz (brother of
the poet Franz Janowitz, FW's friend, who died in World War I).
"Caligari is a hypnotist who orders his somnambulist medium Cesare
to kill a friend of the hero and abduct his girl. After the hero has
uncovered Caligari's machinations, he is revealed to be an inmate of a
mental institution whose director is Dr. Caligari" (*Filmlexikon*, vol. 2,
ed. Liz-Anne Bawden; German edition ed. Wolfram Tichy [Reinbek
bei Hamburg: Rowohlt Taschenbuch Verlag, 1978]). For suggesting a
kinship between the material of *Schweiger* and the *Caligari* film, I
thank Christoph Tölg of Vienna.

89   *to purchase a small palazzo:* ML, p. 162.

90   *notes for a projected large-scale novel:* From FW's unpublished notebooks,
UCLA.

90   *notion harking back to his schooldays:* See Willy Haas in *Die Kritik* (Prague,

1934–35), p. 15: "Werfel's *epic* work began very early on in terms of thought but was realized relatively late. He had already told me at the gymnasium, before 1910, the outline of his Verdi novel, which he did not complete until 1924, giving me his sketches for the characters of Verdi, Richard Wagner, Hans von Bülow, and Arigo Boito." See also FW's preface to *Verdi: Roman der Oper:* "It is twelve years now since this book was first planned, but the writing of it has always been deferred. There were artistic reasons for hesitation—the hesitation that a historical theme always awakens."

90   *to compose music himself:* See Hermann Fähnrich, "Fünf Kompositionsskizzen von Franz Werfel," unpublished typescript, DL. The five composition sketches by FW that Fähnrich discusses can be found in M-W Coll.

90   *a letter to Kurt Wolff:* KW Archive. From then on, Alma Mahler-Werfel wrote all of FW's business letters to Wolff and, later, those to Paul Zsolnay.

90   *Wolff defended himself vehemently:* See *BeV,* p. 345ff.

91   *"Generally speaking less confident":* See *ZOU,* p. 677.

91   *"And yet writing poems":* Unpublished letter from FW to Rudolf Fuchs in the Prague Literatur-Archiv; I thank Rotraut Hackermüller of Vienna for the reference.

91   *Arthur Schnitzler came:* See Arthur Schnitzler's unpublished diaries, which Peter Michael Braunwarth permitted me to see.

92   *revised his initial mistaken view:* See Unseld, "*Franz Kafka,* op. cit., pp. 182, 281.

92   *He praised* Mirror Man *and* Goat Song: See Gustav Janouch, *Gespräche mit Kafka: Aufzeichnungen und Erinnerungen,* rev. ed. (Frankfurt am Main: S. Fischer Verlag, 1968), p. 185.

92   *one of his dreams:* Kafka wrote to Max Brod in mid-November 1917: "In a recent dream of mine I gave Werfel a kiss" (Kafka, *Letters to Friends, Family, and Editors,* trans. Richard and Clara Winston [New York: Schocken Books, 1977], p. 167). On Kafka's relationship with FW, see also his letter to Milena Jesenská, May 30, 1920: "How about your knowledge of human nature, Milena? I've doubted it several times already, when you wrote about Werfel for instance, and though it does show love and perhaps only love, it's nevertheless erroneous and if one leaves out all that Werfel really is and harps only on the reproach of fatness (which to me, incidentally, seems unjustified. In my eyes Werfel appears every year more beautiful and lovable, though it's true I see him only fleetingly) don't you know that only fat people are trustworthy?" (Kafka, *Letters to Milena,* ed. Willy Haas, trans. Tania and James Stern [New York: Schocken Books, 1953], p. 49).

92   *Kafka's disapproval:* After the two had fallen out over *Schweiger,* Kafka wrote a letter to FW in December 1922 that was probably never mailed (*Letters to Friends, Family, and Editors,* op. cit., pp. 365–66):

"Dear Werfel, After the way I behaved at your last visit, you could not come again. I realized that. And I would surely have written to you before this were it not that letter-writing has gradually become as hard for me as talking, and that even mailing letters is troublesome, for I already had a letter all written for you. But it is useless to go over old things. Where would it end, if one were never to stop defending all one's old wretched mistakes and apologizing for them. So let me only say this, Werfel, which you yourself must know: If what was involved here was only an ordinary dislike, then it might possibly have been easier to formulate and moreover might have been so unimportant that I might well have been able to keep it to myself. But it was a horror, and justifying that is difficult: One seems stubborn and tough and cross-grained, where one is only unhappy. You are surely one of the leaders of this generation, which is not meant as flattery and cannot serve as flattery of anyone, for many a man can lead this society, so lost in its bogs. Hence you are not only a leader but something more (you yourself have said something similar in the fine introduction to Brand's posthumous works, fine right down to the phrase 'joyous will to deception') and one follows your course with burning suspense. And now this play. It may have every possible merit, from the theatrical to the highest, but it is a retreat from leadership; there is not even leadership there, rather a betrayal of the generation, a glossing over, a trivializing, and therefore a cheapening of their sufferings.

"But now I am prattling on, as I did before, am incapable of thinking out and expressing the crux of the matter. Let it be so. Were it not that my sympathy with you, my deeply selfish sympathy with you, is so great, I would not even be prattling.

"And now the invitation: in written form, it assumes an even realer and more magnificent appearance. Obstacles are my illness, the doctor (he definitely rules out Semmering once again, though he is not so definite about Venice in the early spring), and I suppose money too (I would have to manage on a thousand crowns a month). But these are not the chief obstacles. Between lying stretched out on my Prague bed and strolling erect in the Piazza San Marco, the distance is so great that only imagination can barely span it. But these are only generalizations. Beyond that, to imagine that for example I might go to dinner with other people in Venice (I can only eat alone)—even the imagination is staggered. But nonetheless I cling to the invitation, and thank you for it many times.

"Perhaps I will see you in January. Be well. Yours, Kafka"

Kafka also wrote to Max Brod in December 1922, "The play means a great deal to me; it hits me hard, affects me horribly on the most horrible level" (ibid., p. 365).

92   *Kafka identified:* On Kafka's relationship to Otto Gross, see the outstanding work by Thomas Anz, "Jemand musste Otto G. verleumdet haben . . . ," in *Akzente* (Munich), February 1984, pp. 184ff. On Otto Gross,

see also Emanuel Hurwitz, *Otto Gross: Ein Paradies-Sucher zwischen Freud und Jung* (Frankfurt am Main: Suhrkamp Verlag, 1979).

93 *rejection from Arthur Schnitzler:* See Schnitzler's unpublished diaries, which Peter Michael Braunwirth was kind enough to let me read. On December 12, 1922, Schnitzler notes that FW presented him with a copy of his new play *Schweiger* that evening. He finds nothing to praise in this "tortured, confused play" but "a couple of intense spots of dialogue. Telephoned Alma about it; she, too, noted Werfel's lack of concentration." On December 26 Schnitzler says that he has informed FW of his objections to *Schweiger* and that "Alma seemed glad someone spoke honestly with him."

93 *the play premiered in Prague:* See Foltin, p. 49.

94 *"your degenerate seed":* In *Goat Song* Steven Milič says to his wife, "Word-twister, clever one! Who sired him on you? Not my child, he. Well born, my clan, for ten generations!" His wife replies, "How you must have spoiled your seed, by abominations, to have it degrade me so, for I am healthy, and I was healthy when you wooed me" (*DD*, vol. 1, p. 262). See also the note *Alma Mahler thought she knew*, above, p. 261.

A NOVEL OF THE OPERA

96 *end of January 1923:* See "Zufalls-Tagebuch," *ZOU*, p. 679.

96 *Richard Specht (1870–1932):* In 1926, Paul Zsolnay Verlag published Specht's biography *Franz Werfel: Versuch einer Zeitspiegelung*, op. cit. He was also the author of the first monograph on Arthur Schnitzler, *Arthur Schnitzler: Der Dichter und sein Werk* (Berlin: S. Fischer Verlag, 1922).

97 *as a gymnasium student:* In *SL*, pp. 33ff., Max Brod gives a very amusing account of FW's rejection of Wagner at that time.

97 *had to defend his own passion for Verdi:* Unpublished letter from FW to Gerhart Hauptmann, Stiftung Preussischer Kulturbesitz, Berlin.

98 *he read the works:* Notes on FW's research in a notebook dated Venice, 1923, at UCLA; see also an unpublished letter to Kurt Wolff dated June 5, 1923, in KW Archive.

98 *"mid-June 1923":* "Zufalls-Tagebuch," *ZOU*, p. 685.

98 *Convinced he had failed: ML*, p. 159.

98 *Anna Mahler:* At this time, she had already divorced Rupert Koller. A little later she married Ernst Křenek. See Foltin, p. 57. Later editions of *Verdi* depict Fischböck more humanely and far more sympathetically than the first edition of 1924.

98 *Ernst Křenek:* Born in 1900, he made his name with the jazz opera *Johnny spielt auf* (1927).

98 *Hauer ... Schoenberg:* Josef Matthias Hauer, 1883–1959; Arnold Schoenberg, 1874–1951.

98 *"The end. Thank God!":* Manuscript of the first version of *Verdi*, M-W Coll. Also see Hans Kühner, *Giuseppe Verdi* (Reinbek bei Hamburg: Rowohlt Taschenbuch Verlag, 1961), p. 115: "On November 1, 1886,

Giulio Ricordi [Verdi] proclaims, '*Otello* completely finished!!! At last!!!!!!!!' Eight exclamation points seem to him an appropriate expression of deliverance."

98   *thought of Brod's* Tycho Brahe: See *SL*, pp. 202f.

99   *"The book is suspenseful":* Unpublished letter from FW to Kurt Wolff, September 30, 1923; KW Archive.

99   *Jakob Wassermann* (1873–1934): The dedication in the copy of *Verdi* FW gave him reads: "Master *Jakob Wassermann*, with reverential thanks for his productive help with this book. Franz Werfel, Venice, 1924." See *ML*, p. 160.

99   *"I know for certain":* Unpublished letter from FW to Kurt Wolff, Prague, December 3, 1923; KW Archive.

99   *Paul von Zsolnay* (1895–1961): According to Anna Mahler, Zsolnay came up with the idea of starting his own publishing house after Alma Mahler told him in the course of a conversation that all the publishers with whom FW had done business were crooks.

100   *one of the largest theaters in Berlin:* The play was performed at the Theater in der Königgrätzerstrasse, with Ernst Deutsch, a friend of FW's youth, in the title role. FW wrote Alma Mahler on October 29, 1923: "It is truly horrendous that we won't get a penny from such a theatrical success. . . . It is an outrage. . . . Something must be done" (FW/Mahler).

100   *Zsolnay, on the other hand, offered:* On FW's leaving Kurt Wolff Verlag, see Wolff's radio talk on Norddeutscher Rundfunk, May 19, 1962, and *BeV*, p. 349.

101   *Franz Kafka was admitted:* On the history of Kafka's illness, see Rotraut Hackermüller's remarkable study *Das Leben das mich stört* (Vienna: Medusa Verlag, 1984).

101   *Werfel wrote:* Markus Hajek (1861–1941), Julius Tandler (1869–1936).

101   *"Can't anything be done":* Unpublished letter from FW to Max Brod.

101   *a big bouquet of red roses:* Kafka wrote to Brod, probably on April 20, 1924: "[FW] sent me the novel (I was frightfully hungry for a suitable book) and roses. And although I had to ask him not to come (for it's marvelous here for the patients; for visitors, and in this regard therefore also for the patients, horrible), a card from him indicates that he means to come today anyhow; in the evening he is leaving for Venice" (Kafka, *Letters to Friends, Family, and Editors*, op. cit., p. 413). It is not known whether FW actually made this visit to Kierling.

Success and Crisis

104   *"Venice—in Alma's house!":* "Zufalls-Tagebuch," *ZOU*, p. 687.

104   *Carl Moll had added two rooms:* See *ML*, pp. 162f.

104   *two major works:* See "Zufalls-Tagebuch," *ZOU*, pp. 687f.

105   *"historical tragedy* Juarez and Maximilian": *DD*, vol. 1, pp. 385–465.

105   *"He is too colossal a figure":* Unpublished notebook on *Juarez and Maximilian*, M-W Coll.

106 *first long trip:* See "Ägyptisches Tagebuch," *ZOU,* pp. 705ff.; all details of the trip to the Near East have been derived from this diary.

106 *presented with a* fait accompli: On FW's love of travel, see Adolf D. Klarmann, "Franz Werfel, der Dichter des Glaubens," *Forum,* nos. 19–20 (1955), pp. 278f.

107 *ancient, ecstatic dance of the dervishes:* The text "Die tanzenden Derwische" (*EzW,* vol. 1, pp. 285ff.) derives from FW's "Egyptian Diary" but was also published independently in *Ewige Gegenwart* (Berlin: Die Buchgemeinde, 1929) and elsewhere.

109 *a serious artistic crisis:* On Werfel's great crisis in the spring of 1925, see FW/Mahler.

109 *a rather unsuccessful world premiere:* On the Magdeburg premiere, FW wrote to Alma, "Boundless disappointment over *Juarez:* I had firmly expected it to overcome the hostility directed against me" (FW/Mahler).

109 *his dramatic legend* Paul Among the Jews: *Paulus unten den Juden, DD,* vol. 1, pp. 467–534. In May 1928 FW was planning a sequel to the play, *Paul Among the Pagans* (*Paulus unter den Heiden*); see the unpublished notebook titled "Firenze, 1928," M-W Coll.

110 *the title page of his* Paul *notebook:* Unpublished notebook, UCLA.

110 *"Before embarking on a new work":* Unpublished letter from FW to Hugo von Hofmannsthal, M-W Coll.

110 *a clear indication:* ML, p. 170.

110 *a journey to India:* Ibid., p. 171.

110 *Ullstein Verlag in Berlin:* Unpublished letter from Ullstein Verlag to FW, January 5, 1925: "We permit ourselves to recapitulate the content of our conversation as follows: You will travel to India in the fall of 1925. At the outset of this trip, Ullstein Verlag will pay you the sum of *10,000 marks.* You undertake to write columns, impressions, etc., from India for our daily newspapers, and for these you will receive honoraria at the highest going rates. . . . Furthermore, you assign to us the option on a novel dealing with the world of India" (UCLA).

110 *a new treatment and translation:* In an unpublished notebook, FW says that Verdi's work requires restoration similar to that performed on old paintings: "to peel off the overpaintings of the theater, to reach the true dramat[ic] coloration of which [Verdi] himself was not aware." The exact descriptive title of the translation was "Freely translated from the Italian by F. M. Piave and adapted for the German operatic theater by Franz Werfel." See also FW, "Meine Verdi-Bearbeitungen," *Die Bühne* (Vienna) vol. 3, no. 105, November 11, 1926; I thank Dr. Kafka (FK letters) for referring me to this article, which has not yet been reprinted.

111 *Alban Berg* (1885–1935): On Berg's relationship with Hanna Fuchs-Robetin, see the exhibition catalogue *Alban Berg* (Vienna: Österreichische Nationalbibliothek, 1985), pp. 83ff. Berg wrote to Hanna Fuchs-Robetin in October 1931, "Not a day passes, not half a day, no

night without my thinking of you, no week in which I am not flooded
with a longing that immerses my entire thinking and feeling and
wishing into a passion that does not seem to me the least whit diminished from May 1925" (ibid.).

111   *Werfel stayed in Berlin:* FW wrote his opinion of Berlin to Paul Zech on
       October 7, 1926: "Berlin is the latrine and dumping ground of all
       Bolshe- and Americanisms that are no longer true or never have been
       true. The clash of the Jews with the Mark Brandenburg has sounded a
       horrendous discord. Because this Berlin that considers itself so real,
       sober, disciplined, and productive is in fact the most fantastic imprint
       of irreality. . . . Berlin is an unworldly hypersophisticated Jew's dream
       of the validity of what he regards as modern and radical: in the
       economy and in art!" (Edschmid, *Briefe des Expressionismus,* op. cit.,
       p. 16).

111   *meeting with Willy Haas:* Haas, "Der junge Werfel," M-W Coll.

111   *"without concentration and pretty much in despair":* FW, unpublished letter
       to Arthur Schnitzler, Breitenstein, June 7, 1926; I thank Peter Mi-
       chael Braunwarth of Vienna for pointing it out to me.

112   *it began to be rumored:* For instance, Arnold Zweig wrote to FW on
       October 18, 1926: "First of all: I have not been spreading a rumor.
       Among my closest acquaintances there are two who many years ago,
       out of an inner need . . . , converted to Catholicism. . . . One of these, a
       critically minded man not at all given to gossip, told me with absolute
       certainty that you had converted" (UCLA).

112   *Sigmund Freud:* I am not familiar with Freud's letters to FW, but their
       contents can be clearly extrapolated from FW's replies in M-W Coll.

113   *Stefan Zweig:* Unpublished letter from Zweig to FW: "The idea is genius,
       the realization great—sometimes colored by an unconscious partisan-
       ship, the one with which our blood has stricken us, despite all our
       resistance to it. . . . You have laid bare the decisive wound. . . . The
       undoubtedly tremendous success will be merely a vehicle for carrying
       the argument farther into the world. All in all: how successful you
       have been in so much! You are practically the only one in this genera-
       tion who has an 'oeuvre' with annual rings. . . . In old friendly feeling
       and entirely warmed by the experience of the world you have given
       me—most truly, Your Stefan Zweig" (UCLA).

113   *talk of the town in New York:* See *Die Literatur,* June 1926, p. 546: "As an
       immediate consequence of the enthusiasm for Werfel, another theatri-
       cal enterprise tried to stage *Schweiger* in English translation. However,
       its performance ended up putting a damper on that somewhat stri-
       dent acclaim."

113   *"A Portrait of Giuseppe Verdi":* ZOU, pp. 358ff.

113   Pogrom: *EzW,* vol. 2, pp. 336ff. FW incorporated this prose piece in his
       novel *Barbara,* chapter 6. See also "Erguss und Beichte," *ZOU,* pp.
       690ff., from which we learn that *Pogrom* harks back to a scene FW had
       actually experienced.

113 The Kingdom of God in Bohemia: *DD,* vol. 2, pp. 7–90.
113 The Man Who Conquered Death: *EzW,* vol. 2, pp. 7ff.
113 *peculiarities and eccentricities:* FW wrote to Alma in the spring of 1925:
     "The old one and Klara welcomed me. The old one, who looks quite
     pitiful, started weeping hideously right away, and it took a long time to
     calm her down. Without delay she then told me about old Gubsch's
     death. Despite the horrible subject, this was grotesque, as she kept
     transposing words in the Czech manner and insisted on saying 'Baby-
     lon' instead of 'pavilion.' According to her, her hospitalized husband
     had died of hunger. Klara, with her strong slave face, stood beside her,
     casting her slightly cross-eyed glance that did not really glisten with
     tears down onto her dirty bodice" (FW/Mahler). See also FW to Alma
     Mahler in Jungk, ed., *Das Franz Werfel Buch,* op. cit., p. 428; and FW,
     "Zufalls-Tagebuch," *ZOU,* p. 663: "Today the old Gubsch woman came
     to show me her family treasures."

BARBARA, OR REALITY

117 *imitated Hauptmann's sartorial style:* MD conversations.
117 *Imperial Palace:* The luxury hotel still exists, under the same name. FW
     liked to work in spacious rooms; see *ML,* p. 180.
117 *a cycle of novellas: A Man's Secret (Geheimnis eines Menschen),* published by
     Paul Zsolnay in 1927. The original title of the cycle was to be *The Ages
     of Life (Die Lebensalter),* M-W Coll. In addition to *The Man Who Con-
     quered Death, Poor People,* and *The House of Mourning,* the cycle con-
     tained *Estrangement, Severio's Secret (Geheimnis eines Menschen),* and *The
     Staircase (Die Hoteltreppe). Estrangement* was originally titled *The Sister's
     Love (Die Liebe der Schwester).* The story describes the intense relation-
     ship between Erwin, a musician, and his sister Gabriele, which is
     terminated by Erwin's domineering wife, Judith. It is a parable of the
     relationship between Alma, FW, and his favorite sister, Hanna. Child-
     hood memories figure prominently in this story (see also FW's idea for
     a novella he wanted to call *The Sister (Die Schwester)* in "Zufalls-
     Tagebuch," *ZOU,* pp. 666f.). *Severio's Secret* was the first novella FW
     wrote in Santa Margherita. It was based on an actual occurrence: Al-
     ma's stepfather, Carl Moll, already a recognized painter, had once
     fallen victim to a notorious Roman forger of statuary by the name of
     Alceo Dossena, who had been deceiving the world's most renowned
     connoisseurs of art for years. Dossena inflicted particular damage on
     an art dealer in Venice whom FW knew personally, and the novella's
     locale is, therefore, Venice (author's conversations with Anna Mahler).
117 Poor People: *EzW,* vol. 2, pp. 235ff. The earlier short story "Knabentag"
     (*EzW,* vol. 1, pp. 57ff.) reflects similar moods.
117 *Erna Tschepper:* See p. 243.
117 *the novella* The House of Mourning: *EzW,* vol. 2, pp. 181ff. FW's poet
     Peppler is a caricature of the Prague poet Paul Leppin; see Gold-
     stücker, *Weltfreunde,* op. cit., p. 225. See also Egon Erwin Kisch's one-

act play *Piccaver im Salon Goldschmied,* first performed in Prague in 1926, which takes place in the bordello on Gamsgasse.

118 *culminated in a novel:* The character of the successful Schulhof corresponds to FW's friend Ernst Deutsch. On the genesis of *Class Reunion,* see also Alma Mahler's version in *ML,* p. 180, with which I disagree.

118 *other professors of the Stefansgymnasium:* In this context, Willy Haas promulgated an anecdote for which there is no corroboration, as the Professor Millrath mentioned by Haas does not appear in the teachers' lists Dr. Kafka consulted in Prague (FK letters). FW's German teachers had other names. It is possible that the story is true and Haas only misremembered the name: "Werfel had a wonderful talent of reproducing other voices which he remembered even after decades: a source of inexhaustible amusement for both of us in those hours of our later life. There was only one of the professors we did not love in any way, as either a funny or serious memory. He was our German professor Millrath. . . . Werfel was his chosen victim. He never missed an opportunity to make Werfel look foolish in front of the class for some trivial reason and hardly ever gave him more than 'Unsatisfactory' on his German essays. [This statement does not correspond with the facts.] We remembered him well, and I asked, 'What happened to Millrath?' 'You won't believe this,' said Werfel, 'he is now the theater critic of the *Wiener Arbeiterzeitung* and pans all my plays.' One has to grant that the man is consistent" (Haas, "Der junge Werfel," M-W Coll.).

119 *Palace of Justice burned:* See Elias Canetti, *Die Fackel im Ohr: Lebensgeschichte, 1921–1931* (Munich: Carl Hanser Verlag, 1983), pp. 274ff. On Alma Mahler's political orientation, see *ML,* for instance, p. 170: "Austria is already lost. Perhaps a cesarean would save it: joining up with Germany." In 1928 she visits Margherita Sarfatti, Benito Mussolini's mistress and thus "the uncrowned queen of Italy": "We noted once again that only a worldwide organization could help. She was of the opinion that an international fascism based on the national one would be possible only if the fascists in other countries were wise enough, like Mussolini, to leave the Jewish question alone. And that had been my express purpose in coming to see her, to discuss this question. . . . 'At long last we have a leader [this refers to Mussolini]—it was almost too late! But even more important than his genius is his character!' She shouted these two sentences in rapid succession."

119 *a large selection of his poems: Gedichte* was published by Paul Zsolnay Verlag in 1927; quotation appears on p. 446.

119 *champagne parties: ML,* pp. 177ff.

119 *"merely a tenant":* Unpublished notebook, M-W Coll.

121 *Alfred Engländer:* The original name of the writer Peter Altenberg, a friend of FW's, was Richard Engländer. It is possible that FW was thinking of Altenberg when he gave his character that name.

121 *death by starvation:* See Franz Blei, *Erzählung eines Lebens* (Leipzig: Paul List Verlag, 1930) pp. 346ff.

121   *This time, it seems, he manages:* See Hautmann, "Franz Werfel: *Barbara oder Die Frömmigkeit* und die Revolution in Wien 1918," op. cit., pp. 469ff.: "It must not be forgotten that a large sector of the public and all his fellow writers in the time between the wars knew about Werfel's faux pas in November 1918. It can be imagined how embarrassing the scuttlebutt 'he sided with the Communists' must have been to a man of Werfel's allegiance to bourgeois pacifist thinking. This is probably why he created an *apology*—masterfully told—for his contemporaries and posterity, in *The Pure in Heart,* in which the character of Barbara appears rather like a religious figurehead for a political autobiography."

121   *The erstwhile anarchist:* See Albert Soergel and Curt Hohoff, *Dichtung und Dichter der Zeit: Vom Naturalismus bis zur Gegenwart* (Düsseldorf: Bagel, 1964), vol. 2, p. 491: "The novel contains the schema of Werfel's evolution from a disappointed revolutionary to a homeless conservative, from intellectual nihilism to Catholicism."

121   *had rarely been described in a more gripping fashion:* See *Radetzkymarsch* (1932) and *Kapuzinergruft* (1938), by Joseph Roth. Both, however, appeared after *Barbara.*

121   *Between February and May 1929:* "*Santa Margherita,* February 4, 1929— arrived at noon, *my old room* (*House of Mourning, Severio's Secret, The Staircase, Class Reunion*) Hotel Imperial" (unpublished notebook, M-W Coll.).

122   *resigned from the Jewish community:* The verso of FW's birth certificate (original in M-W Coll.) bears this notation: "Vienna, June 27, 1929. Notification of withdrawal from the Mos. [Mosaic] faith community acknowledged on the basis of the law of May 25, 1868, R. G. Bl. No. 49, for Chief Administration Officer: [Signature]." The document is stamped "Magistratisches Bezirksamt f. d. I. Bezirk, Wien."

122   *Franz Werfel and Alma Mahler's civil wedding:* See *ML*, pp. 201f., 205.

122   *Hugo von Hofmannsthal's sudden death:* On July 15, 1929.

122   *"Now we have lost":* FW's eulogy appears in *ZOU*, pp. 428f.

122   *While Werfel spent an evening at the opera:* See *ML*, pp. 211f.

122   *Mrs. Tina Orchard:* Below a photograph in an album that belonged to Alma Mahler-Werfel is the legend, in her handwriting: "1930. Tina Orchard, the cause of *Die Geschwister von Neapel—Grazia.*" On the photograph itself are the words "To my dearest Alma and Franz Werfel, with Tina's love."

123   *Tolstoyan dimensions:* See Foltin, p. 70.

123   *Heinz Liepmann:* "One should perhaps send him abroad, without a lot of money, to Canada or northern Russia, anywhere with a cold climate. One would have to protect him from the opera and satiation, all just for the sake of the lightning he created when we were younger and more helpless" (*Die Weltbühne,* December 24, 1929). See also Herbert Ihering in *Das Tage-Buch,* December 14, 1929: "Franz Werfel has long since become one of these false priests of the word. He was a poet. He

274 *Notes*

was intoxicated with language. He was a creator of language. But this
language intoxication affected him like a sweet poison, like opium. It
put him into a state in which the words escaped him. Sound without
sense. Tone without meaning. A soothsayer without content. A prophet
without a goal. . . . We have had enough. Enough compromises, enough
prattle. One of the powerful driving forces of literary life, the masculine
resilience of the intellectual will, has been extinguished."

123 *Karl Kraus: Die Fackel,* nos. 827–33, pp. 96–102.

123 *Willy Haas: "Werfels neuer Roman," Die literarische Welt,* no. 49 (1929),
pp. 5f.

123 *Ernst Polak:* MD conversations. But see also Hartmut Binder, "Ernst
Polak, Literat ohne Werk," *Jahrbuch der deutschen Schillergesellschaft,*
vol. 23 (Stuttgart, 1979), pp. 366–415. Polak was also the editor of
some of Hermann Broch's works, including *The Sleepwalkers.* Polak's
influence and critical collaboration should not be underestimated. An
orgy scene in *The Pure in Heart* probably took place much as described
by FW in Ernst Polak's Vienna apartment at Lerchenfelderstrasse 113
(*Barbara oder Die Frömmigkeit,* pp. 590–99.

123 *Kisch replied:* "Werfel's powers of memory are admirable, and since genius is memory, the book is important. As far as Ronald Weiss is
concerned, the conversations I had with Werfel have been reproduced
here with the accuracy of a phonograph record. Only in places Werfel
counterpoints some things. . . . Two characters have been accorded
more praise, and they deserve it. Gebhard (the psychoanalyst Otto
Gross) and Krasny (the poet Otfried Krzyzanowski) receive their
handsome and well-deserved memorial" (*Wiener Allgemeine Zeitung,*
December 4, 1929).

124 *Gina Kranz:* See also her autobiography, *Und was für ein Leben . . . ,* op. cit.
She died on December 23, 1985.

HOHE WARTE

126 *At the beginning of 1930:* Werfel is mistaken when he claims in an afterword to *Musa Dagh* that the work "was conceived in March 1929 during
a stay in Damascus." In his unpublished diary, Arthur Schnitzler notes
on January 19, 1930, that FW and Alma are leaving for Egypt "tomorrow" but then crosses the word out and writes "soon" above it. See also
an interview FW gave the Viennese daily *Neue Freie Presse* (April 2,
1930) on his return from the Near East trip: "Ist das jüdische Aufbauwerk gefährdet? Eindrücke von einer Palästinareise: Aus einem Gespräch," *ZOU,* pp. 278ff. In an unpublished letter dated February 19,
1930, answering an inquiry concerning FW, Paul Zsolnay wrote that
FW was on an extended trip abroad (Zsolnay Archive).

126 *first to Egypt:* Details of the second Near East trip are derived from *ML*
and from FW's interview "Ist das jüdische Aufbauwerk gefährdet?"
ZOU, pp. 278ff.

127 *Werfel had repeatedly heard about the genocide:* In an interview given to a
newspaper published by Armenians in exile, FW claimed that he had

thought about writing a novel about the fate of the Armenians as long ago as World War I: "I read about it then in the major European newspapers and promised myself that I would one day write a historical novel about this subject. In Syria I met some young Armenians in extremely unhappy circumstances—I could see the destroyed greatness of their people and their persecution in their eyes" (M. A. Iytschian, "Die armenophilen Wellen"). I thank Artem Ohandjanian of Vienna for the reference and the translation.

127 *Count Bertrand Clauzel:* In his diary entry of April 27, 1929, Arthur Schnitzler notes that he was invited to visit Clauzel in the company of Franz Werfel, Alma Mahler, Berta Zuckerkandl, and others. FW probably knew Clauzel quite well; Alma Mahler-Werfel even calls him "a friend" (*Mein Leben*, p. 210).

127 *The play* The Kingdom of God in Bohemia: FW began the first version on March 26, 1930.

127 *not to produce a historical genre painting:* "Wo liegt das Reich Gottes in Böhmen? Franz Werfel über sein Hussitendrama," interview in the Vienna *Neue Freie Presse*, December 15, 1930. See also "Wie mein *Reich Gottes in Böhmen* entstand," *Neues Wiener Journal*, October 5, 1930; I thank Michael Salzer of Stockholm for pointing out this interview of his with FW.

128 *There was nothing in this world:* FW to Kurt Wolff, March 25, 1930 (*BeV*, pp. 349ff.).

128 *Wolff's reply:* Kurt Wolff took three months to reply to FW: "Could be it was my own fault for having gone about things wrongly, could be it was bad luck.... The fact is that I have worn myself out and paid for this publishing enterprise with my life's blood these last six years" (ibid., pp. 351ff.).

129 *Mesrop Habozian* (1887–1974): From 1931 until 1971, the archbishop was head abbot of the Vienna Mekhitarist monastery. On FW's research, see also George Schulz-Behrend, "Sources and Background of Werfel's Novel *Die vierzig Tage des Musa Dagh*," *The Germanic Review*, vol. 26, no. 2 (April 1951), pp. 111ff.

129 *Werfel began his research . . . in June 1930:* See unpublished notebook for *Musa Dagh*, M-W Coll.

129 *talking to a reporter:* See *Neues Wiener Journal*, October 5, 1930.

129 *world premiere of* The Kingdom of God: This took place on December 6, 1930. See Foltin, pp. 71f.

129 *violent disagreements:* See *ML*, pp. 220f., and Arthur Schnitzler's unpublished diaries. On December 1, 1930, Schnitzler talked with Anton Wildgans, the director of the Burgtheater, and the latter unburdened himself to Schnitzler about the clashes between FW and Albert Heine.

130 *Raoul Auernheimer and Felix Salten:* See the reviews in the *Neue Freie Presse*, December 9, 1920, and the *Wiener Sonn- und Montagszeitung*, December 8, 1930.

130 *A few weeks later:* See Arthur Schnitzler's unpublished diary of January 14, 1931.

130   *he returned . . . to Santa Margherita:* See "Gespräch mit Franz Werfel über
       Die Geschwister von Neapel," ZOU, p. 601: "I began to write the book in
       February in Santa Margherita."
130   *"Neapolitan story":* FW originally wanted to call the work *Novel in Naples*
       (*Roman in Neapel*). Talking to A. D. Klarmann, FW called this novel his
       "favorite work" (*DRM,* p. 27).
130   *"The waters of a story":* Unpublished notebook, M-W Coll.
130   *"Art and Conscience":* The lecture was later retitled "Realismus
       und Innerlichkeit"; see *ZOU,* pp. 16ff. FW gave the lecture in May
       1931 in the auditorium of the new Hofburg; see the *Neue Freie Presse,*
       May 7, 1931.
131   *a big move:* See *ML,* p. 225.
131   *The purchase of the ostentatious building:* From the record FW made of a
       conversation after a quarrel with his brother-in-law Ferdinand Rieser,
       June 18, 1942: "From my 'rich' father I received only one larger sum,
       to wit, 40,000 schillings in the year 1931 when we bought the house on
       Steinfeldgasse" (M-W Coll.).
131   *In the salon of this mansion:* See *ML,* and Hubert Mitrowsky, "Sontag-
       nachmittage auf der Hohen Warte," *Die Presse* (Vienna), August
       21–22, 1965; see also Elias Canetti *Das Augenspiel: Lebensgeschichte,
       1931–1937* (Munich: Carl Hanser Verlag, 1985).
132   *"we should call my book a fairy tale":* See "Gespräch mit Franz Werfel über
       Die Geschwister von Neapel," ZOU, p. 601. In the summer of 1932 there
       were negotiations for a film of the book; A. E. Liecho was to be its
       director; three film companies also expressed their interest in the
       Verdi novel at the beginning of the 1930's (Zsolnay Archive).
132   *magnificent parties:* Author's conversations with Anna Mahler. Elias Can-
       etti, Hubert Mitrowsky, and Alma Mahler-Werfel also describe these.
       Enthusiastic accounts of these festivities were also provided to me by
       Adrienne Gessner.
132   *She devised her guest lists for success:* Author's conversations with Adrienne
       Gessner.
132   *Arthur Schnitzler's mistress:* After a visit to the villa at Hohe Warte, Schnitz-
       ler notes in an unpublished diary entry for June 15, 1931, ". . . have
       rarely if ever seen a more beautiful and at the same time pleasant
       [house]. Incredibly cheap purchase. Garden, terrace." When Schnitz-
       ler and his mistress were on their way back home, she burst into bitter
       tears—not only out of envy for the Werfels, but generally "because of
       the relationship between Alma and Werfel. Painful." Clara Katharina
       Pollaczek (1875–1951) was a writer and translator.
133   *cerebral hemorrhage:* Only four days before his death, Schnitzler had
       written to FW to thank him for sending him *Die Geschwister von
       Neapel* and to say that he was looking forward to reading it soon (M-W
       Coll.).
133   *Werfel delivered a eulogy: ZOU,* pp. 436ff.
133   *extended reading tour:* Zsolnay Archive.

133   *he had to flee:* See Foltin, p. 74, and *ZOU*, p. 14 (Foltin erroneously gives the year as 1932).

133   *"I have to admit":* Neues Wiener Journal, May 15, 1932.

133   *a very different idea:* Zsolnay Archive.

134   *"Can Mankind Survive Without Religion?":* The lecture appeared later under the title "Can We Live Without Faith in God?" ("Können wir ohne Gottesglauben leben?"), *ZOU*, pp. 41ff.; see also "Interview über den Gottesglauben, *ZOU*, p. 605ff.

134   *a large family reunion:* ADK notes. Bernhard Kussi was born April 18, 1832, and died July 17, 1932 (FK letters). FW wrote the following dedication in the copy of *Verdi* he gave to his grandfather: "This book that deals with a wonderful flowering of old age I dedicate to my dear beloved grandfather *Bernhard Kussi,* who is himself a rare and wonderful flower of age. Franz Werfel, Pilsen, Dec. 1924" (FK letters).

134   *the abolition of serfdom:* ADK notes.

134   *"Not to take life for granted!":* All quotations are from an unpublished 1932 notebook in M-W Coll. In the same notebook FW writes that it seems to him as if the present has given the world indigestion, so that it is now burping up the past. The fascists are "arse-crawlers" courting the "mobs of youths," but the socialists are no better, being entirely meretricious as well. FW goes on to reminisce that in his childhood every citizen had recognized the authority of the state and given the word "fatherland" an almost sacred meaning—whereas nowadays only the tawdriest horde consciousness holds sway, and all the "wild masses" do on festive occasions is to "yell themselves hoarse." On "horde consciousness," see *The Revolt of the Masses,* by José Ortega y Gasset, which had appeared in German translation the previous year. The influence of this book on FW is evident.

THE FORTY DAYS OF MUSA DAGH

137   *These suspicions were sufficient reason:* On the genocide of the Armenians, see "Der Prozess Talaat Pascha": Reihe pogrom (Göttingen, 1980); and "Der verleugnete Völkermord an den Armeniern 1915–1918: Die deutsche Beteiligung," in the journal *Pogrom,* vol. 10, no. 64. See also Schulz-Behrend, "Sources and Background of Werfel's Novel *Die vierzig Tage des Musa Dagh,*" op. cit.

137   *exterminate the entire Armenian population:* "In one of the edicts signed by Talaat there is this statement: 'The goal of deportation is the void.' In accordance with such orders care was taken to ensure that, of the entire population that was transported from the East Anatolian provinces to the South, only some 10 percent arrived at their supposed destination; 90 percent were murdered along the way, died of hunger or exhaustion, or, in the case of women or girls, were sold by the gendarmes and dragged off by Turks and Kurds" ("Der Prozess Talaat Pascha," op. cit., p. 57).

138   *Dikran Andreasian:* See his article "Suedije: Eine Episode aus der Zeit der

Armenierverfolgungen," in *Orient: Monaltschrift für die Wiedergeburt des Ostens*, nos. 4–5 (1919), pp. 67ff. Dikran Andreasian's counterpart in the novel is Aram Tomasian.

138 *Dr. Johannes Lepsius:* See his *Bericht über die Lage des armenischen Volkes in der Türkei* (Potsdam: Tempelverlag, 1916), and "Mein Besuch in Konstantinopel: Juli–August 1915," *Orient*, nos. 1–3 (1919), p. 21ff.

138 *children's games, crafts:* See FW's unpublished notebooks for *Musa Dagh*, M-W Coll.

138 *Werfel's passionate interest:* ADK notes.

138 *Ernst Polak researched:* MD conversations.

139 *traveled to several German cities:* Zsolnay Archive.

139 *"Interlude of the Gods":* See Foltin, p. 74.

139 *At the beginning of his readings:* The original of the unpublished text FW presented as an introduction for his readings is at UCLA.

139 *Alma stayed in the hotel:* See *ML*, p. 235.

139 *"Unfortunately, not all that bad":* Author's conversations with Anna Mahler.

140 *"The terrible events in Germany":* Alma Zsolnay-Pixner kindly permitted me to see FW's marginalia to the original manuscript.

140 *Heinrich Mann (1871–1950):* At the beginning of December 1932 FW had read the fifth chapter of *Musa Dagh* in Berlin at the Akademie für Dichtung. Heinrich Mann was very impressed by the projected novel. During his stay in the capital of the Reich, FW petitioned the academy to issue a public warning against a history of German literature that had appeared in an edition of millions of copies, and said that this scurrilous book testified to the Nazi tendency of its author, Paul Fechter, slandering not only Jewish authors of the present but also treating Schiller, Goethe, Nietzsche, and Hauptmann with the same cynical scorn. Heinrich Mann took up FW's initiative and wrote up the warning to be issued by the Prussian Academy of Arts. Hitler's rise to power prevented its publication.

140 *Gottfried Benn:* 1886–1956.

140 *members of the literary section:* Alfred Döblin (1878–1957), Thomas Mann (1875–1955), Ricarda Huch (1864–1947).

140 *Werfel, however, signed:* On the events surrounding FW's declaration of loyalty, see Inge Jens, *Dichter zwischen rechts und links: Die Geschichte der Sektion für Dichtkunst der Preussischen Akademie der Künste* (Munich: R. Piper & Co. Verlag, 1971).

141 *In a letter . . . to his parents:* See Eduard Goldstücker, "Ein unbekannter Brief von Franz Werfel," in *Austriaca: Beiträge zur österreichischen Literatur: Festschrift für Heinz Politzer zu Seinem 65. Geburtstag* (Munich: Max Niemeyer Verlag, 1975). About his work on *Musa Dagh*, FW wrote his parents on March 24, 1933: "The world I am describing (and never really got to know) has to be right, convincing, and consistent, and this will cost me endless labors in studying and gathering information."

141 *book burnings:* See Joseph Wulf, *Literatur und Dichtung im Dritten Reich* (Berlin: Ullstein Taschenbuch Verlag, 1983). Strangely enough, three

of Werfel's books had been exempted from the burnings: *Verdi, The Man Who Conquered Death,* and *The Pure in Heart.*

142 *"An idea conceived in fifteen minutes":* Unpublished notebook, UCLA.

142 *music festival in Florence:* On FW's ability to retain his good spirits even during the greatest political crises, see Foltin, p. 75: "When Gottfried Bermann Fischer met Werfel in Rapallo in April 1933, he was struck by the optimism of the latter. On May 5, 1933, Werfel was expelled from the Prussian Academy of Arts by its president, Max von Schillings, on a directive issued by the Nazi minister of culture, Bernhard Rust. He did not realize the full significance of this. Sinclair Lewis and his then wife, the journalist Dorothy Thompson, who visited Werfel and Alma that month, found the poet in a jovial mood—as if the politics of the authoritarian neighboring states did not concern him."

142 *True, he felt most abandoned:* FW/Mahler.

142 *Johannes Hollnsteiner:* 1895–1970.

142 *Polak advised him:* MD conversations.

143 *revising some passages . . . as many as eight times:* MD conversations.

143 *November letter from Prague:* After many years' absence, FW gave a reading in the city of his birth on November 16, 1933, at the Urania, presenting *Musa Dagh* and poems.

143 *Rudolf Werfel was afraid:* Details of FW's Prague visit at the end of 1933 are from FW/Mahler.

144 *German booksellers:* Thus, for instance, the Freiburger Bücherstube wrote to Paul Zsolnay Verlag on December 5, 1933: "Only a short while has passed since the publication of the new Werfel, and we are pleased to inform you today that we regard the book as absolutely Werfel's strongest, and what's more, as one of the best books of the year. All the more reason to regret that the circumstances and the unfolding of propaganda put such restrictions on one. Nevertheless we have practically sold out the copies we received and are pleased to send you our reorder. . . . In any case, we wish to thank you for finding the courage to publish this book in these times. With German greetings!" (Zsolnay Archive).

144 *Werfel wrote to the association's general directorate:* The Zsolnay Archive has a copy of the original letter.

144 *Grete von Urbanitzky:* In his December 11, 1933, letter to Frau von Urbanitzky, FW writes: "I would be much obliged if you would provide the necessary information about me. I know that you have followed my work and have a clear idea of my human integrity. . . . I would like to add that nothing has changed in my attitude and that I refuse, as I have always done, to participate in political battles" (copy in Zsolnay Archive).

145 *Gerhart Hauptmann . . . seemed intent:* FW/Mahler. Hauptmann even told FW about a plan to write a polemic against Nazism.

145 *there were moves afoot:* In the Zsolnay Archive there is, for instance, a letter dated February 3, 1934, in which a German bookseller, Rolf

Heukeshoven, explicitly warns the publisher that "in the next few days" the public will probably "be presented with an edict" regarding *Musa Dagh:* "A Turkish journalist and writer of my acquaintance who lives in Germany is concerned about this book and will shortly ask the appropriate authorities to have it banned. Of his detailed reasons for this, I know only that the book is aggressively directed against Turkish circles and the Turkish people in general. It would be extremely regrettable for the book trade if the ban were to come through, since the book itself is entirely untendentious and the ban would only satisfy the wish of this one gentleman, of whom we do not even know whether he is acting in the name of the Turkish people. Perhaps my brief notes on the matter will be useful to you in acting to prevent that step. It would be a great loss not to have the book available any longer." It is possible that the Turkish journalist in question was a certain Falich Rifki Bey, a close associate of the president of Turkey; in a newspaper article he had chastised the German authorities for not banning or at least deploring Werfel's book, considering that Turkey had been a German ally in World War I. In any event, Herr Heukeshoven's warning arrived too late: a few days later the book was being confiscated everywhere in the German Reich.

146   *"I now stand on the ruins of myself"*: Unpublished letter from FW to Anna Moll, UCLA.

BAD TIDINGS

148   *Prince Starhemberg:* Ernst Rüdiger, prince of Starhemberg, had participated in Adolf Hitler's coup d'etat attempt in Munich in 1923. On the civil war of 1934, see *ML*, p. 241: "The workers' paper kept on agitating for civil war. It was an outrage how they provoked the government. . . . Eight days earlier Prince Starhemberg had told me that if Dollfuss would not act against the workers' continued aggression, he and Fey would go it alone without Dollfuss."

148   *three hundred people were killed:* Some sources cite 1,200 dead and 5,000 injured on the workers' side alone.

148   *Kurt von Schuschnigg* (1897–1970): Acting as minister of justice, he imposed death sentences on nine leaders of the Schutzbund, a Socialist paramilitary organization. When Chancellor Dollfuss wanted to decorate him for this "performance of his duty," Schuschnigg refused to accept. See Franz Theodor Csokor, *Zeuge einer Zeit: Briefe* (Munich: Langen Müller Verlag, 1964), p. 81.

148   *"Bolshevism is the worst"*: See Jungk, *Das Franz Werfel Buch*, op. cit., pp. 431ff.

149   *He hoped that the world would come to an end:* Unpublished letter from FW to Felix Costa at Paul Zsolnay Verlag, February 26, 1934. In this letter FW also says:

"Please don't be annoyed with me for asking you a couple of immodest questions.

"—Where, when, why did the ban of *Musa Dagh* come about?

"—Have you done anything about it? Or is there nothing to be done?—Does it hurt the rest of my work?—

"—Can anything be done to gain advantage from the ban in other German-speaking countries?—

"—How high are the present sales of *M.D.*—and how have they changed in the weeks since the ban?—" (Zsolnay Archive).

149 *Meyer W. Weisgal:* An impassioned lifelong Zionist, Weisgal (1894–1977) came to America as a boy. In the 1940s he became secretary to Chaim Weizmann, who in 1948 was elected first president of the state of Israel.

149 *Werfel's plan:* FW/Mahler; and see *Der Weg der Verheissung, DD,* vol. 2, pp. 91–177.

150 *suddenly very ill:* On Manon's polio, see *ML,* pp. 243ff.

150 *After only two days:* "After eight days respiratory paralysis set in, and this first death was averted only thanks to the rapid and energetic actions of my daughter Anna Mahler, who in a downpour of rain located an oxygen machine in a distant pharmacy" (ibid., pp. 245f.).

150 *memorizing long theatrical parts:* See FW's prose text "Manon," in *EzW,* vol. 3, pp. 392ff.

150 *in Leopoldskron Castle: ML,* p. 254. The castle had once belonged to an uncle of Alma's father, the novelist and parliamentarian Alexander Schindler.

151 *he seemed rather disappointed:* Details of Weisgal's reaction come from my conversations with Gottfried Reinhardt (see pp. 156–58). Alma Mahler-Werfel describes this meeting in *ML,* p. 254: "Franz Werfel traveled to Salzburg in the summer of 1934 to discuss the whole thing once more with Max Reinhardt and Kurt Weill. A couple of rich East European Jews were also present, and Werfel read the rough draft of the play to them. Afterward, one of these gentlemen approached Werfel and said, 'That was very nice, Herr Werfel, but you have to make an angrier God—a God of vengeance!'"

151 *Werfel expressed his approval:* See *Wiener Sonn- und Montagszeitung,* August 6, 1934, p. 7. From now on, writers in the German Reich referred to Austria as the "Jew-ridden corporate state" (my thanks to Professor Norbert Leser of Vienna).

151 *Julius Bab:* Unpublished letter from FW to Bab, August 28, 1934, in the Leo Baeck Institute, New York.

151 *Up to two hundred guests:* Among the guests was Guido Zernatto, the leader of the "Fatherland Front" and also a minister without portfolio in Schuschnigg's government; in this context, see also Robert Musil, *Tagebücher* (Reinbek bei Hamburg: Rowohlt Verlag, 1983), vol. 1, p. 831 (autumn 1934): "The chancellor had attended a lecture given by Werfel that apparently was full of hot air. The poet speaks to the Führer." The reference is to FW's lecture on Verdi, which he delivered in Vienna at the end of November 1934 as "Verdi und wir"; see "Verdi in unserer Zeit," *ZOU,* pp. 353–58.

152 *in an elegiac letter:* See Klaus Mann, *Prüfungen: Schriften zur Literatur,* ed. Martin Gregor-Dellin (Munich: Ellerman Verlag, 1986), pp. 286f. Klopstock was recruited to the team of physicians attending Manon Gropius.

152 *"When I fetch childhood":* From "Erster Schultag," *DlW,* pp. 426f.

152 *A physician had told him:* See "Manon," *EzW,* vol. 3, pp. 392ff.

152 *Barbara Šimůnkova:* According to FK letters, she died on March 23, 1935.

152 *"Please wait":* From "Die getreue Magd," *DlW,* pp. 413f.

152 *"The Transfigured Maid":* In ibid., pp. 413f.

152 *Her funeral:* See the Viennese dailies of April 23 and April 24, 1935, and Elias Canetti, *Das Augenspiel,* op. cit., pp. 214ff.

152 *"the most difficult time":* Unpublished letter from FW to Ludwig Hatvany of Budapest; I thank Rotraut Hackermüller for referring me to it.

153 *"I started this in 1932":* Unpublished notebook, M-W Coll.

153 *a grand tour of Italy:* See *ML,* p. 251: "In Vienna, the tear-filled atmosphere of mourning after Manon's death robbed us of what shreds of contentment we had left ... and we decided to travel, with Anna Mahler, to Italy, first of all to Rome. But Rome didn't help."

153 *"A charming, delicate woman":* See *Wiener Sonn- und Montagszeitung,* July 15, 1935.

153 *able to express its rage:* See *Arbeiterzeitung* (Brünn), July 21, 1935: "While the victims of dictatorship were on hunger strike in the jails, in order to defend their human dignity against brutality, the *Sonn- und Montagszeitung* published an article by Franz Werfel in which he ... celebrates the chancellor as *the incarnation of humanity.* This deserves a place as a record in the history of *disgusting literary deeds.* People, defenseless yet unbroken, are using the only weapon left to them in their fight against their tormentors: their health. People are refusing their meager fare in order to protect against violations of humanity. People are starving in dungeons, but the Werfels are gorging themselves at the crib and licking the hand that feeds them. Incarnations of the dregs of the human psyche!"

154 *"I'm not exaggerating":* See *Wiener Sonn- und Montagszeitung,* August 12, 1935.

154 *Werfel sent him the final version:* The final version of the drama and FW's letter to Max Reinhardt are housed in the theater collection of the Österreichische Nationalbibliothek, Vienna.

154 *Armenians living in exile:* One of these many celebrations took place January 5, 1936, at the Pennsylvania Hotel in New York; the host was the prelate of the Armenian Church in the United States. The testimonial dinner had an extensive program, including musical performances. Rabbi Stephen Wise was also present on this memorable evening. The invitation bore the words: "He is a God-sent friend who with a singularly keen understanding has penetrated the depths of the soul of a race fighting for liberation from the annihilating force of tyranny and shedding its very life's blood in the struggle" (library of the Mekhitarist monastery, Vienna).

154 *he had not for a moment felt like a stranger:* See *ZOU*, pp. 544f.

155 *this year of grief:* On August 11, 1935, Maria Glaser Bondy, FW's child-hood sweetheart, died of breast cancer (FK letters).

155 *Alban Berg had died:* On December 24, 1935.

155 *About $400,000:* See the interview with FW in the *Wiener Sonn- und Montagszeitung*, March 2, 1936. A further disappointment for FW was that Metro-Goldwyn-Mayer had yielded to Turkish pressure and boy-cott threats, and had decided not to make a movie of *The Forty Days of Musa Dagh*.

156 *When they arrived in Paris:* See *ML*, pp. 257f.

156 *"a Vienna that was like a cemetery":* Unpublished letter from FW to Rudolf Kommer, March 6, 1936 (manuscript collection of the Öster-reichische Nationalbibliothek, Vienna).

JEREMIAD

159 *"Yesterday, late at night":* ZOU, p. 773.

159 *"American edition of my novellas":* Published in 1937 by Viking Press, *Twilight of a World* contains *Poor People, Class Reunion, Estrangement, Severio's Secret, The Staircase, The Man Who Conquered Death, The House of Mourning*, and *Not the Murderer*. FW wrote a prologue to the volume, "An Essay upon the Meaning of Imperial Austria" ("Ein Versuch über das Kaisertum Österreich," *ZOU*, pp. 493ff. On the transitional notes, see *EzW*, pp. 379ff.

159 *Alma and Johannes Hollnsteiner:* Previously, in Zurich, FW and Alma had met up with Hollnsteiner, who was lecturing on "Germanness and Christianity"; see Thomas Mann, *Tagebücher 1935–1936* (Frankfurt am Main: S. Fischer Verlag, 1978), p. 287 (April 5, 1936). In Locarno, Hollnsteiner celebrated mass for Manon one year after her death (*ML*, p. 258).

159 *"I thought of the legends":* ZOU, pp. 755–73. See also *ML*, p. 258.

159 *an outline of the life:* ZOU, pp. 773–83.

159 *Werfel had an idea:* Unpublished notebook, a sequel to the one reprinted in *ZOU*, titled "Gedanken, Einfälle, Notizen zum Plan des Proph-etenromans," UCLA.

160 *haunted by insistent déjà vu:* During his stay in New York, FW apparently received as a gift a novella by Irene Untermeier-Richter that dealt with the theme of déjà vu; it impressed him considerably and inspired his frame story (see Alma Mahler-Werfel's unpublished diary, M-W Coll.). Evidently this frame displeased Alma particularly, and after FW's death she republished the novel without it, and without even mention-ing that it had existed; see *Jeremias: Höret die Stimme* (Frankfurt am Main: Fischer Verlag, 1956; part of the *Gesammelte Werke*, in single volumes).

160 *supplementary characters:* FW's unpublished notebook (UCLA) also con-tains other references to models for various minor characters: he intended to model a female journalist in the frame story after Dorothy Thompson, and a prophetess and traveling companion of Jeremiah's

after Else Lasker-Schüler; an "obese joker" known among the priests
as an enemy of God who dressed up his "blasphemous paradoxes in
. . . orthodox views" was to be a caricature of Egon Friedell. Manon,
too, was to be immortalized as the chaste beauty Zenua, an Egyptian
girl whom Jeremiah wants to marry. Alma Mahler-Werfel tells about a
Negro boy who became the model for the character Ebedmelech: "In
1935 I read a newspaper advertisement seeking a foster home for a
musically talented Negro child. . . . I wanted the little fellow for
Manon, who was lying paralyzed in her bed, and she got very excited.
. . . He danced all day, on the street, in the house, he was really unable to take a normal step. I knew immediately that I would not be
able to keep this child. . . . Franz Werfel was very interested in the
boy and gave him form and content in the Jeremiah novel" (*ML*,
pp. 247f.).

160 *among the most compelling:* One must not underestimate the influence of
Thomas Mann on the Jeremiah novel; the first two novels of Mann's
tetralogy *Joseph and His Brothers* had already been published at this
time. In *Monatshefte für deutsche Literatur*, vol. 30, no. 8 (December
1938), Wolfgang Paulsen writes: "It is hardly surprising that Thomas
Mann's great biblical novels, the Joseph books . . . became a model for
any similar effort. . . . However, Thomas Mann is a particularly risky
model because his style in its unique meticulousness cannot be seriously repeated or even hinted at. And that is exactly what Werfel has
tried to do. . . . Psychologically, very understandable—but artistically
catastrophic." Paulsen cites numerous similarities, quotes from
Werfel's book, and goes on to say: "But even subtler similarities and
correspondences can be found. Even Jirmija's position in the parental
home is definitely a 'Joseph' situation. Here and there one finds echoes
of the bourgeois-artist opposition that was a leitmotiv in Thomas
Mann's early work." Mann and FW had also become closer personally
during the last few years. From time to time Mann considered a move
from Switzerland to Austria, and Alma Mahler-Werfel and Johannes
Hollnsteiner had already petitioned Schuschnigg in the matter, so
that there were no obstacles to Mann's immigration; see Mann, *Tagebücher 1935–1936*, op. cit., pp. 286, 289, 299.

161 *Karl Kraus died in Vienna:* On June 12, 1936.

161 *"Title still undecided":* Manuscript of *Jeremias*, M-W Coll.

161 *The chancellor visited:* MD conversations.

162 *completed the second draft:* Once again, FW collaborated with Ernst Polak
on the final version. The 1937 Austrian edition bore the title *Höret die
Stimme;* an edition in Germany the following year was titled *Jeremias:
Höret die Stimme.*

162 *to his sister:* At the time, Marianne Rieser's play *Turandot* was premiering
at the Zurich Schauspielhaus. On May 31, 1937, on the occasion of the
world premiere of Alban Berg's opera *Lulu* at the Zurich Stadttheater,
FW gives his lecture "Preface to Alban Berg" ("Vorrede auf Alban

Berg"), which he repeated at the Zurich Tonhalle on June 2; see Thomas Mann, *Tagebücher 1937–1939* (Frankfurt am Main: S. Fischer Verlag, 1980), p. 593. Werfel's text for this lecture is considered lost.

162 *a kind of farewell garden party:* See the *Neues Wiener Journal*, June 13, 1937, p. 5. The guest list included Prince Alexander Dietrichstein, Prince Hohenlohe, Ida Roland, the vicomte de Montbas, Bruno Walter, Carl Zuckmayer, Egon Wellesz, Alexander von Zemlinsky, Ödön von Horváth, Franz Theodor Csokor, and Hermann Broch.

162 *PEN Congress:* See Foltin, p. 78.

162 *Despite this vehement difference of opinion:* Marta Feuchtwanger told me in a conversation: "Werfel certainly attacked Lion terribly—we couldn't figure out why. After his speech he was introduced to us. Lion and I had agreed that both of us would act as if it hadn't mattered at all. I didn't want us émigrés to appear divided. And Werfel was charming and also pretended that nothing had happened. Then Lion invited him to visit us at our hotel the next day. As soon as he got there, they of course started talking politics—that was inevitable—and Werfel immediately started raging against Russia. I didn't usually interfere, but in order to help Lion, who was a little embarrassed because he didn't want to contradict his guest, I said, 'Well, in Russia, as there are no class differences, there really are only poor people. In Russia, poverty is very widespread.' And Werfel yelled at me, 'Be quiet! You don't know anything about politics!' I became frightened and didn't say anything else. And Lion, he was a little too polite, he didn't really say anything, either. Suddenly Werfel went down on his knees in front of me and shouted, 'Oh, please forgive me! Can you forgive me?' Now I was embarrassed, and Lion ordered some caviar." To my question "Perhaps that was how Werfel related to his wife as well?" Frau Feuchtwanger replied, "It certainly was. I was there to experience it often enough. Both of them would really scream at each other, but the next moment they were the best of friends."

162 *Ben Huebsch . . . James Joyce:* Huebsch (1873–1945) describes the meeting with Joyce in his unpublished memoirs (Manuscript Division, Columbia University, New York). See also Joyce's unpublished letter to FW, Paris, June 24, 1937 (M-W Coll.): "Dear Mr. Werfel: Since you were kind enough to inscribe your book for my son I hope you will accept the copy of my daughter's illuminations in Chaucer which I asked my publisher to send you. Wir wissen noch nicht bestimmt wohin wir gehen sollen heute abend. Wenn sie C [?] sehen im Laufe des Tages vielleicht wird er es wissen. Freundliche Grüsse James Joyce [We do not know yet where we will be going tonight. If you see C in the course of the day perhaps he will know. Friendly regards James Joyce]." Foltin's assumption (p. 79) that Joyce and FW weren't able to communicate is erroneous.

162 *Werfel gave a speech:* See Milan Kundera, "The Central European Tragedy," *New York Review of Books,* April 26, 1984, p. 36: "[FW] ended his

speech with a proposal. . . . Not only was this proposal rejected, it was openly ridiculed. Of course, it was naive. Terribly naive. . . . However, this naive proposal strikes me as moving, because it reveals the desperate need to find once again a moral authority in a world stripped of values. It reveals the anguished desire to hear the inaudible voice of culture, the voice of the *Dichter und Denker* [poets and thinkers]."

163 *"After I had been working"*: Newspaper interview in the manuscript collection of the Österreichische Nationalbibliothek, Vienna).

163 One Night: *DD*, vol. 2, pp. 179–240.

163 *Each of the play's characters:* MD conversations.

164 *reunion dinner:* I owe the description of that evening to a letter from Helen Wolff of New York.

164 *"Of Man's True Happiness"*: ZOU, pp. 86ff. FW wanted to go on a grand lecture tour of the United States in 1938 with this lecture and the earlier "Realism and Inwardness" and "Can We Live Without Faith in God?"

1938

167 *"I've been rushed"*: Unpublished letter from FW to Stefan Zweig, January 25, 1938; M-W Coll.

167 *"The Friend of the World Does Not Know How to Grow Older"*: DlW, pp. 477f.

167 *collection of his essays:* See unpublished 1938 notebook, UCLA.

167 *"Thoughts on Tomorrow's War"*: ZOU, pp. 291ff.

167 *visits to nearby Naples:* While in Naples, FW also visited the famous Italian philosopher Benedetto Croce (1866–1952), an opponent of Mussolini, whose works had probably influenced FW's lectures in recent years. See also *ML*, p. 270.

167 *scenes and dialogues for a possible sequel:* See unpublished 1938 notebook, UCLA.

167 *nine-year-old Franca:* See unpublished 1938 notebook, UCLA; see also *ML*, p. 270.

168 *difficult to part from Alma:* See FW/Mahler.

168 *Disturbed by the noise:* See unpublished 1938 notebook, UCLA.

168 The Lost Mother: *DD*, vol. 2, pp. 489ff.

169 *"the weightiest and most complex of all"*: FW/Mahler.

170 *"This Sunday"*: ZOU, p. 743.

170 *"for the third time since '33"*: Ibid. FW is referring to Hitler's rise to power and also to the death of Manon Gropius.

170 *Alma fled Vienna:* Author's conversations with Anna Mahler; but see also *ML*, pp. 247f.

170 *They then went to Zurich:* See unpublished 1938 notebook, UCLA; but see also *ML*, p. 276.

170 *the Viennese dailies:* See, for example, *Wiener Montagsblatt*, April 4, 1938.

170 *he wrote to Kurt Wolff:* Unpublished letter, KW Archives.

171 *In the Rieser household:* See unpublished correspondence between FW and Marianne Rieser, copies in M-W Coll.

171   *Paris . . . Amsterdam . . . London:* See unpublished 1938 notebook, UCLA. They remained in Zurich until April 29, in Paris until May 6, Amsterdam until May 9, and in London until May 30, 1938.

171   *Gottfried Bermann Fischer:* on the signing of the contract with FW, Fischer (born 1897) recalls: "I went to London in 1938 and signed the contract with him there. His relationship to Zsolnay was unclear then, but Zsolany didn't have a publishing house anymore, or at least it had been quasi-impounded by the Nazis. And Werfel and I were of the opinion that he was free to sign" (author's conversation with G. B. Fischer in Camaiore, Italy). In his memoirs Fischer says of the contract: "On my return flight to Stockholm I carried an important contract. Franz Werfel, who was staying in London, . . . had signed on with me. I was grateful for his trust" (*Bedroht, bewahrt: Der Weg eines Verlegers* [Frankfurt am Main: S. Fischer Verlag, 1967], p. 168).

171   *no plans for an extended work:* G. B. Fischer permitted me to see the unpublished correspondence between FW and him. In one of the letters, soon after the signing of the contract, FW announces a political essay titled "In the Final Hour" ("In letzter Stunde"), which was never written.

171   *Werfel liked London:* Author's conversations with Anna Mahler.

171   *the Werfels took lodgings:* See unpublished 1938 notebook, UCLA; but see also *ML,* p. 278. The Hotel Royal-Madeleine on rue Pasquier still exists; the building has been modernized, the name retained.

171   *"the face of a dead man":* See "Beim Anblick eines Toten," *EzW,* vol. 3, pp. 28ff.

172   *the burial took place:* Alice Herdan-Zuckmayer, Carl Zuckmayer's widow, told me: "In Paris, we all got together for Horváth's funeral. Before the event we sat in the Café Weber, Alma, Werfel, my husband, and I. And Alma said to Franzerl, 'Listen, I won't let you go to that funeral.' And my husband said, 'Alma, that's out of the question, he's on the list, he has to speak, just like me.' But Alma retorted, 'First one dies, then the other. No, Franz mustn't go.'" The funeral took place on June 7, 1938. Horváth's remains were transferred to an honorary grave in Vienna's Central Cemetery in the spring of 1988.

172   *In mid-June:* See unpublished 1938 notebook, UCLA; but see also *ML,* p. 278.

172   *Pavillon Henri IV:* The hotel in St. Germain-en-Laye still exists, under the same name. After his heart attack and until the spring of 1940, FW often returned to it, as Alma and he were traveling back and forth between the South of France and Paris.

172   *Alma was meanwhile traveling:* Author's conversation with Anne Marie Meier-Graefe-Broch, St. Cyr; but see also *ML,* p. 280.

173   *"I feel more ill than ever":* ZOU, p. 743.

173   *Four weeks after the attack: ML,* p. 280.

173   *"Ballad of an Illness": DlW,* pp. 470f.

173   *"The Greatest Man of All Time":* FW later retitled this poem "The Greatest

German of All Time" ("Der grösste Deutsche aller Zeiten"); *DlW*, p. 482.

173 *two of the dramatic sketches: EzW*, vol. 3, pp. 40ff., 46ff. In the same volume, see also "Par l'Amour" (pp. 51–58), "Anlässlich eines Mauseblicks" (pp. 37–39), and "Die arge Legende vom gerissenen Galgenstrick" (pp. 7–27).

173 *"When I manage to get some work done":* Unpublished letter from FW to Carl Moll, in DL.

173 Illness That Leads to Life: See *Cella oder Die Überwinder, EzW*, vol. 3, pp. 65–304.

174 "Danger: *echoes of* Musa Dagh": Unpublished notebook for *Cella,* UCLA.

174 *He liked the harsh, flat landscape:* See FW's poems "Das Bauernboot" and "Der Neusiedlersee," *DlW*, pp. 437f. See also poem sketches in an unpublished notebook titled "Eisenstadt, 1932," M-W Coll.

174 *a mood of wintry grief:* See Richard Christ's afterword to *Cella oder Die Überwinder: Versuch eines Romans* (Berlin and Weimar: Aufbau-Verlag, 1970), pp. 326f.

174 *"high point of horror and shame!":* ZOU, p. 743. In an unpublished letter to his parents dated October 14, 1938 (DB), FW writes: "I suffer unspeakably for Bohemia, which has been butchered by vicious stupid and cowardly 'allies.' I am choking on the horrifying fate that has already caught up with tens of thousands and threatens all, all."

174 *"I feel more for Bohemia":* ZOU, p. 743.

174 *Werfel contacted the Czech consul:* See unpublished letter to his parents, September 15, 1938, in DB. After October 28, 1918, the date of Czechoslovakia's independence from Austria-Hungary, FW was a Czech citizen.

175 *"drops in the bucket":* See unpublished letter from FW to his parents, October 14, 1938, in DB.

175 *Financially . . . in good shape:* "Recently we have had some good economic experiences. Alma has received a very tidy sum from the Composers' Guild in Vienna, and *Juarez* is being bought for a film in America. None of it is splendiferous, but it'll help us through the coming year without our having to touch our ultimate reserves" (ibid.).

175 *a Hollywood movie:* The film, titled *Juarez,* was produced by Warner Brothers in 1939.

175 *"Israel's Gift to Humanity":* ZOU, pp. 322ff.

175 *reunion with his parents:* FW/Mahler. On his father's gift of money, see note to p. 131.

176 *"The new year stands before us":* See Fischer, *Bedroht, bewahrt,* op. cit., pp. 173f.

177 *his antifascist novel* The Oppermanns: There seems to be a rumor prevalent among German literary scholars that FW felt that Feuchtwanger's trilogy *Der Wartesaal—Erfolg, Die Geschwister Oppermann,* and *Exil—* surpassed his own undertaking both artistically and politically. However, there is no evidence that FW ever thought so. Lion Feucht-

wanger's widow Marta told me, when I asked her about it, "I don't think that's true. At least, I never heard anything about it."

HEAVEN AND HELL

179　*"Yet another infernal outrage!": ZOU,* p. 744.

179　*"Prague occupied by the* boches!":　In May 1938 Rudolf Werfel had instructed his lawyer to register Werfel & Böhm's export director, Erich Fürth, as a partner of the firm. On June 16, 1939, Rudolf Werfel, then in Rüschlikon, tried to transfer all his shares in the firm to Fürth. Three days later, the partners Rudolf Werfel and Benedikt Buöhm were stripped of all rights to the firm by the occupation authorities; for a short time, Fürth figured as the only partner. On the basis of an edict issued by the Gestapo, Staats-polizeistelle Prague, on September 22, 1939, Fürth was deposed and replaced by Erich Kraft. In an official statement by the circuit civil court of Prague, Kraft was appointed "commissar director" and manager, and in the fall of 1941 a certain Karl Schmachtl, Diplomingenieur, purchased the glove factory in the "Aryanization program" (FK letters).

179　*appointed honorary president:*　Robert Neumann (1897–1975), Werfel's friend from the Vienna years, who had also fled to France, offered the honorary presidency to him in December 1938. Werfel told Neumann that although he had always avoided such positions, he would accept this one, hoping to be able to use it to "ease the tribulations of some" (see unpublished correspondence between FW and Robert Neumann, in the Dokumentations archiv des österreichischen Widerstands, Vienna). In this context it should be mentioned that an organization of Austrian émigré writers and intellectuals, the Liga für das geistige Österreich (League for Intellectual Austria), sponsored a reading by Franz Werfel in January 1939 in the Salle Chopin in Paris as the first event arranged by the group. The full house in the Salle Chopin consisted of Austrian monarchists, communists, Spanish Civil War veterans, and supporters of Schuschnigg. Before reading his poems and sections of his Jeremiah novel, FW delivered a short lecture titled "No Humanity Without Divinity" ("Ohne Divinität keine Humanität," *ZOU,* pp. 546ff.). He deplored, as so often before, the godlessness prevalent in Europe and said the world had not experienced a comparable decay of values since the decline of the Roman Empire: most people worshiped "success and power" as their deities and were prey to "every kind of quasiheroic criminality." In Prussia, a "new paganism" had arisen that strove to "get rid of old Israel, as if this were 600 B.C.," the era of Nebuchadnezzar and the destruction of Jerusalem. Nevertheless Werfel believed that these very refugees, the "expelled ones," would in their exile contribute to the preparation of a future "new world consciousness" among all nations. Werfel's speech disappointed primarily the socialists and communists in his audience, who had disapproved of his Christian world view since before the fall of Austria; they also felt that his words were lacking in political commitment. In view of the deadly threat of Hitler's Germany, his critics found his idealistic philosophizing about a renewal of the world inappropriate. I thank Dr. Elisabeth Freundlich, one of the organizers of the event, for describing it to me.

179   *he had told his publisher:* GBF.

179   *"Alma and I":* Letter dated April 20 or 29, 1939, GBF.

180   *not just a "stopgap":* GBF. In a radio interview with NBC, Los Angeles, on March 16, 1941, FW said: "You ask me if I have woven any particular 'message' into this book. I am indeed aware that all my books, realistic as they are, contain a hidden message. The symbolism of *Embezzled Heaven* is very simple. Old Teta is nothing but the soul of mankind in its naive longing for immortalization, which becomes cheated out of heaven—i.e., out of its metaphysical grounding—by the modern intellect and then regains that heaven after a via dolorosa" (*ZOU*, p. 612).

180   *strain caused by an abandoned work:* In *Embezzled Heaven* FW says of *Cella* (without letting the reader know that the subject is that fragment): "The whole plan [seemed] insincere and without meaning. . . . It was a very bulky novel, and I had already written about five hundred pages in the sweat of my brow. I did not possess the moral strength to destroy the stack of sheets that lay upon my table, nor had I the patience to extract the good from the bad and begin afresh. The only true method in art is to assume the labor of Penelope, yet the aspect of the world was changing every few weeks, so that what yesterday seemed to be truth was today revealed as illusion. . . . Nonetheless I tried. Every morning I sat down with a groan to write."

180   *didn't usually believe in his work:* GBF.

181   *One of the first:* See Hartmut Binder, "Ernst Polak: Literat ohne Werk," *Jahrbuch der deutschen Schillergesellschaft,* vol. 23 (Stuttgart, 1979), pp. 366–415.

181   *friends and fellow exiles:* Ludwig Marcuse (1894–1971), Arnold Zweig (1881–1968), Wilhelm Herzog (1884–1960). See Herzog's *Menschen, denen ich begegnete* (Berne and Munich: Francke Verlag, 1959). FW and Herzog had been acquainted since 1914, when Herzog arranged a reading for FW in Munich. They had met frequently in Leipzig and Vienna. Herzog was the publisher of *März*, a well-known literary journal. Friedrich Wolf (1888–1960) was a homeopath and prescribed herbal medications for FW's cardiac problems.

181   *Werfel and Feuchtwanger had regular arguments:* See unpublished text written for Feuchtwanger's sixtieth birthday in 1944, UCLA. Looking back, FW muses, "Neither one of us managed to convince the other. I was strident, you were relaxed. I would get excited, you were calmness personified. I became insulting, you were unshakably even-tempered. Had a witness to our protracted arguments been unfamiliar with the language, he would no doubt have considered truth to have been on your side, because not I but *you* were the very image of superiority, and

a charming sort of superiority at that. You never lost your temper, you
would smile and laugh even after my worst attacks."

181 *"any man, woman, and child":* Quoted in Tilman Zülch, *Zeitschrift Pogrom,*
nos. 72–73 (May 1980), pp. 297f.

182 *After Hitler's attack:* See *ZOU,* p. 744; but see also *ML,* pp. 297f.

182 *During an interrogation:* See *ZOU,* p. 745.

182 *Werfel volunteered:* GBF.

182 *"The Hitler gang":* GBF.

182 *moved from Zurich to Vichy:* See unpublished letter from FW to his parents, in DB. After a visit with his parents, he told Wilhelm Herzog that
Sanary seemed like paradise compared to Vichy (Herzog, *Menschen,
denen ich begegnete,* op. cit., pp. 438ff.).

183 *One of the first to respond:* "It is of course a good and appropriate idea. I
admire Werfel's work with all my heart and would be happy to see the
Swedish Academy reward it, but I do not believe it will do so. I have to
refrain from participation in the petition because I have repeatedly
voted for *Hesse,* whose chances are better and in whom a non-Reich
Germanness and a higher German tradition would also be honored."
See Herzog, *Menschen, denen ich begegnete,* op. cit., p. 440; see also
Thomas Mann, *Briefe 1937–1947,* ed. Erika Mann (Frankfurt am
Main: S. Fischer Verlag, 1963), p. 133.

183 *"tricky little marital story":* GBF.

183 April in October: See Jungk, ed., *Das Franz Werfel Buch,* op. cit.,
pp. 202ff. FW originally wanted to call the novella *Confusions of a Day
in October (Wirrnisse eines Oktobertags)* or *Confusions of a Day in April (Die
Verwirrungen eines Apriltages).*

183 *"relationship with a Jewess":* Unpublished notebook, UCLA. My personal
guess is that the character of the civil servant Leonidas may have been
inspired by a public figure in Vienna: before 1938, FW knew a section
chief, Dr. Leodegar Petrin, who was possibly even employed in the
Ministry of Education, Leonidas's workplace. Otherwise he bears
characteristics reminiscent of Sebastian in *Class Reunion.*

183 *most positive Jewish character:* See Max Brod in *Die Zeit,* January 20, 1955:
"Vera Wormser [appears] unique among Werfel's numerous Jewish
characters; she has a nobility of both intellect and feeling, and is
determined, selfless, immune to insult. . . . Not a 'broken Jewish type'
but fully aware of her worth, with a healthy mind; at the same time
reticent, modest, mildly forgiving, and above all, beautiful and en-
chanting."

184 *"The treacherously attacked land":* ZOU, pp. 555f.

184 *Jules Romains . . . asked Werfel:* ML, p. 301.

184 *lived in constant fear:* Ibid.

184 *Lion Feuchtwanger . . . interned:* See Lion Feuchtwanger, *Unholdes Frankreich: Meine Erlebnisse unter der Regierung Pétain* (London, 1942);
republished under the title *Der Teufel in Frankreich* (Rudolstadt:
Greifenverlag, 1954; Berlin: Aufbau-Verlag, 1982; Munich, Vienna:
Langen Müller Verlag, 1983).

184 *a run for Spain:* See *ML,* pp. 303ff., on the flight from Sanary to Lourdes.

184 *After an odyssey with many mishaps:* But see also *Jacobowsky und der Oberst, DD,* vol. 2, pp. 241–340.

185 *Vicky von Kahler:* Letter from the Kahlers to FW and Alma Mahler-Werfel, May 12, 1945, M-W Coll.: "The times when the rooms of a United States consulate seemed as fascinating as the Venusberg are long past, and there is some fading even of such impressions as the merciless orgiastic rain of Biarritz, the nocturnal figures in Hendaye, the 'Jessas, jetzt ham's uns' ["Jeez, they've got us now"] on the road to Pau."

185 *arrived in Lourdes:* See *ML,* and FW's preface to *Das Lied von Bernadette,* pp. 7ff.

185 *new safe-conducts:* See unpublished letter from FW to his parents, in DB.

186 *American Guild for German Cultural Freedom:* FW to Prince Löwenstein, in the Dokumentationsarchiv des österreichischen Widerstands, Vienna. I am grateful to Dr. Ulrich Weinzierl of Vienna for this information.

186 *Werfel's parents . . . moved to Bergerac:* See unpublished letter from FW to his parents, in DB.

187 *a kind of vow:* See FW's preface to *Das Lied von Bernadette,* p. 8: "One day in my great distress I made a vow. I vowed that if I escaped from this desperate situation and reached the saving shores of America, I would put off all other tasks and sing, as best I could, the song of Bernadette." Father Georg Moenius, a close friend of the Werfels in exile in California, gave the following account in a radio broadcast on Bayerischer Rundfunk in 1952: "One evening in the summer of 1939 I had come from Lourdes to Paris to visit Werfel in his small hotel behind the Madeleine. On the way, I had been reading Zola's novel about Lourdes, in which so little attention is paid to the religious experience. Werfel was most eager to learn my impressions of Lourdes. Still in a quandary between my actual experiences and my reading of Zola, I told him that *he* ought to write a book about Lourdes one day. Neither one of us could have imagined how soon and under what circumstances this would indeed happen" (manuscript of talk in M-L Coll.). In this connection, see also Schalom Ben-Chorin in *Aufbau* (New York): "Not hesitant and doubtful, but noisy and irreverently ridiculing the miracle, . . . Egon Erwin Kisch walked the streets of Lourdes in 1934, shortly after Bernadette's canonization. 'Ich bade im wundertätigen Wasser' ['I Bathe in the Miracle-working Water'] is the title of his report. . . . Kisch does not see the miracle as Werfel does. He does not see the touching figure of little innocent Bernadette. . . . He sees the negative, and it, too, should be seen. He notes, 'The Holy Virgin has been rather ungracious to her village of grace. The victims of certain processions lie in mass graves. And over there on the road of the Stations of the Cross is a memorial for the Catholics from Bourbon who lost their lives on August 1, 1922, in a train collision on their pilgrimage to Lourdes. Even the holy grotto was not spared: in June

1875 a flood entered it and destroyed the altar, the image of Mary, and all entrances.' "

187   *In Marseilles the Werfels stayed:* Varian Fry, *Surrender on Demand* (New York: Random House, 1945); German edition *Auslieferung auf Verlangen* (Munich: Carl Hanser Verlag, 1986), p. 16. See also Mary Jayne Gold, *Crossroads Marseilles, 1940* (New York: Doubleday, 1980). In an ironic turn of fate, other refugees approached FW in his desperate straits: see Ivan George Heilbut, "Franz Werfel in Marseille," *Stuttgarter Zeitung*, August 27, 1955: "In the afternoon I stood in front of the Hôtel Louvre & Paix on the Canebière. . . . Then I entered the foyer, which was teeming with German officers." Heilbut needed to give Werfel's name as a guarantor to the U.S. Consulate and was hoping that Werfel could help him and his family to escape. "I presented my request. He remained silent. He hesitated. Then, in a muted voice: 'I can't do it; my name has been used up here. . . . No, I can't do any more. I can't even receive visitors. I run the danger of surveillance everywhere.' . . . I shall never forget Werfel's tense expression, his compressed lips, his big blue eyes staring straight ahead as he moved through the crowd of German officers. . . . 'We're trapped,' he said quietly."

187   *The personal intervention:* See unpublished letter from FW to his parents, August 10, 1940, in DB. Evidently FW's sister Mizzi and the American publisher Ben Huebsch also played a role: "Mizzerl and my American friends did tremendously good work."

187   *"Nous sommes . . . :* "We are in a *terrible situation*—we are practically prisoners. . . . If you possibly can: Help us!" Louis Gillet (1876–1943) was an art historian and critic.

188   *a young American Quaker:* See Fry, *Auslieferung auf Verlangen*, op. cit. Untenable and definitely untrue is Alma Mahler-Werfel's claim that Fry undertook his rescue mission halfheartedly: "The Americans had sent a man, Mr. Fry, who was supposed to help all of us. He did so but was quite rude and morose. . . . The only thing Mr. Fry really did for us was to transport the luggage of the five of us across the border" (*ML*, pp. 314f.). FW wrote his mother on January 19, 1941, "I owe him a great deal."

188   *Lion Feuchtwanger had been freed:* See Stefan Jaeger and Volker Skierka, *Lion Feuchtwanger: Eine Biographie* (Berlin: Quadriga Verlag, 1984); but see also Marta Feuchtwanger, "Die Flucht," in Lion Feuchtwanger, *Der Teufel in Frankreich* (1983), op. cit., pp. 255ff.

188   *"forced to make decisions":* Unpublished letter from FW to his parents, August 29, 1940, in DB.

188   *causing the plan to be aborted:* See Fry, *Auslieferung auf Verlangen*, op. cit., p. 70.

188   *in a large restaurant:* Author's conversation with Professor Golo Mann, Kilchberg/Zurich.

188   *The next day:* On details of the escape, see above all *ML*, pp. 316–18.

Alma Mahler-Werfel's narrative of the escape is mostly reliable, as Golo Mann confirmed to me; but see also Fry, *Auslieferung auf Verlangen*, op. cit., pp. 79ff., and Gold, *Crossroads Marseilles, 1940*, op. cit.

191 *He had been saved:* Varian Fry claims that German agents were sighted in Port Bou the very next day. Two weeks after the Werfels crossed the Pyrenees, Walter Benjamin arrived in Port Bou, where Spanish officials threatened to deliver him to the Gestapo. By the time the decision was made to let Benjamin cross the border, he had committed suicide; see Jaeger and Skierka, *Lion Feuchtwanger*, op. cit., p. 210. The philosopher Carl Einstein and the writer Ernst Weiss also committed suicide at about the same time in the Pyrenees region.

191 *"Alma managed surprisingly well":* Alice Herdan-Zuckmayer told me: "Alma was so weak during the crossing of the Pyrenees that these sturdy students sent out by President Roosevelt had to *carry* her across. . . . That wasn't so easy."

"I'M AN AMERICAN"

193 *"Now, having almost reached the Statue of Liberty":* Unpublished letter from FW to his parents, October 12, 1940, in DB.

193 *morning of October 13:* See the American daily newspapers for October 14, 1940, and Thomas Mann, *Tagebücher 1940–1943* (Frankfurt am Main: S. Fischer Verlag, 1982), p. 165.

193 *might endanger those still trapped in France:* In his interviews with American journalists, Lion Feuchtwanger had been less cautious. When he arrived in New York ten days earlier on the American passenger ship *Excalibur,* he described to the reporters the possible routes across the passes of the Pyrenees and thus greatly endangered the rescue committee's work: the Gestapo took note and sent additional agents to the region between Cerbère and Port Bou.

194 *this autumn of 1940:* FW also met Meyer Weisgal again, who tried to persuade him to revive the *Eternal Road* project. According to Thomas Quinn Curtiss of Paris, the Werfels attended the premiere of *The Wedding March*, Erich von Stroheim's film about Vienna, which displeased Alma in particular.

194 *Stefan Jacobowicz:* Author's conversation with Gottfried Reinhardt; and see *Jacobowsky und der Oberst, DD*, vol. 2, pp. 241–340.

194 *"We're doing wonderfully":* Unpublished letter from FW to his parents, December 5, 1940, in DB.

194 *over 150,000 copies:* Ibid.

194 *fund-raising dinners:* See Thomas Mann, *Tagebücher 1940–1943*, op. cit., pp. 172f. (October 13, 1940).

194 *"Our Road Goes On": ZOU*, pp. 333–37.

195 *In and around Los Angeles:* Author's conversations with Albrecht Joseph, Los Angeles; but see also John Russell Taylor, *Strangers in Paradise: The Hollywood Emigrés* (New York: Holt, Rinehart & Winston, 1983).

195   *Erich Wolfgang Korngold:* The composer was born in Brünn in 1897 and
        died in Hollywood in 1957.
195   *"Before Christmas":* Unpublished letter from FW to his parents, Decem-
        ber 6, 1940, in DB.
195   *Mr. and Mrs. Loewi:* See *ML,* pp. 246, 322; see also Thomas Mann,
        Tagebücher 1940–1943, op. cit., pp. 887f.
195   *6900 Los Tilos Road:* The house is still there, essentially unchanged.
195   *natural acoustics:* Author's conversations with Albrecht Joseph, Los An-
        geles.
195   *August Hess:* Author's conversations with Albrecht Joseph and Professor
        Gustave O. Arlt, Los Angeles.
196   *"The Riviera is just trash":* Unpublished letter from FW to his parents, end
        of February 1941, in DB.
196   *food was delivered to the house:* Ibid. See also *SU,* p. 66.
196   The High Song of Bernadette: FW also thought of *The Beautiful Song of
        Bernadette* (*Das schöne Lied von Bernadette*); see the manuscript of the
        first version, begun January 14, 1941, finished May 18, 1941, M-W
        Coll. On *Bernadette,* see also the legends about saints written after
        Manon Gropius's death, *ZOU,* pp. 755–73, and *ZOU,* pp. 773ff.
196   *"Almost decided on Bernadette":* Unpublished notebook, UCLA.
196   Our Holy Shepherdess Bernadette: The correspondences between this
        book and Werfel's novel are extraordinary—great possible thesis ma-
        terial! Belleney's book can be found in Box 28, UCLA.
196   *Ben Huebsch ... shared his misgivings:* Author's conversations with Al-
        brecht Joseph, Los Angeles.
196   *Varian Fry was involved:* Unpublished letters from FW to his parents and
        to his sister Hanna von Fuchs-Robetin, in DB.
197   *"I'm an American":* *ZOU,* pp. 611ff.; the typescript of the radio program is
        at UCLA. See also FW's vehemently anti-American speeches from the
        1930s in *ZOU,* pp. 16–109.
197   *on March 22, 1941:* "Declaration of Intention," Document 108819,
        UCLA. The entry under "race" is "Hebrew."
197   *Departing from his usual practice:* Author's conversations with Albrecht
        Joseph, Los Angeles.
198   *"true genius of a girl":* GBF.
198   *"daily, hourly self-mortification":* Unpublished letter from FW to Hanna
        von Fuchs-Robetin, July 21, 1941, in DB.
198   *"a terrifying lecture tour":* See the poem "Eine Prager Ballade," *DlW,*
        pp. 488f.: "Dreamt on the train from the state of Missouri to the state
        of Texas. . . . 'Not to worry, my young sir, via Königsaal and Eule / I'll
        drive you directly across the Atlantic.' "
198   *On July 31, 1941:* ADK notes. Hanna von Fuchs-Robetin wrote to her
        brother in August 1941: "Now, in the pain that we are all feeling, I am
        certain that he went in order to make it easier for poor beloved
        mother. . . . Will she have the strength to survive all the complications
        of this trip? Will she be able to travel at all?" (M-W Coll.).

198 *Alma started up her salon:* Author's conversation with Riccarda Zernatto of
      Vienna, widow of the politician and author Guido Zernatto.

198 *bitter recriminations:* Author's conversations with Anna Mahler and Al-
      brecht Joseph.

199 *the German edition of* The Song of Bernadette: See Thomas Mann, *Tage-
      bücher 1940–1943"* op. cit., p. 378 (January 15, 1942): "The evening
      with Werfel's novel, with a degree of indignation." In this context,
      Gottfried Reinhardt told me: "Thomas Mann and Werfel met at Salka
      Viertel's place in L.A. Mann said he did not understand why Werfel
      claimed in the book that Bernadette had *seen* the mother of God. Why
      hadn't he said that Bernadette Soubirous had *imagined* that she had
      seen the Virgin? A *vision* . . . And Werfel said, 'Because she *saw* her!'
      Thomas Mann got very excited, in his brittle, northern German,
      puritanical fashion. That someone could have the chutzpah to claim
      that Bernadette *had* seen the Virgin! But Werfel didn't give an inch. It
      was a wonderful afternoon."

199 *"People here":* Unpublished letter from FW to his mother, 1942, in DB.

199 *letter from Stefan Zweig:* Unpublished letter from Zweig to FW and Anna
      Mahler-Werfel, November 20, 1941 (UCLA): "I had . . . a regular
      nervous *breakdown.* [The fact] that I could no longer find my identity
      in all the absurdities that this time imposes on us—to be a writer, a
      poet in a language in which one is not permitted to write, . . . detached
      from everything that was home, . . . dragging suitcases from one place
      to the next, with no books, no papers . . . —all that depressed me
      horribly, and on top of that . . . that I was unable to work in this
      nomadic life with a storm overhead and coming through the seams of
      the tent. . . . So I managed to write my life story [*Die Welt von Gestem
      (The World of Yesterday)*)]—or as much of it as I care to tell others"
      (UCLA).

200 *far more stimulating:* See unpublished letter from Stefan Zweig to FW and
      Alma Mahler-Werfel, December 25, 1941 (UCLA).

200 *"It is appalling!":* Unpublished letter from FW to his mother, 1942,
      in DB.

200 *At a memorial service:* "Stefan Zweigs Tod," *ZOU*, pp. 459ff.

200 *turned into a treatment:* At the time FW was already collaborating with his
      friend Friedrich Torberg (1908–1979); in an unpublished letter of
      October 1941, FW tells Torberg to set the story wherever he wants:
      "India or China, I don't care" (Friedrich Torberg Archive, Marietta
      Torberg, Vienna). FW and Torberg were apparently also planning a
      very different kind of movie project. Torberg wrote to FW on July 9,
      1943: "The next thing was yet another offer by Skirball to pay a
      writer's advance of $3,000 for the Czech aviator film; in case nothing
      came of that film, the $3,000 would be a down payment on another
      'Werfel property,' and once again, and quite clearly, he was thinking of
      the Zorah Pasha script" (M-W Coll.). FW paid Torberg regularly for
      his collaboration. I thank Marietta Torberg for the information about
      her late husband.

201   *"The Love and Hatred of Zorah Pasha":* The 170-page typescript is in the possession of Marietta Torberg.

201   *another 100,201 copies:* Telegram from Ben Huebsch to FW, May 28, 1942, M-W Coll.

201   *flare-up of an old family antagonism:* Unpublished correspondence between FW and Mizzi Rieser, M-W Coll. How perturbed FW really was by this incident becomes evident from a passage in a letter to Hanna von Fuchs-Robetin, dated August 22, 1942 (DB): "As you know, dearest Hannerl, I had to endure some unpleasant nervous crises (on her part) and correspondence with Mizzi a while ago. She and especially Ferdi accused me of being cold and indifferent toward them and that I, in my boundless ambition (to which Alma is 'welded'—that's a quotation), have done nothing and will do nothing for Mizzi's *Eugenia*. This whole business, even though it isn't 'all that serious,' as you wrote, has bothered me quite a bit. The accusation is unjust. . . . There's no doubt that Mizzi isn't only very talented but also of a passionate, torn, ecstatic temper. She is only deficient in certain prerequisites that are hard to acquire later on: reading, education, criticism, intellectual order. . . . Please write me what you think and what I should do."

203   *"the bedrooms were below":* See *SU,* pp. 49, 87: "Because of the previously mentioned fear of the sun, the houses of this city were not built above, but deep down under, the ground. . . . The more personal and the more intimate the purpose of a room, the deeper it lay buried in the bowels of the earth, quite the reverse of the custom of a period that located its bedrooms on the upper floors. The more private these people wished to be, the farther they withdrew."

204   *Fritz Kortner* (1892–1970): Austrian character actor and director who returned to Germany after the war and had a distinguished film and stage career.

204   *Leonhard Frank* (1882–1961): Novelist and short story writer best known for *Der Mensch ist gut* and *Links, Wo das Herz ist.* In 1937 he emigrated from Austria to Paris, and in 1940 from Paris to Los Angeles, where he met Werfel.

DANCE OF DEATH

206   *Cyrill Fischer* (1892–1945): See *ZOU,* pp. 468ff. According to ADK notes, Fischer resisted, from a Catholic viewpoint, both the Austrian Socialist "Friends of Children" movement and the Nazi experiments in the education of children and adolescents. Fischer, by the way, checked the *Bernadette* manuscript for theological mistakes.

206   *Old Mission:* The Franciscan monastery, founded by Junipero Serra in 1786, is still one of Santa Barbara's main attractions. A large Indian cemetery (the Indians had been converted by the monks) adjoins the mission building.

206   *"a charming Spanish-style hotel":* Unpublished letter from FW to Hanna von Fuchs-Robetin, August 22, 1942, in DB. The Biltmore still stands, practically unchanged.

206 *"Scheeben's 'Secret of Predestination' "*: Matthias Joseph Scheeben, *Mysterien des Christentums* (Freiburg im Breisgau: Herder, 1911), chapter 10, "Das Mysterium de Prädestination."

206 Jacobowsky and the Colonel: *DD*, vol. 2, pp. 241–340.

206 *Reinhardt's son Gottfried:* Gottfried Reinhardt told me: "I told Werfel, in my father's house in Pacific Palisades, 'Herr Werfel, I think that that would be material for a terrific play, and my friend Sam Behrman is of the same opinion, but he thinks that *you* should write it.' But Werfel said, 'No, that isn't my kind of thing, I can't write that.' And Alma was immediately hostile. She didn't want him to deal with such mundane stuff. So then I suggested that Behrman and I would write the play—with the one request that we'd get together one more time for Werfel to tell us the whole story. Behrman, by the way, suggested that any proceeds should be divided fifty-fifty with Werfel. One of the main characters in the play was created by *me*—the female lead Marianne. She did not occur in Werfel's story. I felt that we should have some love interest, so we came up with Marianne, a kind of incarnation of France."

207 *sent completed scenes to Albrecht Joseph:* Author's conversations with Albrecht Joseph, Los Angeles. Most of the details on *Jacobowsky* are derived from these conversations. Joseph is of the opinion that the upsets and strains caused by the play cost FW years of his life.

207 *George Marton:* I have drawn on an unpublished manuscript by Marton, which his widow, Hilda Marton, kindly put at my disposal.

207 *"a big Jewish novel":* Unpublished letter from FW to Hanna von Fuchs-Robetin, August 22, 1943, in DB.

208 *"purest force sent by God":* See "Vorwortskizze zu *Das Lied von Bernadette*," *ZOU*, p. 525. (Adolf D. Klarmann's translation of "Brief an den Erzbischof Rummel von New Orleans, Louisiana," *ZOU*, pp. 892f., is inexact.)

208 *"Even for a Jew":* See unpublished notebook, UCLA. At the end of fairly extensive theological reflections (which would later return in the 1944 collection of fragments *Theologumena*), FW says, "These reflections do not belong to the novel proper. Alfred Engländer in *The Pure in Heart* would have been the man to voice them."

208 *wrote . . . to Rudolf Kommer:* This unpublished letter, dated October 3, 1942, is preserved in the manuscript collection of the Österreichische Nationalbibliothek, Vienna.

209 *the Werfels moved:* See *ML*, p. 331.

210 *Thomas Mann was also a frequent visitor:* See Mann, *Tagebücher 1940– 1943*, op. cit., p. 564 (April 17, 1943): "With K [Katia] and Erika at Romanoff's, supper (bad duck) treated by the Werfels. Later at their house; reading of the final chapter of the Moses with strong impression in amusement and seriousness." See also p. 482 (October 5, 1942): "For supper Werfels. Dramatic performance from his French comedy of catastrophe, much enjoyed by the children." Professor

Ernst Haeussermann of Vienna told me that FW presented *Jacobowsky and the Colonel,* acting out all the parts.

210 *a flood of letters:* Some of these can be found in the Werfel Collection at UCLA.

210 *writing to his mother:* Unpublished letter in DB.

210 *remark at a dinner party:* See Mann, *Tagebücher 1940–1943,* op. cit., pp. 505f. (December 7, 1942).

210 *Clifford Odets* (1906–1963): American actor and playwright; see *Weltliteratur im 20. Jahrhundert: Autorenlexikon,* ed. Manfred Brauneck (Reinbek bei Hamburg: Rowohlt Taschenbuch Verlag, 1981), vol. 3, p. 961: "With the one-act play *Waiting for Lefty* (1935) Odets became the main American representative of proletarian drama concerned with the class struggle."

211 *surrounded by "vultures":* Unpublished letter from Alma Mahler-Werfel to Friedrich Torberg, Torberg Archive, Marietta Torberg, Vienna.

211 *"I am not really one who believes in dreams":* The first page of first draft of the "travel novel" (UCLA) bears the title *A Short Visit to the Distant Future (Ein kurzer Besuch in ferner Zukunft).* See *SU.*

211 *"reluctance to work":* FW abandoned not only *The One Who Stayed* but also a novel he had promised to write for the Baha'i religious community at a meeting with a Mrs. Chanler and a Mr. Mizza Ahmed Sohrab in mid-March 1943.

211 *In only six days:* "I wrote these 40¼ pages (106 typewritten pages) in the course of 5 to 6 days in May in the year 1943 in *Sta Barbara* in California, at the Hotel Biltmore close by the Pacific Ocean, where I could hear the surf at night while I was working" (insertion on p. 41 of the first draft of *SU,* UCLA). For a useful synopsis of the narrative see Lore B. Foltin and John M. Spalek, "Franz Werfel," in Spalek and Joseph Strelka, eds., *Deutsche Exilliteratur seit 1933* (Berne, 1976), pp. 644–67.

212 *wearing the tailcoat:* "For the wedding of his sister Hanna Fuchs-Robetin, he returned home unexpectedly from the front at 5:00 in the morning and was fixed up by the bride. Received tails and top hat from his father. The description of his resurrected corpse in *Star* [*of the Unborn*] reminded [Albine Werfel] of that episode" (ADK notes). See also p. 287 above.

213 *"In only a few days":* GBF.

214 *"I have* squeezed out *everything":* Unpublished letter from FW to Albrecht Joseph, UCLA. He also says: "Don't worry about Marianne! She *can't* have any *active* function and *shouldn't.* Her suffering for France grows gradually up to the last act. All realistic details would be a distraction for this *3d voice,* as they would be padding and superfluous!"

214 *corresponded with Max Brod:* See *SL.*

214 *frequently visiting the set:* Professor Gustave O. Arlt of Los Angeles told me, "Fox paid Werfel for being on set as, so to speak, an 'expert.' "

214 *became a movie enthusiast:* Author's conversations with Gustave O. Arlt.
214 *Jennifer Jones:* She received the Oscar for her performance as Bernadette.
214 *rewritten several times:* See Foltin, p. 103.
214 Word of Life on Earth: *DlW,* pp. 483ff.
214 *Rudolf Voigt* (1899–1956): Teacher and author.
214 *memories of the Prague years:* In the summer of 1943 in Santa Barbara, FW
       also wrote the novella *Géza de Varsany, or: When Will You Get a Soul at
       Long Last? (Géza de Varsany, oder: Wann wirst du endlich eine Seele bekom-
       men?).* Stylistically, it is reminiscent of *Poor People.*
214 *"In the year five":* From "Sechs Setterime zu Ehren des Frühlings von
       Neunzehnhundertfünf," *DlW,* p. 489.
215 *an honorary doctorate:* FW immediately had calling cards printed: "Dr.
       h.c. Franz Werfel" (author's conversations with Gustave O. Arlt).
215 *Two days after Werfel's birthday:* See *ML,* p. 338.
215 *Biltmore Hotel menu:* At UCLA.
215 *Max Reinhardt's sudden death:* See *ML,* p. 342, and FW's text for Max
       Reinhardt's seventieth birthday, *ZOU,* pp. 466ff.
216 *"Dance of Death": DlW,* p. 497.
       A million copies: On November 29, 1943, before the height of the
       Christmas sales, Ben Huebsch wrote to Alma Mahler-Werfel (M-L
       Coll.) that at least 802,000 copies of *Bernadette* had already been sold,
       and probably many more.
216 *Numerous, often page-long telegrams:* At UCLA.
217 *The Broadway premiere:* For the premiere, FW wrote a far from honest
       introductory text in which he says: "Finally, a brave man took pity on
       my Jacobowsky. This parfit knight was the excellent playwright Clif-
       ford Odets. . . . Even though the god of the theater finally did not let
       his adaptation reach the stage, I am grateful to him for many valuable
       suggestions. . . . My old friend, the Theatre Guild, purchased the
       honorable Jacobowsky, and from then on, his fate took a turn for the
       better. At the same time, a man dear to me appeared out of the clouds
       of his sensitivity and reticence, and declared himself willing to guide
       the still errant Jacobowsky, whom he had known and appreciated from
       the very beginning, into the limelight. This was the witty and highly
       regarded playwright S. N. Behrman" (*ZOU,* pp. 264ff.).
217 *He told a reporter:* Newspaper interview in the *Green Sheet Journal* (Mil-
       waukee, Wis.), March 17, 1944. The headline: "Ailing Bernadette
       Author Writes About 101944 A.D."

"The Book Must Be Finished"

221 *Franz Werfel's horoscope:* M-W Coll.
221 *"Theologumena": ZOU,* pp. 110–95.
221 *"On the Subject of Theodicy":* Unpublished sketches titled "Fragmente zum
       Kapitel Theodizee," intended as part of a larger essay work, *Krisis der
       Ideale,* at UCLA. An example: "As arrogant as it may sound, millions

of good people have been pursued by misfortune, but since the beginning of the world no bad person has been lucky." These theodicy fragments were written between 1914 and 1920.

221 *He began to dictate:* From Albrecht Joseph's 1944 diary (in his possession).

222 *another coronary occlusion:* Ibid.

222 *moved back to Santa Barbara:* See the manuscript of the first draft of *SU* (UCLA): "Today, July 10, 1944, I am back again in Sta Barb. Biltmore (bungalow) trying to continue the travel novel."

222 *Dr. Spinak:* Author's conversations with Albrecht Joseph; but see also *ML.* On "Schwammerl," see Rudolf Bartsch's novel of that title (Vienna: Alfred Keller, 1910).

222 *taken over by the American military:* See the manuscript of the first draft of *SU* (UCLA): "Biltmore taken over by military: July 16, 44—we had to leave."

222 *El Mirasol:* The hotel and its bungalows no longer exist. On the site, in the middle of Santa Barbara, there is now a city park, the Alice Keck Memorial Garden.

222 *"in the most remote future":* Letter dated August 8, 1944, GBF.

222 *dictated by a powerful imagination:* See Thomas Mann, *Die Entstehung des Doktor Faustus* (Amsterdam: Bermann-Fischer Verlag, 1940), pp. 140f.

223 Goat Song: See note *the theme of* our *time,* p. 263 above.

223 *talked to Alma three or four times daily:* See unpublished letter from Alma Mahler-Werfel to Adolf and Isolde Klarmann, M-W Coll.

224 *"humorous-cosmic-mystical world poem":* Unpublished letter from FW to Ben Huebsch.

224 *"I'm working, sluggishly":* Unpublished letter to Friedrich Torberg, Torberg Archive, Marietta Torberg, Vienna.

224 *"Wild West stories":* ADK notes, conversation with Kurt Wolff.

224 *Jewish reviewers:* See, for example, Ludwig Marcuse, "In theologischen Schleiern," *Aufbau* (New York), March 9, 1945.

224 *Max Brod wrote a letter:* M-W Coll.

225 *Werfel . . . wrote back:* M-W Coll.

225 *Carl Moll committed suicide:* Author's conversations with Anna Mahler; see also *ML,* p. 367.

226 *"The defeat of Germany":* ZOU, pp. 337ff.

226 *"To the German People":* ZOU, pp. 626f.

226 *Ernst and Anuschka Deutsch pleaded with him:* Author's conversation with Anuschka Deutsch, Berlin.

226 *"sweat of anxiety and embarrassment":* See Friedrich Torberg, *In diesem Sinne . . .: Briefe an Freunde und Zeitgenossen* (Munich: Langen Müller, 1981), pp. 433ff.

226 *forgive him for his long absence:* See Jungk, ed., *Das Franz Werfel Buch,* op. cit., p. 436.

227 *an incarnation of his own son:* See FW's 1919 story "Spielhof": "Suddenly he felt that . . . he was holding something warm, small, and tender in his hand. It was a child's hand. A small child was looking at him. . . . It was his lost dream" (*EzW,* vol. i, p. 155).

227   *planned a final, twenty-seventh chapter:* Last page of the manuscript of the
       first draft of *Stern der Ungeborenen* (UCLA).

227   *"a ride across Lake Constance":* See Annemarie von Puttkamer, *Franz
       Werfel: Wort und Antwort* (Würzburg: Werkbund Verlag, 1952), p. 148.

227   *August Hess drove Werfel:* See *ML*, p. 360.

227   *There was an owl:* From my conversation with Lady Isolde Radzinowicz,
       Adolf D. Klarmann's widow, I gather that FW saw the presence of that
       owl in front of his window as a certain omen of death; and see *ML*,
       pp. 110f. In his "Secret Diary," August 2, 1918, FW wrote: "I remem-
       ber that when I spent the night for the first time in her country house,
       we heard a strange bird go on making a sawing or scraping noise for
       hours. I thought that it was a bad omen for her. I did not tell her this."

227   *a letter from . . . Johannes Urzidil:* Dated August 10, 1945 (UCLA).

228   *One week after his return:* I derive the description of the last days and
       hours of FW's life from an unpublished letter from Alma Mahler-
       Werfel to Adolf Klarmann, M-W Coll.

228   *"A Greeting to Salzburg": ZOU*, pp. 627f.; according to Adolf Klarmann,
       these are the last words FW wrote before his death.

228   *receiving visitors:* They were a Mr. and Mrs. Byrn, musicians (according to
       a letter from Alma Mahler-Werfel to Isolde and Adolf Klarmann,
       M-W Coll.).

228   *selection of favorite poems: Gedichte aus den Jahren 1908–1945* (Los Angeles:
       Pazifische Presse, 1946).

228   *"The Conductor":* See *DRM*, p. 41: "Through the poem . . . runs the pencil
       stroke of him who was called away." The poem appears in FW, *Gedichte
       1908–1945*, op. cit.

231   *a typescript by Willy Haas:* The quotation is given in slightly edited form.

232   *in July 1975:* This was in fulfillment of Alma Mahler-Werfel's wish. Her
       mortal remains had been brought to Vienna in 1964 and buried in the
       Grinzing cemetery, next to Gustav Mahler and Manon Gropius. Arme-
       nian circles in the United States raised the money for the transfer of
       FW's bones, as the Austrian government could not see its way to pay
       for it. The memorial grave, with a headstone designed by Anna Mah-
       ler, can be found between those of the musician Hans Swarowsky and
       the composer Egon Wellesz, a friend of Werfel's in the Vienna days.
       Every year students of the Armenian Mekhitarist order in Vienna
       make a pilgrimage to the grave on the day of Werfel's death. A few
       steps away from Werfel's grave, in the Czech Domestics' Cemetery, lies
       Agnes Hvizd—"Teta Linek" from *Embezzled Heaven*—sharing her
       grave with seven others. (See Dietmar Grieser, *Piroschka, Sorbas & Co.:
       Schicksale der Weltliteratur*, op. cit., pp. 235ff.)

232   *The director of the Austrian Society for Literature:* Dr. Wolfgang Kraus is still
       director of the society. The description of his experience at the airport
       is derived from my conversation with him.

Select Bibliography:
Works by Franz Werfel

GERMAN EDITIONS:

Der Abituriententag: Die Geschichte einer Jugendschuld [*Class Reunion*]. Berlin, Vienna, Leipzig: Paul Zsolnay Verlag, 1928.

Barbara oder Die Frömmigkeit [*The Pure in Heart*]. Berlin, Vienna, Leipzig: Paul Zsolnay Verlag, 1929.

Die Dramen. Edited by Adolf D. Klarmann. 2 vols. Frankfurt am Main: S. Fischer Verlag, 1959.

Erzählungen aus zwei Welten. Edited by Adolf D. Klarmann. Vol. 1, *Krieg und Nachkrieg.* Stockholm: Bermann-Fischer Verlag, 1948. Vol. 2. Berlin and Frankfurt am Main: S. Fischer Verlag, 1952. Vol. 3. Berlin and Frankfurt am Main: S. Fischer Verlag, 1954.

Das Franz Werfel Buch. Edited by Peter Stephan Jungk. Frankfurt am Main: S. Fischer Verlag, 1986.

Die Geschwister von Neapel [*The Pascarella Family*]. Berlin, Vienna, Leipzig: Paul Zsolnay Verlag, 1931.

Jeremias: Höret die Stimme [*Hearken Unto the Voice*]. Frankfurt am Main: S. Fischer Verlag, 1956.

Das Lied von Bernadette [*The Song of Bernadette*]. Stockholm: Bermann-Fischer Verlag, 1941.

Das lyrische Werk. Edited by Adolf D. Klarmann. Frankfurt am Main: S. Fischer Verlag, 1967.

Stern der Ungeborenen: Ein Reiseroman [*Star of the Unborn*]. Stockholm: Bermann-Fischer Verlag, 1945.

Verdi: Roman der Oper [*Verdi: A Novel of the Opera*]: Berlin, Vienna, Leipzig: Paul Zsolnay Verlag, 1924.

Der veruntreute Himmel [*Embezzled Heaven*]. Stockholm: Bermann-Fischer Verlag, 1939.

Die vierzig Tage des Musa Dagh [*The Forty Days of Musa Dagh*]. Berlin, Vienna, Liepzig: Paul Zsolnay Verlag, 1933.

Zwischen Oben und Unten [*Between Heaven and Earth*]. Stockholm: Bermann-Fischer Verlag, 1946.

Zwischen Oben und Unten: Prosa, Tagebücher, Aphorismen, Literarische Nachträge. Munich and Vienna: Langen Müller Verlag, 1975.

ENGLISH EDITIONS:

Between Heaven and Earth [*Zwischen Oben und Unten*]. Translated by Maxim Newmark. New York: Philosophical Library, 1944.

Class Reunion [*Der Abituriententag*]. Translated by Whittaker Chambers. New York: Simon and Schuster, 1929.

Embezzled Heaven [*Der veruntreute Himmel*]. Translated by Moray Firth. New York: Viking Press, 1940.

Embezzled Heaven: A Play in a Prologue and Three Acts. Adapted by Laszló Bus-Fekete and M. H. Fay. New York: Viking Press, 1945.

The Eternal Road: A Drama in Four Parts [*Der Weg der Verheissung*]. English version by Ludwig Lewisohn. New York: Viking Press, 1936.

The Forty Days of Musa Dagh [*Die vierzig Tage des Musa Dagh*]. Translated by Geoffrey Dunlop. New York: Viking Press, 1934.

Goat Song: A Drama in Five Acts [*Bocksgesang*]. Translated by Ruth Langner. The Theatre Guild version. Garden City, N.Y.: Doubleday, Page, 1926.

The Grand Tour. Based on S. N. Behrman's adaptation of *Jacobowsky and the Colonel.* Book by Michael Stewart and Mark Bramble. Music and lyrics by Jerry Herman. New York: Samuel French, 1979.

Hearken Unto the Voice [*Jeremias: Höret die Stimme*]. Translated by Moray Firth. New York: Viking Press, 1938.

Jacobowsky and the Colonel: Comedy of a Tragedy in Three Acts [*Jacobowsky und der Oberst*]. Translated by Gustave O. Arlt. New York: Viking Press, 1944.

Jacobowsky and the Colonel. Original play by Franz Werfel, American play based on same by S. N. Behrman. New York: Random House, 1944.

Juarez and Maximilian: A Dramatic History in Three Phases and Thirteen Pictures [*Juarez und Maximilian*]. Translated by Ruth Langner. The Theatre Guild version. New York: Simon and Schuster, 1926.

The Man Who Conquered Death [*Der Tod des Kleinbürgers;* British title, *The Death of a Poor Man*]. Translated by Clifton P. Fadiman and William A. Drake. New York: Simon and Schuster, 1927.

The Pascarella Family [*Die Geschwister von Neapel*]. Translated by Dorothy F. Tait-Price. New York: Viking Press, 1935.

Paul Among the Jews [*Paulus unter den Juden*]. Translated by Paul P. Levertoff. London: Diocesan House, 1928.

Poems. Translated by Edith Abercrombie Snow. Princeton, N.J.: Princeton University Press, 1945.

The Pure in Heart [*Barbara oder Die Frömmigkeit;* British title, *The Hidden Child*]. Translated by Geoffrey Dunlop. New York: Simon and Schuster, 1931.

The Song of Bernadette [*Das Lied von Bernadette*]. Translated by Ludwig Lewisohn. New York: Viking Press, 1942.

The Song of Bernadette: A Play in Three Acts. Dramatized by Jean and Walter Kerr from the novel by Franz Werfel. Chicago: The Dramatic Publishing Company, 1944.

Star of the Unborn [*Stern der Ungeborenen*]. Translated by Gustave O. Arlt. New York: Viking Press, 1946.

Twilight of a World. Translated by H. T. Lowe-Porter. Contains *Poor People, Class Reunion, Estrangement, Severio's Secret, The Staircase, The Man Who Conquered Death, The House of Mourning, Not the Murderer.* New York: Viking Press, 1937.

Verdi: A Novel of the Opera [*Verdi: Roman der Oper*]. Translated by Helen Jessiman. New York: Simon and Schuster, 1925.

Index of Names

Index of Works

NOVELS AND NOVELLAS

PLAYS

POETRY